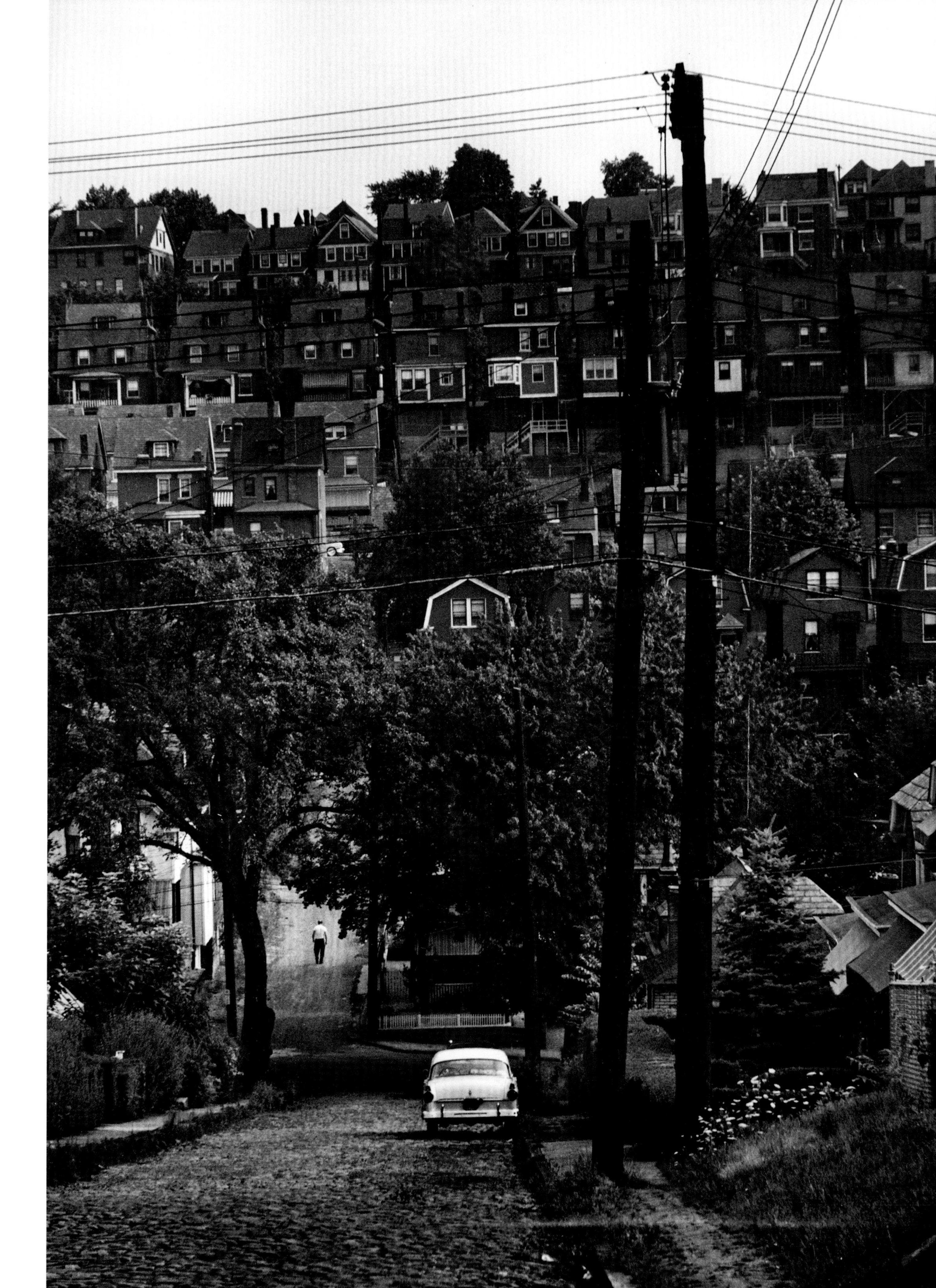

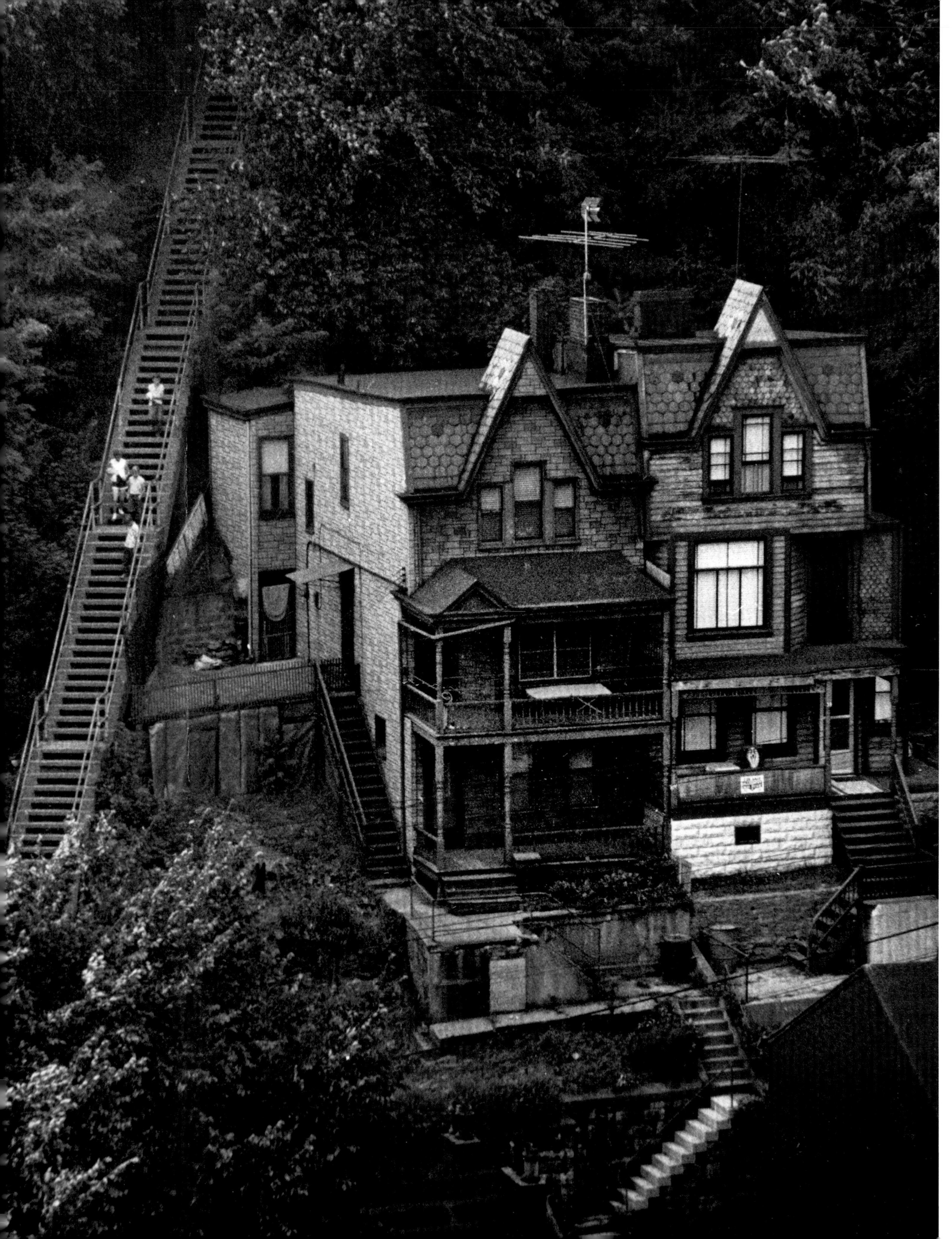

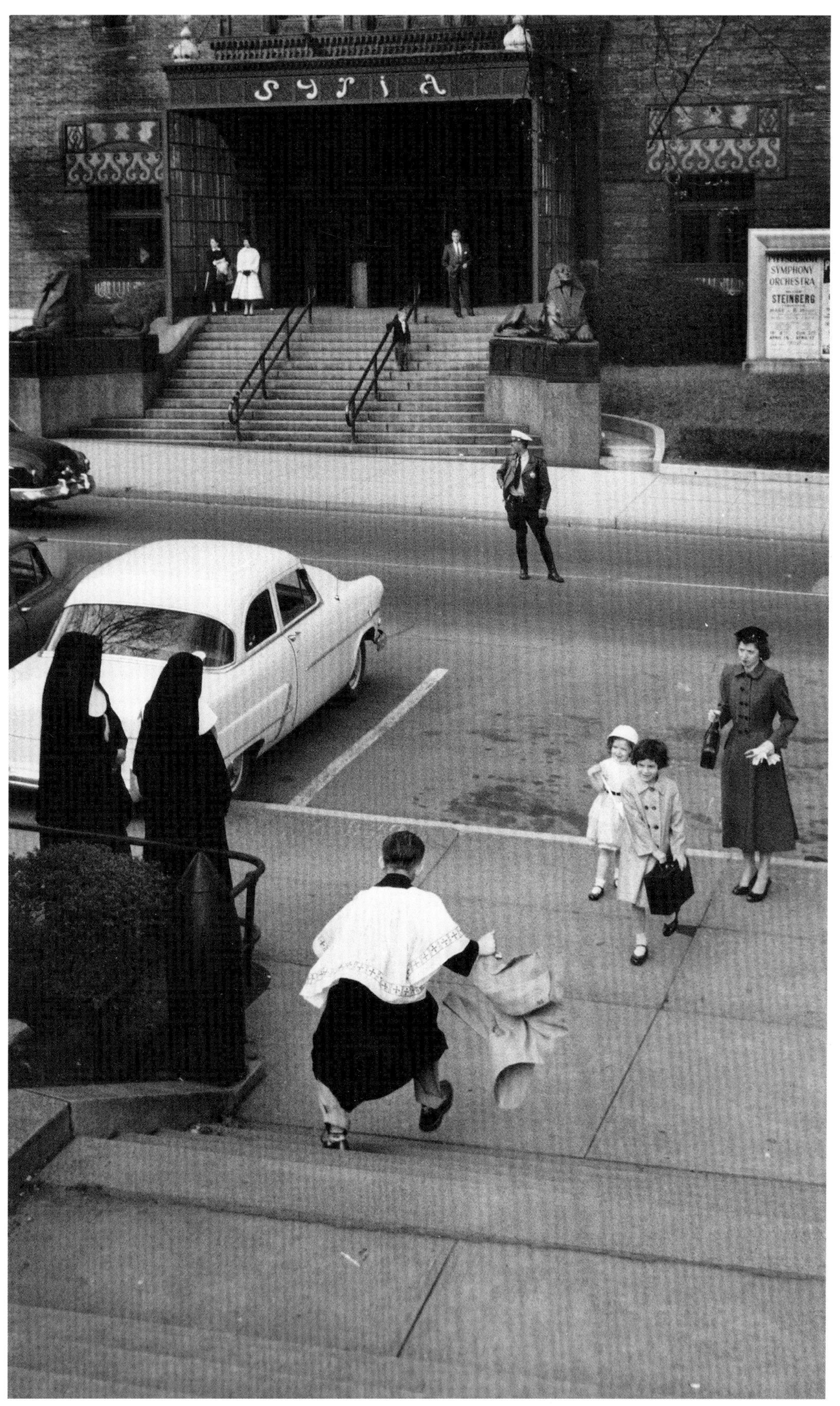
syrIa
SYMPHONY
ORCHESTRA
STEINBERG

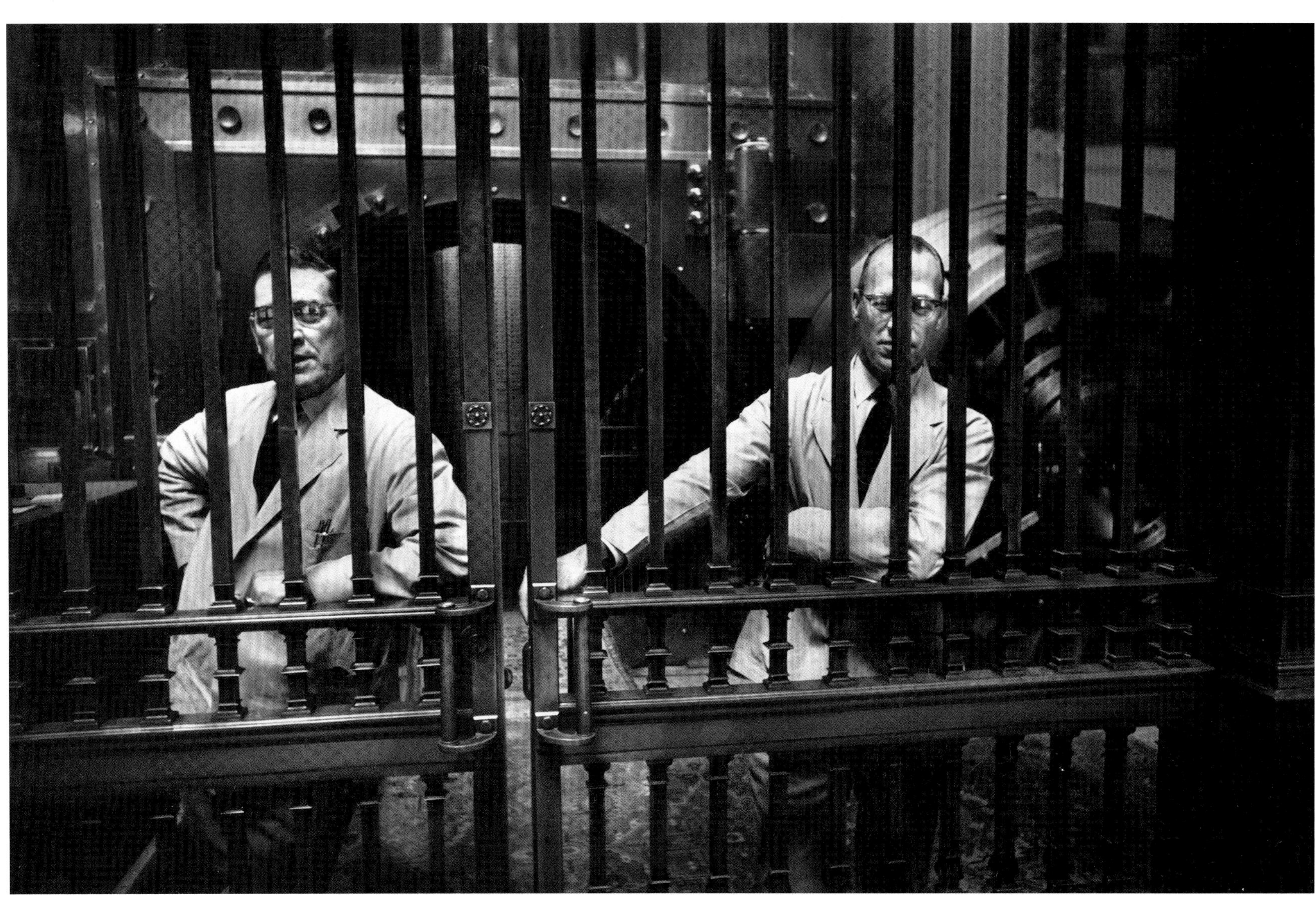

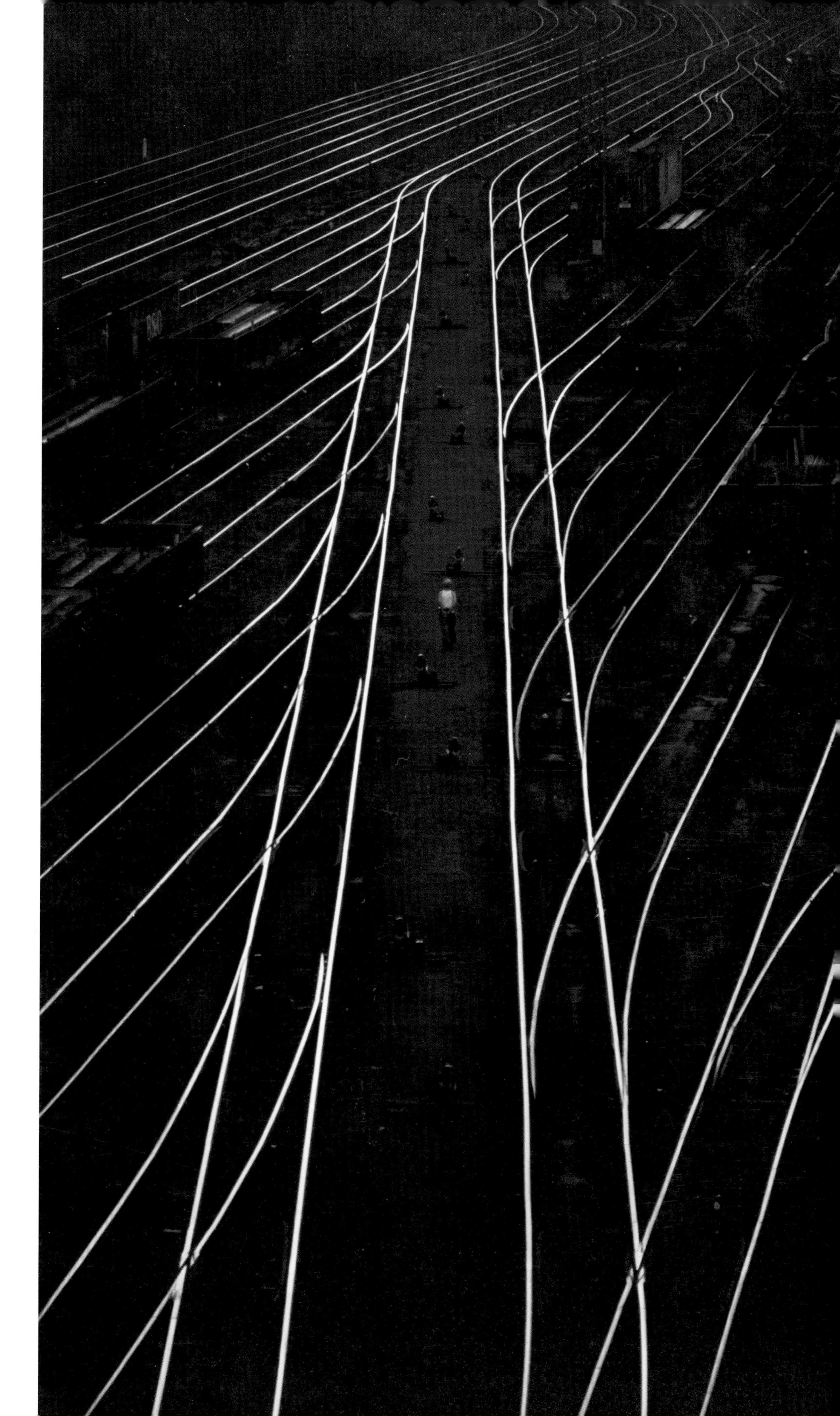

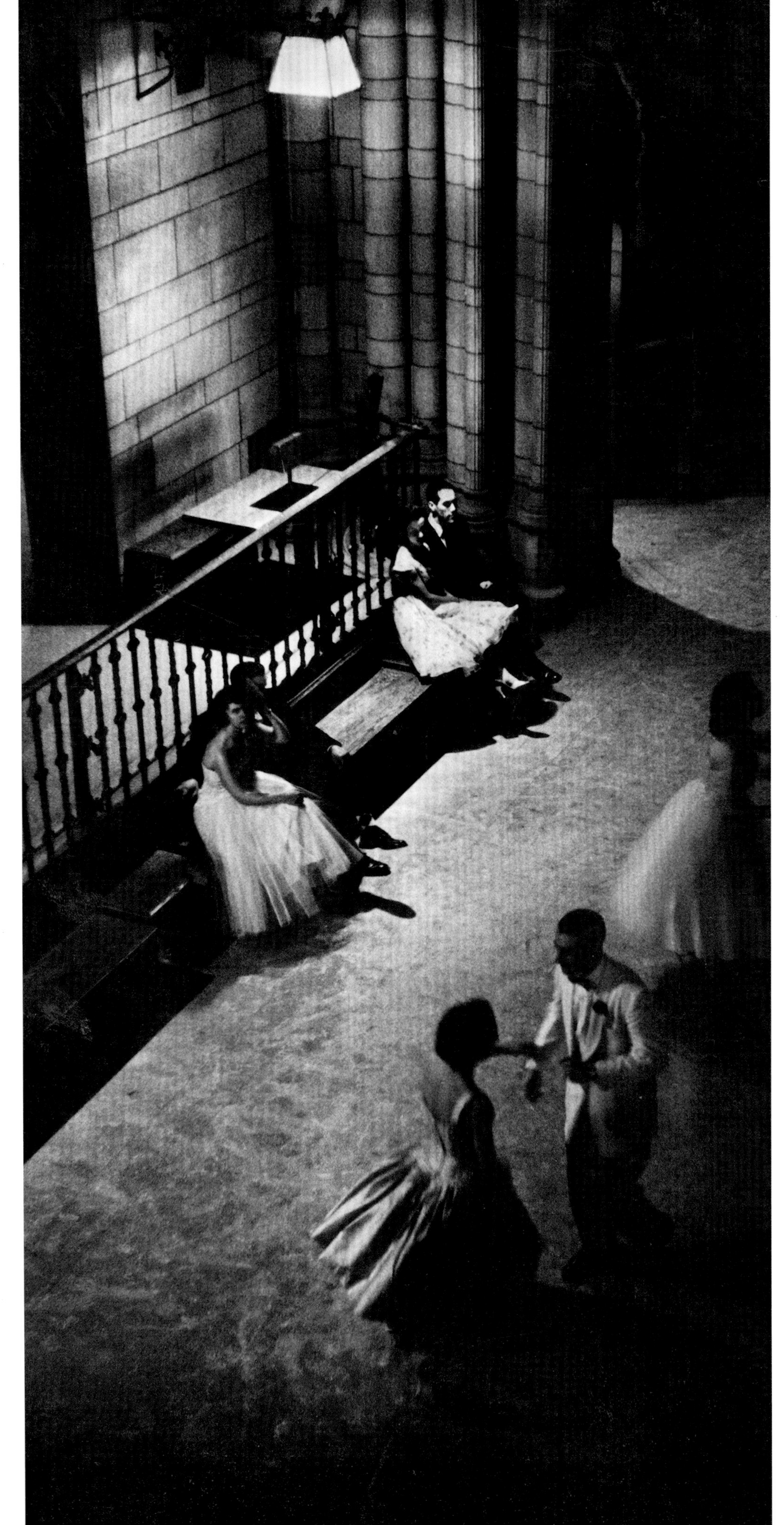

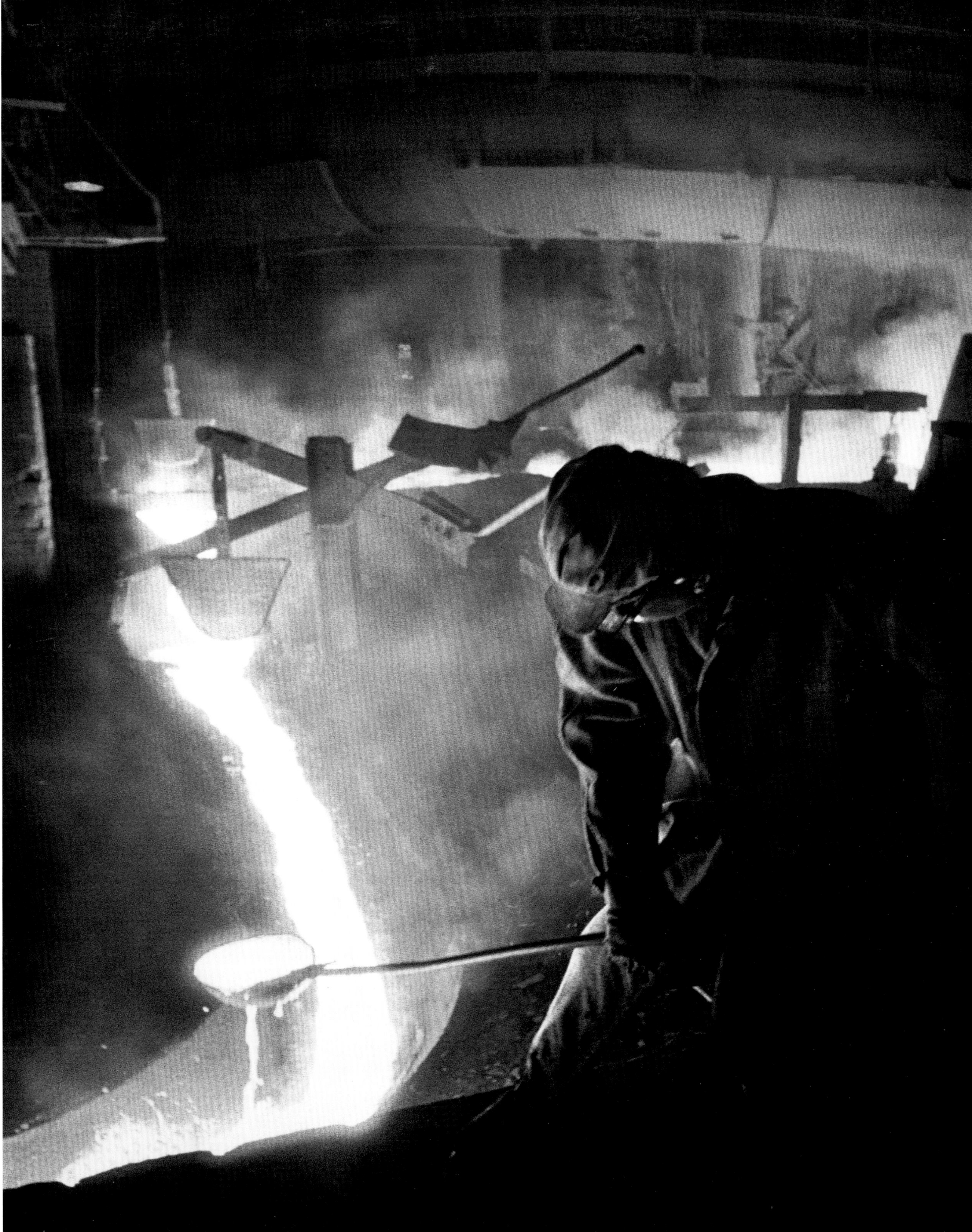

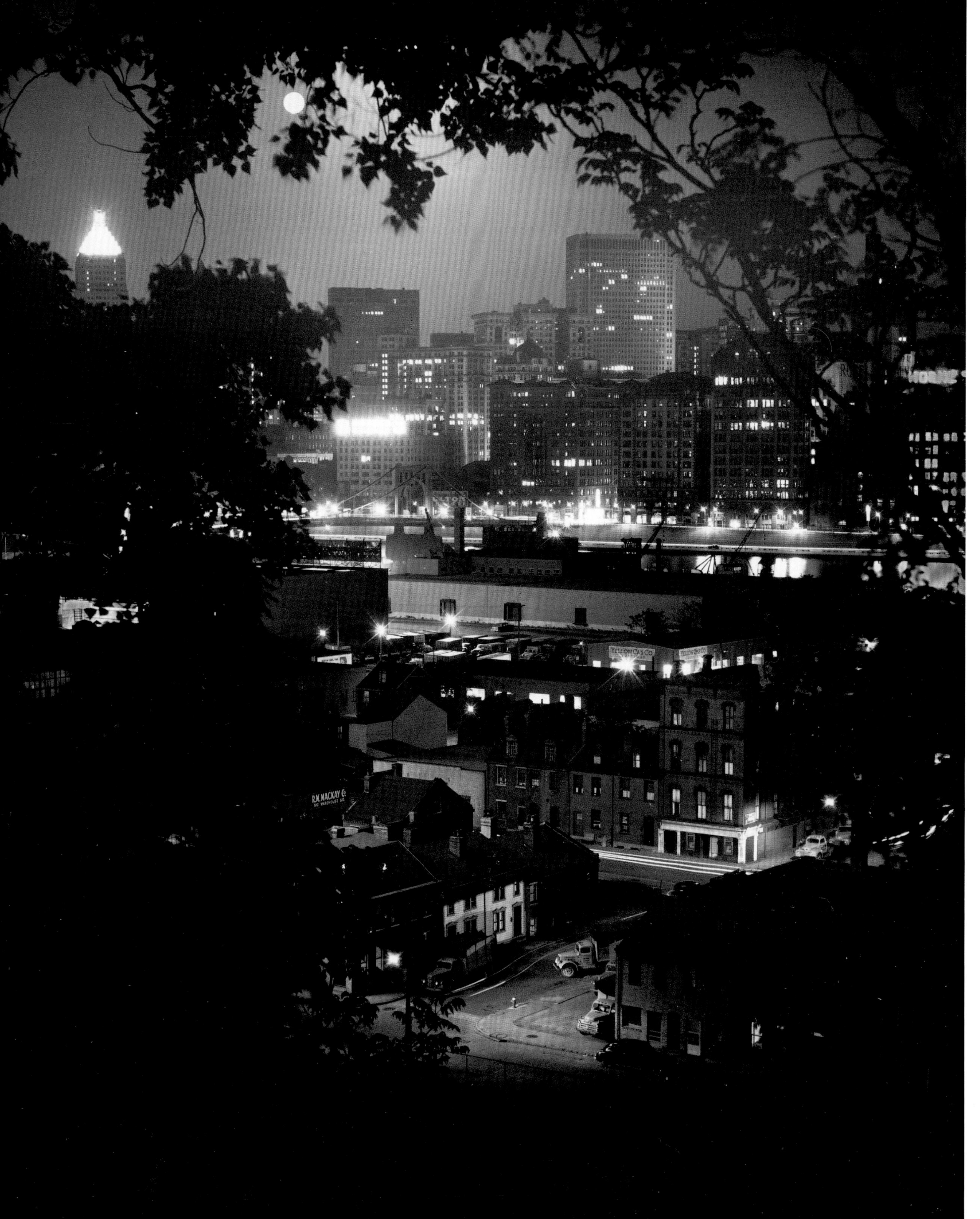

YELLOW CAB CO.
R.M. MACKAY C?

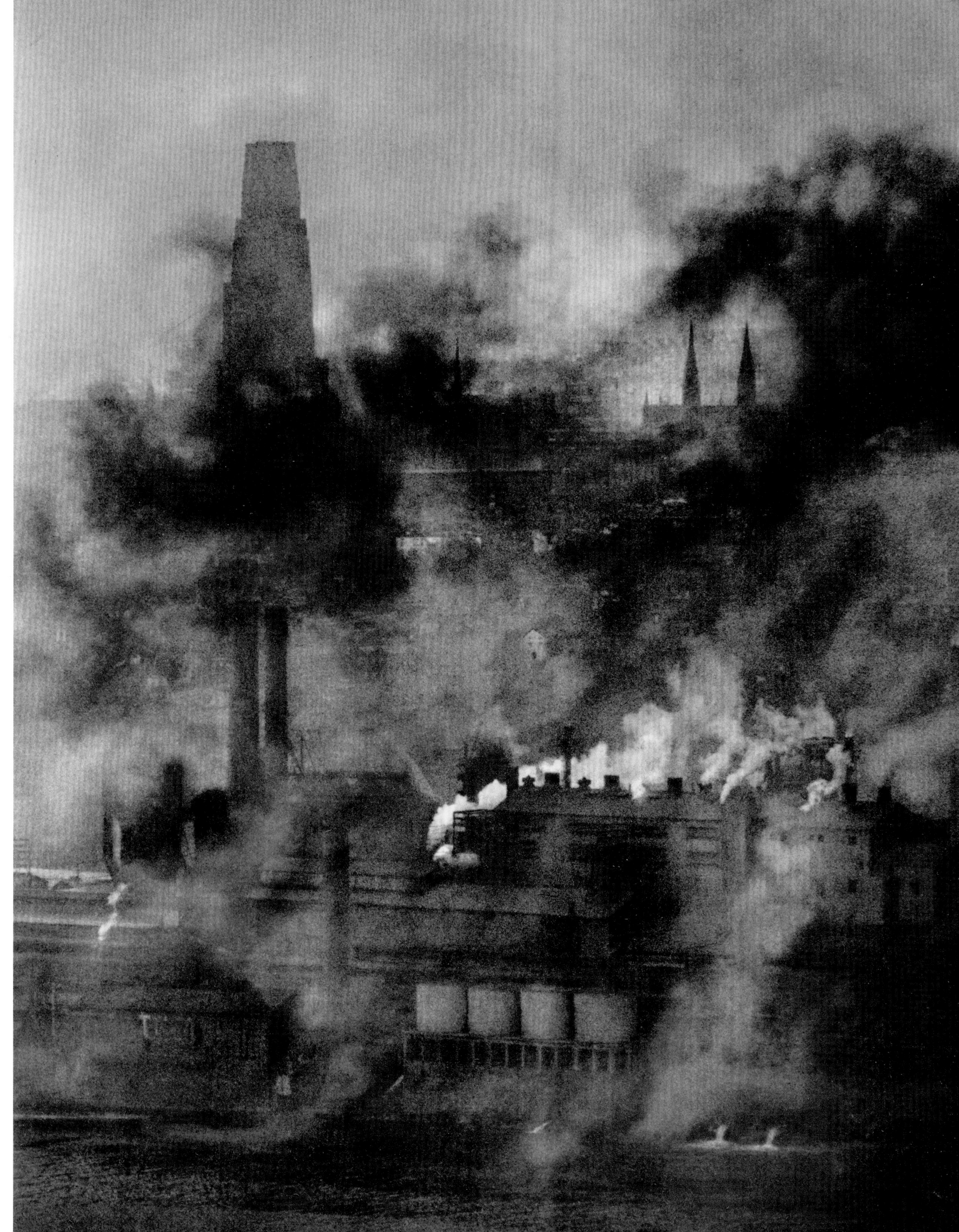

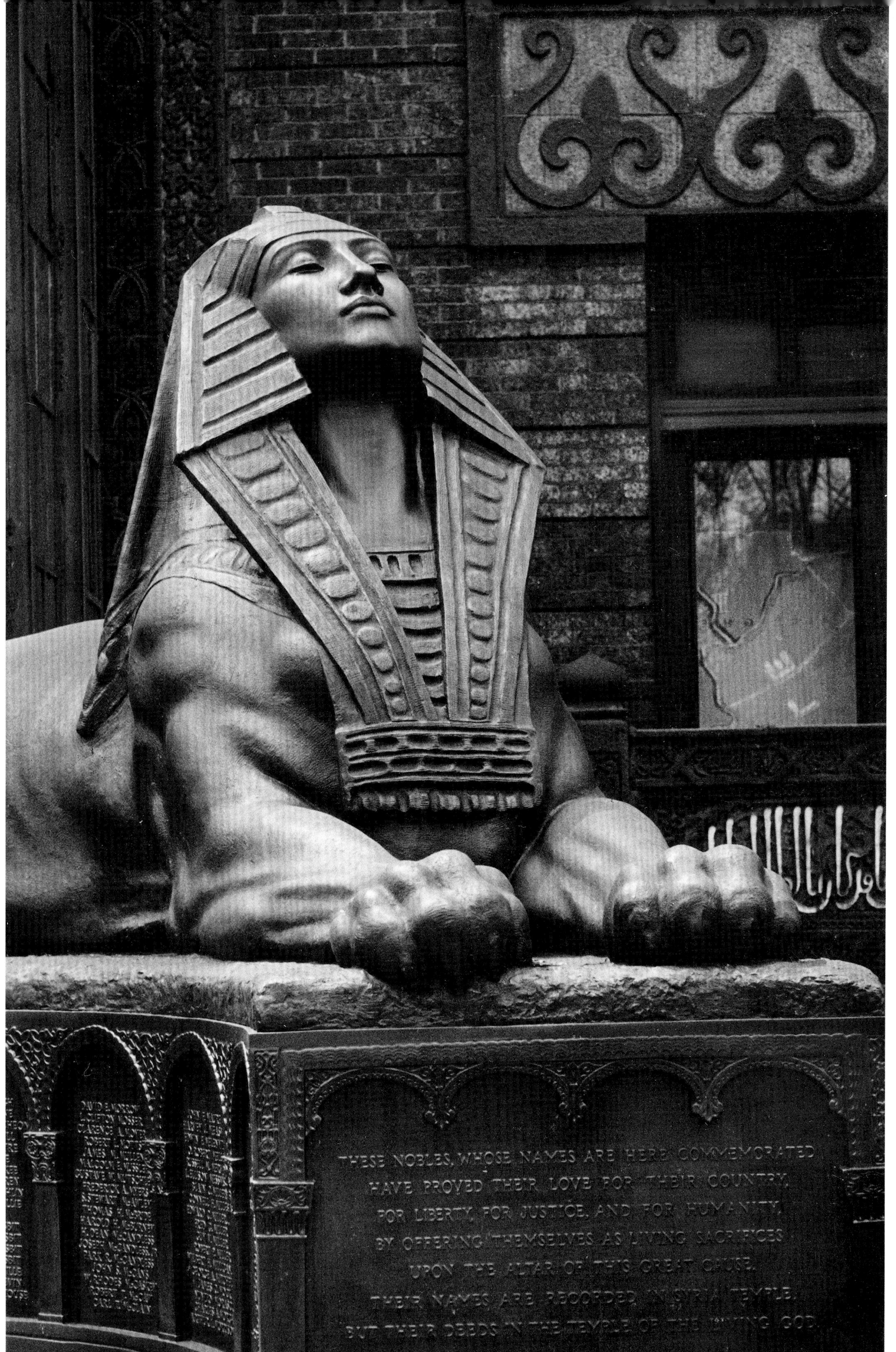

THESE NOBLES, WHOSE NAMES ARE HERE COMMEMORATED
HAVE PROVED THEIR LOVE FOR THEIR COUNTRY,
FOR LIBERTY, FOR JUSTICE, AND FOR HUMANITY,
BY OFFERING THEMSELVES AS LIVING SACRIFICES
UPON THE ALTAR OF THIS GREAT CAUSE.
THEIR NAMES ARE RECORDED IN OUR TEMPLE,
BUT THEIR DEEDS IN THE TEMPLE OF THE LIVING GOD.

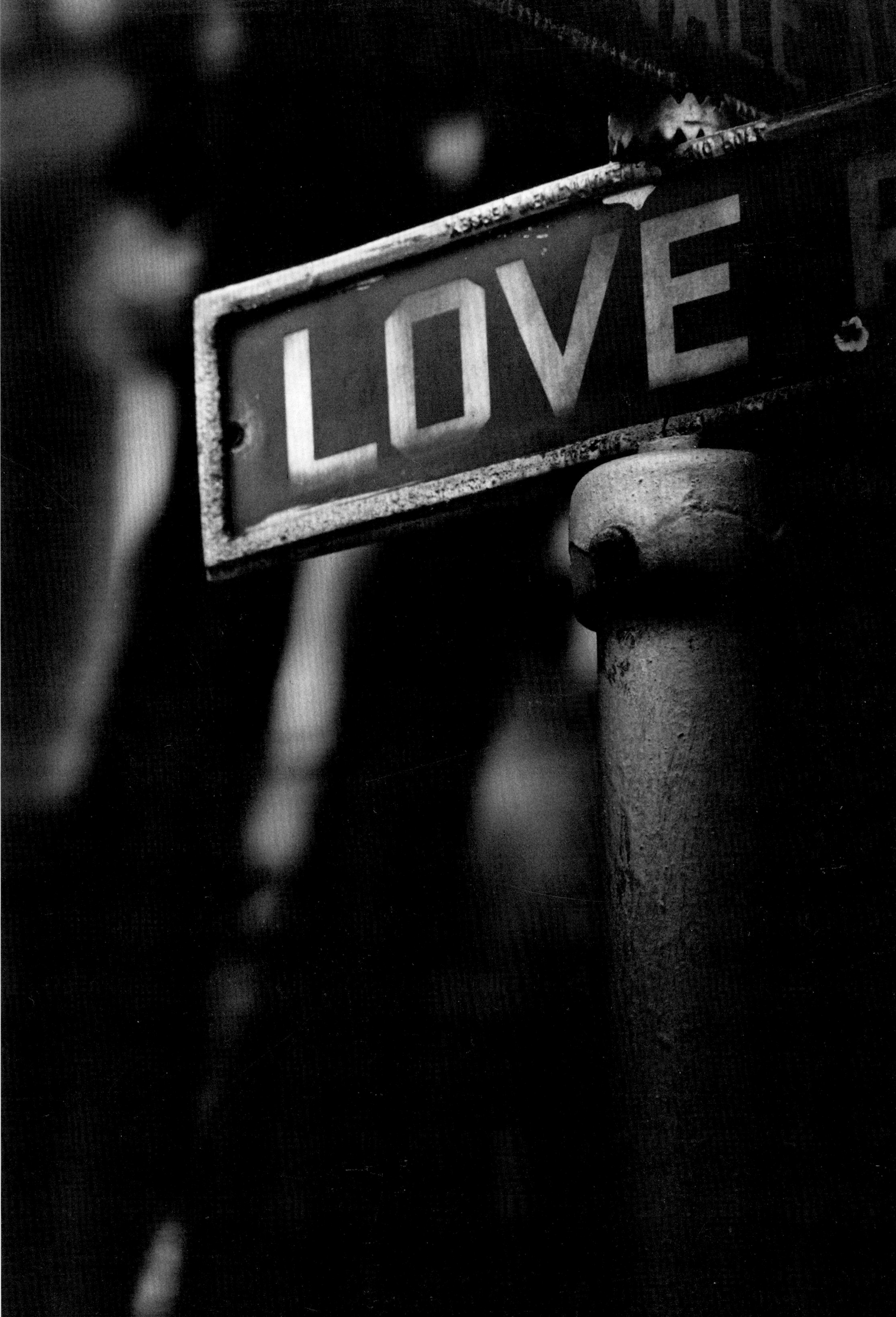

LOVE

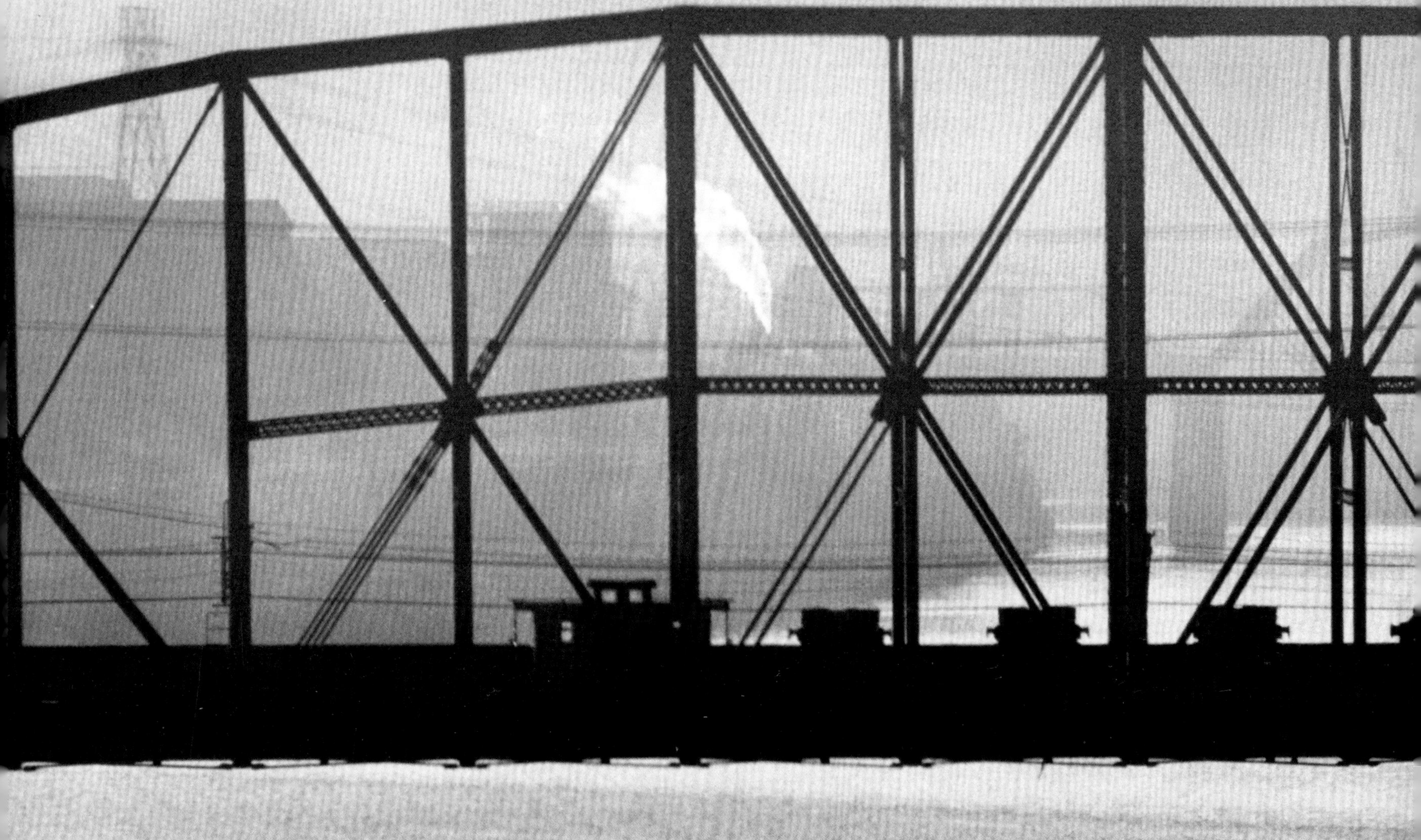

# DREAM STREET: W. EUGENE SMITH'S

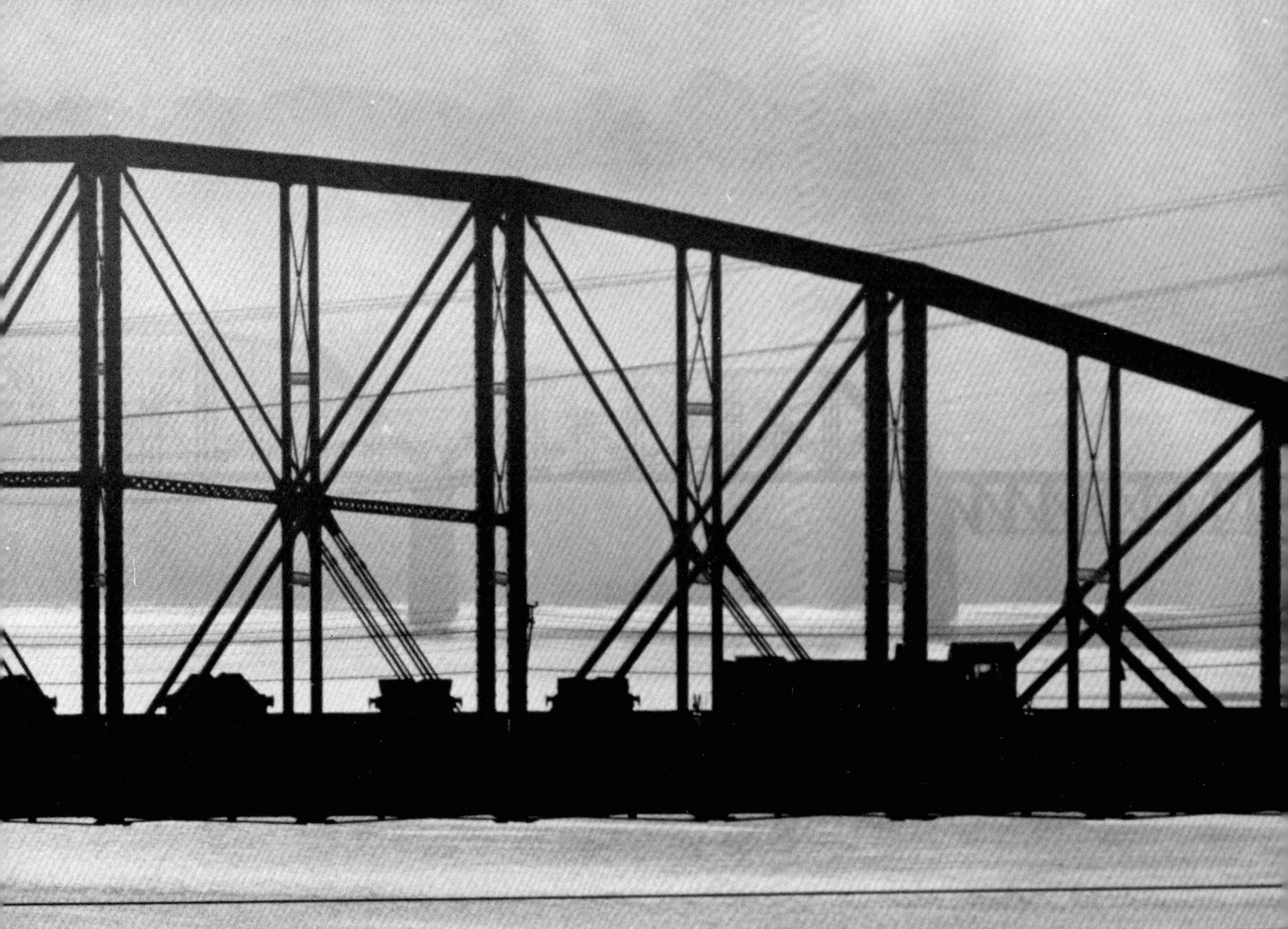

# PITTSBURGH PROJECT

EDITED BY SAM STEPHENSON
WITH A FOREWORD BY ROSS GAY
THE UNIVERSITY OF CHICAGO PRESS
CHICAGO · LONDON

The University of Chicago Press, Chicago 60637
The University of Chicago Press, Ltd., London

*Dream Street: W. Eugene Smith's Pittsburgh Project*
© 2001 by Sam Stephenson, the Center for
Documentary Studies, and the Heirs of W. Eugene
Smith

"W. Eugene Smith and Pittsburgh"
© 2001 by Sam Stephenson

"'Man-Breaking City': W. Eugene Smith's Pittsburgh"
© 2001 by the Heirs of Alan Trachtenberg

Foreword © 2023 by The University of Chicago

All photographs © 1955–1957, 2023 by the Heirs of
W. Eugene Smith

All rights reserved. No part of this book may be
used or reproduced in any manner whatsoever
without written permission, except in the case of
brief quotations in critical articles and reviews. For
more information, contact the University of Chicago
Press, 1427 E. 60th St., Chicago, IL 60637.
Published 2023
Printed in Italy

32  31  30  29  28  27  26  25      2  3  4  5

ISBN-13: 978-0-226-82483-3 (cloth)
ISBN-13: 978-0-226-82701-8 (e-book)
DOI: https://doi.org/10.7208
/chicago/9780226827018.001.0001

Originally published by W. W. Norton & Company, Inc., 2001, with
the participation of the Collection and W. Eugene Smith Archive at
the Center for Creative Photography, The University of Arizona.

The publication of this edition was generously supported by the
Jonathan Logan Family Foundation.

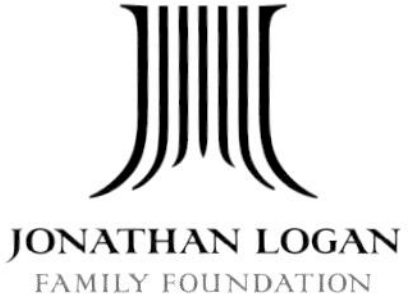


Library of Congress Cataloging-in-Publication Data

Names: Smith, W. Eugene, 1918-1978, photographer. | Stephenson,
    Sam, editor. | Gay, Ross, 1974- writer of foreword. | University of
    Arizona. Center for Creative Photography.
Title: Dream street : W. Eugene Smith's Pittsburgh project / edited
    by Sam Stephenson ; with a foreword by Ross Gay.
Other titles: W. Eugene Smith's Pittsburgh project
Description: Chicago ; London : The University of Chicago Press,
    2023. | "Originally published by W.W. Norton & Company, Inc.,
    2001, with the participation of the Collection and W. Eugene
    Smith Archive at the Center for Creative Photography, The
    University of Arizona." | Includes bibliographical references.
Identifiers: LCCN 2022055151 | ISBN 9780226824833 (cloth) |
    ISBN 9780226827018 (ebook)
Subjects: LCSH: Pittsburgh (Pa.)—Pictorial works. | Pittsburgh
    (Pa.)—History—20th century—Pictorial works. | Pittsburgh
    (Pa.)—Social life and customs—20th century—Pictorial works.
Classification: LCC F159.P643 S67 2023 | DDC 974.8/8600222—
    dc23/eng/20221122
LC record available at https://lccn.loc.gov/2022055151

♾ This paper meets the requirements of ANSI/NISO Z39.48-1992
(Permanence of Paper).

# CONTENTS

# FOREWORD

BY ROSS GAY

Toward the conclusion of Sam Stephenson's excellent introductory essay to *Dream Street* he writes, "What shines through though, irrevocably, in this enormous body of material—the detritus of Smith's spectacular failure—are the prints. They overwhelm it all with their beauty and sheer volume." I find myself drawn to that phrase—*spectacular failure*—a characterization Stephenson uses at least in part because it's what Smith himself felt about this project that consumed him for the better part of three years. Thousands of photographs and a lot of personal wreckage later, all Smith had to show for the effort was a thirty-eight-page photo-essay in *Photography Annual*, which he thought a "debacle."[1]

Smith's ambition was somehow to articulate the "essence" of a major American city, the human beings living there, the land, the world-transforming industry. Looking through *Dream Street*—and this is one of the achievements of Stephenson's arduous work as editor—it is obvious to me that Smith's vision, his reams of work, simply exceeded the bounds of any convention there might have been to contain them. That's to say, he was trying to do something that, quiet as it's kept—especially if you're one of the sensitives, as Smith obviously was—*you can't do*. And so if there is failure, it is the spectacular inadequacy of any form to properly hold Smith's epic attempt.

Almost any form, I should say. Because *Dream Street*, as far I'm concerned, manages to hold or contain—wrong words, too static, too conclusive, too fixed; maybe I should say *regard*; yes, let's say *regard*—Smith's unresolvable, unfinishable project. In the assembly and arrangement of *Dream Street*, which includes not only remarkable photographs omitted from Smith's original photo-essay but a selection of Smith's own letters and other writings on the project—a herculean archival achievement, by the way, for Smith's archives once filled an entire high school gymnasium—Sam Stephenson regards, and so helps us to regard, the Pittsburgh project's spectacular, wonderful impossibility. I would go so far as to say that he regards the true subject of W. Eugene Smith's Pittsburgh photographs: *dreaming*.

Smith's dreaming, yes, which these brilliantly placed letters reveal was fraught with ambition and perfectionism and fear and real trouble—some of which I think (not sure about you) I could say animates my dreams as well. But Stephenson also helps us to regard the way Smith's photos regard the dreaming of those who populate these photos, and not only who populates them dramatically, in the hellfire cauldron of the steel mills or in the courtroom or university or promenade or church or banks.

Much of my family on my father's side lives, incidentally, about sixty miles from Pittsburgh, in Youngstown, kind of a kid sibling city to Pittsburgh. It drew immigrants from the south (my Youngstown people come from Mississippi, etc.), from eastern and southern Europe, and beyond—one small though delicious example is that most every Christmas my mother makes kulachi, a kind of rolled bread filled with walnuts and cinnamon, from a recipe given to my Aunt Butter by a Hungarian neighbor. Their rivers cradle what is perhaps the most obvious kinship between the two cities: Youngstown and Pittsburgh were both booming steel towns, with mills that most everyone worked in or adjacent to. In one of our last conversations, as my grandfather lay dying of blood cancer, he told me a little bit from his bed about working in the mill, which too his father did, all of which was more or less mythology to me, given as only three years after I was born in 1974, Black Monday saw the sudden shuttering of the last mills in Youngstown, one more in an ongoing brutality upon a city and its people.

I'm talking about the dreaming of the man planting a tree, or the young couple pushing a stroller, or the mason holding a brick in prayer, or the girls pulling flowers from the star magnolia tree, or the cement man balancing on a two-by-four leveling his work, or the students in the library listening to records through headphones, or the group of little boys lounging around on a stoop and sidewalk. These are who I find myself most drawn to, because they look neither static nor monumental—they look to be in the midst of their unknowable way. And though they are in the shadows of the mills and millionaires, that is not all they are. That is not all we are. Stephenson, in his curation and arrangement of Smith's photos and correspondence, in his juxtapositions and sequences (in, let's call it, his collaboration with Gene Smith), helps us to see with Smith's tenderest eye, which unfixes these people into the midst of their dreaming.

And in so doing, *Dream Street* unfixes us into ours.

1. Much of what I know of Eugene Smith comes from *Gene Smith's Sink*, Stephenson's beautiful lyric biography of the photographer.

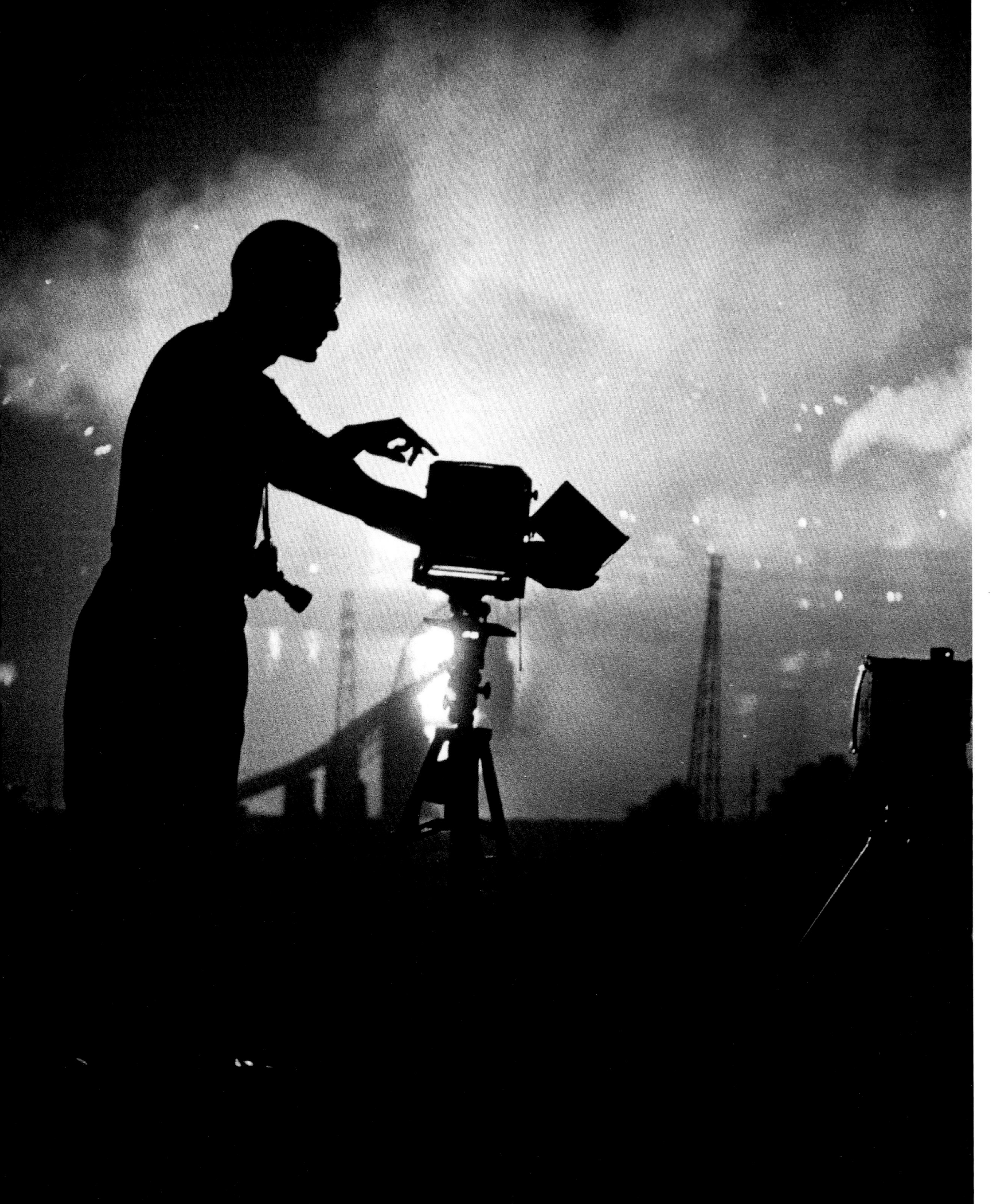

# W. EUGENE SMITH AND PITTSBURGH

BY SAM STEPHENSON



WHEN W. EUGENE SMITH drove to Pittsburgh in early March 1955 he intended to attempt "the greatest of the impossible," an epic study of the city that would lay bare the mores of America at mid-century and set new standards in the medium of photographic journalism. He was thirty-six years old and had recently resigned from his high-salaried job with *Life* magazine, where his World War II combat pictures and groundbreaking photo-essays, along with rancorous fights for editorial control of his work, had made him a legend. Smith went to Pittsburgh for a routine, freelance assignment expected to last three weeks, but he had, in fact, embarked on a personal odyssey that would lead him to make up to seventeen thousand pictures in the city over the better part of 1955, and on return trips in 1956 and 1957. Through the end of 1958, Smith worked obsessively—financing the work himself at the expense of his family's well being—making prints and experimenting with layouts of his essay. He believed he was putting together a magnum opus with no comparison in the history of photography, a work whose lyrical precedents he found in Rilke's *Duino Elegies*, Faulkner's novels, Joyce's *Ulysses*, and Beethoven's Ninth Symphony and late string quartets. In hindsight, it appears that the deep frictions in Smith's professional and personal lives may have fueled photographic ambitions of impossible proportions—ambitions that effectively ended his career in journalism (publishers became wary of his reputation as a maverick) and tangled him fully in the realm of art. It was a twist of fate that Smith concentrated his greatest energies in Pittsburgh, the fortunate match of a brilliant, if sometimes quixotic picture-maker, who was wrestling with fundamental issues of human yearning, economy, and modern mythology, with one of America's most important and arresting industrial cities at its zenith. Though Smith never achieved his goals for the Pittsburgh essay (at least not

for public viewing), he left behind a stunning collection of prints—fragments from his mind's eye.

William Eugene Smith was born in Wichita, Kansas, on December 30, 1918, to William Henry "Bill" Smith and Nettie Lee Caplinger Smith. He had an older brother, Paul, who was stricken with polio. Smith was introduced to photography as a young boy by his mother, who made frequent snapshots of the family, and he quickly took to it. According to his biographer, Jim Hughes, he was working in a household darkroom by the time he was twelve years old. By age fourteen he was making photographs professionally for the Wichita newspapers. In 1934 his photograph of a drought-dried bed of the Arkansas River was published in the *New York Times*. But Smith's teen years were defined by a devastating tragedy. In 1936 his father, whose grain business had been lost a year earlier, drove to a hospital parking lot and blew open his stomach with a shotgun. He did not die until several hours later, after doctors had tried to save him with a blood transfusion from sevente-year-old Gene.

Several months after his father's suicide Smith enrolled at the University of Notre Dame on a special photography scholarship that had been arranged by his mother, who was a devout Catholic, and her priest, who had connections at the university. He dropped out after one year, however, to become a full-time professional photographer in New York City. Smith's first job was as a staff photographer for *Newsweek* magazine, but he was fired in less than a year's time for disobeying orders not to use small-format cameras on assignments. He joined the Black Star Agency in 1938 and did freelance work for many publications, including *Life, Collier's, Harper's Bazaar, Time,* and the *New York Times*. In 1939 *Life* offered him a prestigious position as a full-time staff photographer, which Smith accepted. But he resigned in 1941, citing dissatisfaction with the routine nature of the assignments. At age twenty-three Smith was already exhibiting a restless disposition and a commitment to photography that some would later call megalomania.

Smith tried to join Edward Steichen's naval photography unit in World War II but was denied entry because of his poor eyesight (he wore glasses) and insufficient college education. Instead, he joined the Ziff-Davis Publishing Company and was given assignments in the Pacific Theater. Over the next two years he photographed sixteen missions on the frontlines. In 1944 Smith rejoined *Life* to cover the combat in Guam, Saipan, Okinawa, the Philippines, and Iwo Jima. All told, he spent three years photographing the war from close range.

Smith considered himself a colleague of the soldiers, a full participant in their frightful world. He drank with them and listened to records with them on the frontlines, and his fearless efforts to make pictures during combat sometimes startled them. In his letters Smith describes the chaos of invasions; the odor of decaying corpses; the odd mixture of feral emotions and solemn dignity in soldiers and civilians struggling to stay alive; and warfare's indifferent destruction to humans and nature.

Smith's aesthetic matured during the war. His pictures began to express a benevolent melancholy. His prints, with their ever-deepening contrasts between dark and light, were visual metaphors for the colossal and violent struggle he was bearing witness to, and felt within himself. The night before he was to accompany soldiers on an invasion of Guam in 1944, Smith wrote to Carmen, his wife of four years: "I am searching for that which is real of my heart, and which when completed I can stand humbly to one side of and say, 'This is it, this is how I feel, this is my honest interpretation of the world; this is not influenced by money, or trickery, or pressure—except the pressure of my soul.'" He would make similar statements about nearly all of his work the rest his life.

Smith was hit by fragments of a Japanese bomb while photographing American foot soldiers on a mission in Okinawa in May 1945. He was disabled for more than a year by critical injuries to his head and left hand. His work in the war was over, but the emotional fervor of his photography had taken form.

After a lengthy rehabilitation from his injuries, Smith returned to *Life* magazine as a staff photographer. *Life* was a powerhouse of journalism during the pre-television glory days of the 1940s and '50s, when its weekly circulation peaked at an astounding 8.5 million. Smith undertook more than fifty assignments for the magazine between 1947 and 1954, producing, among them, a handful of photo-essays that are generally considered to be among the most significant in the history of photojournalism. On each assignment Smith spent several days or weeks observing the location and mingling with people before he took his first photograph. His goal was to create picture stories that would bring new and intimate experiences into the homes of *Life*'s readers. He rendered the dedication of a country doctor in Colorado; the nobility of a black nurse-midwife in rural, poverty-stricken South Carolina; and the intricacies of daily life in a Spanish village. He explored the paradoxes of such disparate places as a coal-mining town in Wales, the giant chemical manufacturer Monsanto, and Albert Schweitzer's village hospital in Africa. Smith's pictures resounded with basic human themes: birth, hope, fear, compassion, death, and *Life*'s readers responded with tremendous enthusiasm, even sending unsolicited donations on behalf of the nurse-midwife, Maude Callen, that eventually totaled $28,000, money that was used to build her a new clinic.

Smith's success at *Life*, however, was accompanied by agonizing clashes with the magazine's editors over control of his work. He rejected the editors' notion that a photographer's job was over when the negatives were finished. Smith felt that only he could print pictures from his negatives and arrange layouts true to the integrity of *his* subjects. He was enraged by the slightest dissent from his editors; he stormed out of meetings and repeatedly threatened to quit. He was convinced that the magazine's bureaucratic and commercial pressures stifled his expression and gave superficial treatment to the work he so carefully created. *Life*'s editors countered that Smith was irrational and pigheaded, that other staff photographers did not have such problems with their policies. The magazine's chief editor, Edward Thompson, once wrote to Smith in exasperation, "You seem to get upset by what seem perfectly normal questions to [us]."

Smith became increasingly obsessive during his tenure at *Life*. He started spending less time at his home outside New York City and more in the Manhattan studio where he kept a darkroom. He expended enormous amounts of time and film on assignments others deemed routine. On jobs such as the Monsanto Chemical Company in 1952 or migrant farm workers in Michigan in 1953, Smith spent months making thousands of beautiful, meticulous prints on *Life*'s account—many more than the magazine needed or wanted—all for a layout of a few pages.

Smith consumed excessive amounts of alcohol and amphetamines, especially benzedrine, and went through manic highs and suicidal lows. He often worked for three or four days without sleeping and then would collapse, exhausted. He also suffered from debilitating migraine headaches and once said that the only antidotes to his headaches were work and music. His music collection exceeded twenty thousand vinyl records of all kinds, but especially classical and jazz, which he listened to in his darkroom late at night at thunderous volumes. He read and annotated thousands of newspaper and magazine articles and stacked them in piles. He amassed piles of rubber bands and paper clips. He placed orders of up to fifty books at a time from local bookstores (everything from Sergei Eisenstein's *Film Form,* Charles Baudelaire's *Flowers of Evil,* and the writings of Sean O'Casey and Samuel Beckett to *The Best of Sick Jokes, What Every Songwriter Should Know,* and *How Not to Write a Play*), eventually building a collection of more than eight thousand titles. Wired on amphetamines, a glass of Scotch in hand, Smith would deliver hour-long soliloquies full of wry, self-effacing humor to transfixed guests. To family and friends, even casual acquaintances, he typed four-thousand- to six-thousand-word letters simmering with tremendous aspirations, guilt, and self-justification. In 1951 he wrote to *Life*'s editorial staff: "It is not presumptuous for me to speak in a relative relationship with such as Beethoven, for the capacity of the man, his emotions, his beliefs, his integrity; who is to say I am not a vehicle for these capacities, as acutely intensified as they were in Beethoven?"

Smith, with his affecting pictures, wide audience, and reputation as a maverick who successfully bucked the corporate powers at *Life,* had become a legend: the compassionate photographer as indomitable hero. He fed off of the legend and fueled it. His troubles at *Life,* which he sometimes inflated, gave him motivation for marathon stints in the darkroom, as well as justification for his shortcomings as a husband and father (though not without profound feelings of guilt). These pressures finally took their toll and, in late 1950, at the end of six months of work on "Spanish Village," Smith was committed to Bellevue mental hospital and Payne Whitney psychiatric clinic for three months. The police had found him wandering nude, or wearing only boxer shorts (accounts differ according to Jim Hughes), in the streets of Manhattan, an incident that he later termed a "crack-up." After his release Smith went on, less than a year later, to produce "Nurse-Midwife." But Smith's relationship with the magazine was doomed. The magazine wanted a reliable photographer who could accept the boundaries of assignments and meet deadlines; Smith wanted to change the world with his pictures. In 1953 Smith wrote to his mother, "I have a cult of followers throughout the world who look up to me as the shining light and the protector of integrity and as the one who never compromises my beliefs before pressures of the commercial and outside world. Perhaps this . . . is a reason I am unhappy because I am afraid I will let these people and the world down and it never allows me to quite relax enough to live the life of a human being and it means I must always be at war with what I consider to be evil and wrong."

Smith's conflicts with the magazine reached their peak while he and the editors were trying to condense his mammoth study of Dr. Albert Schweitzer's medical compound in Africa into a publishable essay. He resigned from *Life* at the end of 1954, giving up an annual salary that was more than $25,000 (approximately $124,000 in 2001 dollars). But finally Smith was free to choose his own assignments and make his own pictures.

By February 1955, Smith had joined Magnum, the preeminent cooperative agency for photographers, through which he could seek freelance assignments. Right away he typed an eight-page, single-spaced letter to John Morris, the agency's executive director, outlining seventy-three ideas for potential photo-essays. The letter is a remarkable relic of Smith's sprawling ambitions at the time. The proposed topics range from portraits of famous figures such as Marlon Brando, Billy Graham, Eudora Welty, and Ezra Pound to portraits of unknown individuals, including a minor-league baseball umpire, a bullfighter, a southern minister, and a prostitute, to studies of human habitats, a modest apartment building, a New York City commuter train, an orphanage, and a traveling circus. He also suggested such wide-ranging subjects as "basic research, a very complicated branch of science"; the American coal industry; "Broadway, from its beginning in lower Manhattan to Albany"; Portuguese or Japanese fishing villages; the Japanese industrial complex; "Rome at night"; and "the water-table—the struggle for, and worship of, and the basic need for water." In the middle of all this, Smith made this parenthetical remark to Morris, indicating he was open to assignments not on his list: "Let the project really present itself [so it] can really intrigue and seduce my mind and soul, and I'll throw [my] body into the deal—and it will respond, perhaps aided by a little Benzedrine."

Smith's first job presented itself right away, and he was drawn in immediately. Historian and editor Stefan Lorant, who had been hired by civic and commercial leaders in Pittsburgh to put together a book commemorating the city's bicentennial, needed a photographer. The assignment was to produce one hundred prints, as scripted by Lorant, for the book's chapter on contemporary Pittsburgh. Lorant offered Smith room, board, and a darkroom in the basement of his rental house. He expected Smith to finish the job in three weeks, tops. Smith accepted.

By this time Smith's personal life was crumbling. His mother, always a dominant, if not domineering, presence in his life, died a month before he left for Pittsburgh. The home he shared with his wife, their four children, and a housekeeper in Croton-on-Hudson was strained at best. Smith's son has described being woken at night by the sound of his father sobbing in his darkroom. (In December 1954 a longtime lover in Philadelphia bore him a fifth child, unbeknownst to the rest of his family.) With Smith's departure from *Life* the prospect of economic instability loomed over his family; the housekeeper eventually took a second job to help pay bills in the Smith home. But Smith, free of professional constraints, left for Pittsburgh.

When Smith arrived in the city in early March 1955, Lorant was astounded to see him unload some twenty pieces of luggage, a record player, and hundreds of records and books from his station wagon, all for the projected three-week stay. Smith spent the first month in Pittsburgh wandering the city and reading its history. The three-week deadline passed with hardly a click of his shutter.

Any American city might have been a fascinating topic for a photographic study of the magnitude Smith was preparing. The optimism and hope of the mid-1950s were as prevalent in Pittsburgh as they were everywhere else in America. In fact, Lorant's book was to be a celebration of the "rebirth" of Pittsburgh, a city finally free of its grimy and polluted hard-industrial past.

Smith's imagination was ignited by what he saw in Pittsburgh. The city's three rivers cut deep valleys through the Allegheny foothills, providing what he called "vistas of melancholy." In one glance Smith could see the city's monolithic factories, fiery steel mills, and skyscrapers—monuments to Carnegie, Frick, Mellon, and Heinz—surrounded by the dense, humble neighborhoods of Irish, Dutch, Polish, Slovak, Greek, Russian, Italian, Hungarian, Syrian, German, and African American people, many of them less than two generations removed from their homelands. Like the smokestacks, belfries and spires in each neighborhood reached upward, rising above narrow, winding streets and wood-planked rowhouses. Hillsides were adorned with inclined trolleys or five-hundred-step metal staircases connecting home to the workplace and market. Everything emanated from the riverbanks, which had stunned early European explorers with their natural beauty but which in 1955 were covered with factories, mills, and railroad tracks as far as Smith could see. The haunting and paradoxical elements of the modern world—elements that had been building in his photography since the war—were on full display in Pittsburgh: glory and despair, production and destruction, past and present, human and machine, the individual and the collective, the natural and the man-made. Smith called these "equilibriums of paradox." In his notes, Smith wrote, "In all travels, all experiences, I have seldom so felt the contradictions."

Smith took photographs in Pittsburgh for the better part of 1955 and on return trips to the city in 1956 and 1957, accumulating up to seventeen thousand negatives. After an explosive encounter with Lorant over control of his work, Smith met his obligation by delivering several hundred prints for Lorant to use as he pleased in his book. Then, aided by the rare awarding of two successive Guggenheim fellowships, Smith worked to bring his Pittsburgh pictures into a coherent, publishable form. By late

1955 Magnum realized the immense scale of the Pittsburgh material Smith was accumulating and dispatched a young photographer, Jim Karales, to Smith's home in Croton to help with the darkroom work. Karales stayed for more than two years. The two men met at the darkroom everyday at 3 p.m. and worked until sunrise the following morning.

Smith gradually pared the images down to a set of two thousand meticulous 5 × 7 work prints which he painstakingly arranged, rearranged, and pinned to bulletin boards all over the house. He considered these boards, in their constant, fragmentary state of flux, to be his Pittsburgh essay. He labored to bring each of these images into master-print form, something he achieved for more than six hundred pictures—a heroic accomplishment. In his notes and letters he referred to this body of work as his "greatest" or "finest" set of photographs. "If nothing else, this Pittsburgh layout has the tremendous unity of my convictions," Smith wrote. He seemed to be drawing upon every influence in his life for this essay—the sense of moral tragedy he had gleaned from his war experiences; the stream-of-consciousness narrative techniques of Joyce and Faulkner; the social conscience of O'Casey; the lyrical passion of Rilke; the dissonant rhythms of late Beethoven; and the topsy-turvy chords of Thelonious Monk—a magnum opus that would realize the kaleidoscopic stream of imagery that Smith had created in his mind, a photo-essay of symphonic scale. He also felt an urgent need to prove to *Life*'s editors that he was the visual revolutionary they had been constraining all along.

Smith and Magnum began approaching potential publishers of the project in 1956. Many magazines were interested, including *Life,* but none would agree to his demands for editorial control. He rejected several offers of up to $20,000 for rights to the pictures when his terms of publication were not accepted. It was an excruciating bind for Smith, his family, and Magnum, which had depleted many of its cooperative resources with loans to him. The two Guggenheim grants had made only a dent in Smith's growing debts. In desperation, Smith moved out of the home in Croton in mid-1957, virtually abandoning his family, and into a dilapidated loft building in Manhattan's wholesale flower district. The building, a hangout of jazz musicians who regularly turned up for impromptu all-night jam sessions, was a fitting environment for Smith. There he continued to work on his Pittsburgh essay, making more prints and refining his layouts. Some of the jazz musicians remember waist-high stacks of prints lining the walls of the rat-infested building.

In 1958 Smith found a publisher for the essay, which he had aptly titled "Labyrinthian Walk." *Popular Photography* magazine agreed to give him thirty-eight pages in its *Photography Annual 1959.* Smith was paid only $1,900

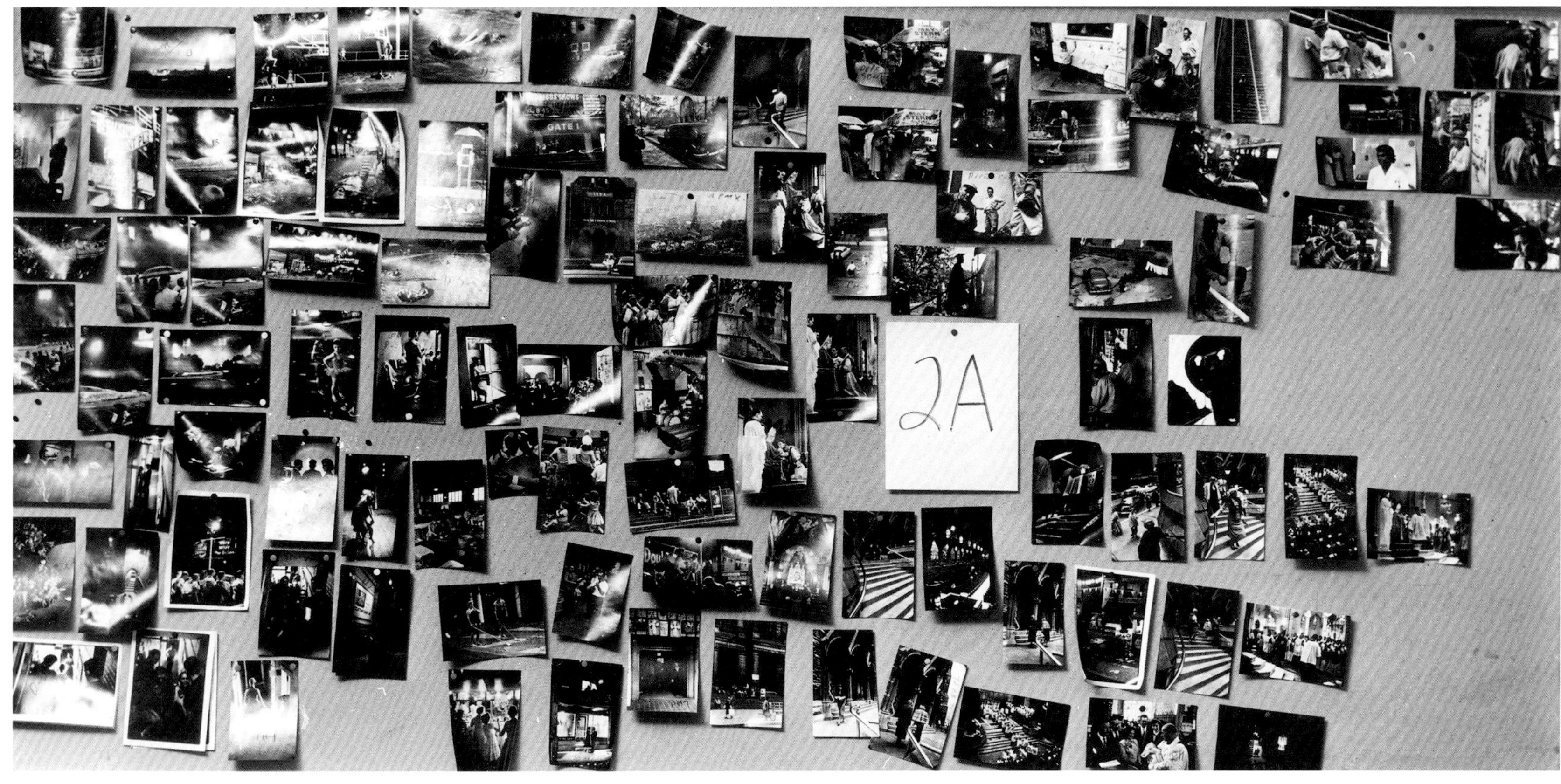

but was given what he wanted, complete control over the layout. He worked continuously to meet *Popular Photography*'s June 1958 deadline. The published layout of eighty-eight pictures with text was mostly Smith's design, but he was extremely dissatisfied—devastated—with the result. The magazine, as a form, simply was not a suitable vehicle for the complex essay that Smith had envisioned. His colossal ambition had fused with a growing sense of inadequacy, no doubt enhanced by his dependencies to alcohol and amphetamines, and prevented him from making final decisions about the composition of the essay that met his satisfaction. In a sense, his dreams for the project had been doomed from the start.

In his letters from the period Smith's despair is clear. To his friend Ansel Adams in November 1958, Smith explained why he was writing: "Among the reasons is my desire to make a personal apology to you (and thus to photography) for the final failure, the debacle of Pittsburgh as printed." To his uncle, Jesse Caplinger, Smith wrote, "My own effort was destroyed through my own failure. Having fought through four years trying, I very bluntly could not work my way through the onslaughts with enough workable strength to complete it right. . . . So, it is a failure." To Leon Miller, a young Pittsburgh resident who had assisted him, Smith wrote, "That I can look to saving my career and life by regaining an income is my present, survival problem. The infinite mistake of Pittsburgh does not take from the fact that the set of

photographs is my finest set. The toll and the toil, for miracles."

For many years Smith kept a Pittsburgh book on his list of projects—even mentioning it in 1978, the year he died—but he never returned to it. Not long before his death he issued an autobiographical statement, almost a self-eulogy, in which he said: "I think I was at my very peak as a photographer in, say, 1958 or so. My imagination and my seeing were both, I don't know if I can think of . . . were 'red-hot' or something. Everywhere I looked, every time I thought, it seemed like it left me with great exuberance and just a truer quality of seeing. But it was one of the most miserable times of my life, for I had little opportunity to put it into real usage."

*Dream Street* is my attempt to gather in one place the most important pictures from Smith's Pittsburgh work. I have relied as much as possible on choices Smith himself made, without attempting to re-create his essay (see Notes to Photographs). In searching to understand Smith's original intentions for this project it became evident that "Labyrinthian Walk," the layout that Smith designed for *Photography Annual 1959* was the clearest indicator of his plans. "Labyrinthian Walk" is reproduced in the back of this book, but this eighty-eight-picture photo-essay tells only part of the story.

At the Center for Creative Photography in Tucson (CCP), 653 master prints are in Smith's archive; another

572 are part of the collection at the Carnegie Museum of
Art in Pittsburgh. In addition to these exquisite prints
there are some 6,000 meticulous 5 x 7 work prints, 400
contact sheets, and 17,000 negatives, all providing significant clues as to Smith's intentions. In CCP's collection
were key photographs for understanding what Smith
struggled to accomplish in Pittsburgh. The photographs
of his bulletin boards show ever-evolving montages of
hundreds of images and communicate Smith's cinematic
sense of the world. I looked at sketches and partial dum-
mies of what would eventually become "Labyrinthian
Walk"—Smith's best attempts to transfer the bulletin-
board arrangements to print—but much of that material
only raises more questions than it answers.

Smith also left behind an archive of written materials
in which he gives alluring glimpses at, but no definitions
of, his dreams for the project: marked-up street maps of

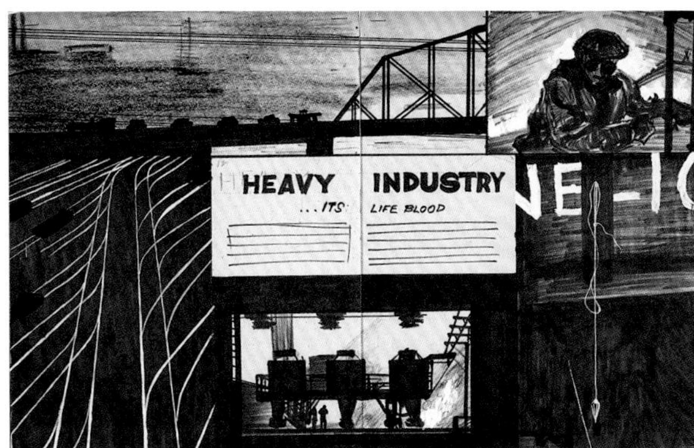


Pittsburgh from 1955; thousands of 3 x 5 notecards with
comments scribbled in pencil ("get names from ceme-
tery," "learning, yearning, sperming," "send layout to
Faulkner, Camus, Beckett"); many drafts of text meant to
accompany the pictures; two Guggenheim grant applica-
tions; dozens of clipped and annotated magazine and
newspaper articles; and hundreds of letters.

What shines through, irrevocably, in this enormous
body of material—the detritus of Smith's spectacular
failure—are the prints. They overwhelm it all with their
beauty and sheer volume. Smith may not have achieved
his essay but surely these prints redeem his labor, and
leave a trail for an editor to follow. I often felt I might be
overreaching but my astonishment at seeing these master prints was profound. I then began to recognize that
Smith's work prints were, to a large degree, as beautifully
crafted and carefully detailed as the masters; *the work
that went into this project.* If we could have seen those
bulletin boards pinned in turn with all two thousand of
these 5 x 7 work prints, we might have seen Smith's essay.
Now all we have are a mammoth set of prints. When
Smith was paring down his work prints into a smaller set
of master prints he commented that the result was a
"synthesis of the whole." This book is my speculation, or
approximation, of that synthesis.

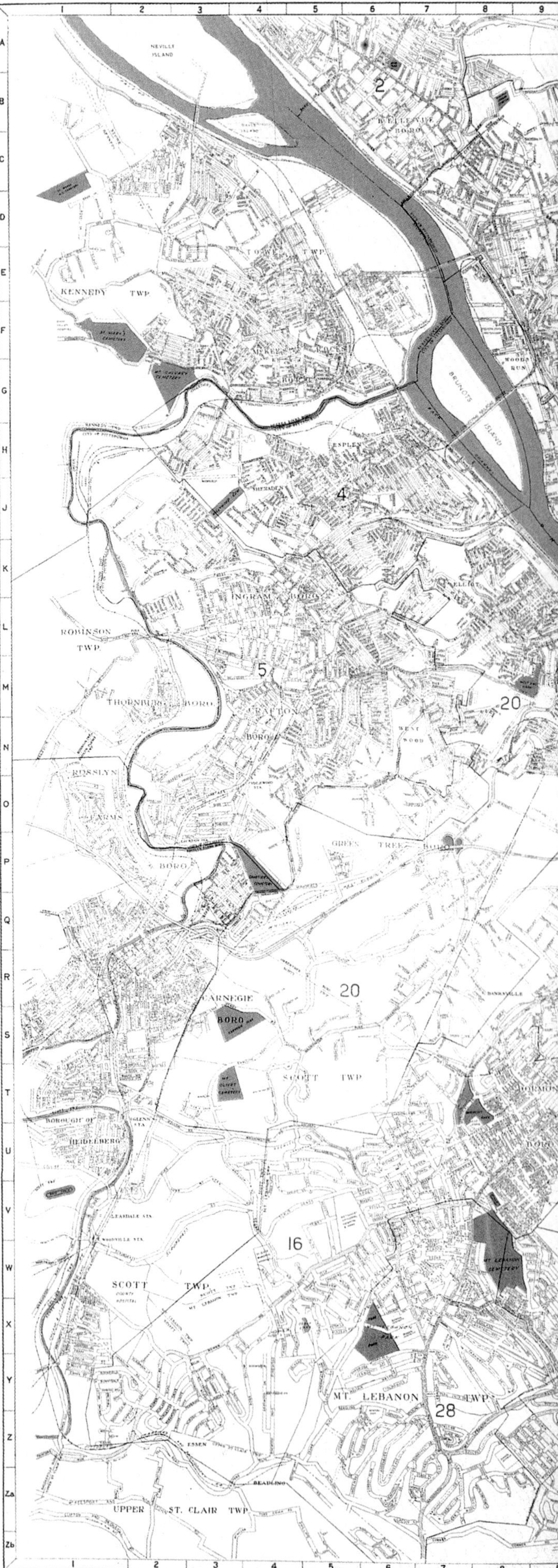

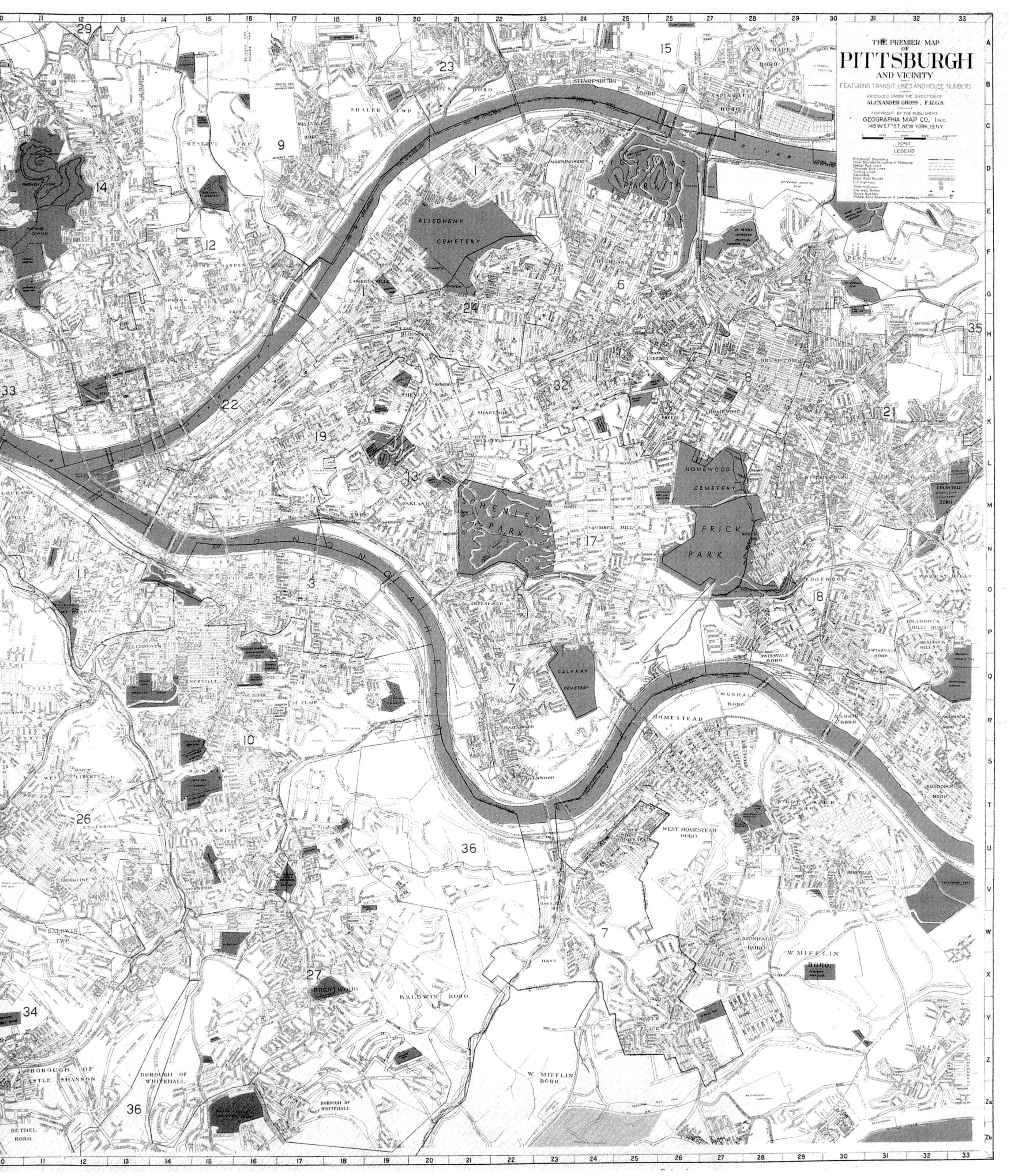

THE PREMIER MAP
OF
PITTSBURGH
AND VICINITY
FEATURING TRANSIT LINES AND HOUSE NUMBERS
PRODUCED UNDER THE DIRECTION OF
ALEXANDER GROSS, F.R.G.S.
COPYRIGHT BY THE PUBLISHERS
GEOGRAPHIA MAP CO., INC.
145 W.57TH ST., NEW YORK, 19, N.Y.
SCALE
LEGEND
Pittsburgh Boundary
Other Boundaries outside of Pittsburgh
Feeder Bus Lines
Through Bus Lines
Trolley Lines
Railroads
Main Auto Routes
U.S. Highways
State Highways
One-way Streets
House Numbers
Postal Zone Boundaries & Zone Numbers

Feb. 1, 1955

Dearest Mother,

I am as calm as a sleepy lagoon, although that, and I, may conceal a volcano on the verge of eruption. Who said to you, of the possibilities of my being fired, or of firing. After all it is my eight bucks (owed) against their eight billion (a figurative figure), and what could be more even than a grain of wheat against the miller's stone—I speak not of mill stones dangling from a chain around my neck. Shed no tears of compassion for only tragedy awaits—but as yet it awaits not for me. It may be that we are walking hand in hand, tragedy and I, and desperation makes three. Though my stomach quivers like a professional belly dancer, the dancer is paid and mine is caustic(ing). All is not lost, instead, I have thrown it away, lightly, dancingly, trippingly away—though I calculate it may return as would a friendly boom-a-rang, and if it doesn't, let me rest six months to lift the rubble of collapse from about my head.

In other words, don't get perturbed—difficulty, but not destruction is at hand. And everyone shall get their money, as well.

Learn me once—this you never done—and even credit the pioneer stock from which you gave to me. I do many regrettable things, and may prove the point that heaven and hell can exist within one human body—yet in my work, and the responsibility I choose to assume in it, I will not make the compromise that defiles (in my arbitrary viewpoint) that responsibility, nor that work—try to understand—that my mind has long been made up, irrevocably so, and that I have a talent which others need for their commercial ends; and because mine is an exceptional talent, or rather, a small talent forced high by exceptional stubbornness in utilizing it, that these people think twice and twice again (though they might hate me, rather than respect the conscience that I sometimes flaunt by example) before they have the courage of saying, to hell with that guy—for to take the courage of that decision diminishes their own security, just a shaving less. And I who need the security just as badly as they, have the courage (but oh God how it frightens me at times, with debts, and children four) to gamble that security to protect the purity of my work, or gain a strength to make it work the better in the future. I will work with people for the best way of handling, and do not necessarily insist that mine is the only way but I expect a half-way intelligent attempt on their part, and can not accept another's decision when it is quickly derived from shoddy inattention. For it is my name that is carried to the world under their ineptness, and bearing my name, I must accept full responsibility for what is presented—

Love,
Gene


Letter from Smith to his mother a month after his resignation from *Life* and a month before he accepted the three-week freelance assignment in Pittsburgh

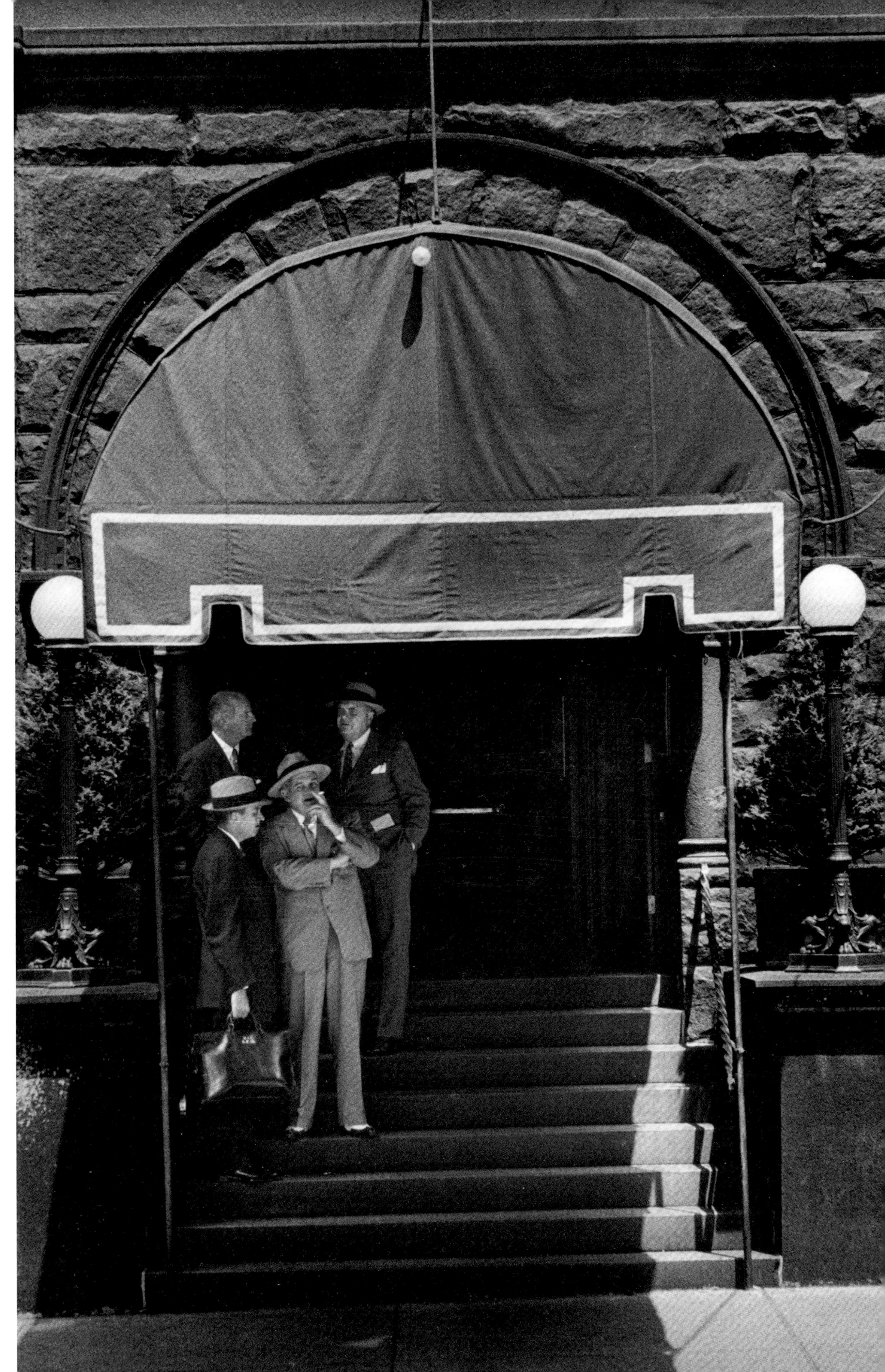

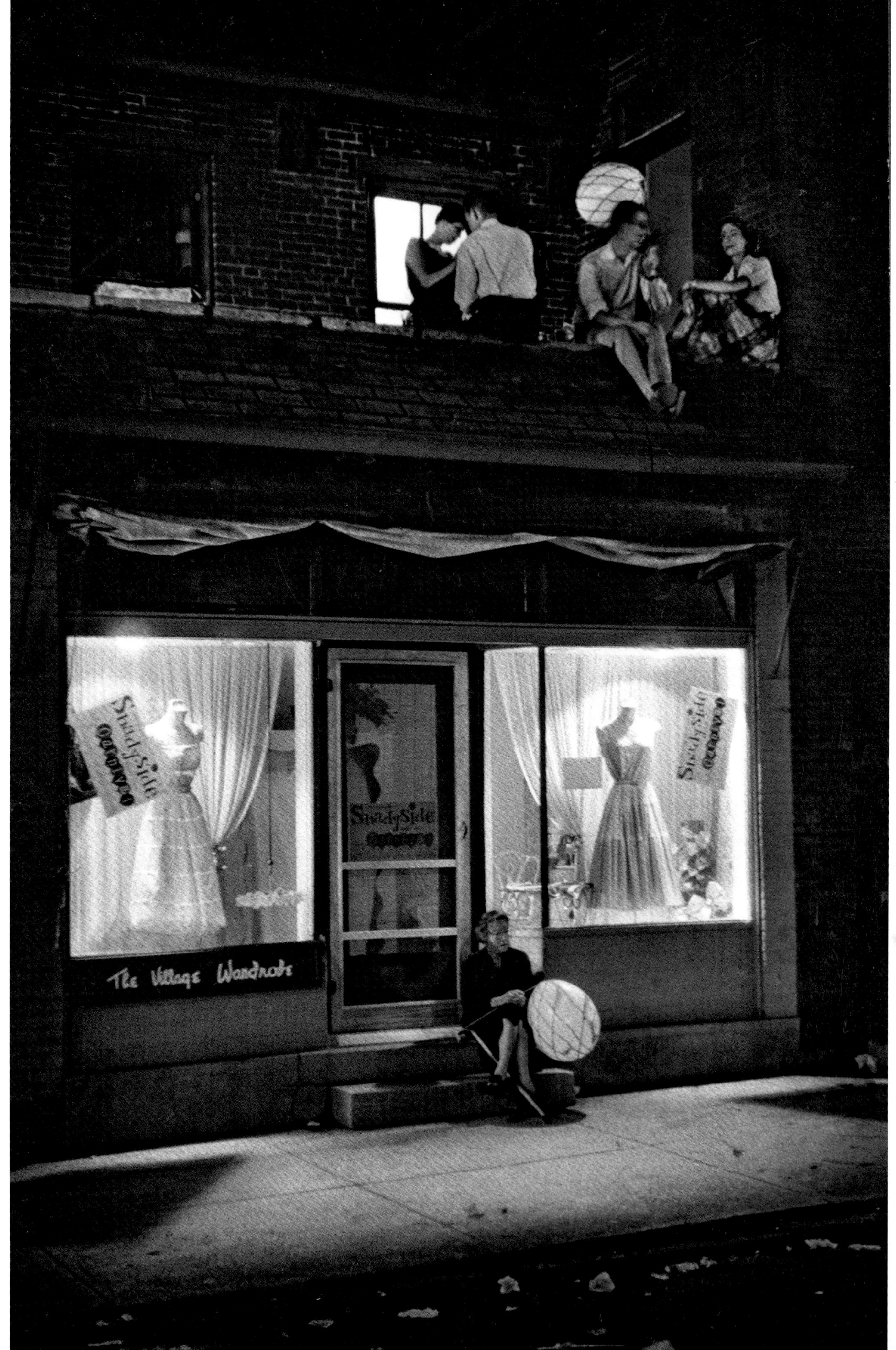
ShadySide
ShadySide
The Village Wardrobe

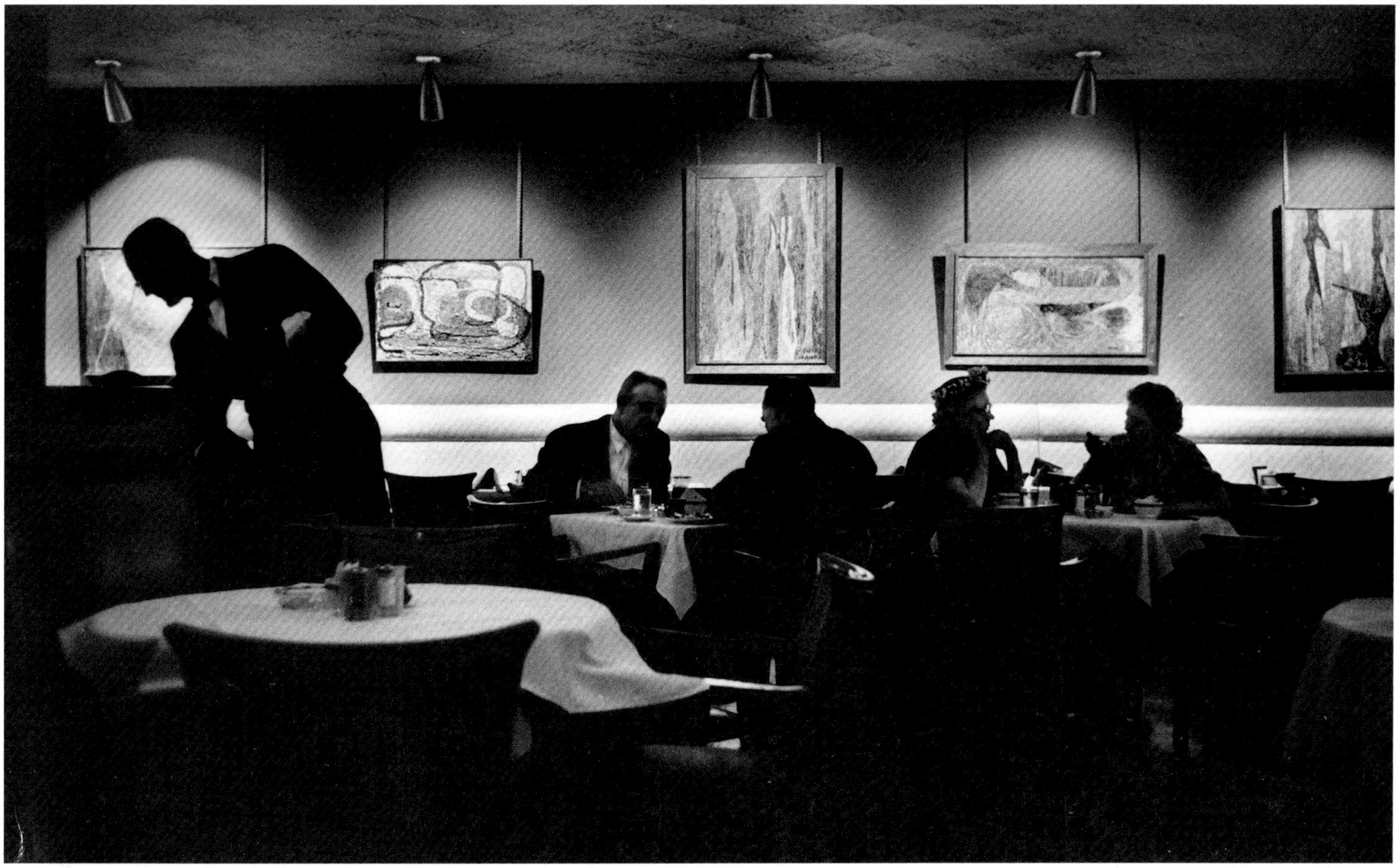

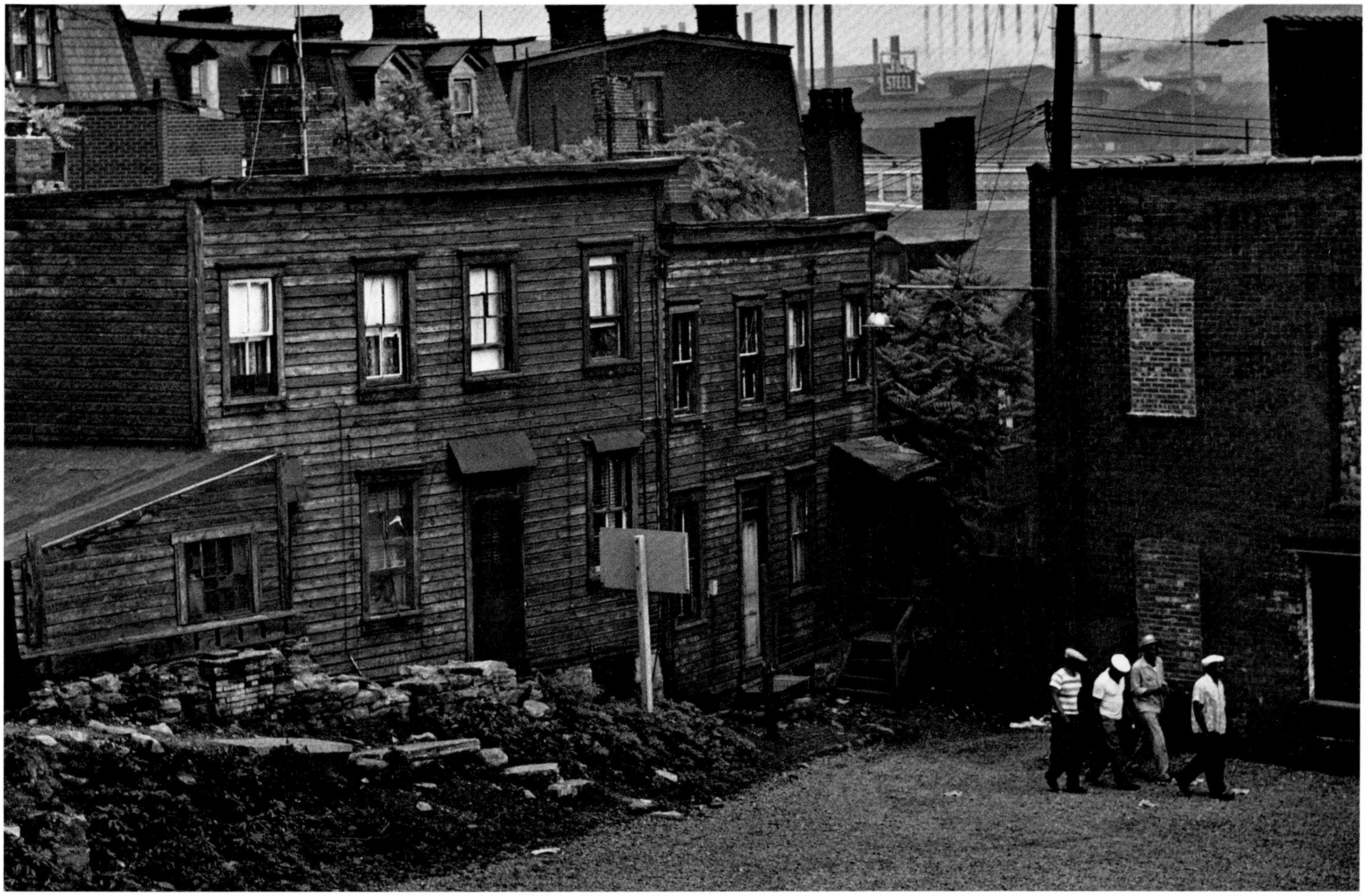

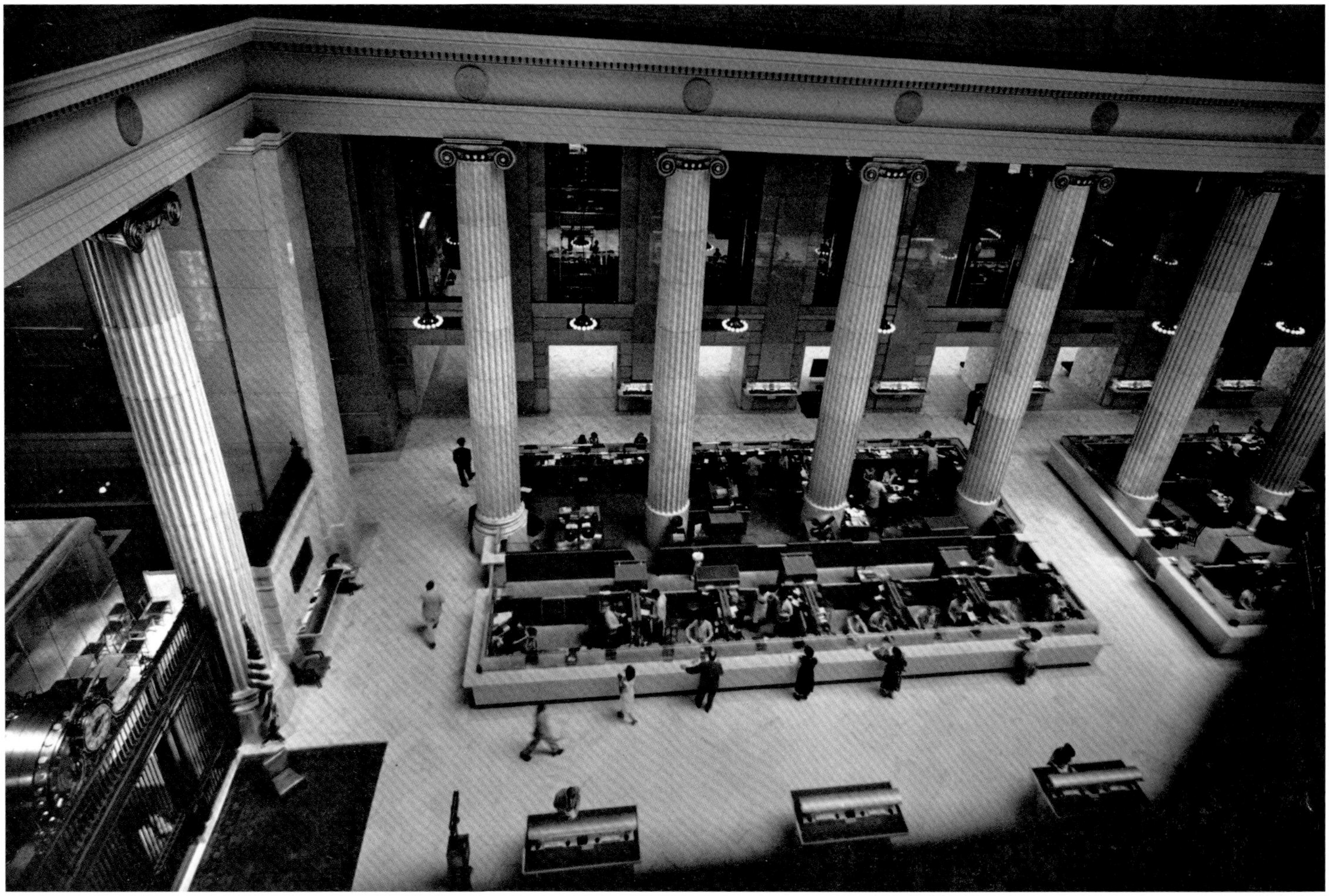

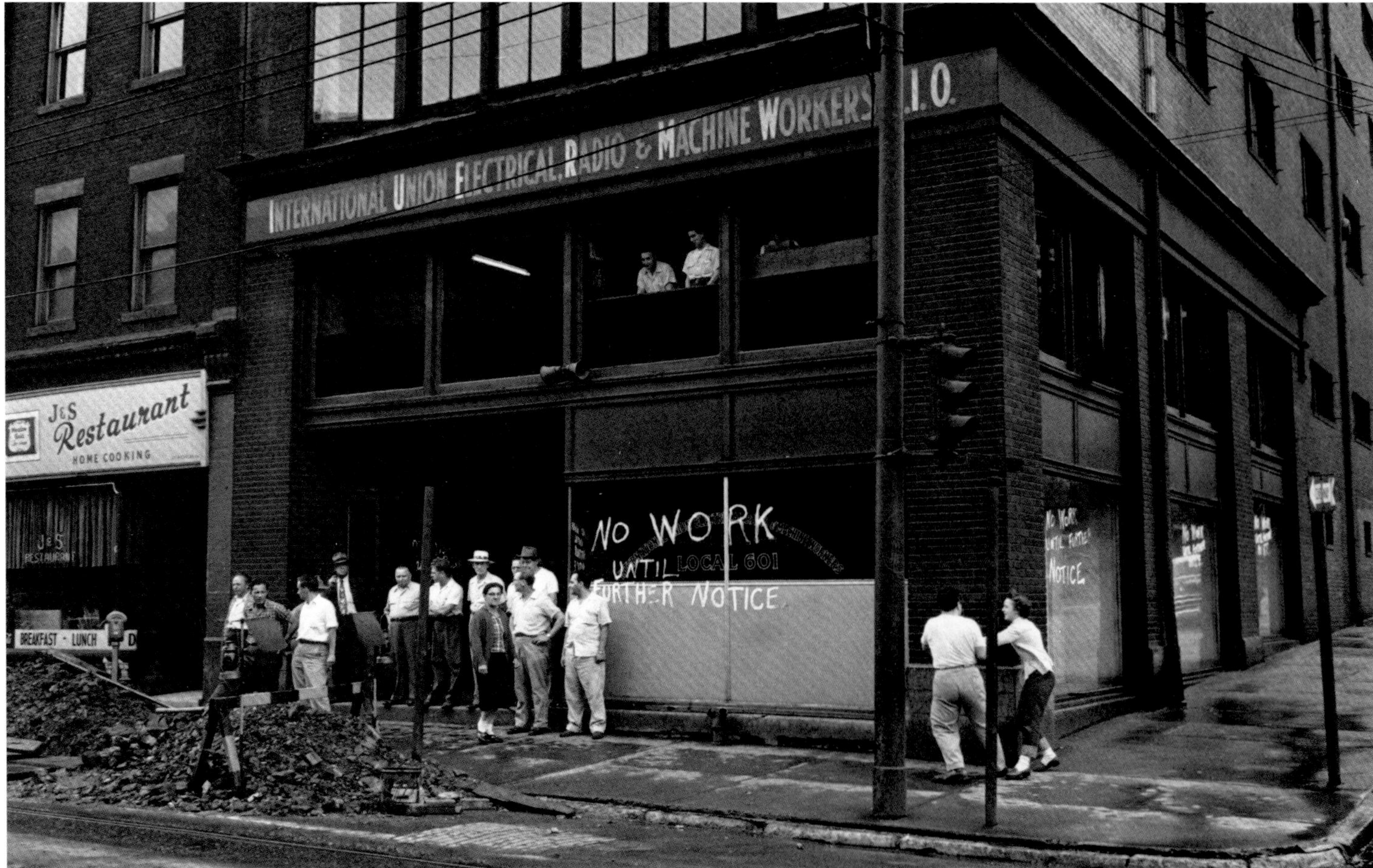

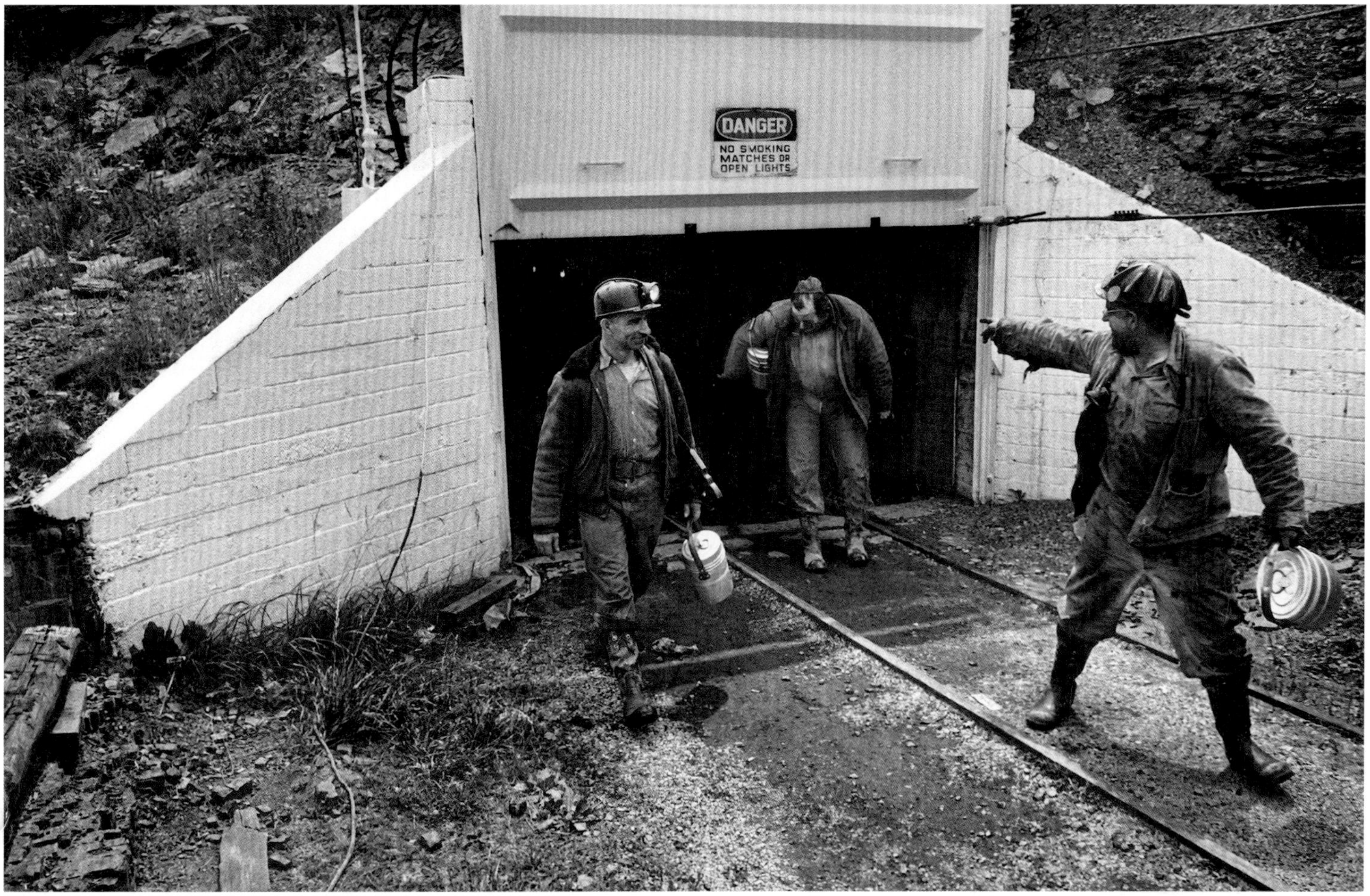

DANGER
NO SMOKING
MATCHES OR
OPEN LIGHTS

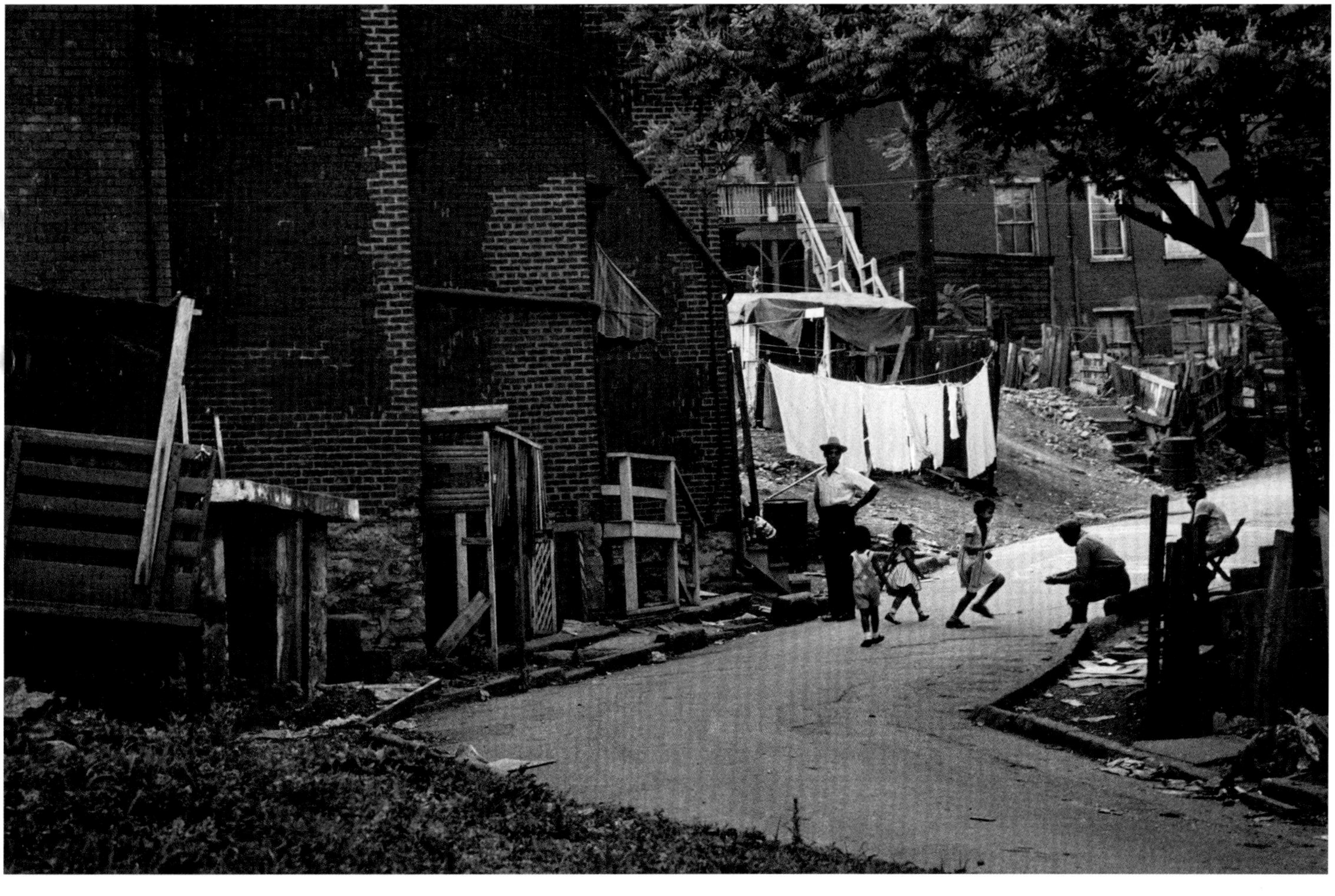

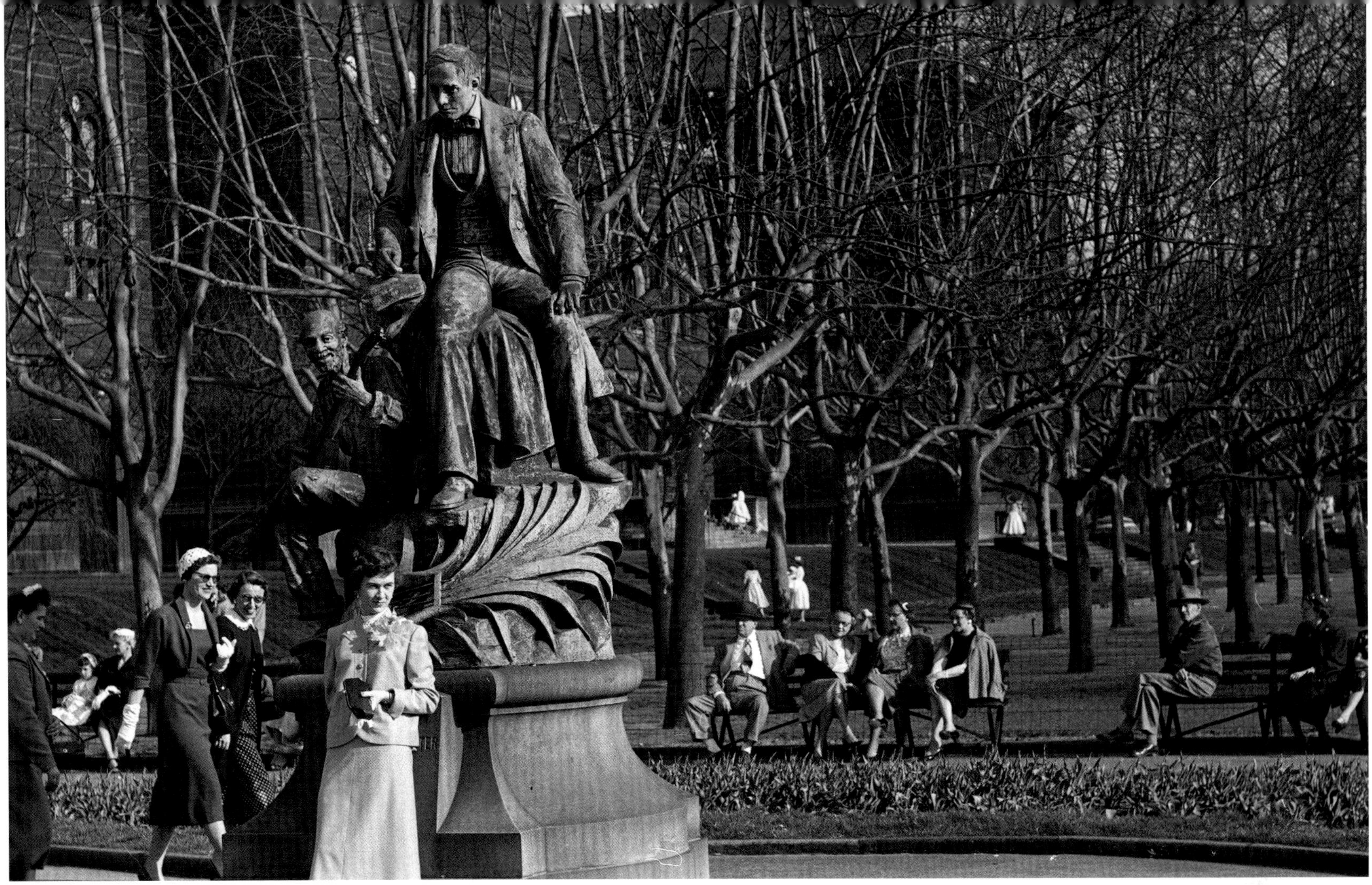

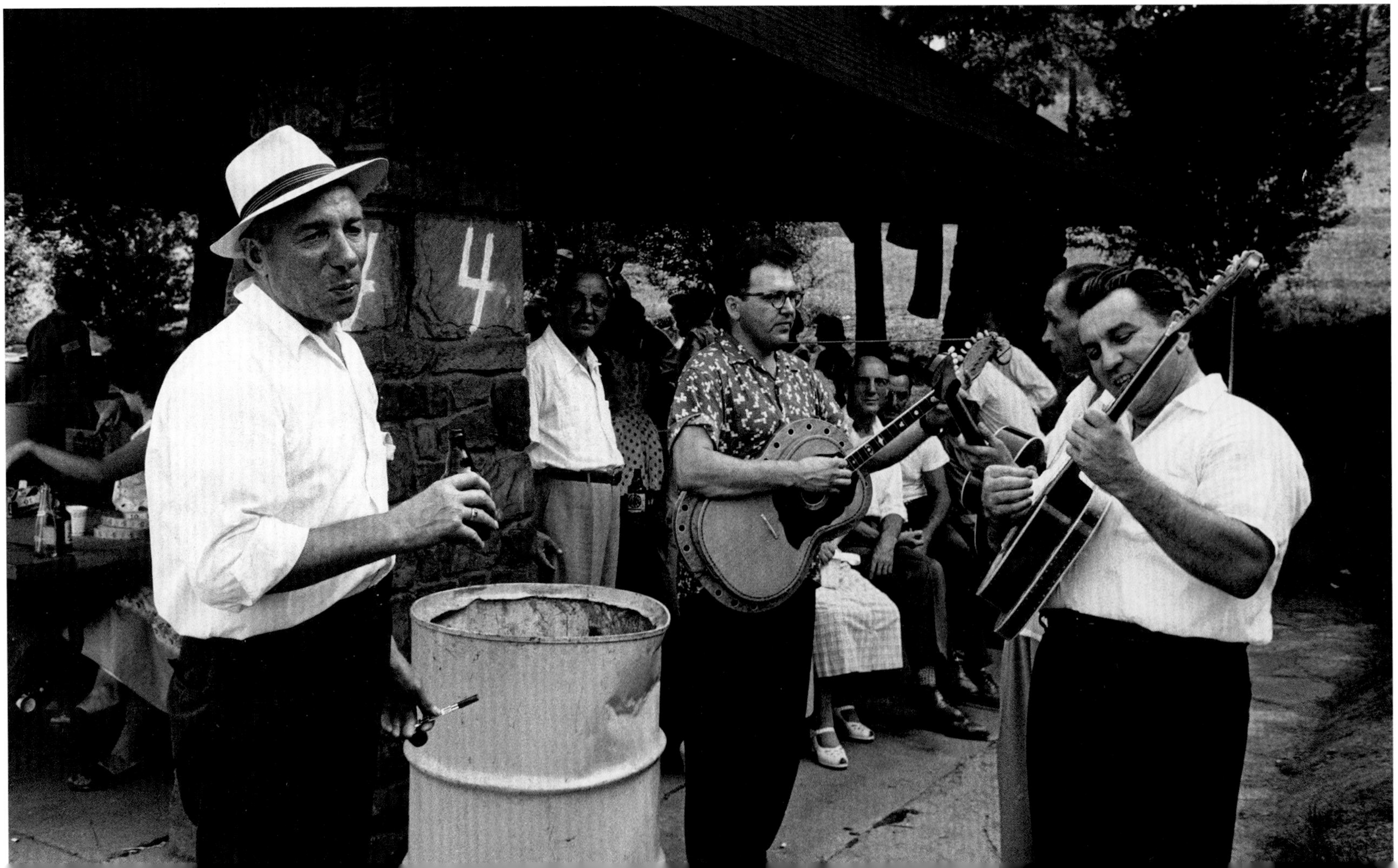

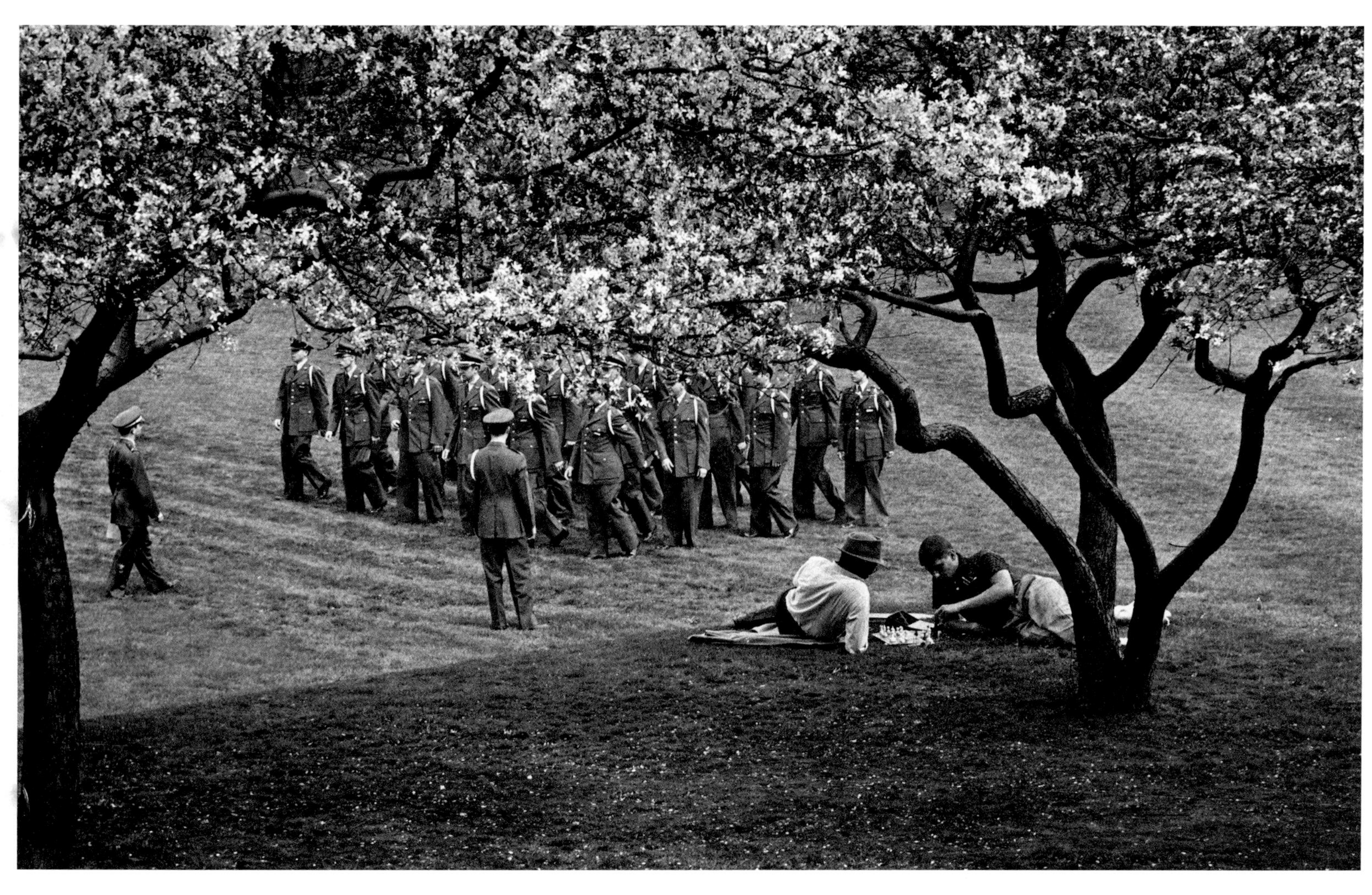

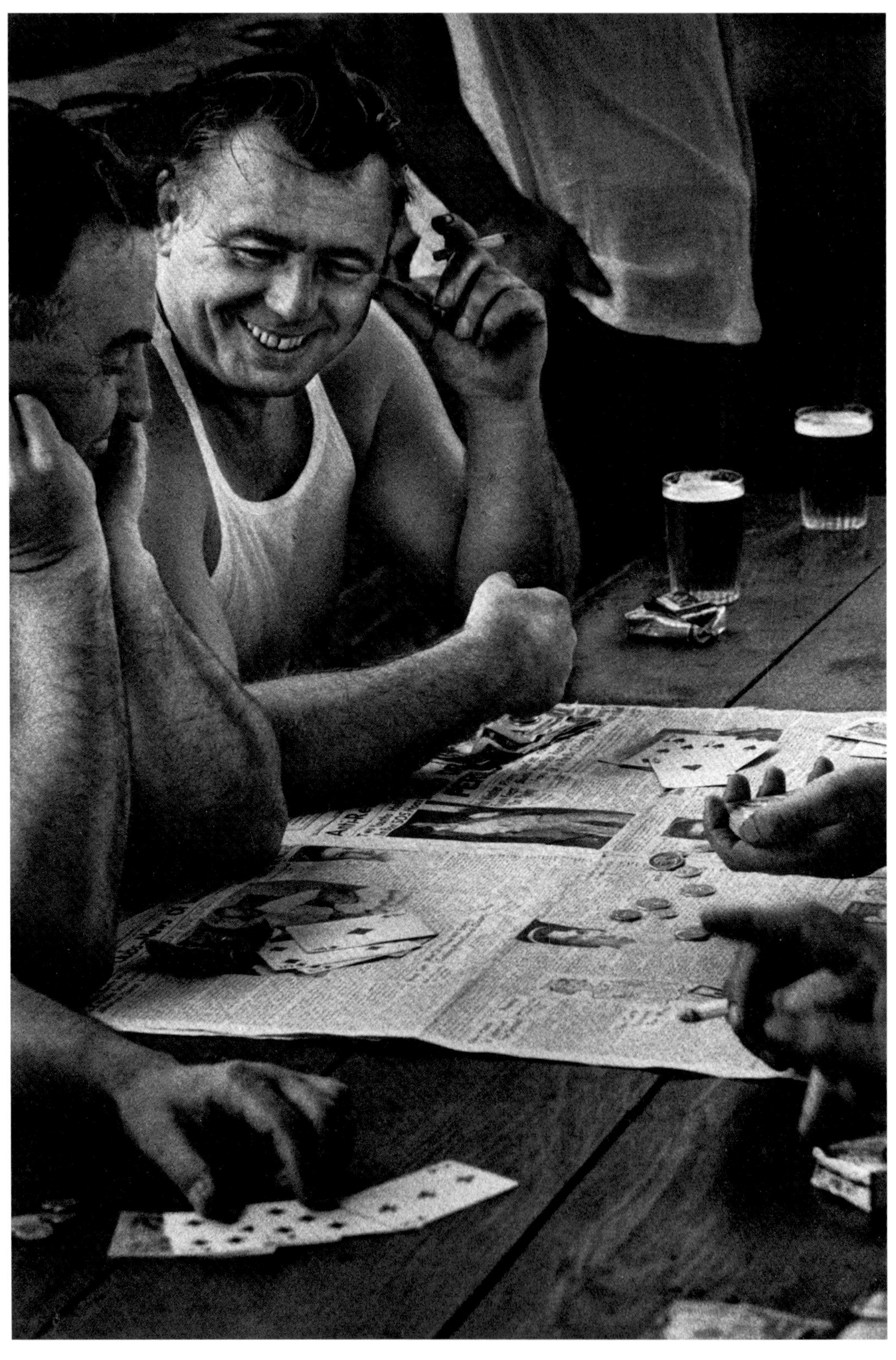

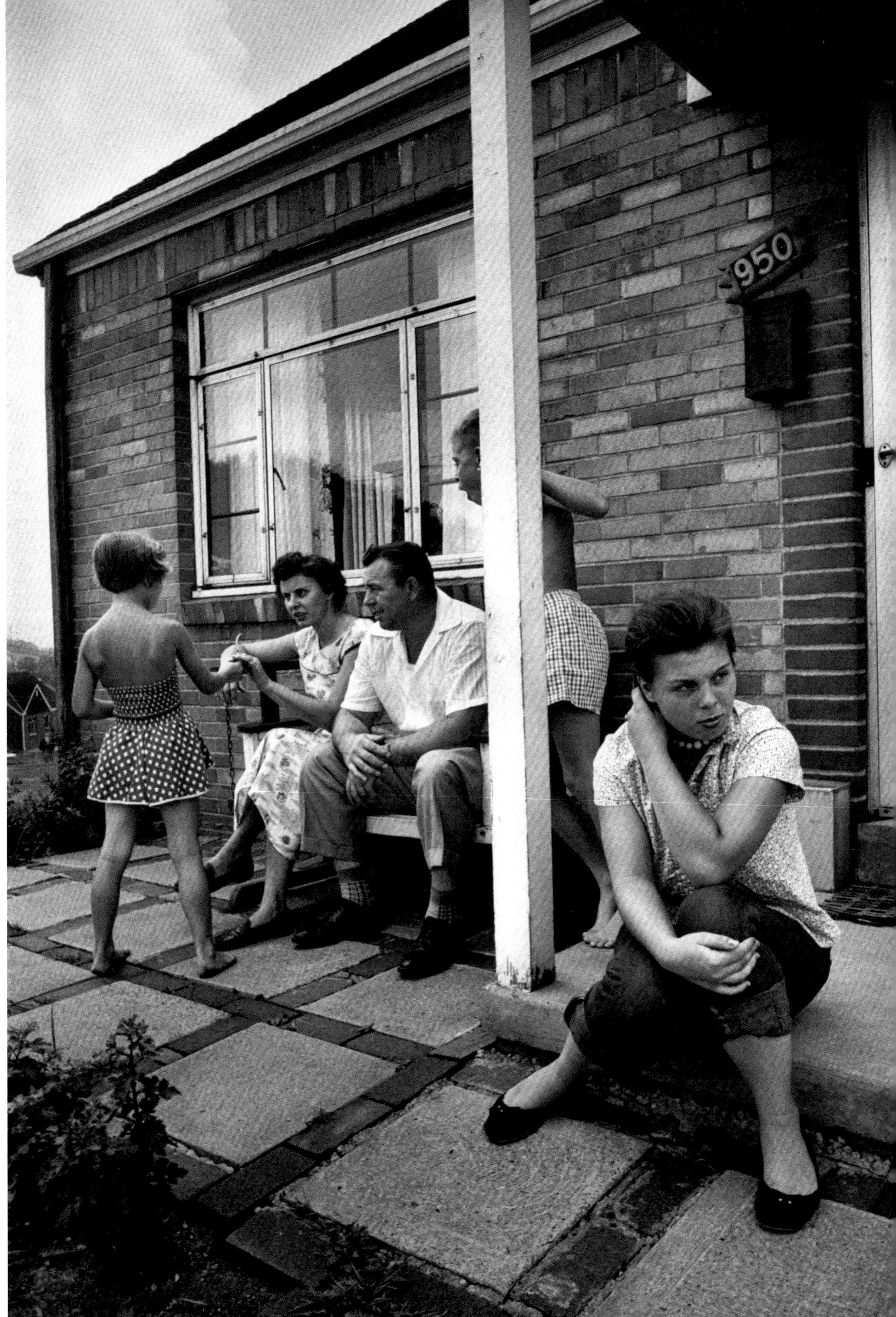
950

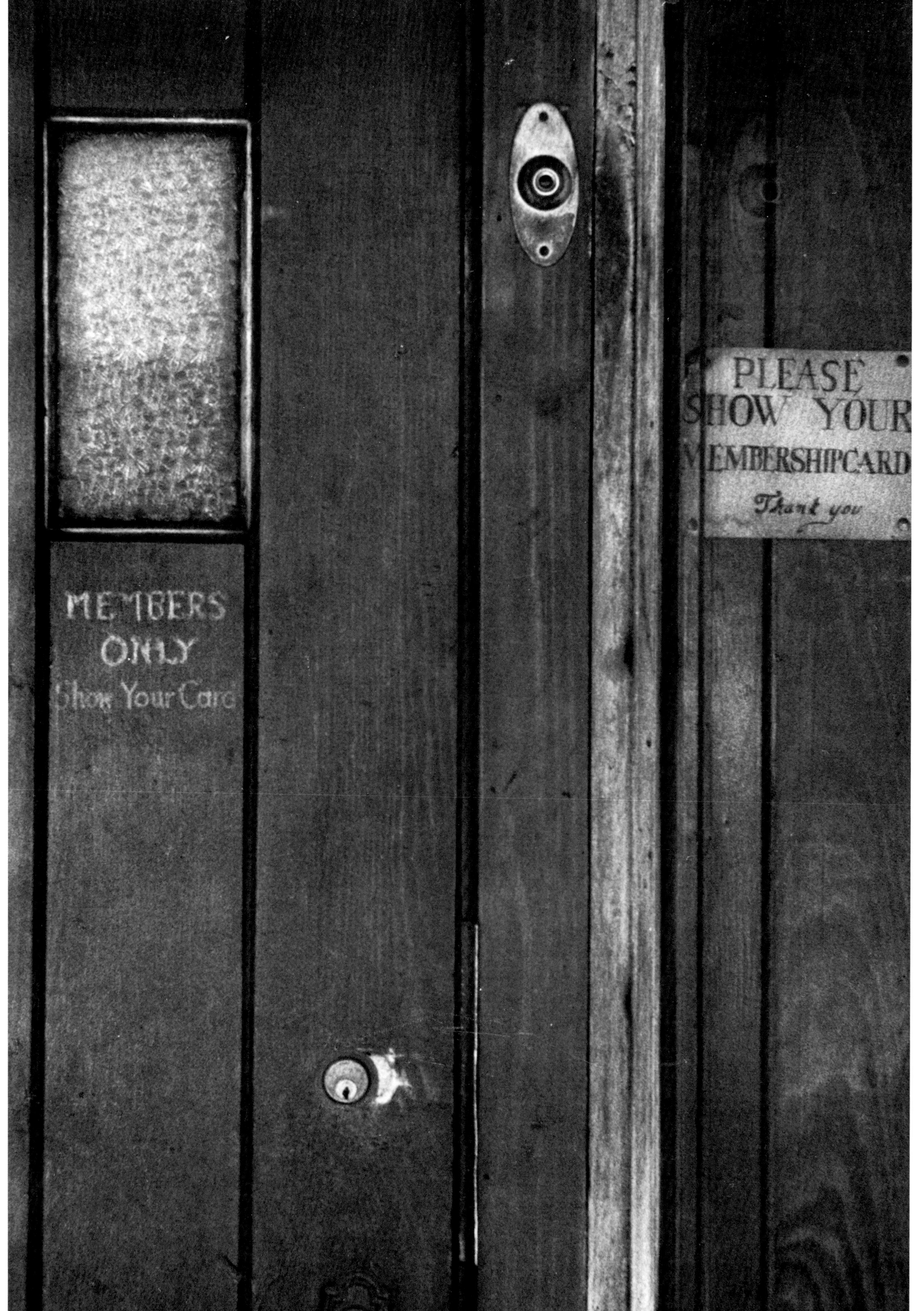
MEMBERS
ONLY
Show Your Card
PLEASE
SHOW YOUR
MEMBERSHIPCARD
Thank you

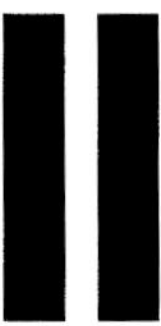

Pittsburgh, the City of. An attempt at photographic insight into the always transitory immediate of a city undergoing existence. Its physical characteristics (and physical portrait) through surface line and detailed feature—through an eloquence of vistas given thought, and by the details of many fragments. The long squat belching of its industries, the blemish of its slums, and how at times both have given way to the cleanliness of cared for greenery in newly built parks close by newly constructed buildings. From the blighted even to how soft with sensual beauty the city can be—seen from high, looking along the buildings and up the river to the moon which has just become fully stated above the horizon. And a further attempt at photographic penetration deriving from study and awareness and participation, a result that would transmit a sense of the city's character, even unto the spirit and the spiritual—and I would have the result derive from a sensible perspective.

From Smith's 1956 application for a fellowship from the John Simon Guggenheim Foundation
—"Plans for Use of Fellowship"

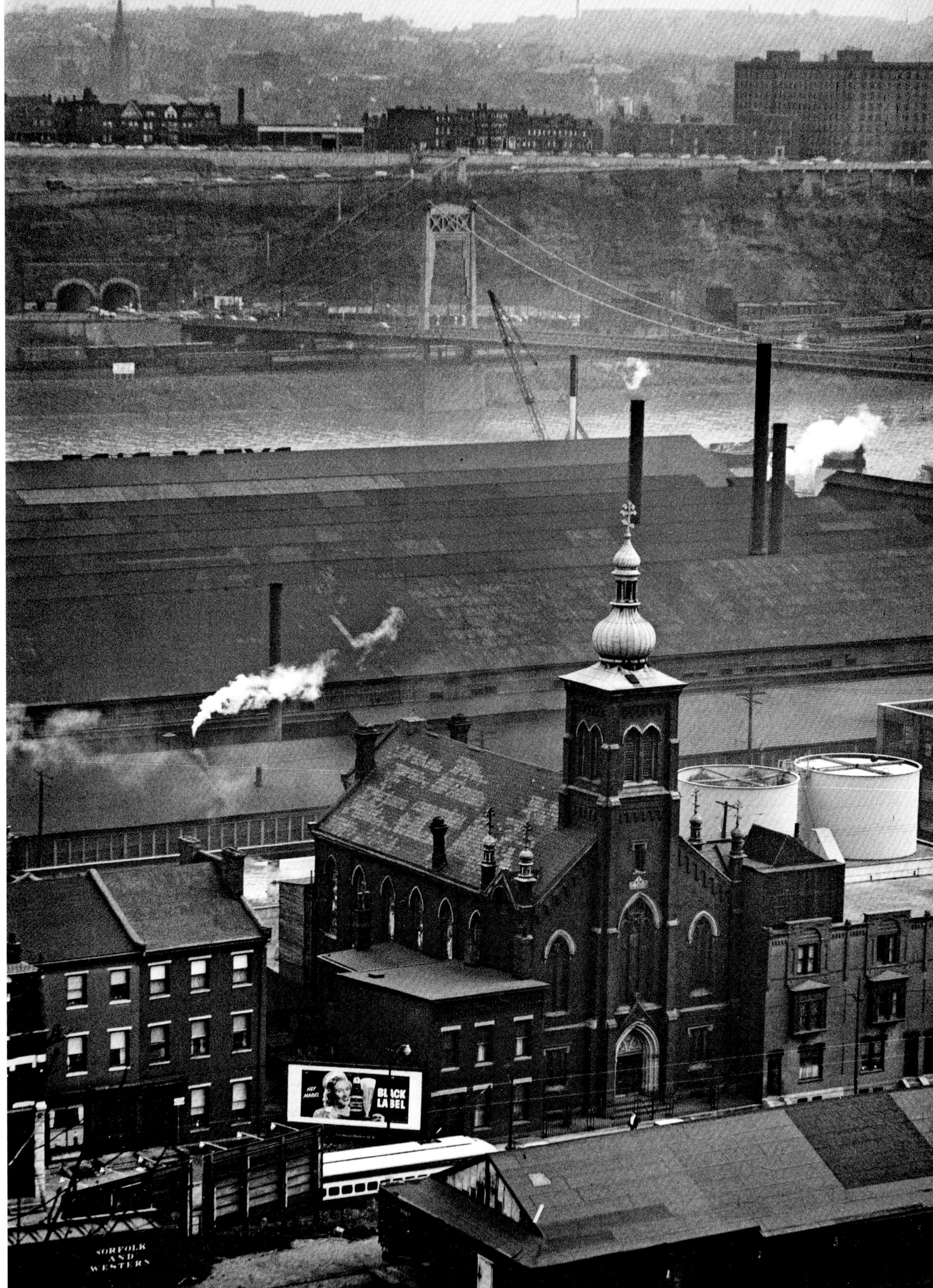

HEY MABEL
BLACK LABEL
NORFOLK AND WESTERN

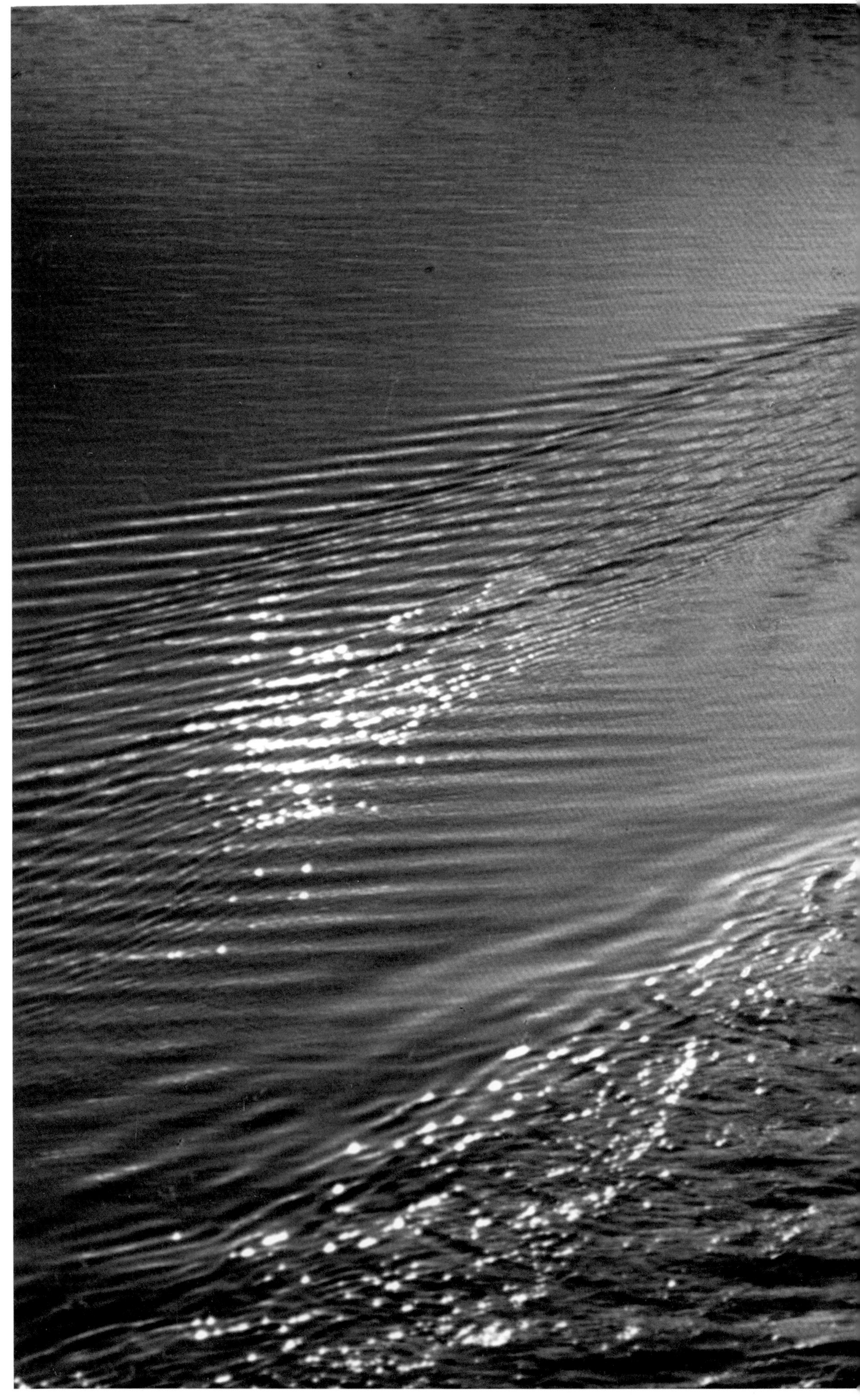

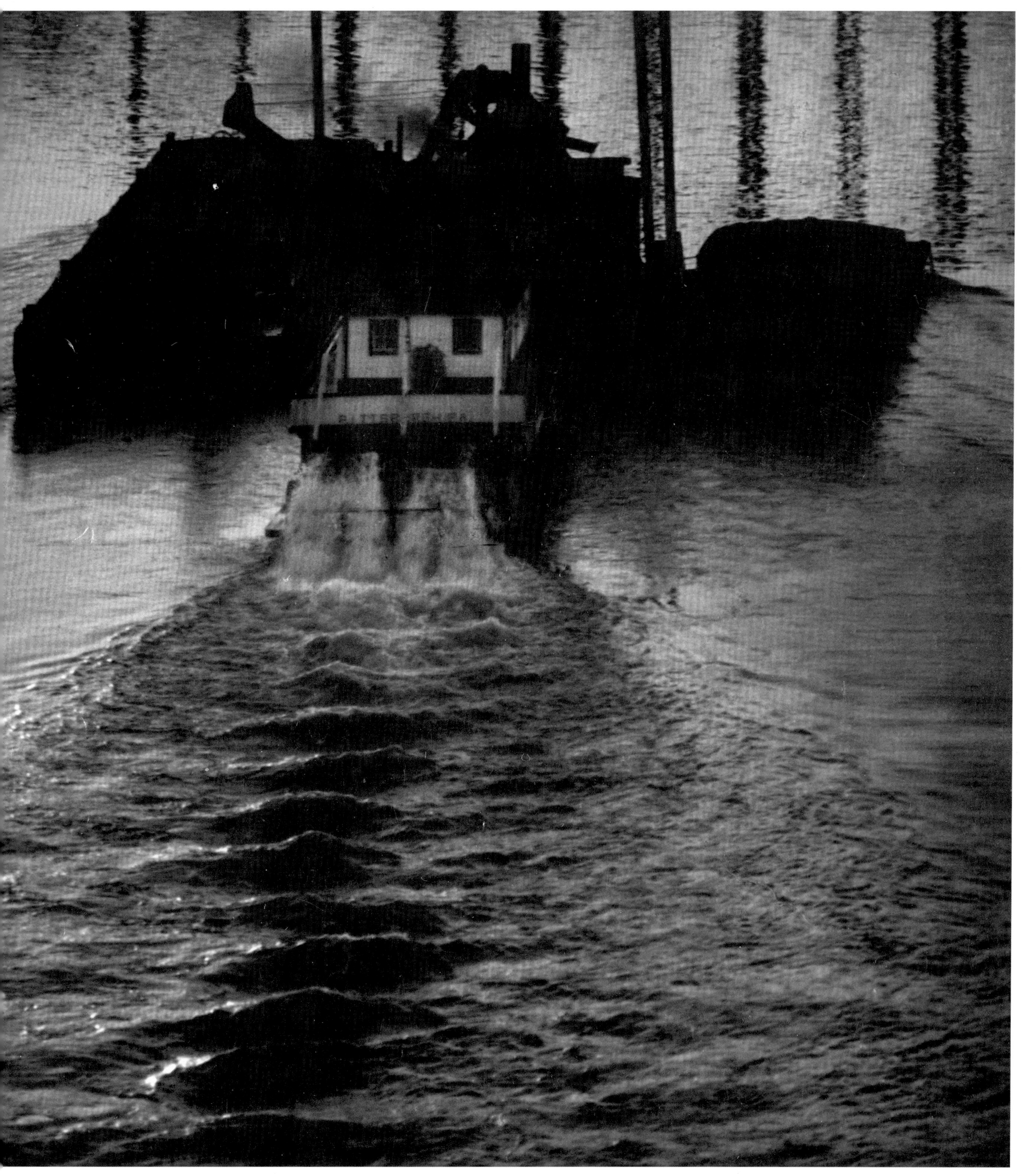

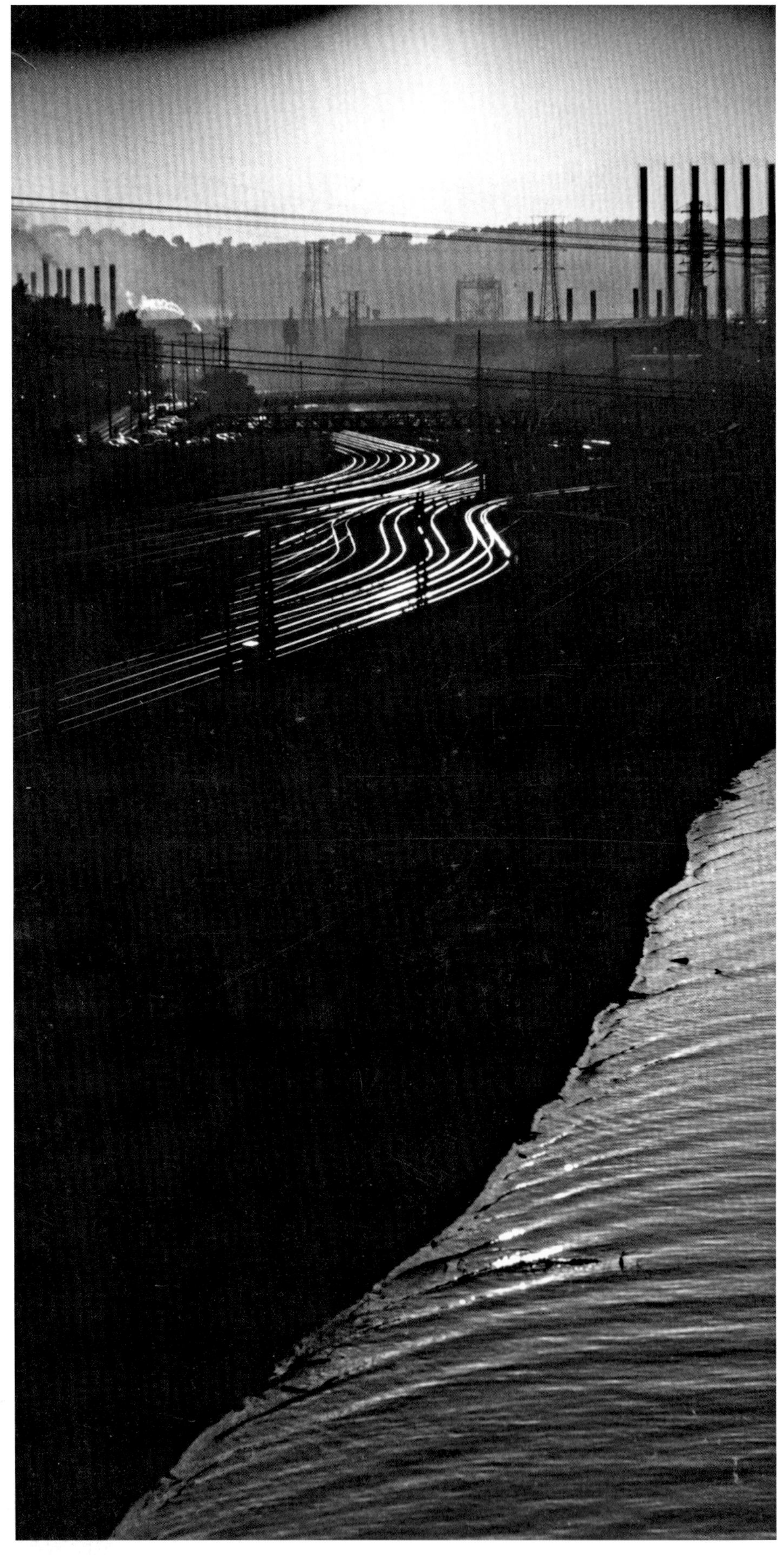

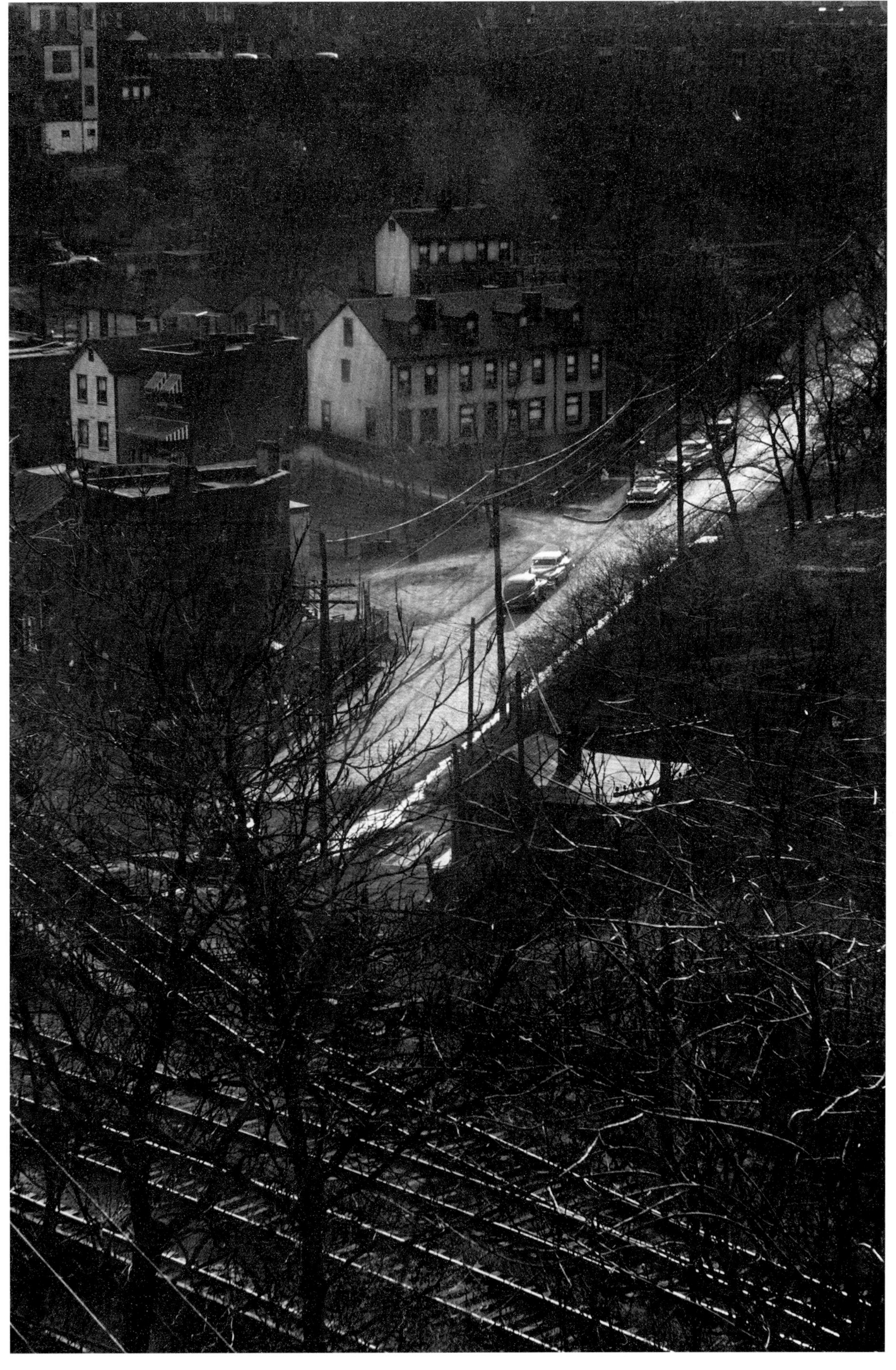

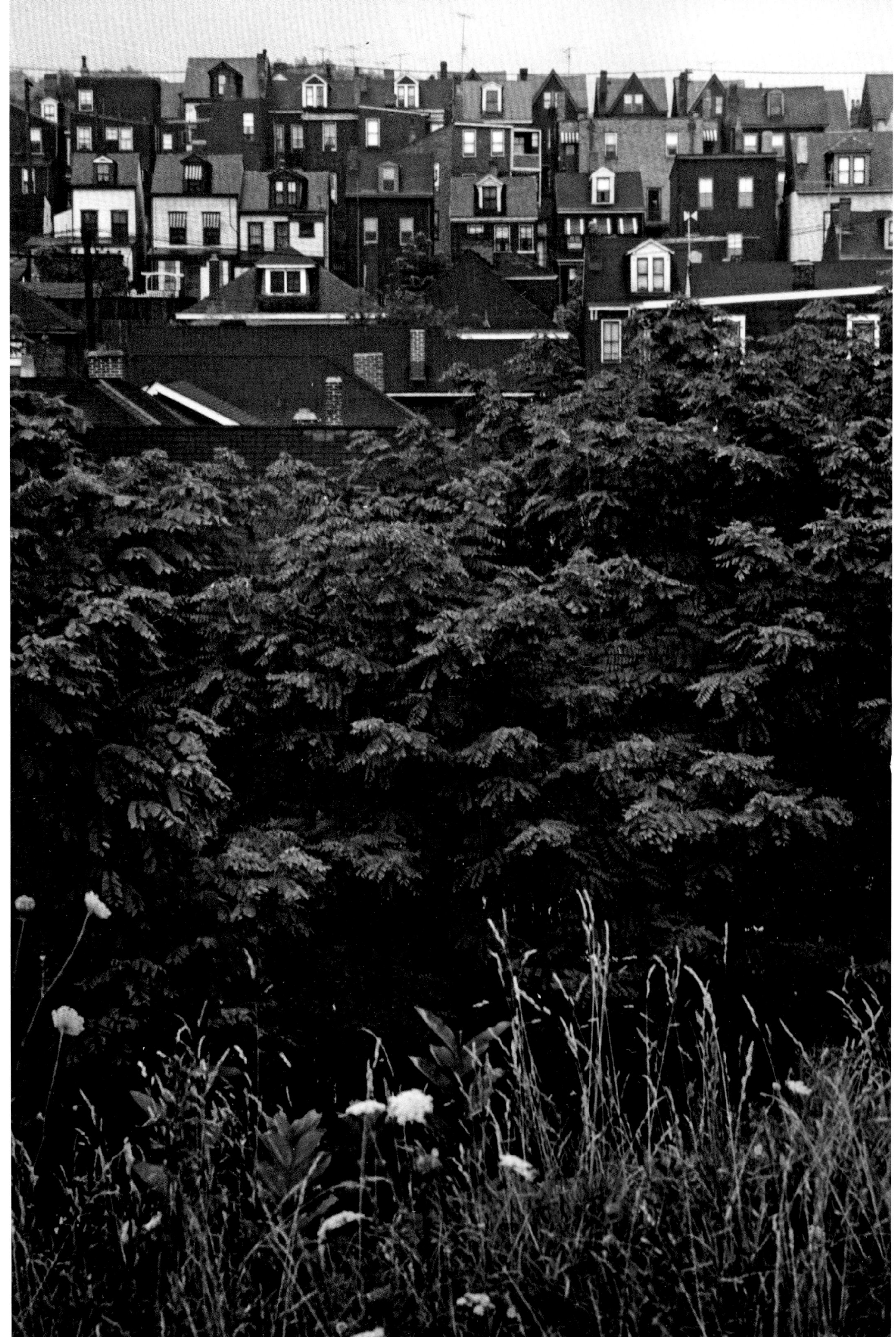

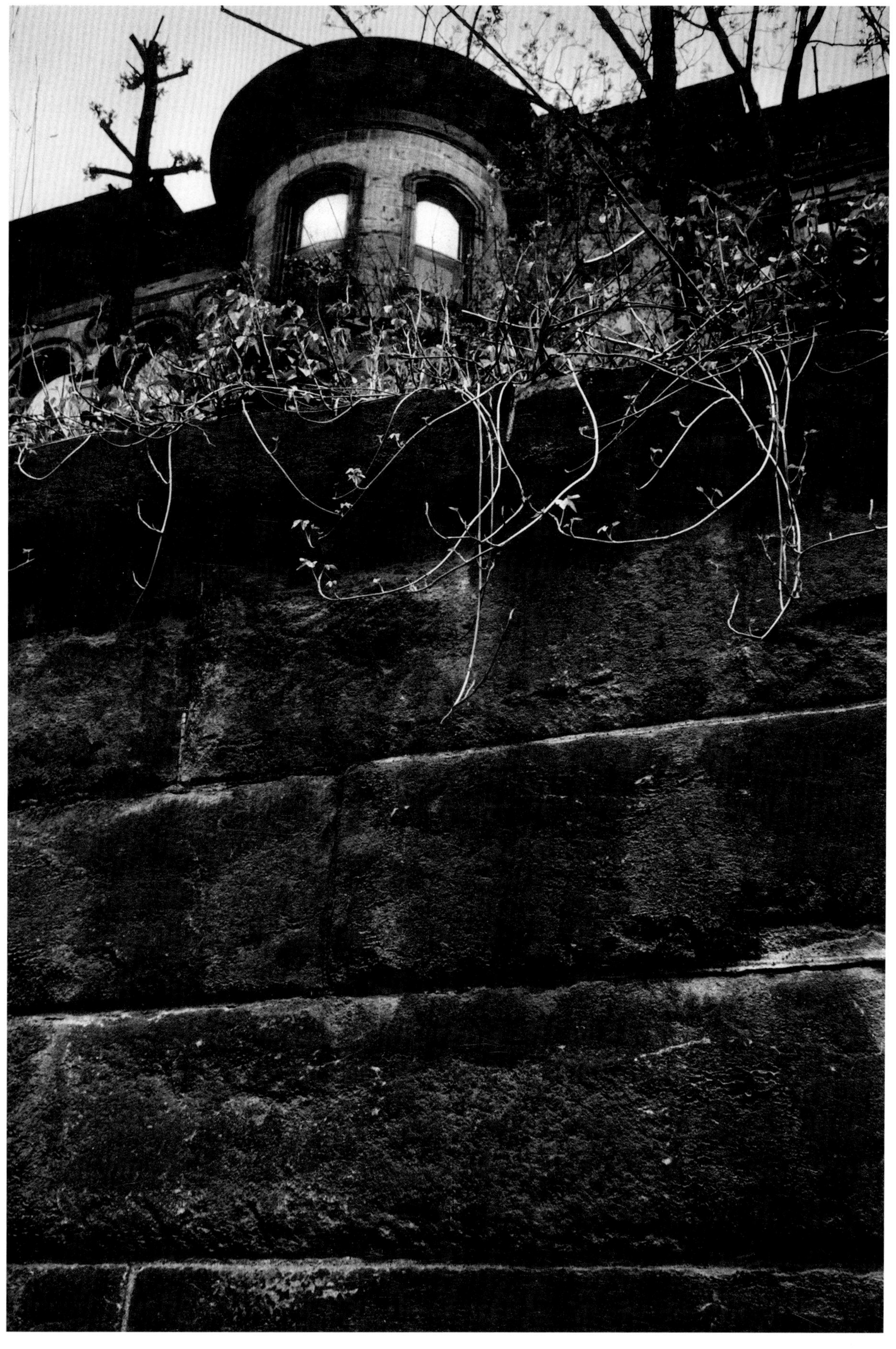

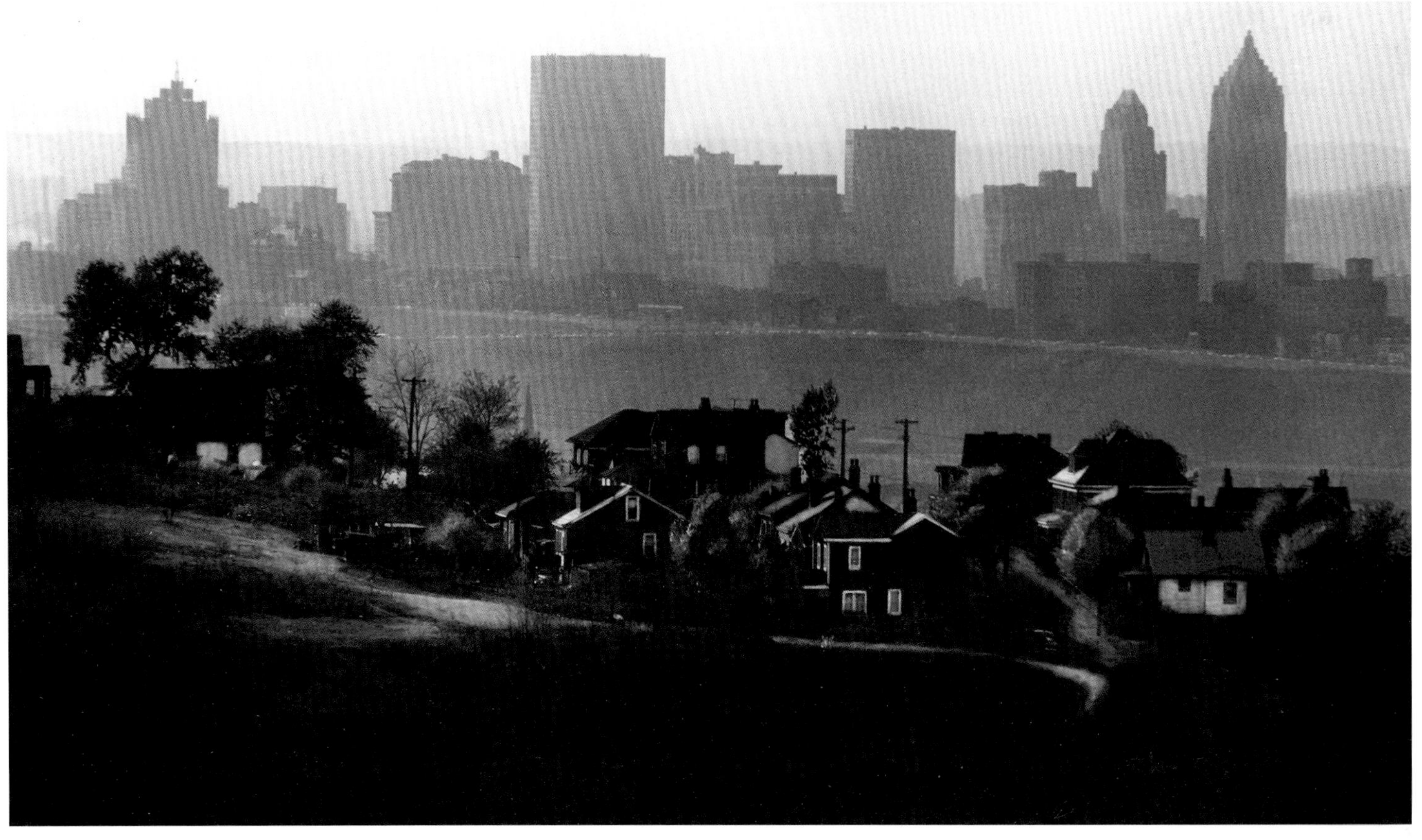

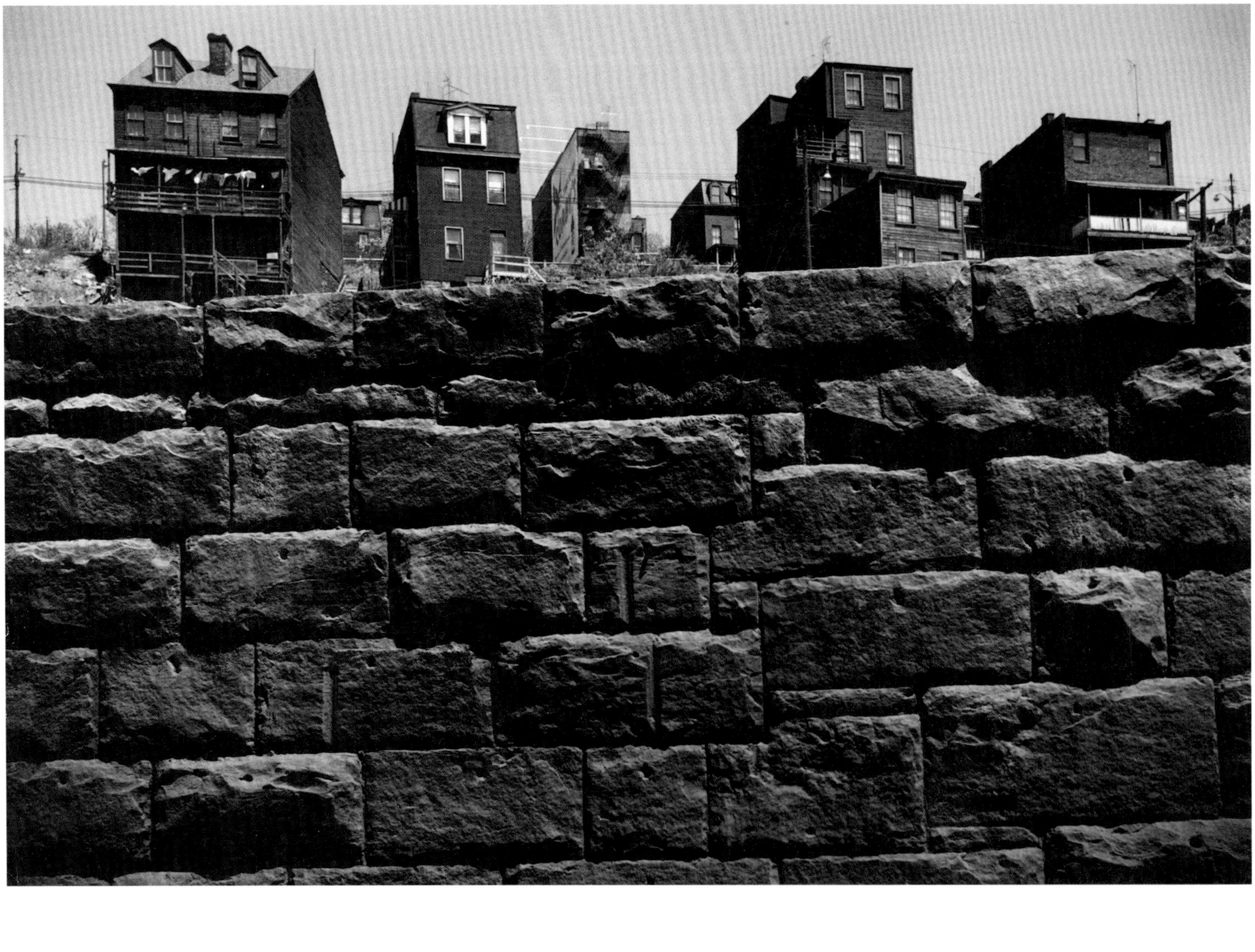

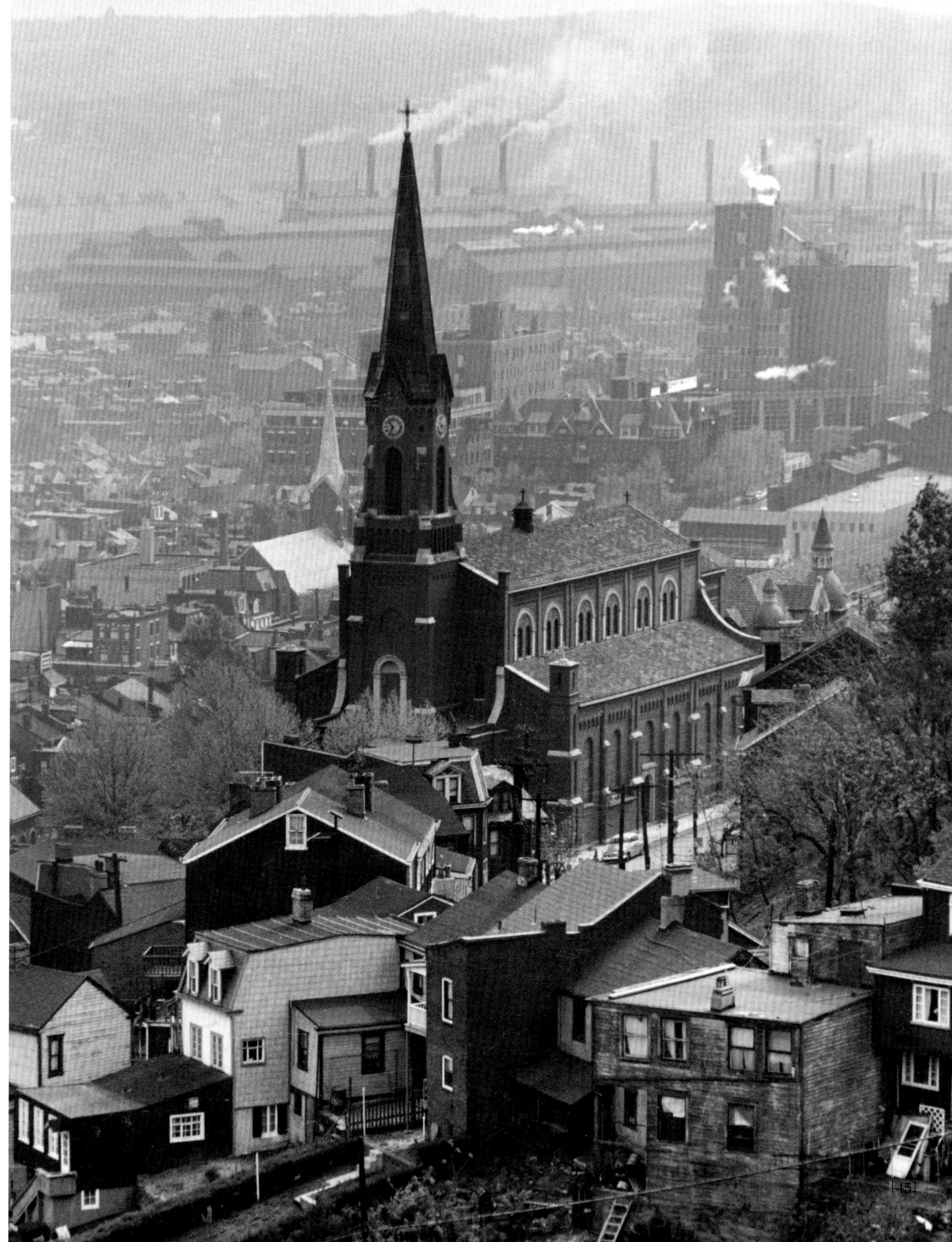

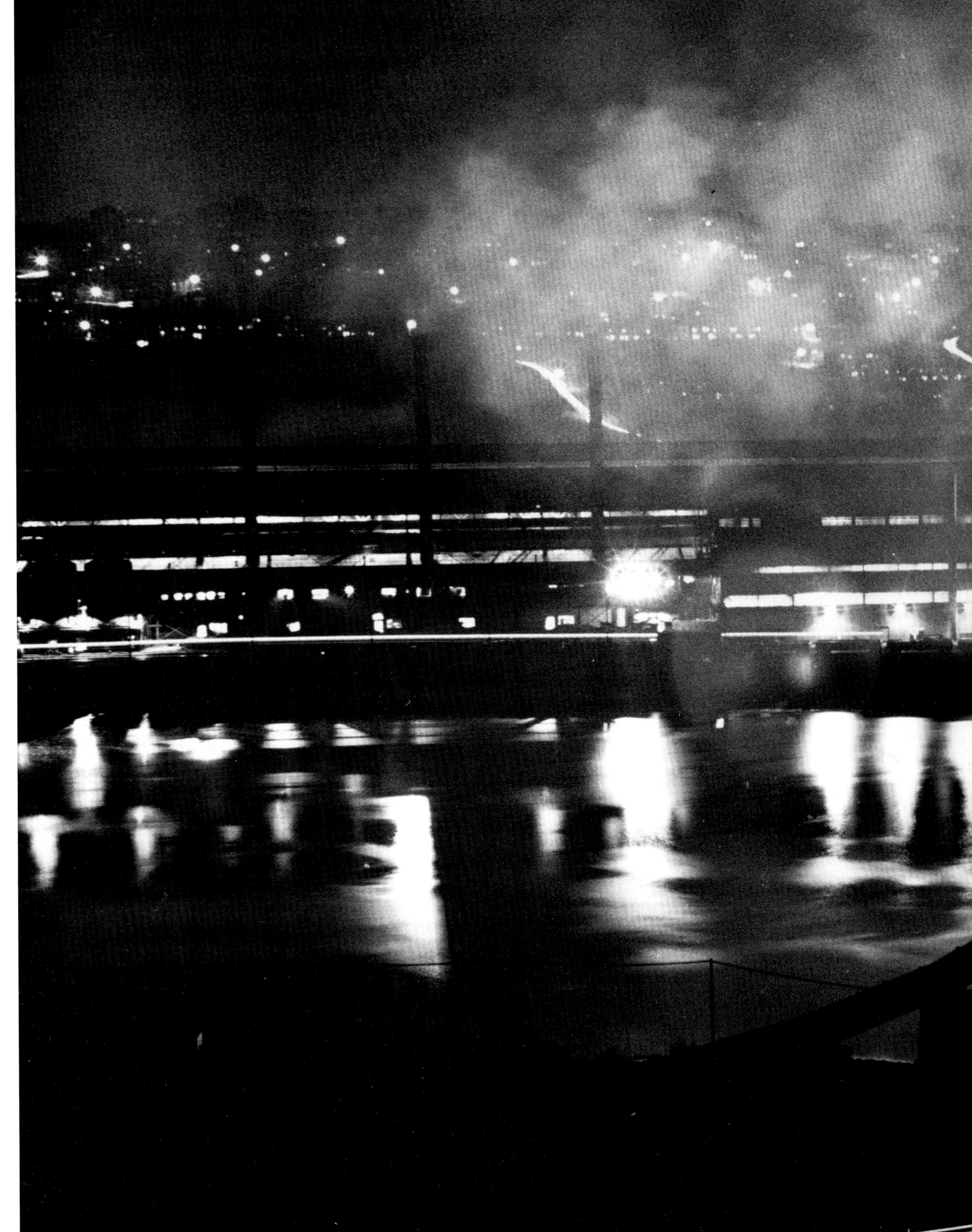

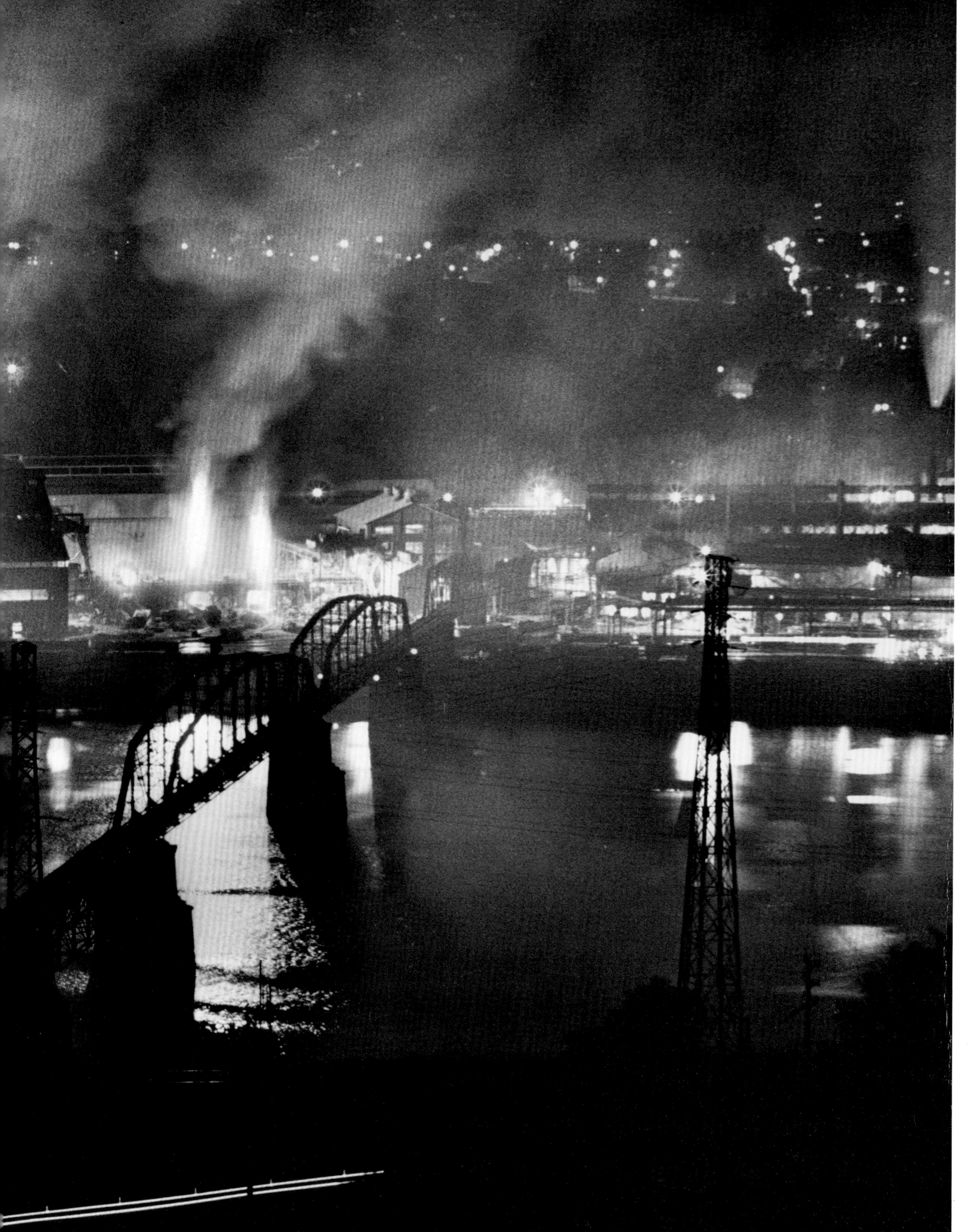

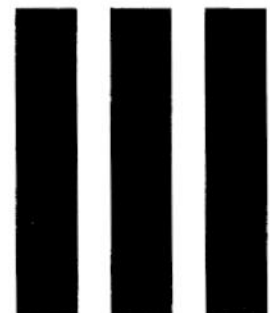

I would search civic pride and civic
shame; specific problems and specific
interests—at odds, at cooperation,
at due process; government, business
management, worker, as qualified
through the infinite mixtures and the
rewards and stresses of being of this
place at this time. I would give the
taste of its very breathing—at work,
at humdrum, at learning, at worship,
at play, at growth (and the decay
which is simultaneous with growth in
every living thing). My intention of
a result—(health, sustenance, talent,
and the variables of fate be willing)
—a strong example of an individual
and functioning American city.

From Smith's 1956 application
for a fellowship from the John Simon
Guggenheim Foundation—"Plans
for Use of Fellowship"

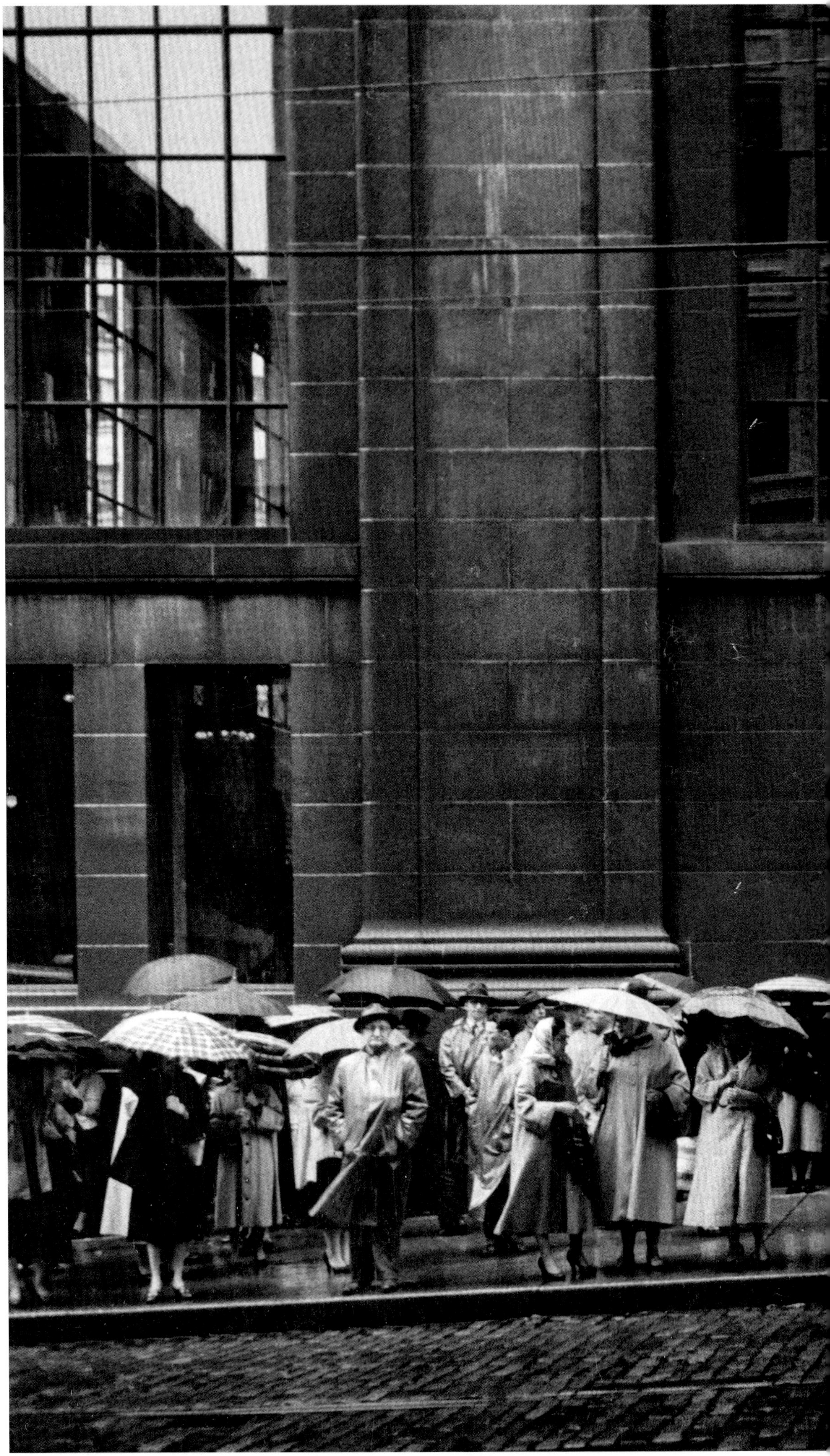

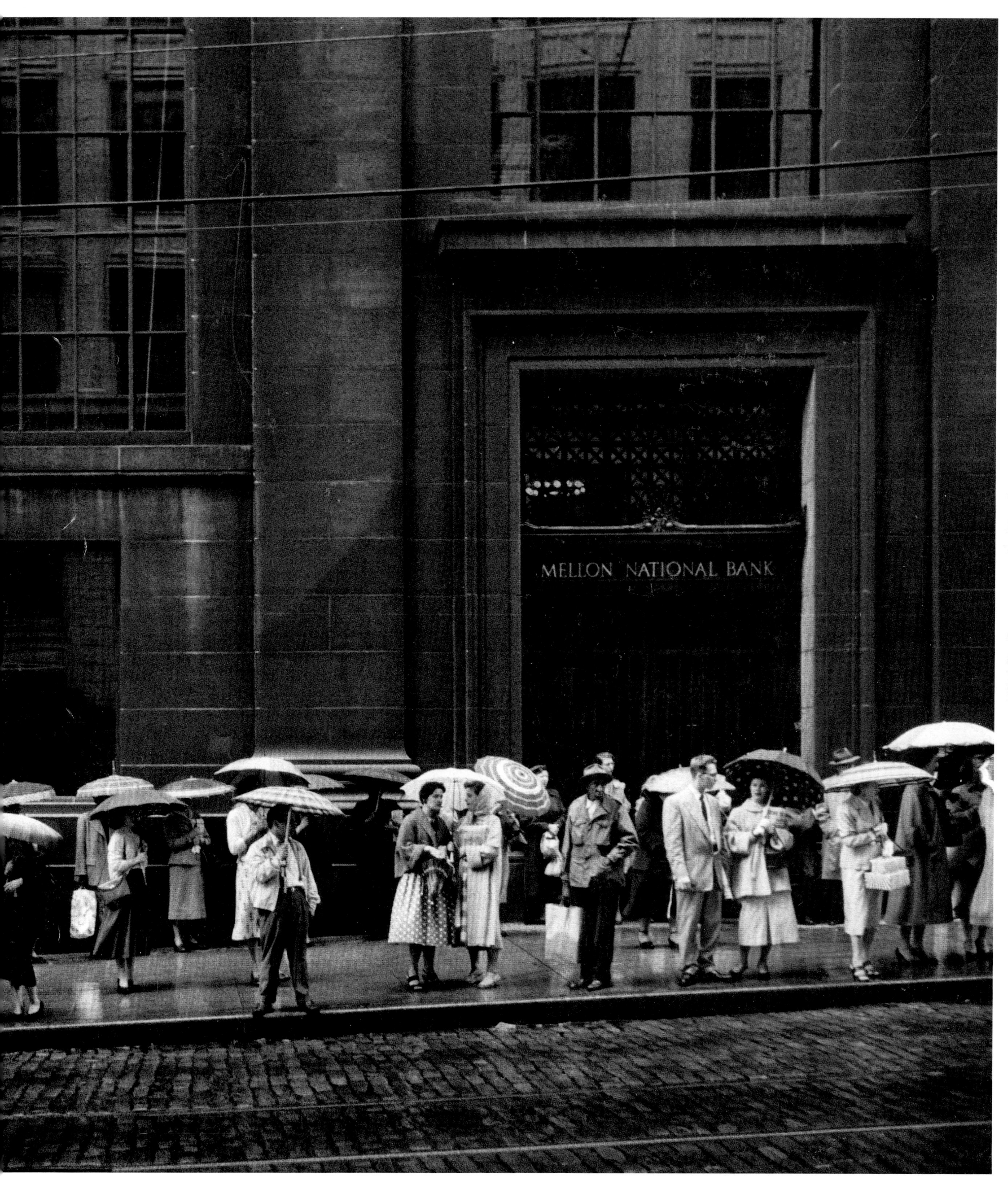

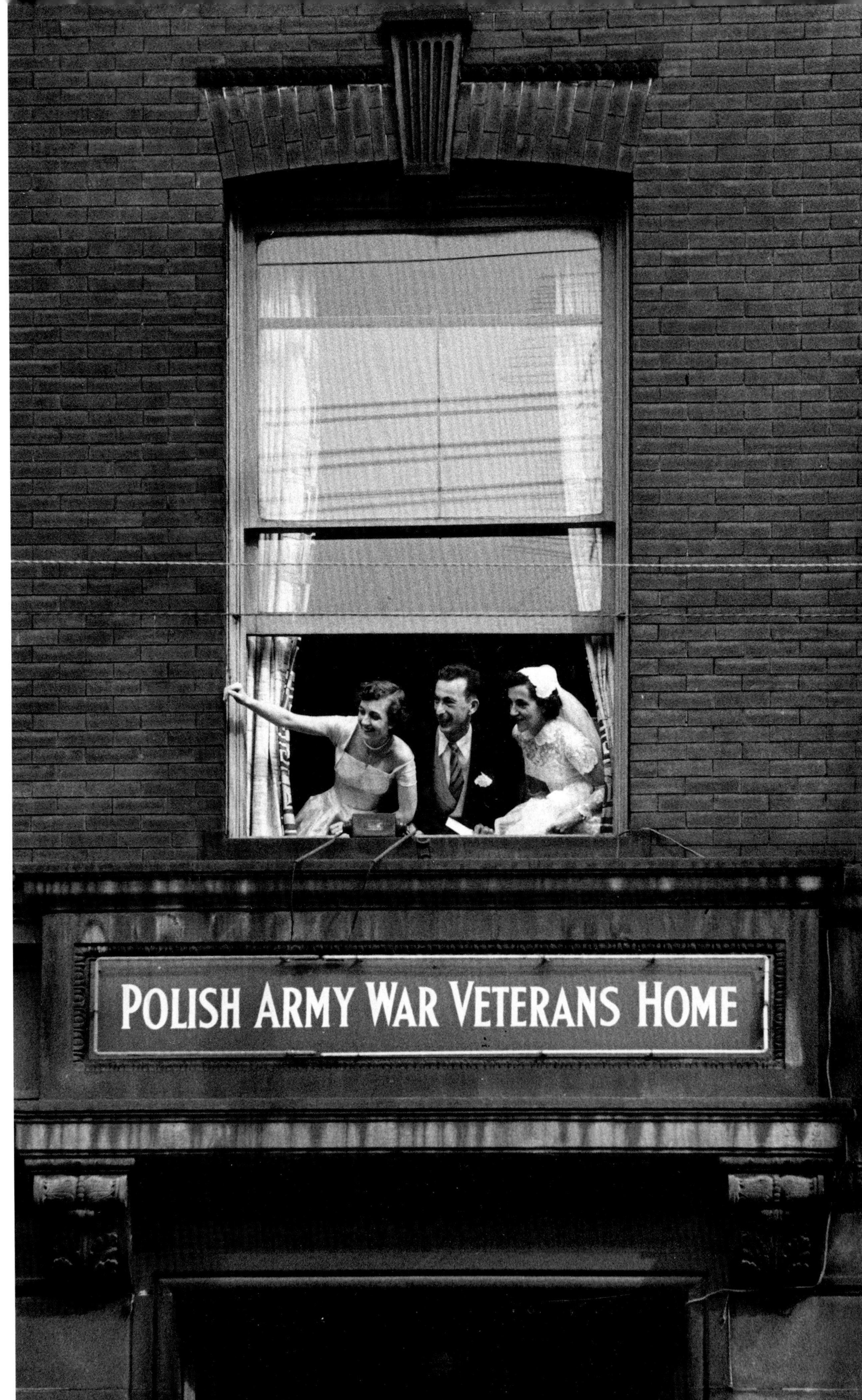
POLISH ARMY WAR VETERANS HOME

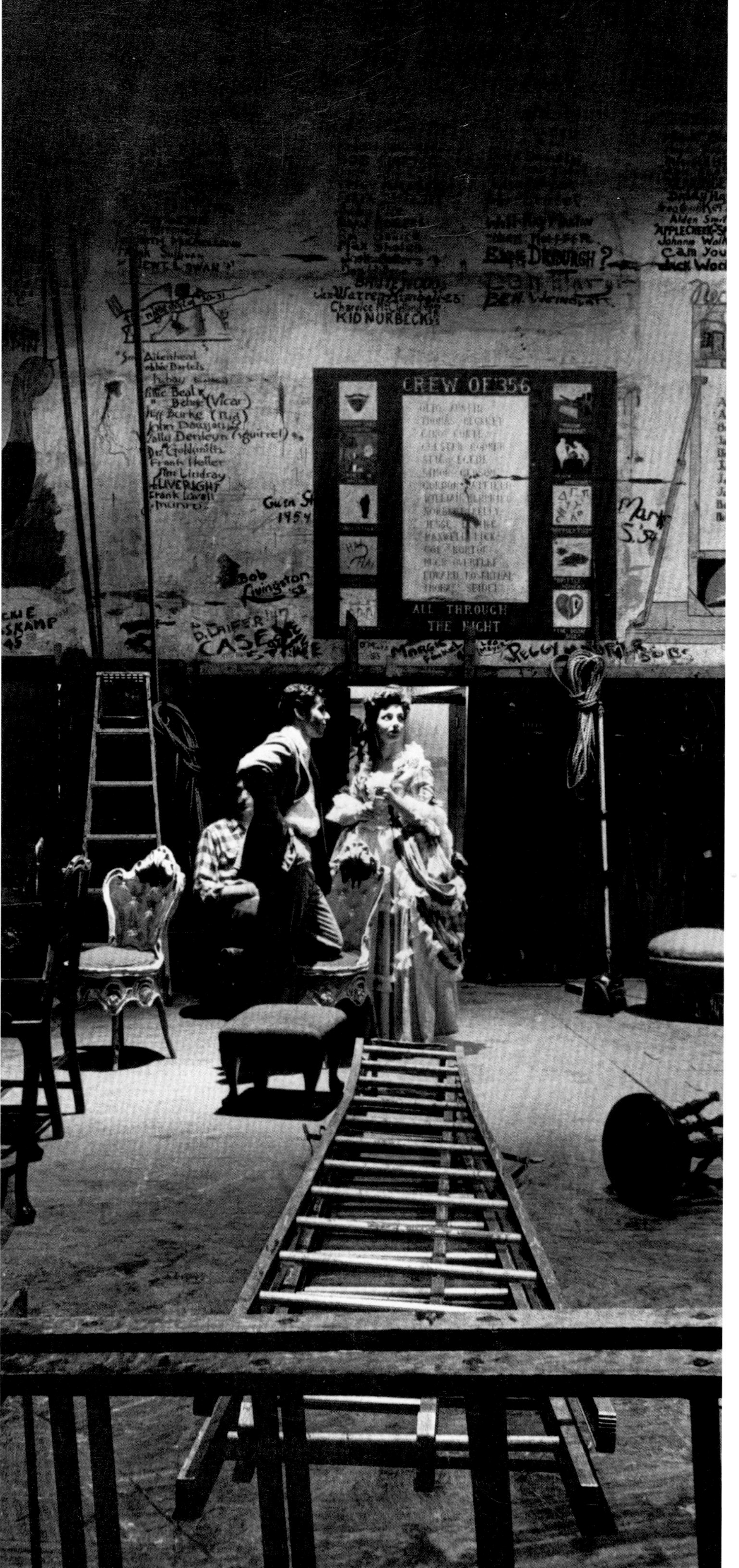


CREW OF 356
ALL THROUGH
THE NIGHT

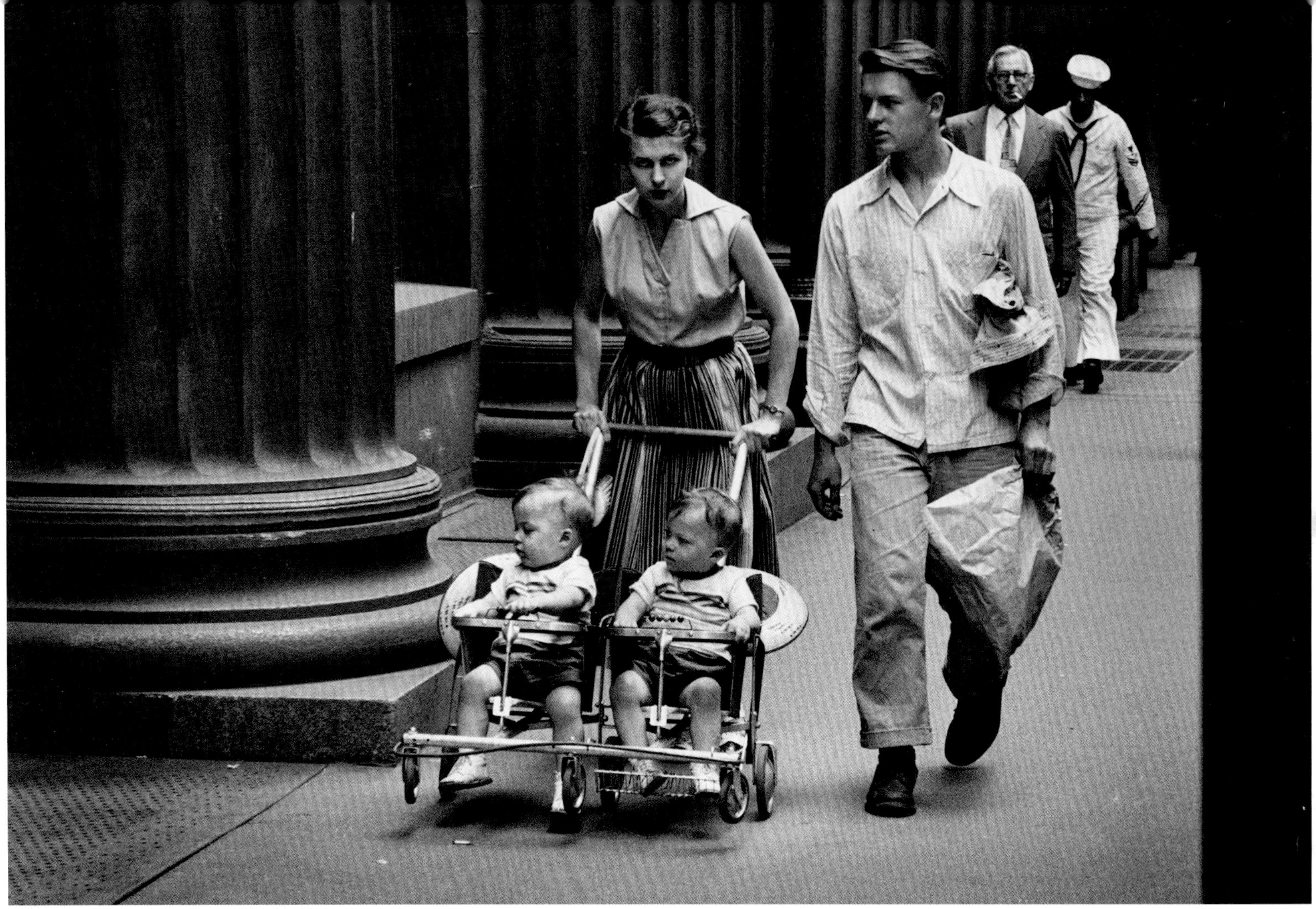

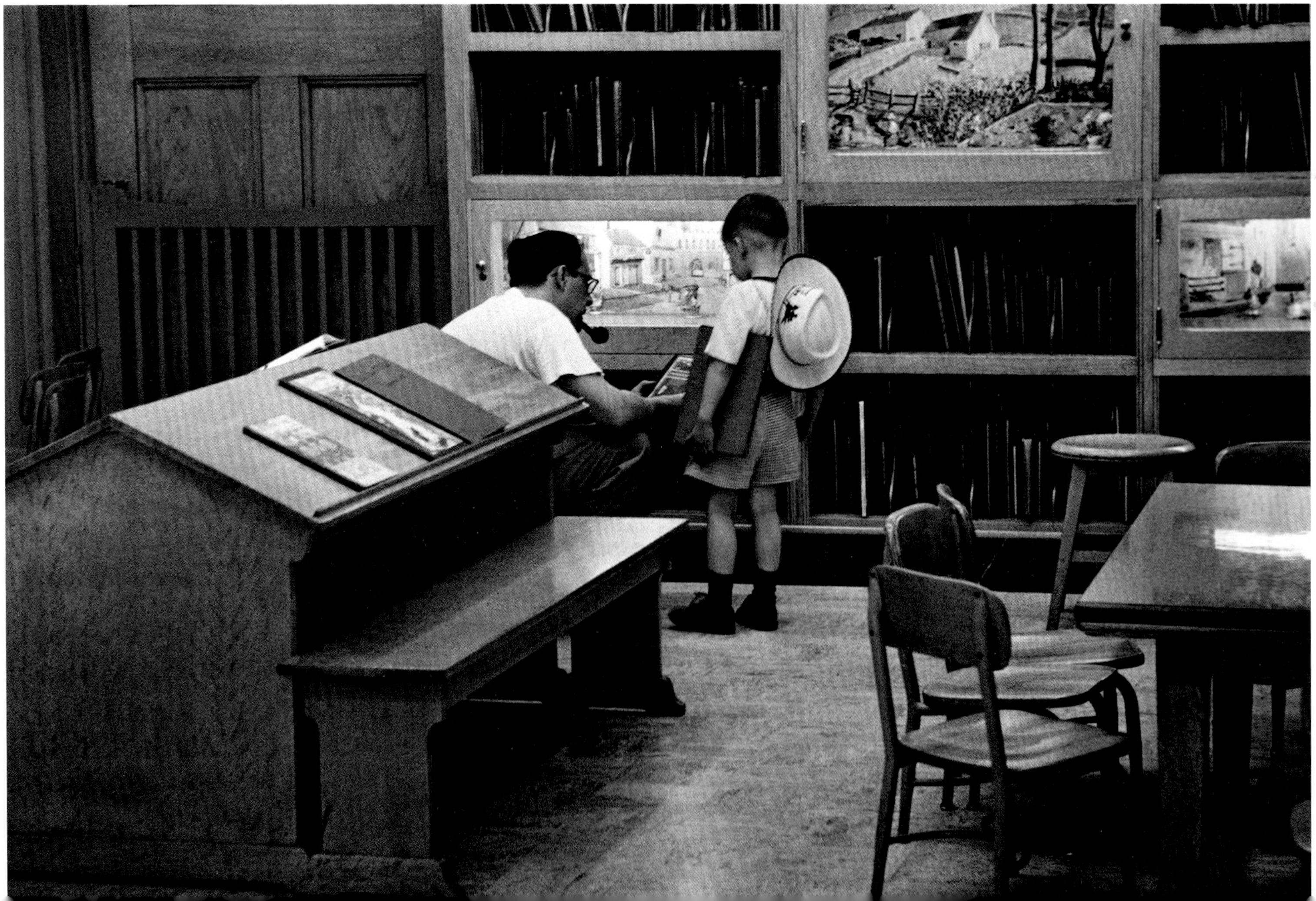

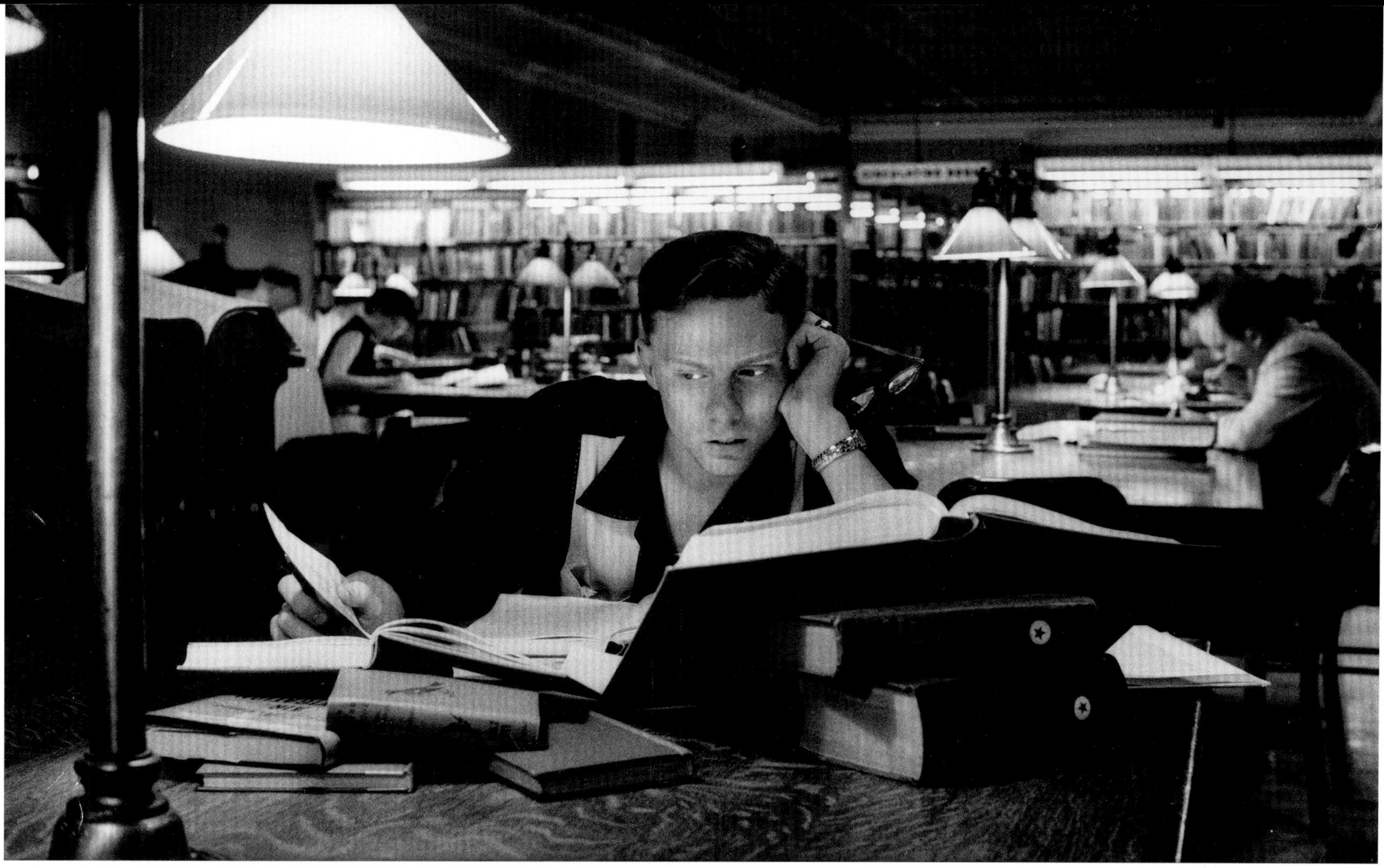

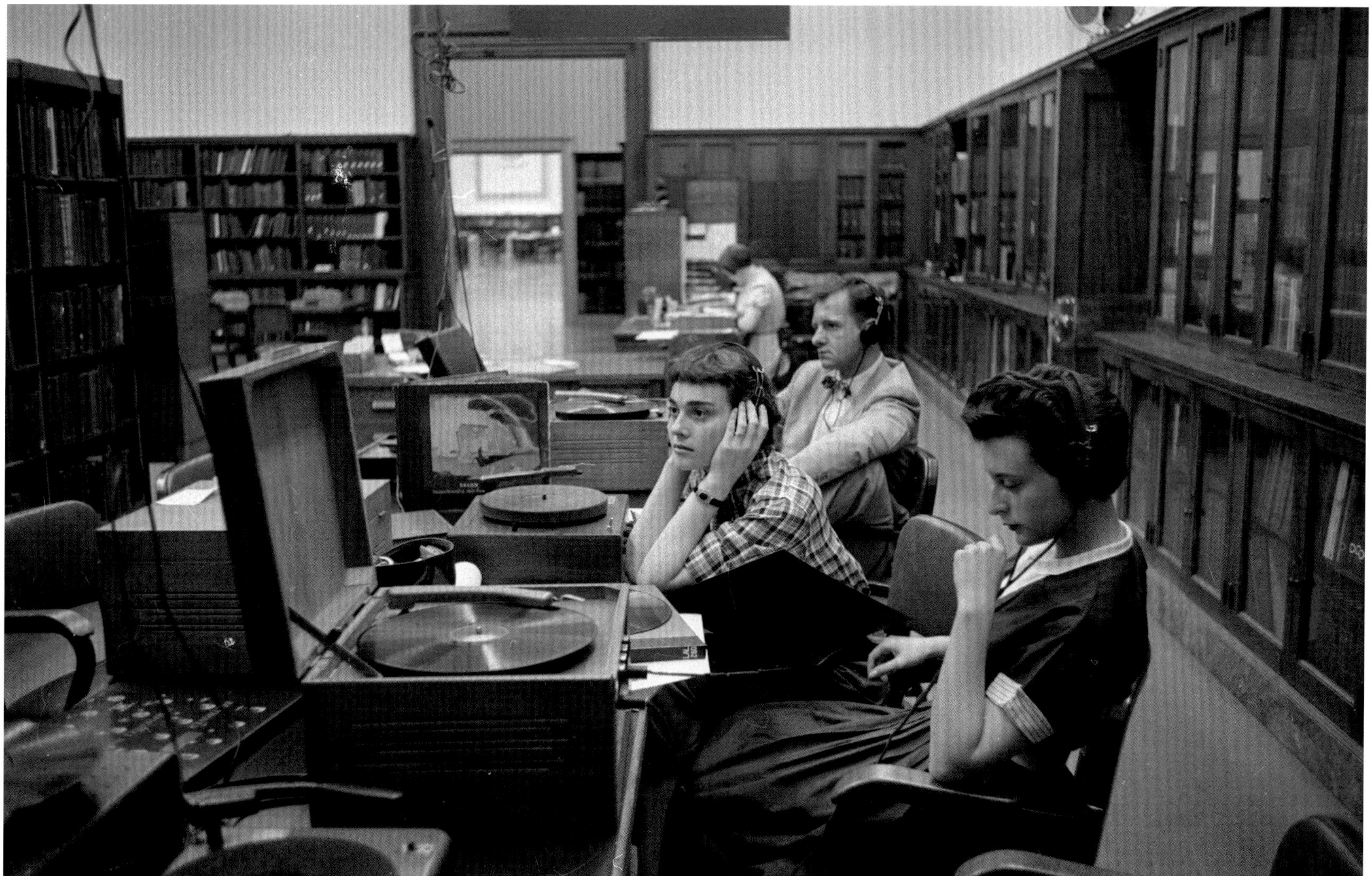

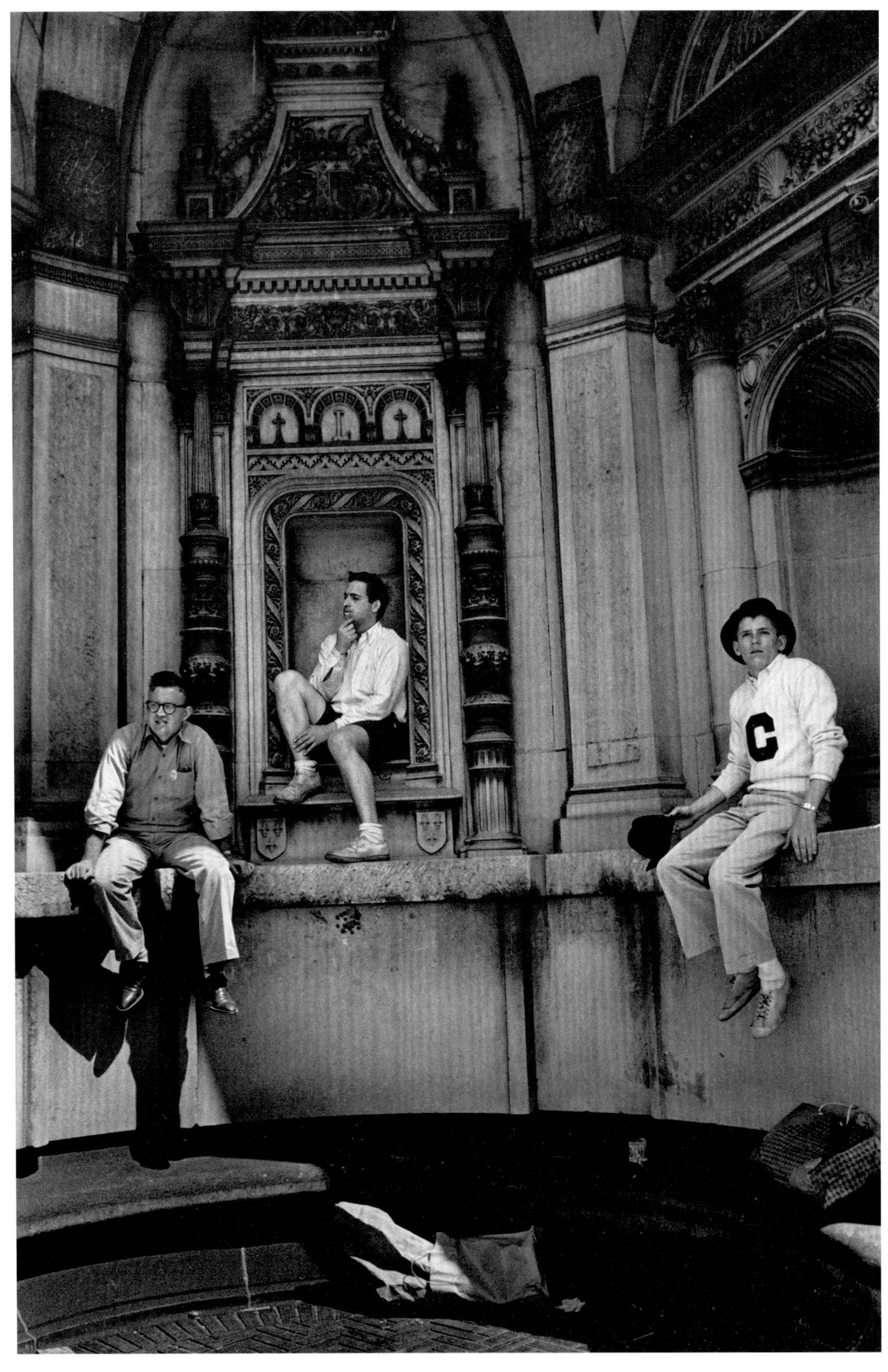

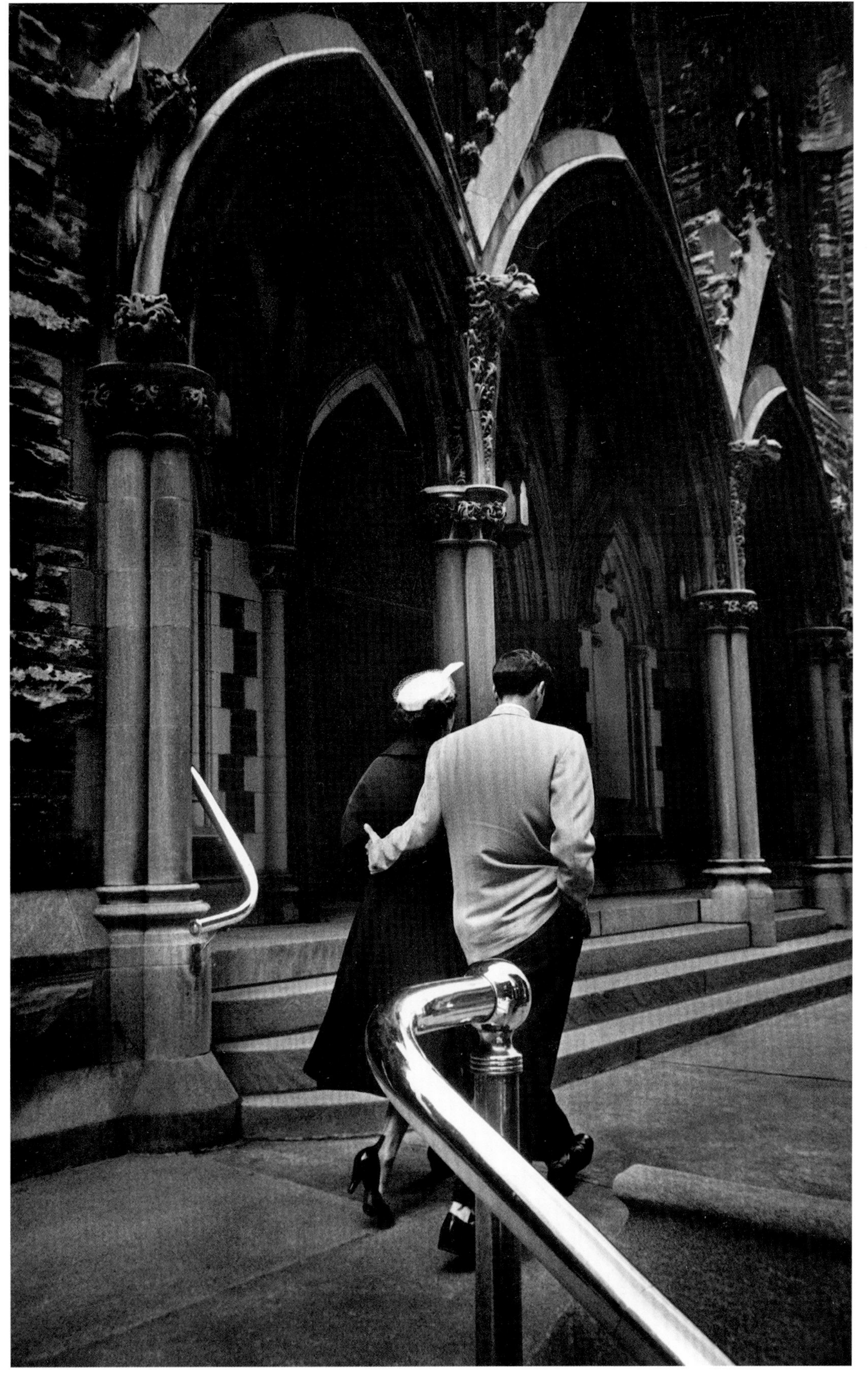

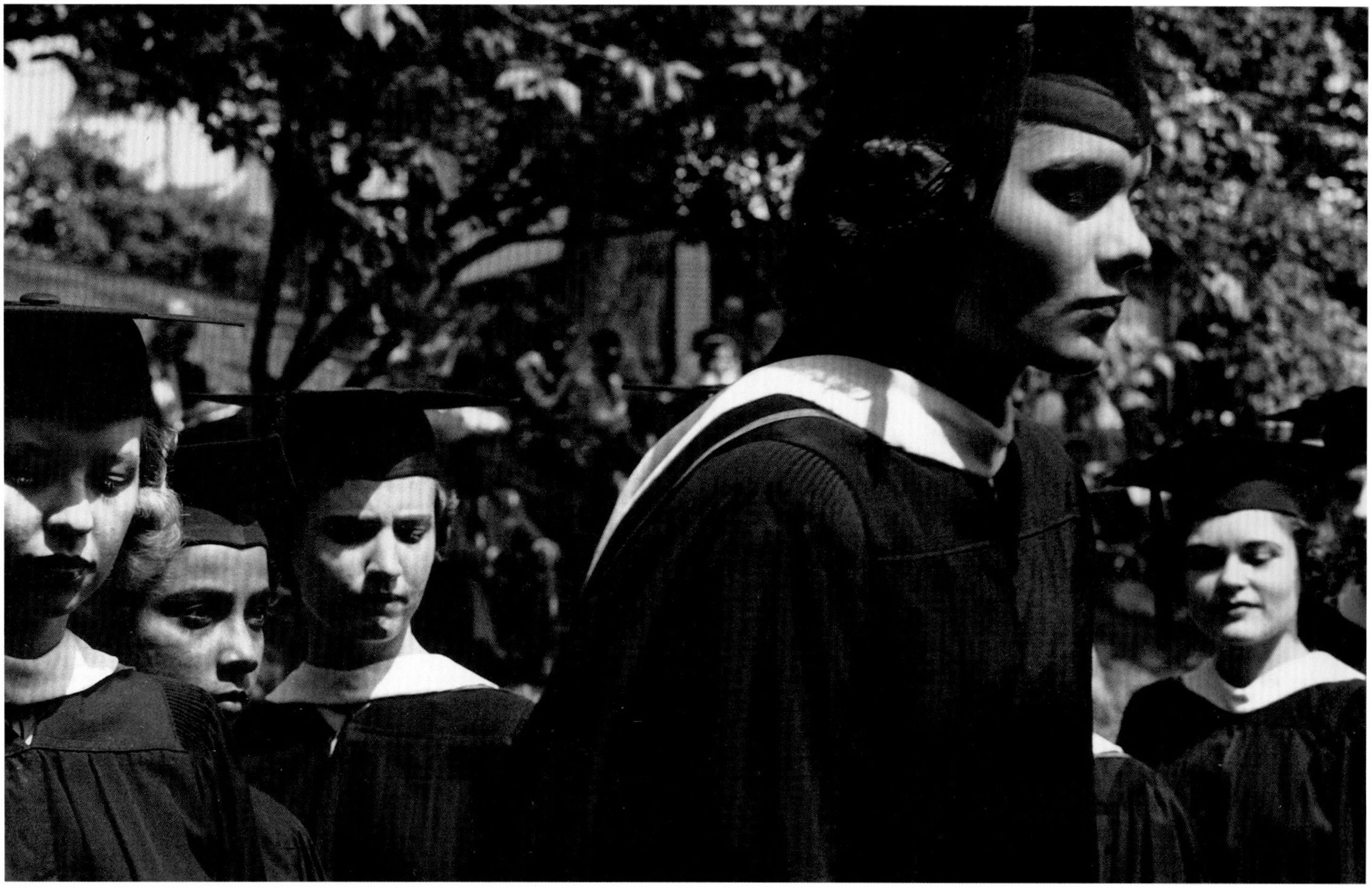

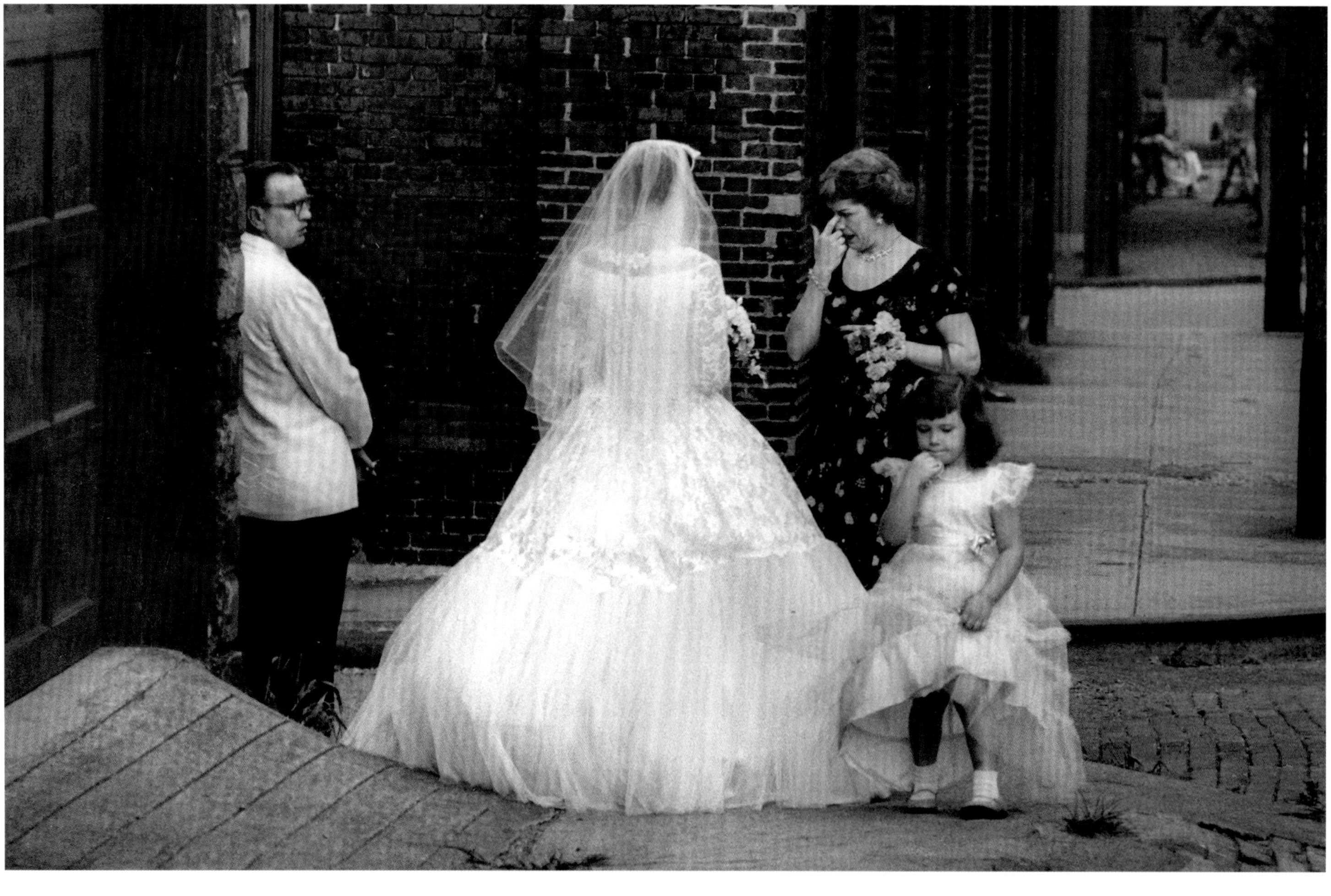

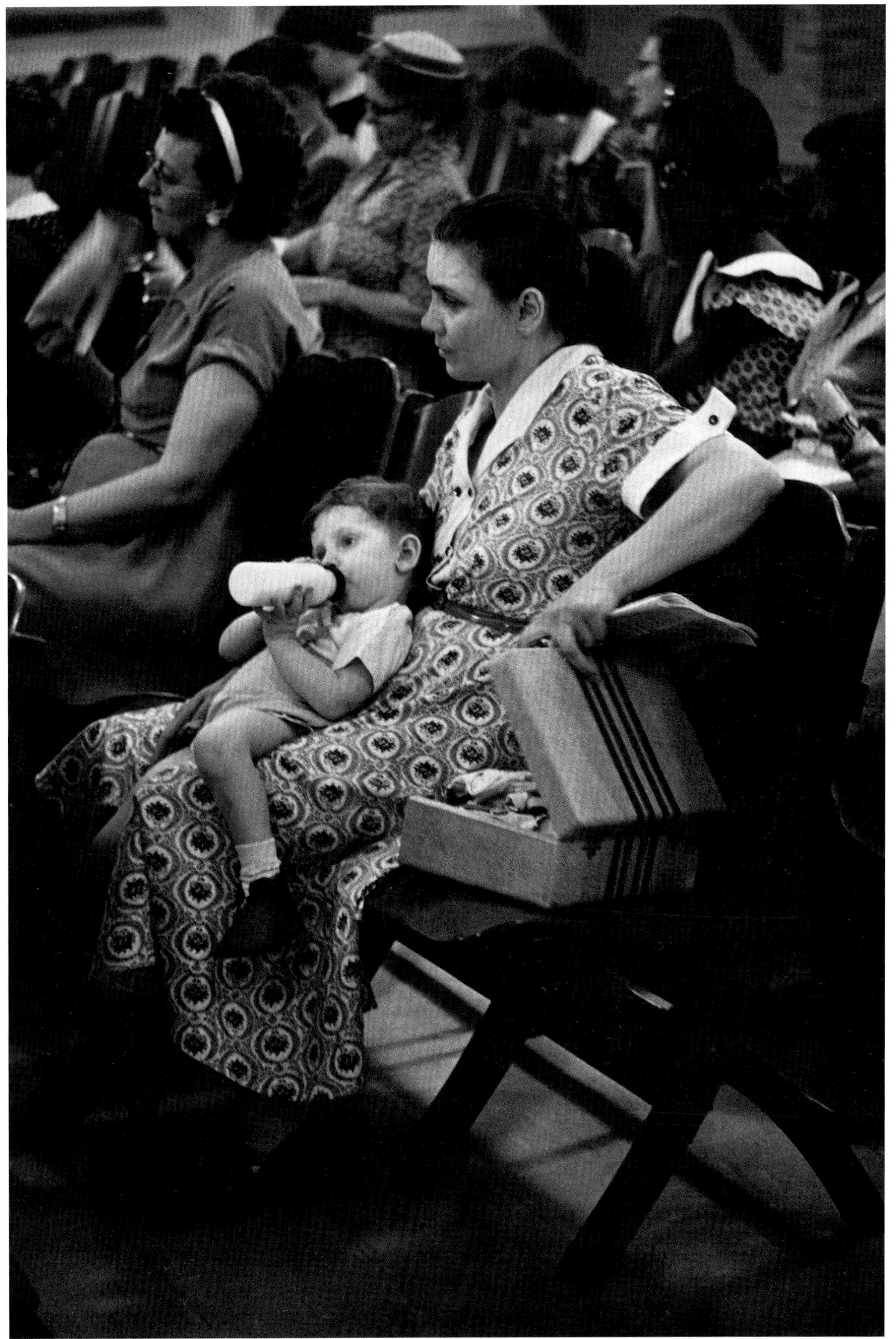

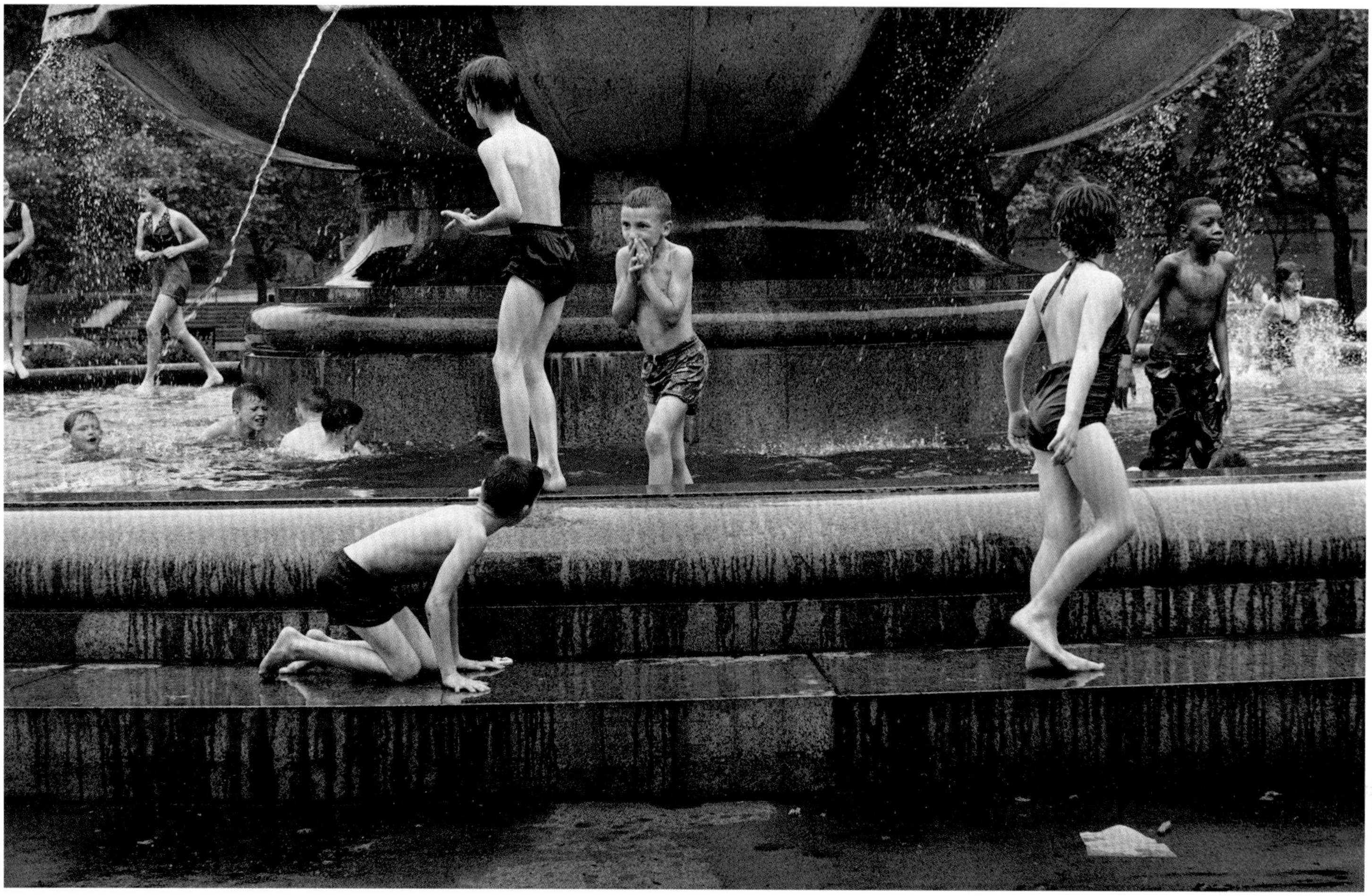

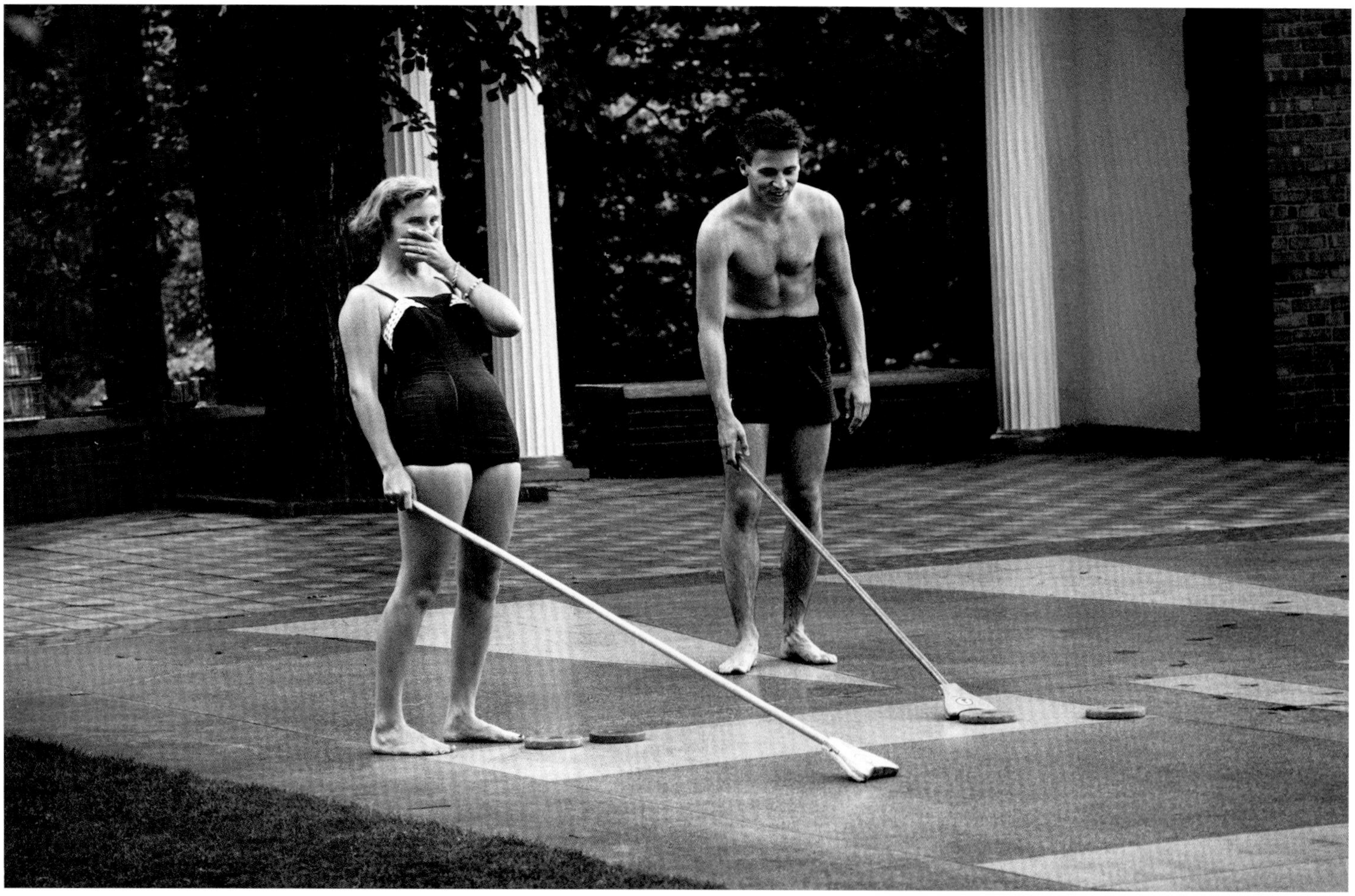

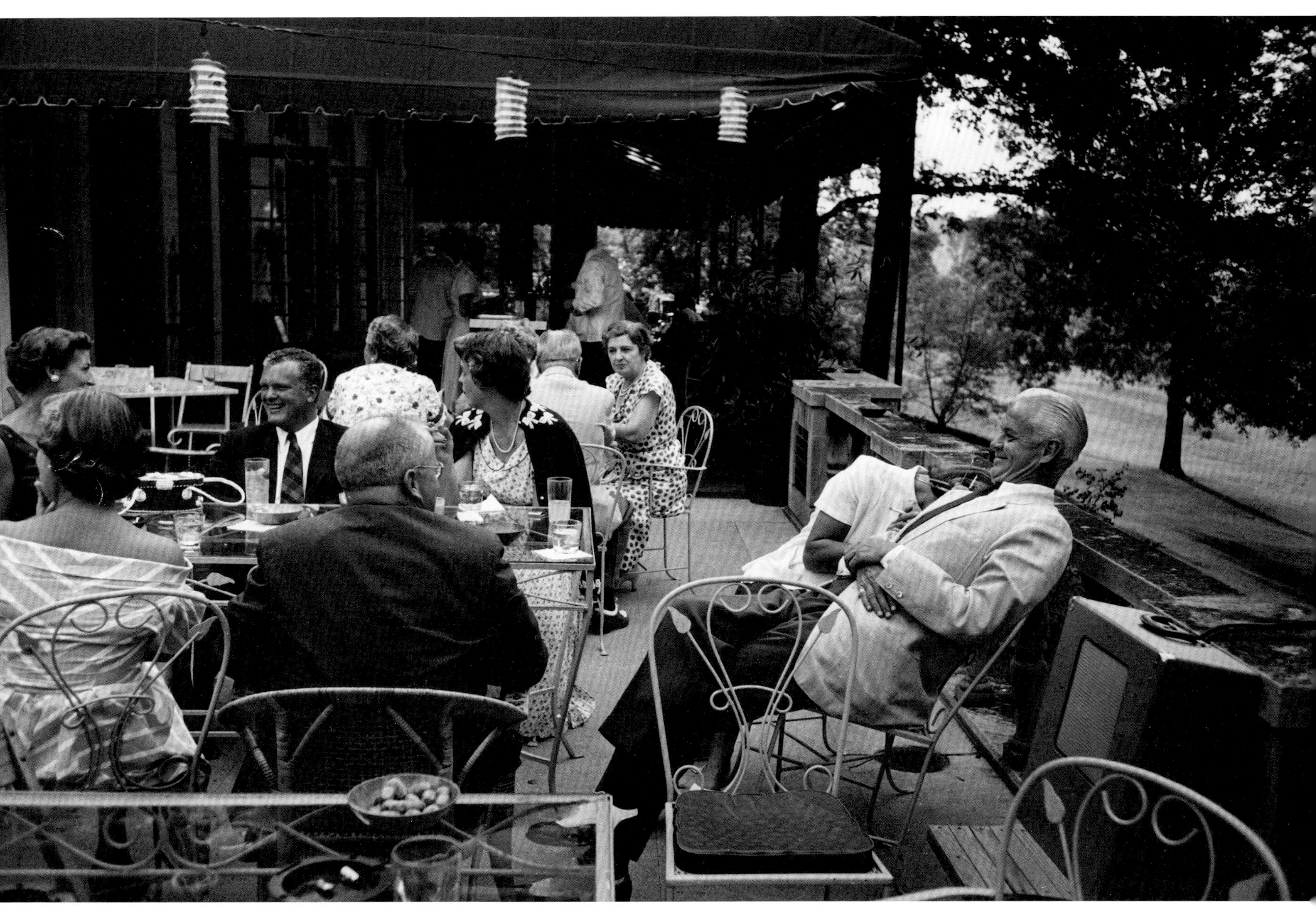

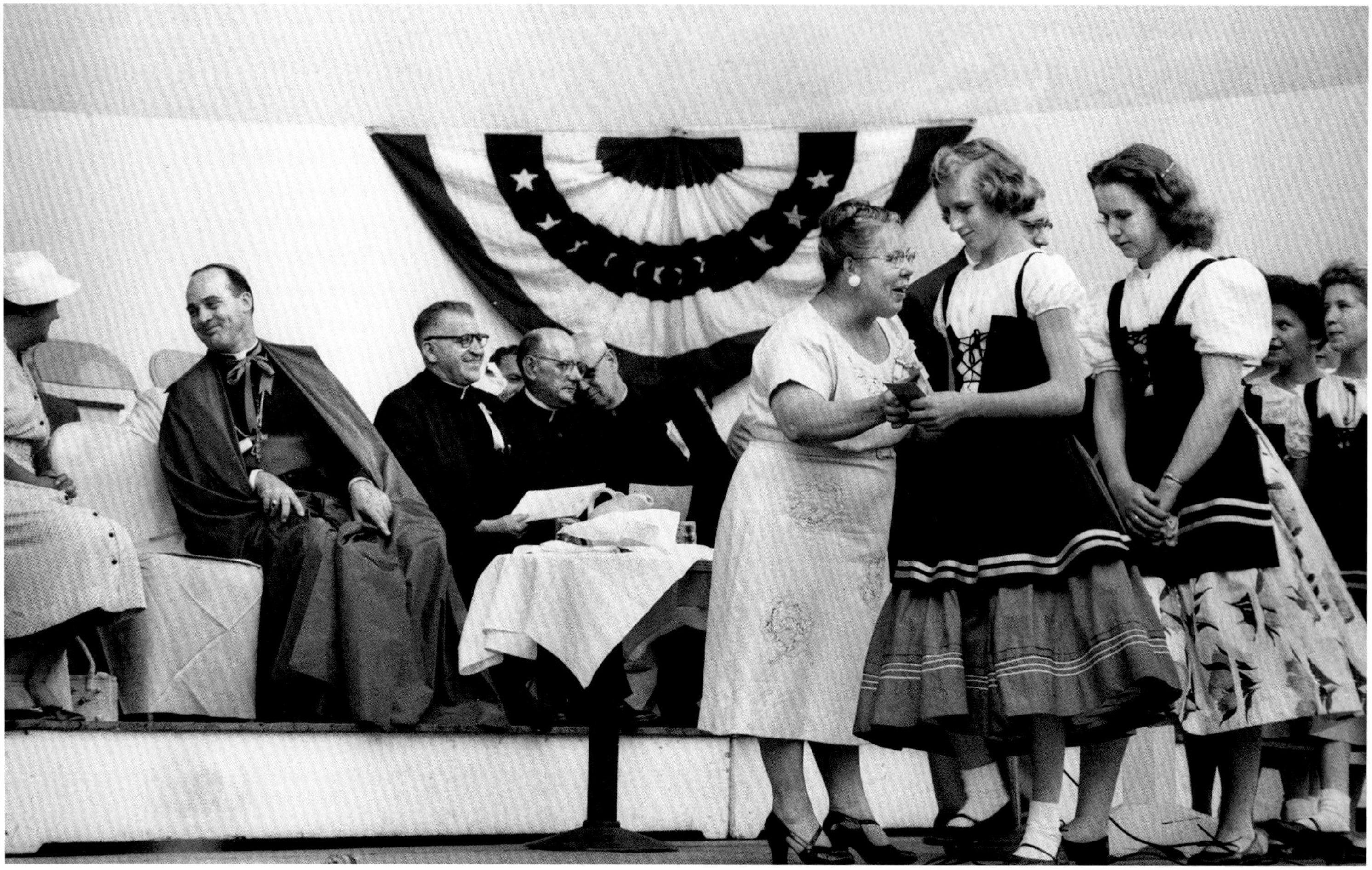

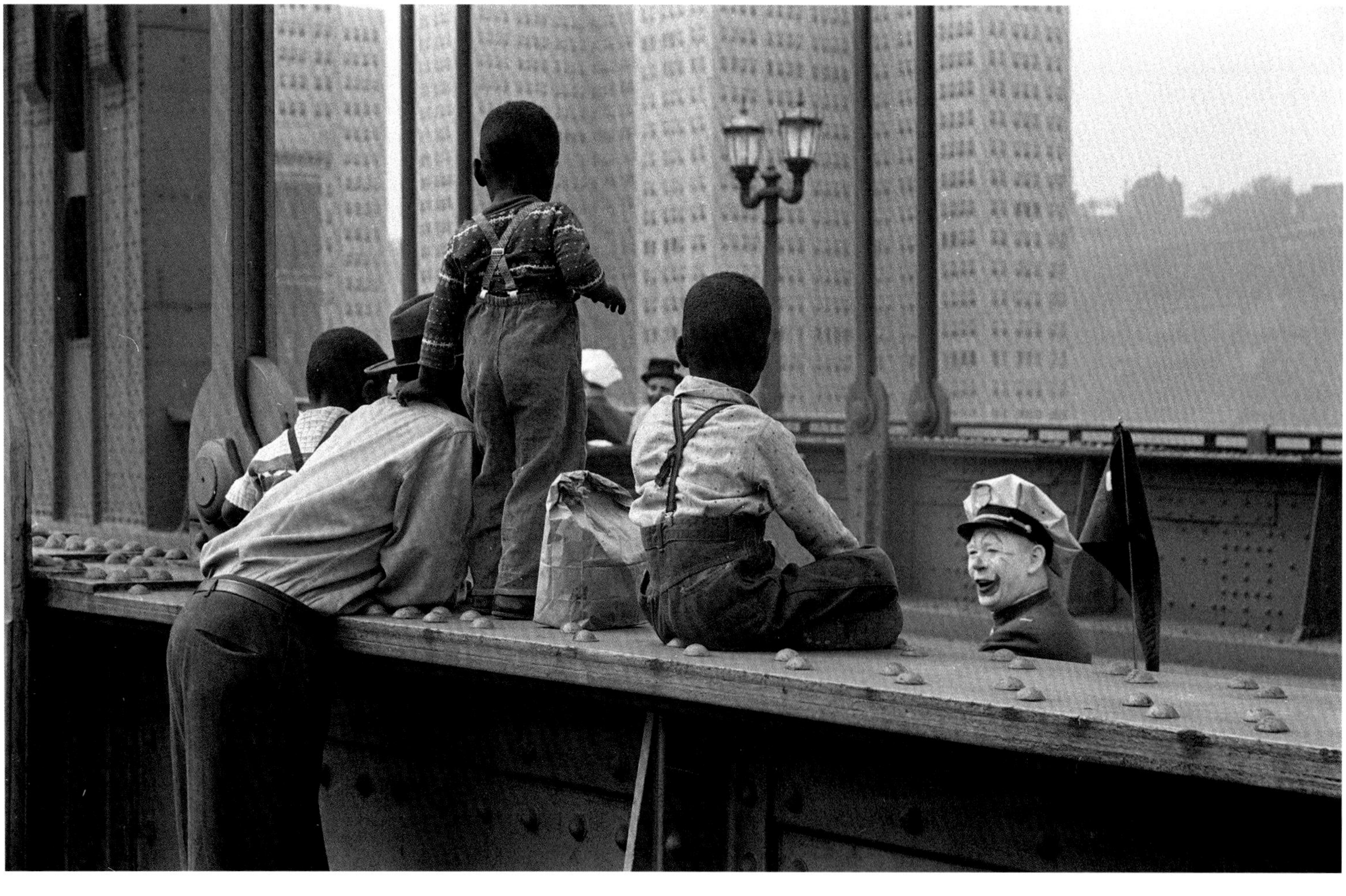

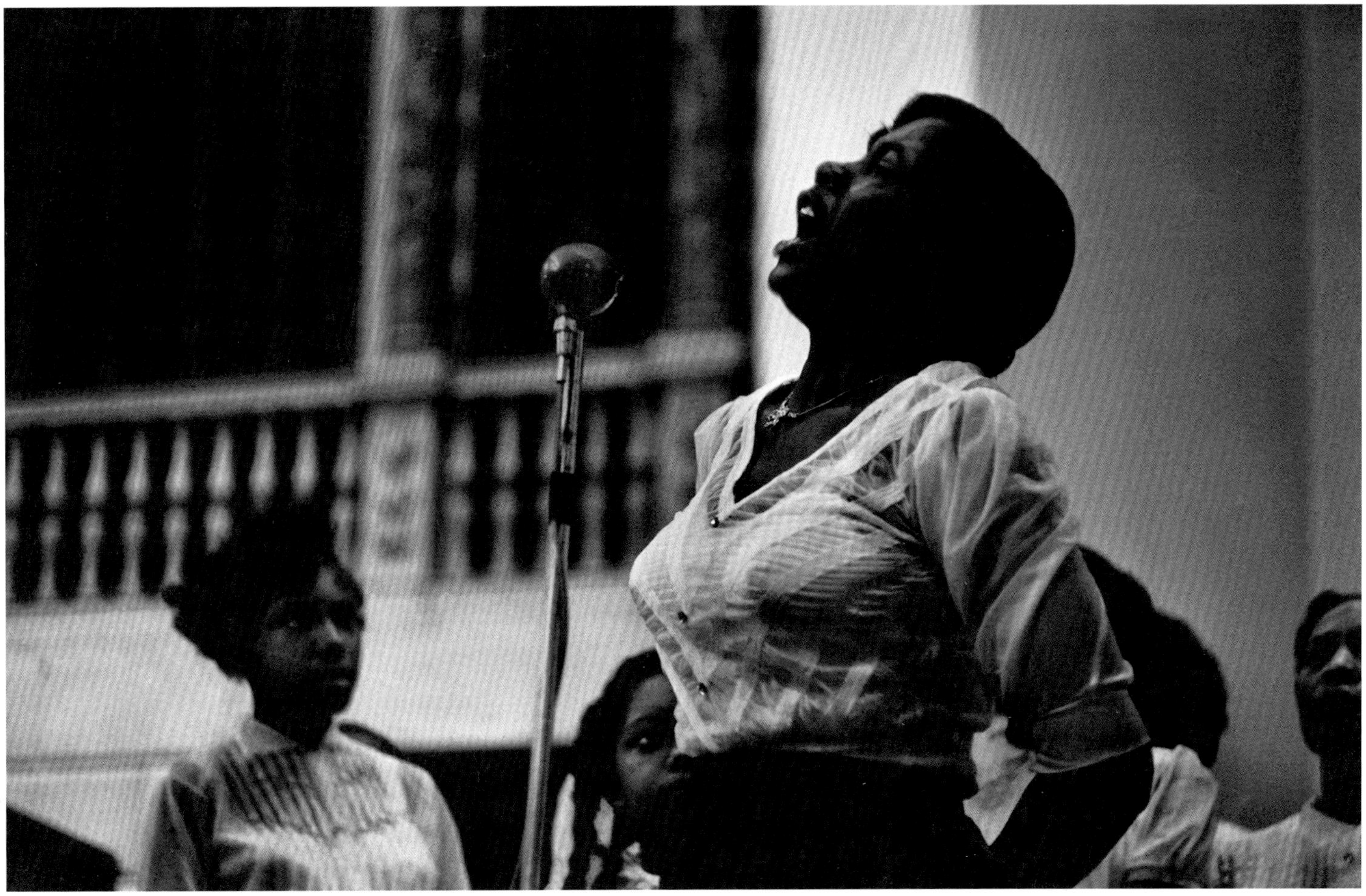

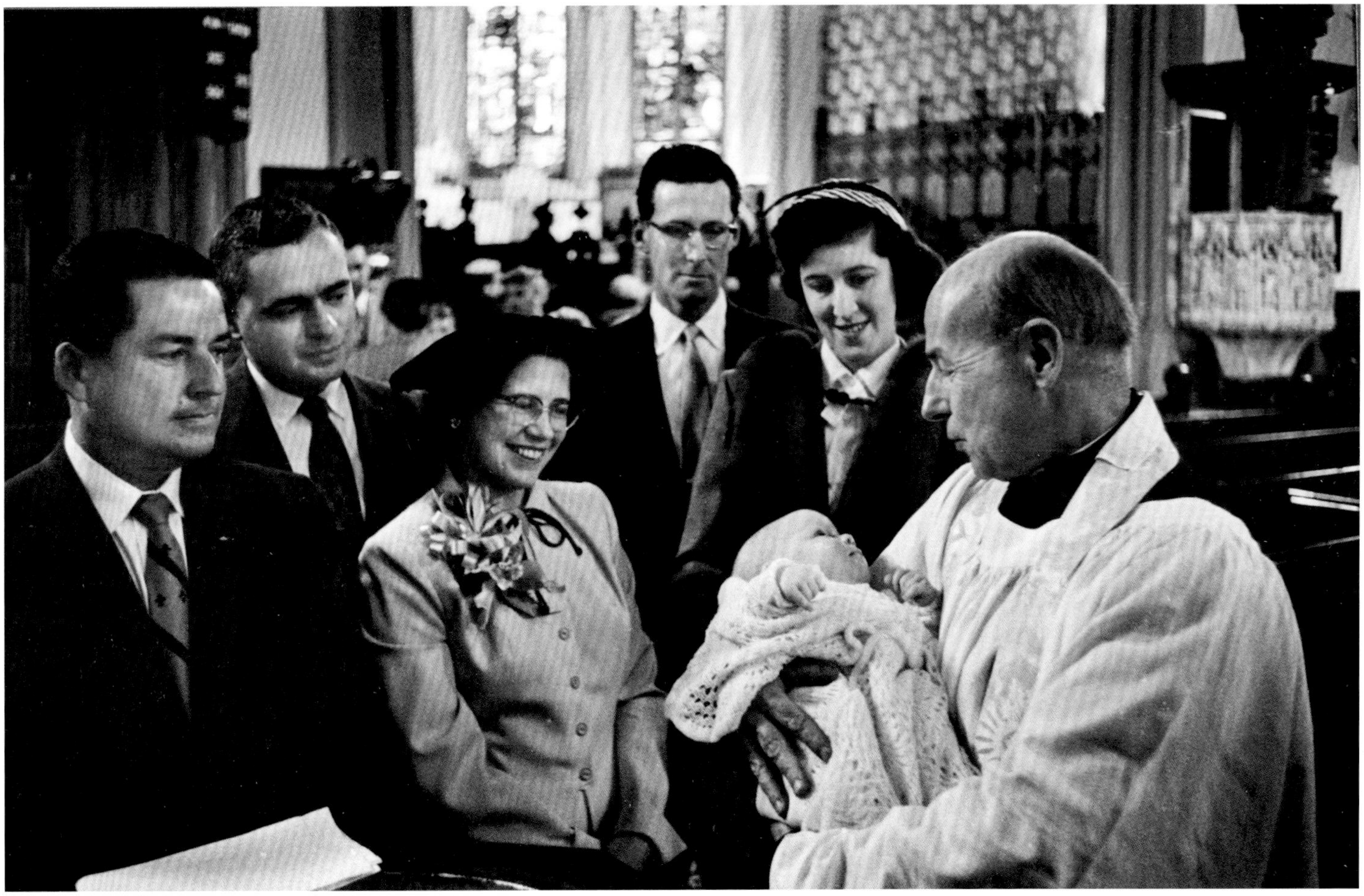

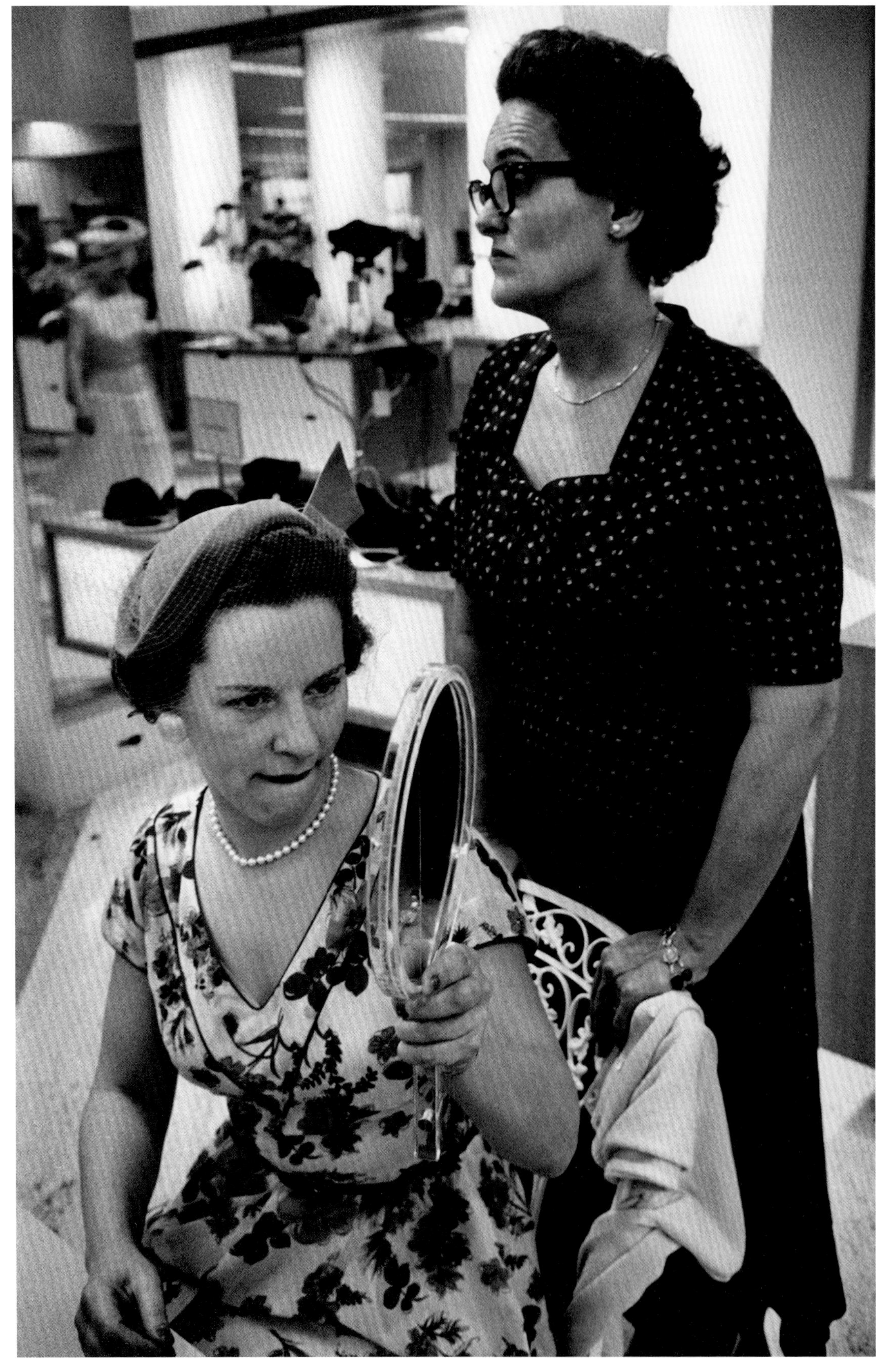

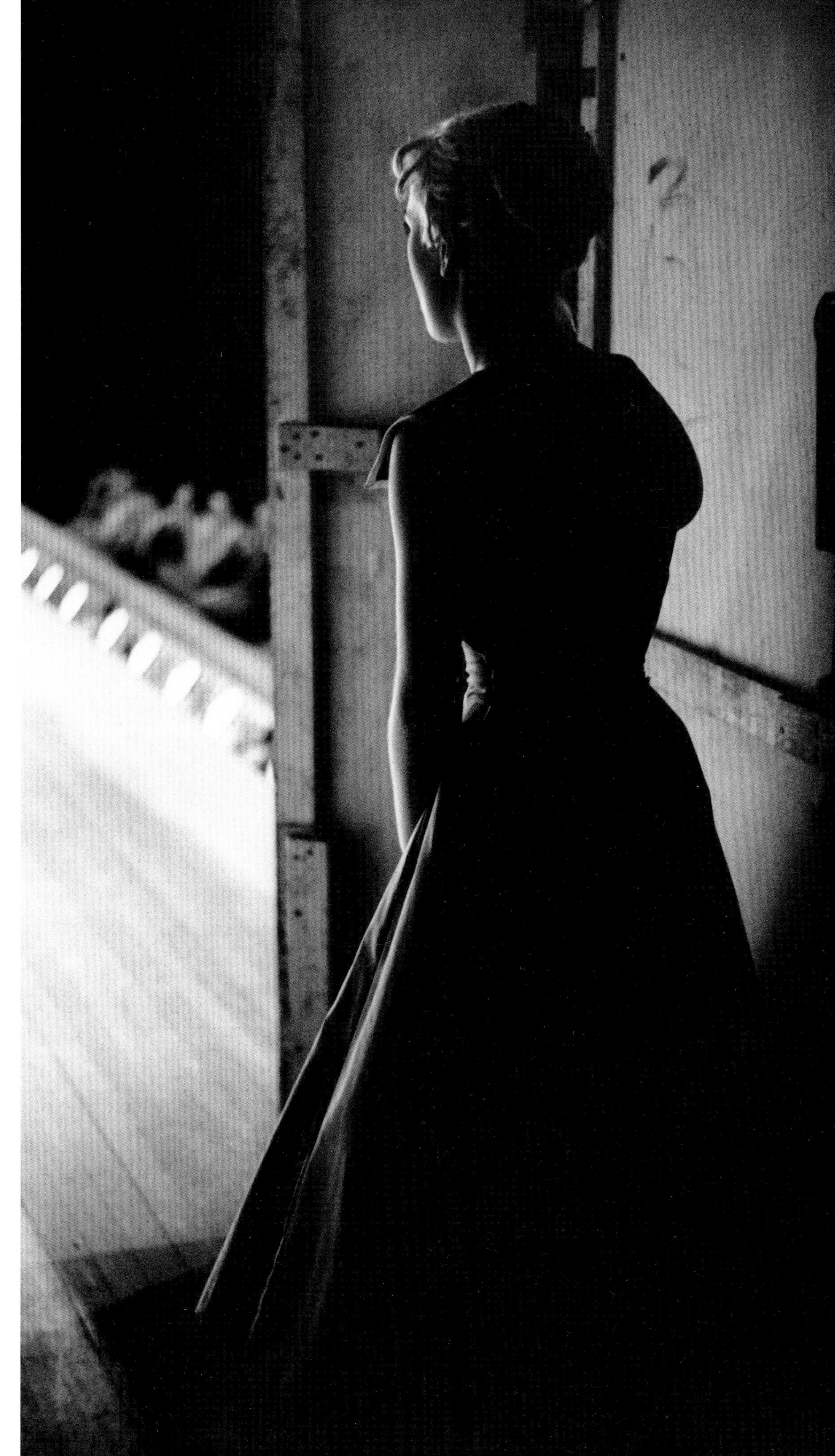

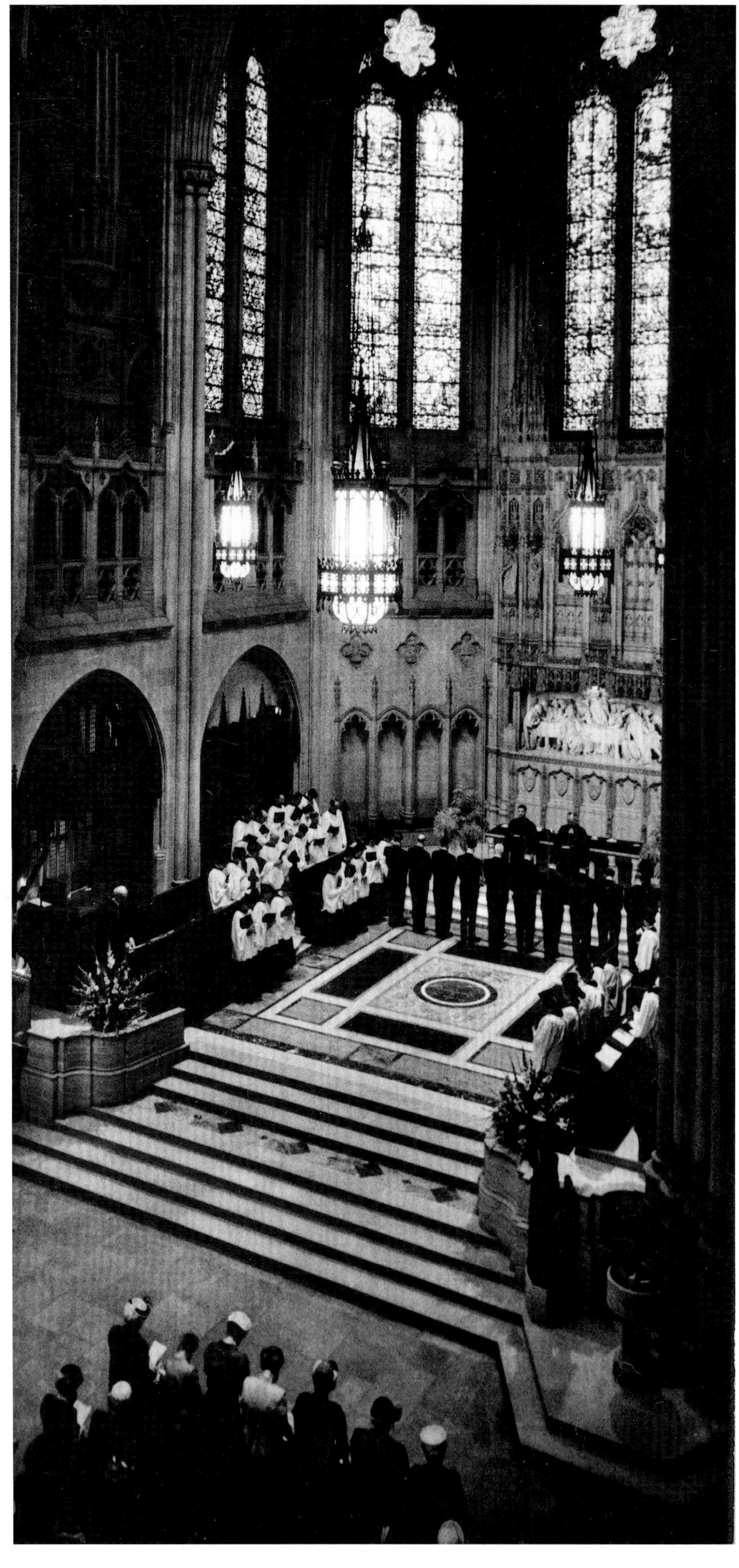

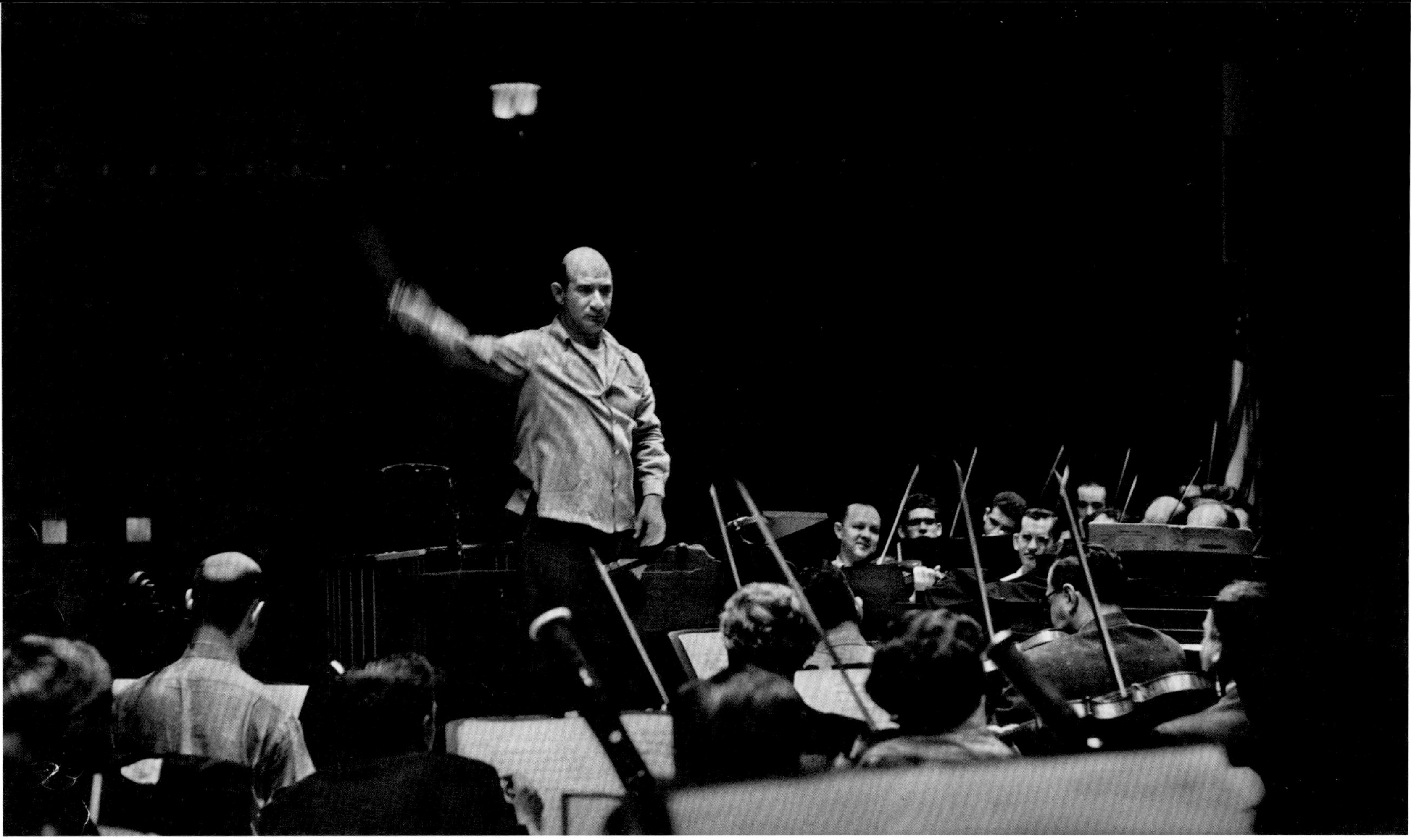

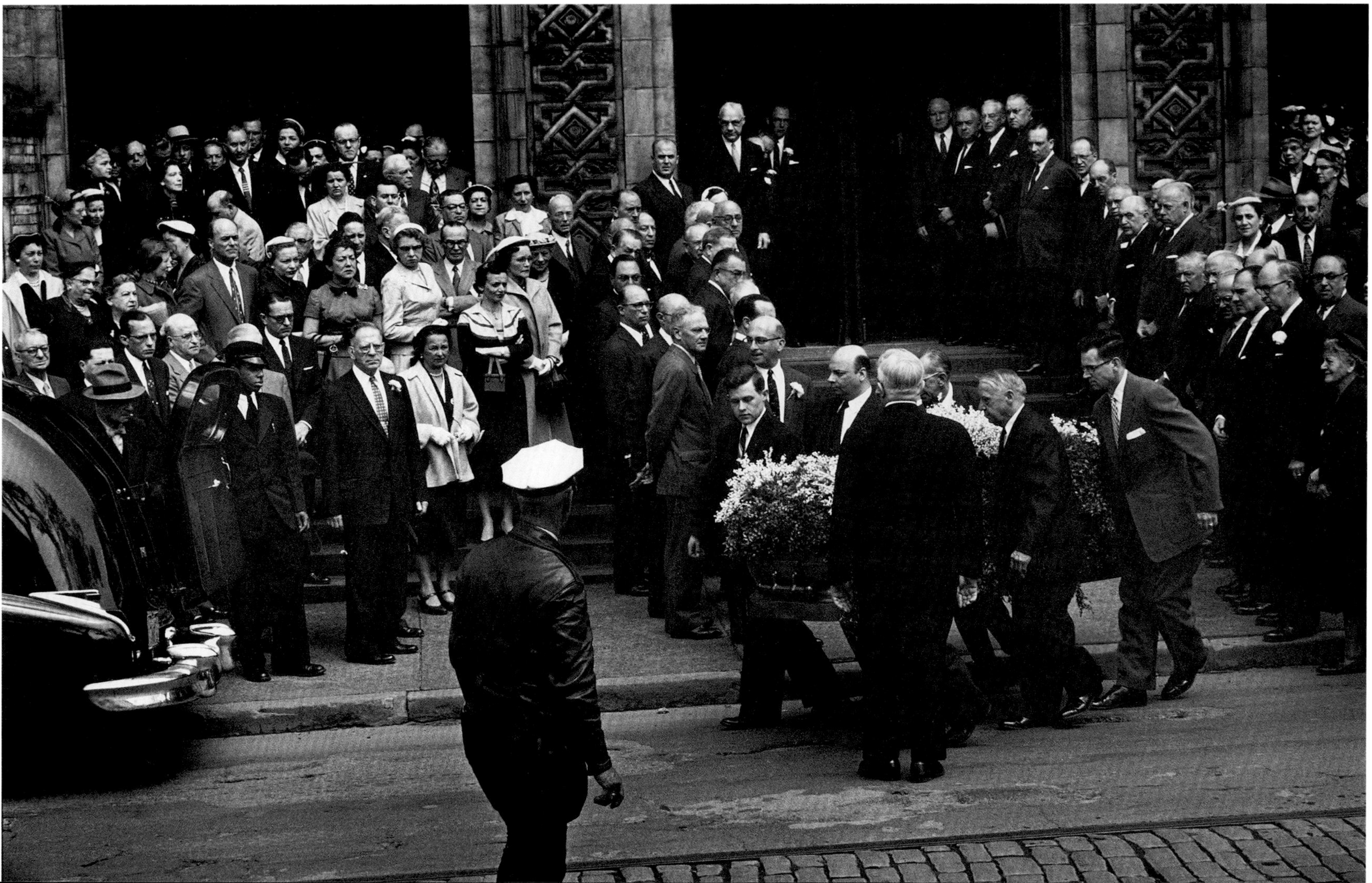

# IV

It would have been good to have you see the Pittsburgh work situation; the board after board filled with several thousand 5 × 7 proof prints, the layout sketches, the fine sets of finished prints (and the howling kids). It might explain of me, much more than is possible to realize by merely seeing the finished work accompanied by my wordy complaints and apologies. Without judging of it, I know of no photographer working or thinking in photography as I do. I wonder why I continually apologize that others do not understand, except that I do hate misinterpretation.

Excerpt from Smith's letter to Norman Hall, editor of the London-based magazine *Photography*, March 19, 1956

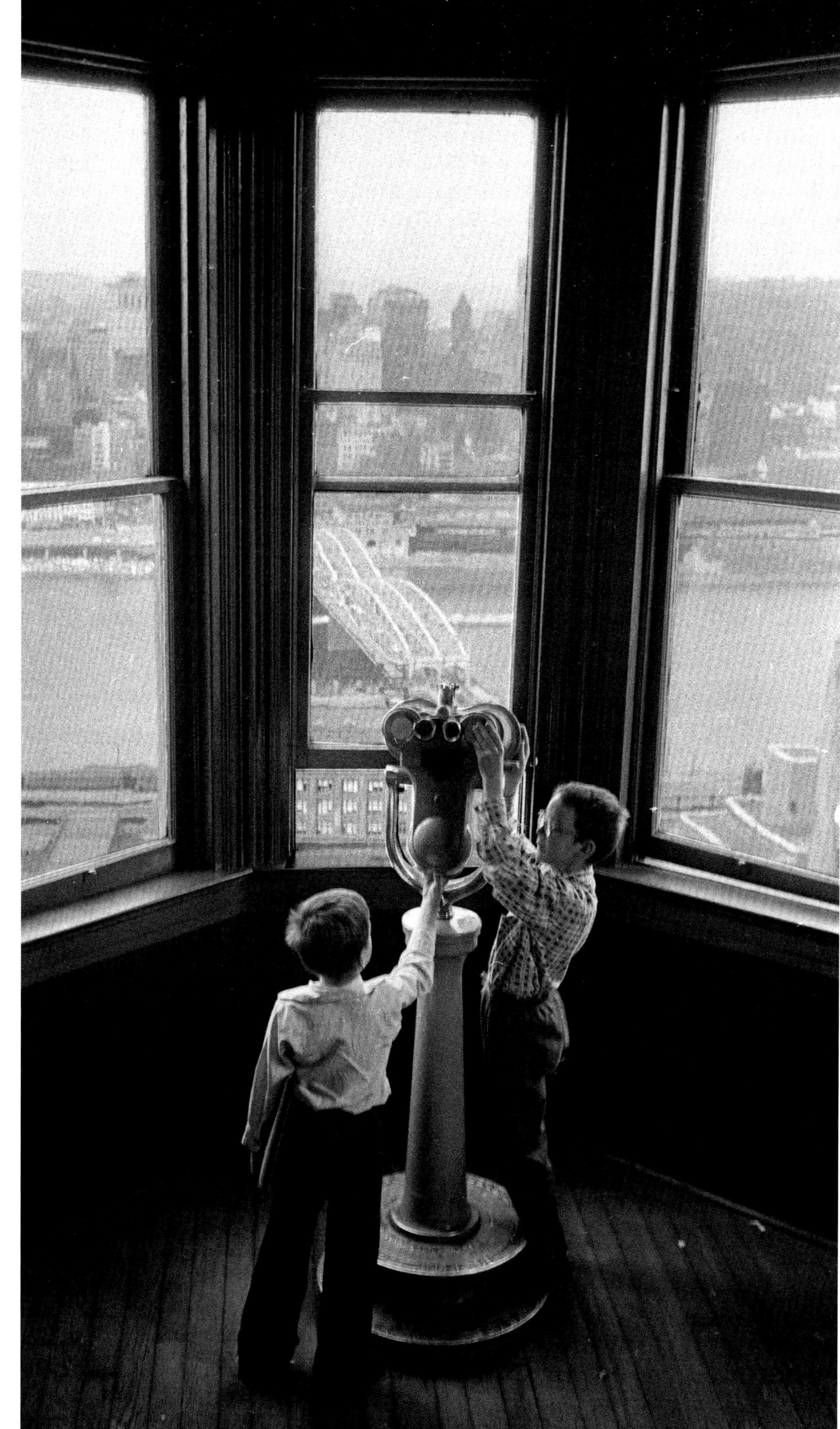

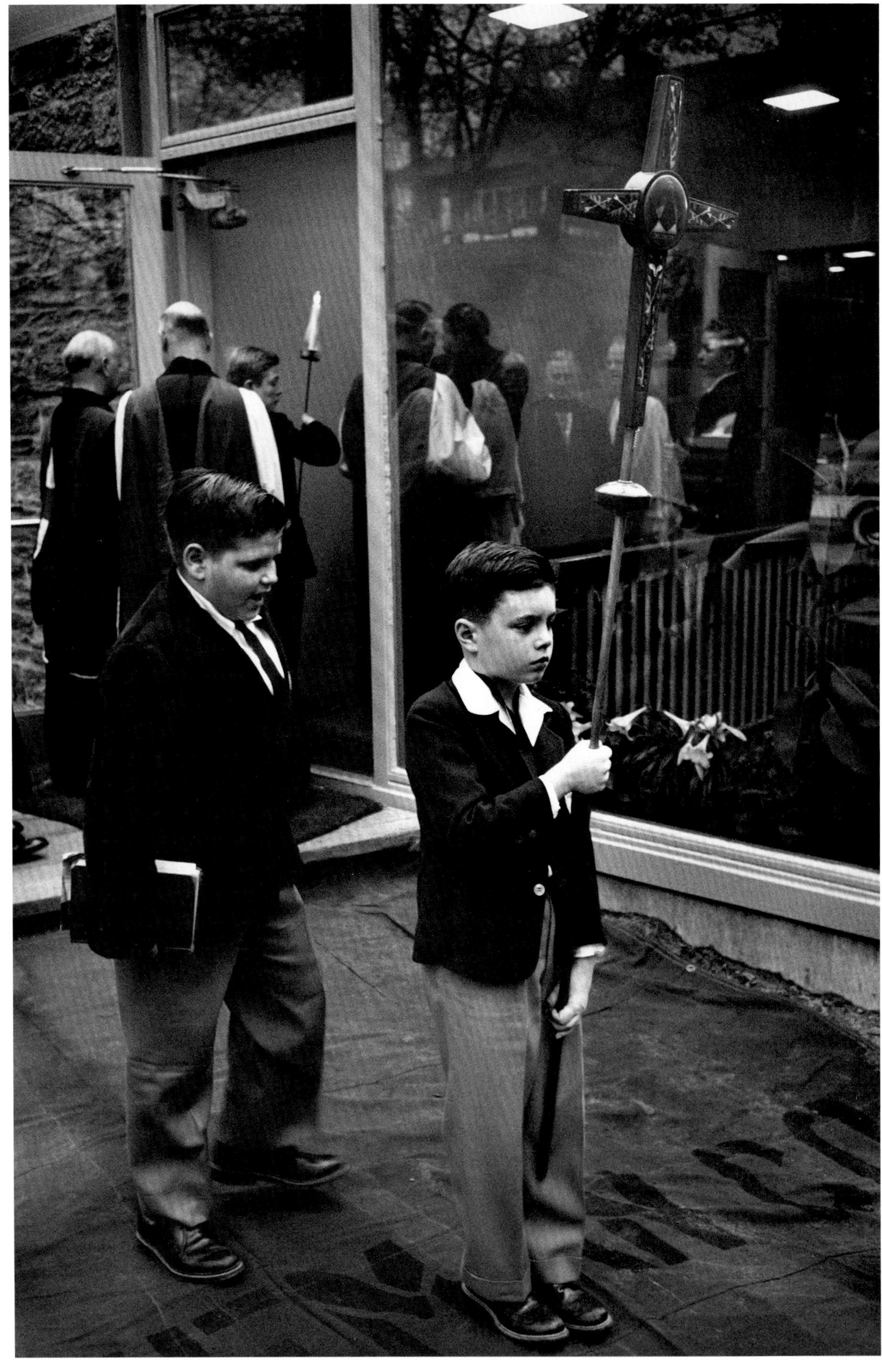

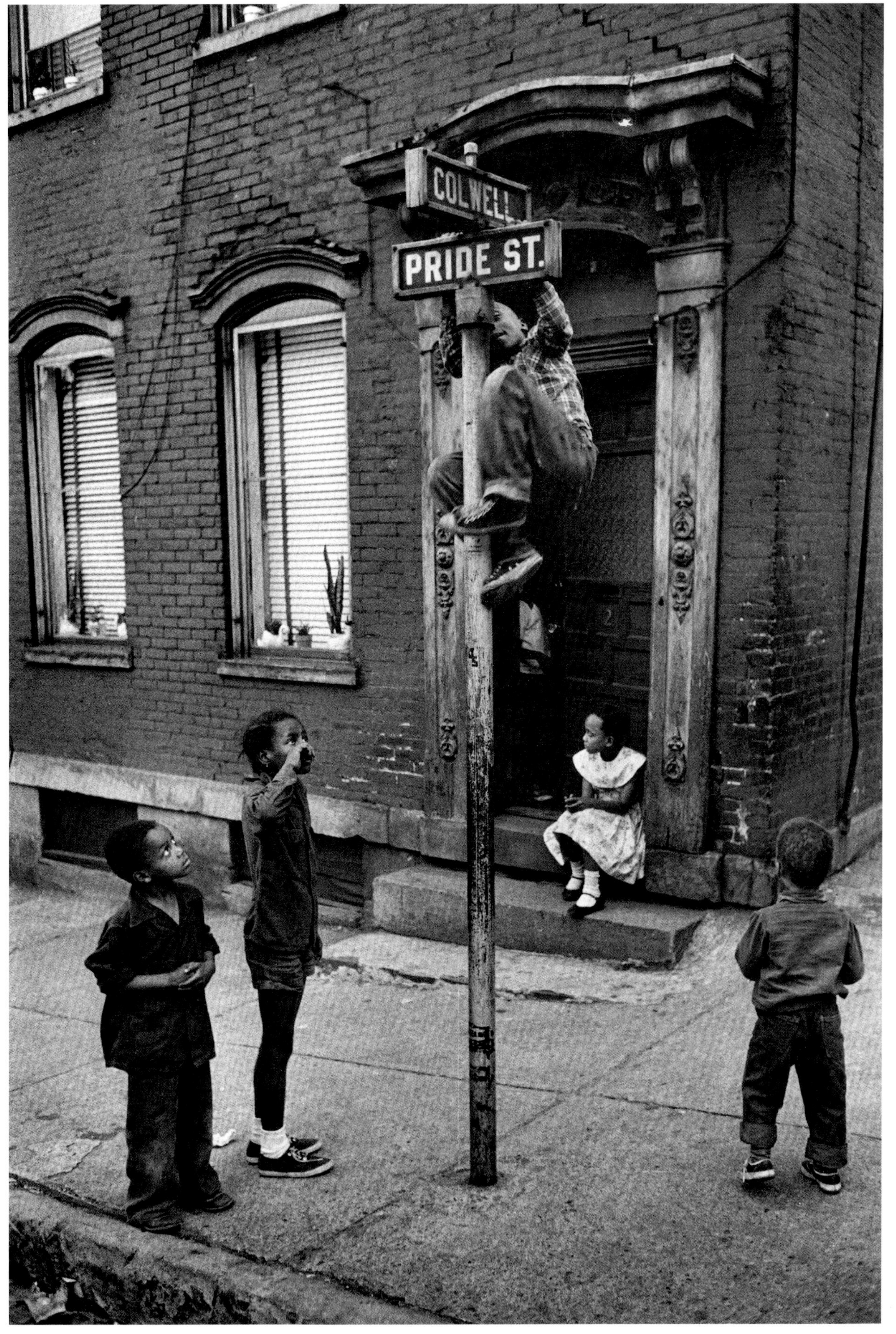
COLWELL
PRIDE ST.

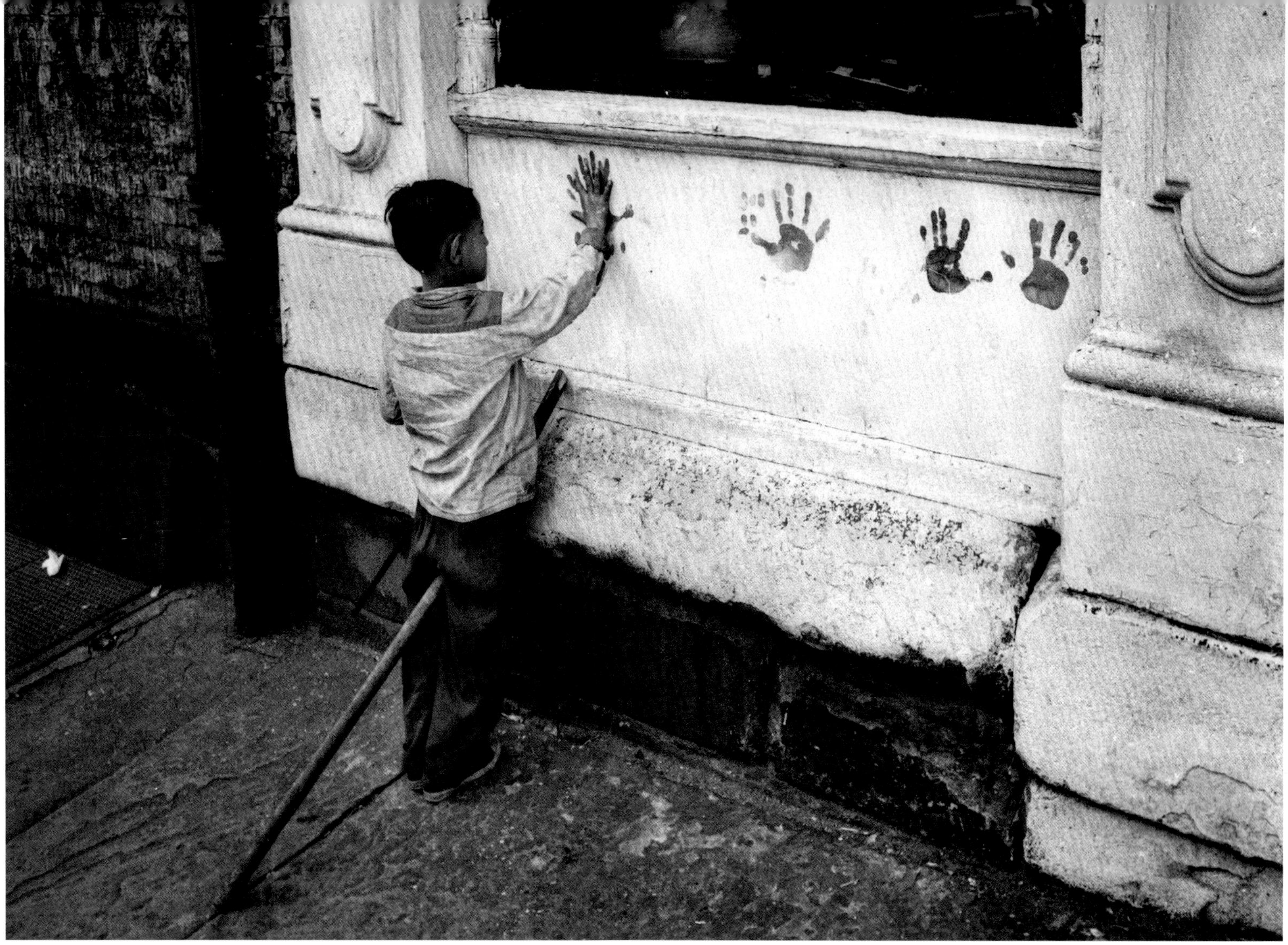

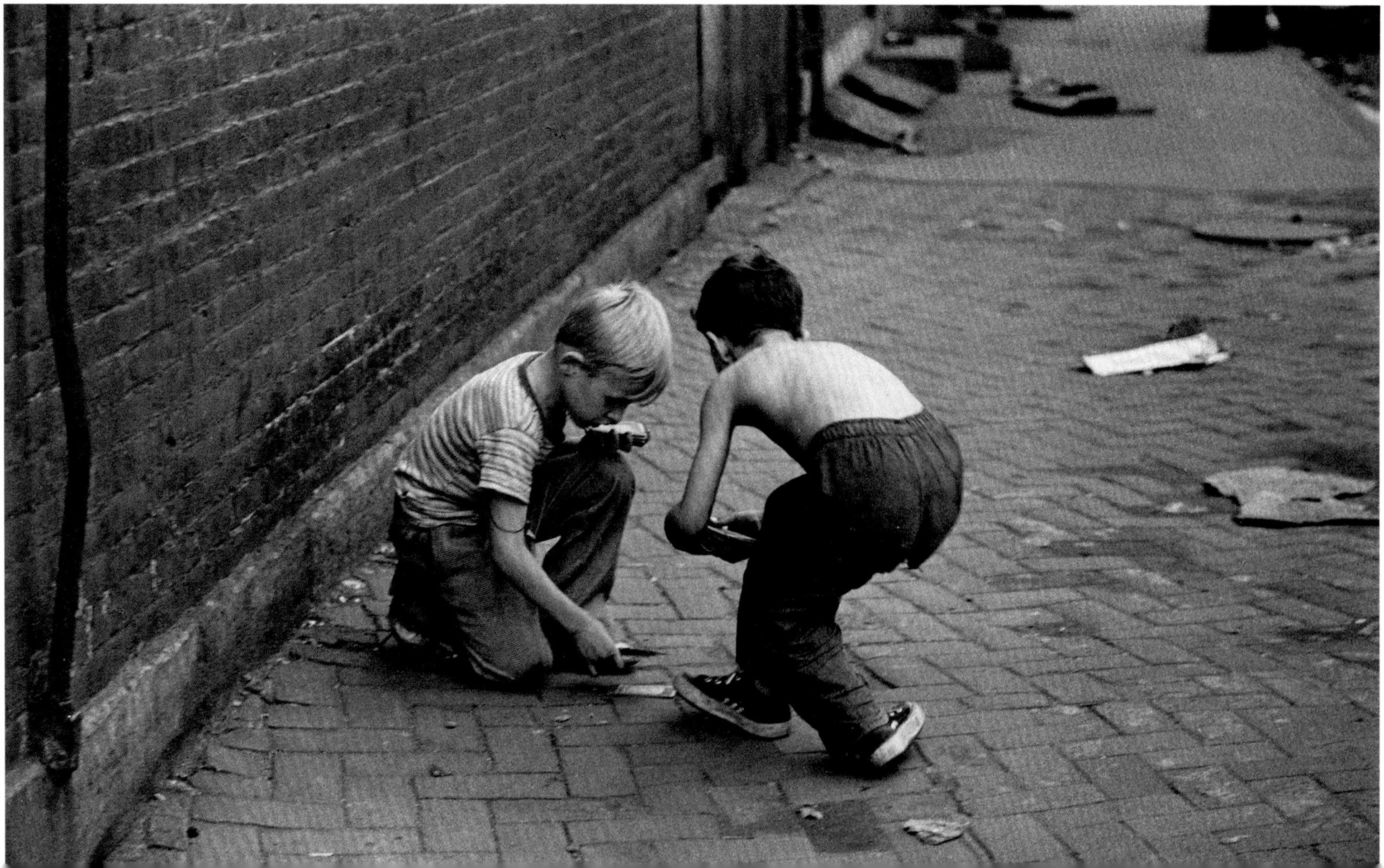

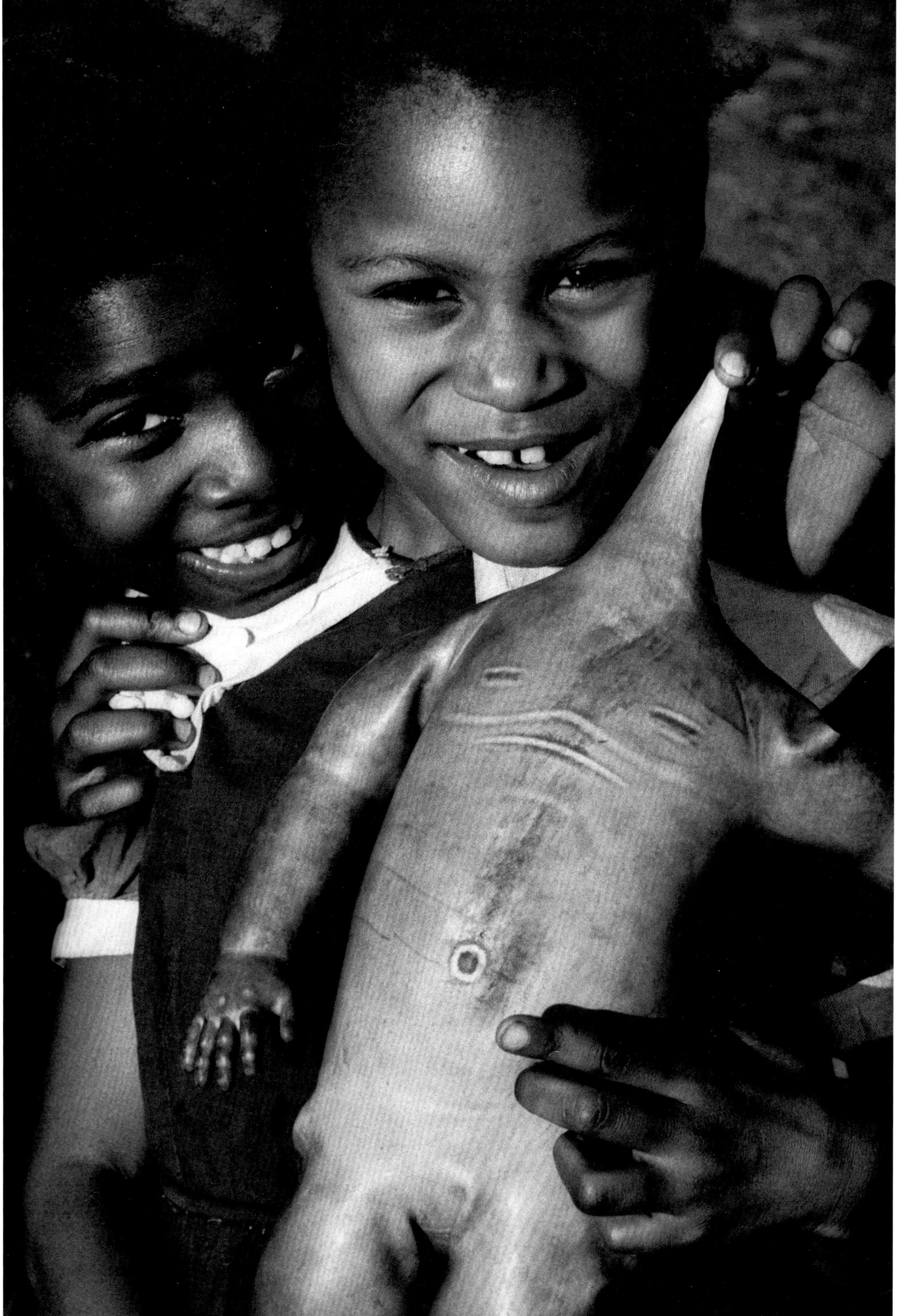

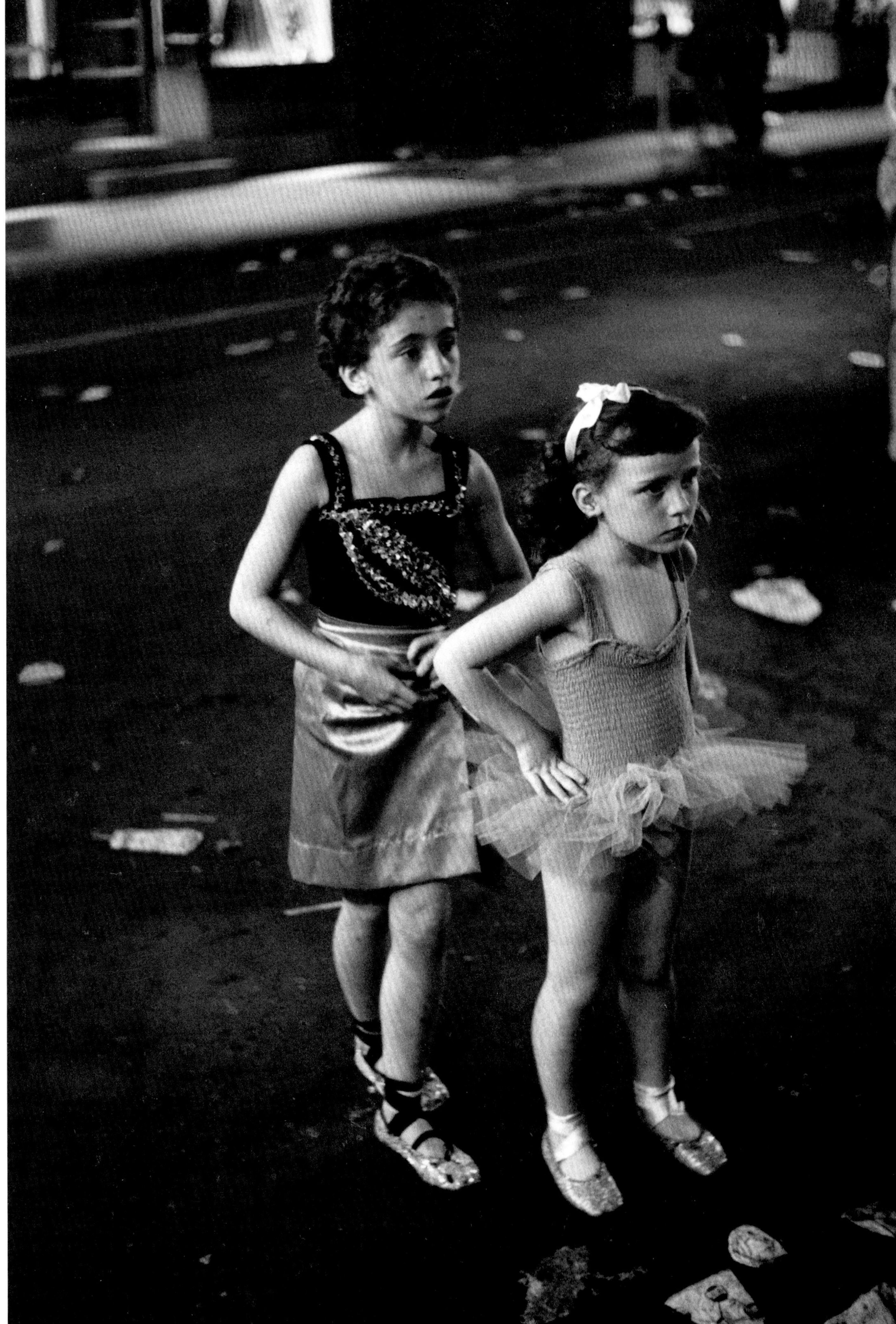

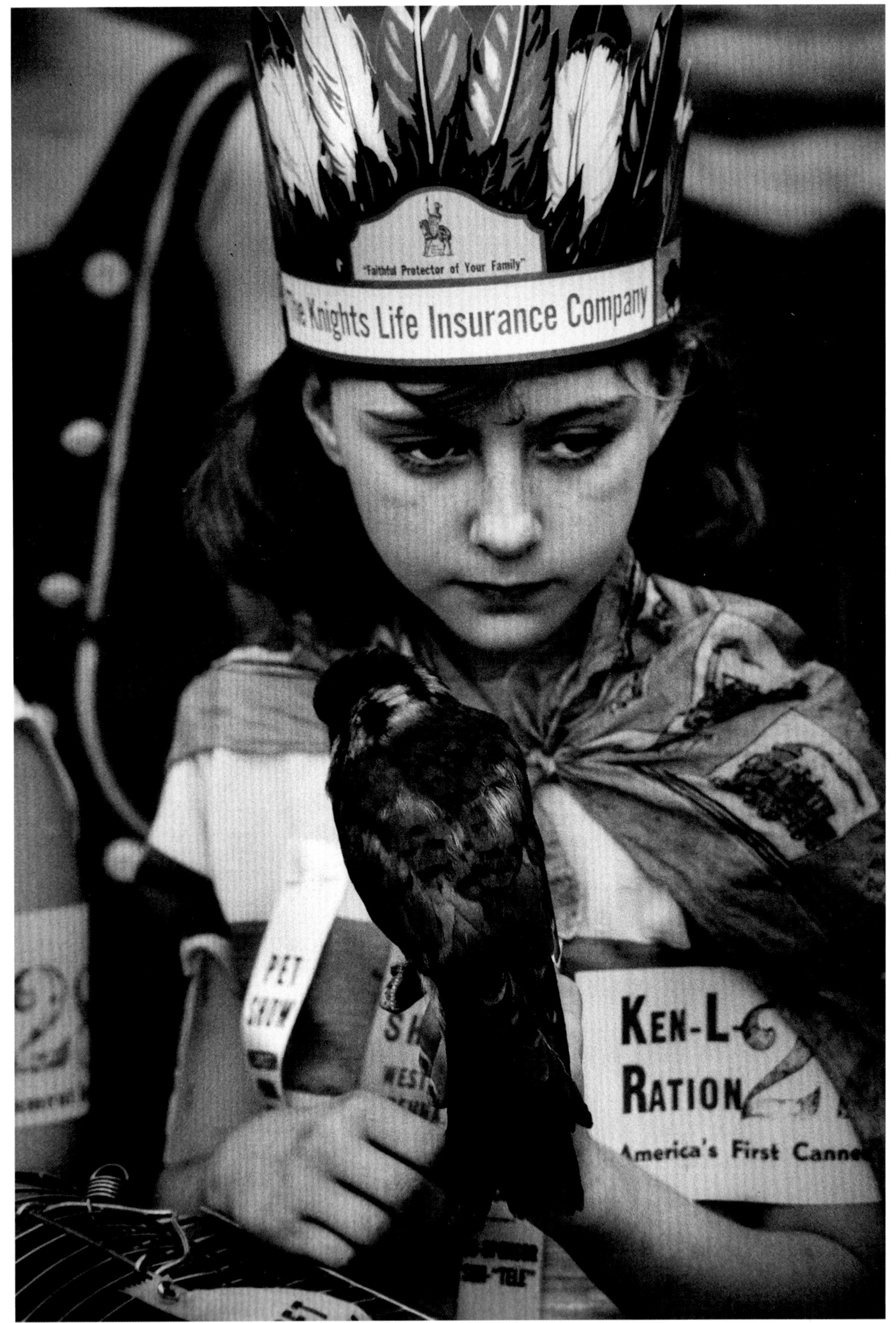
"Faithful Protector of Your Family"
e Knights Life Insurance Company
PET
SHOW
WEST
KEN-L
RATION 2
America's First Canne

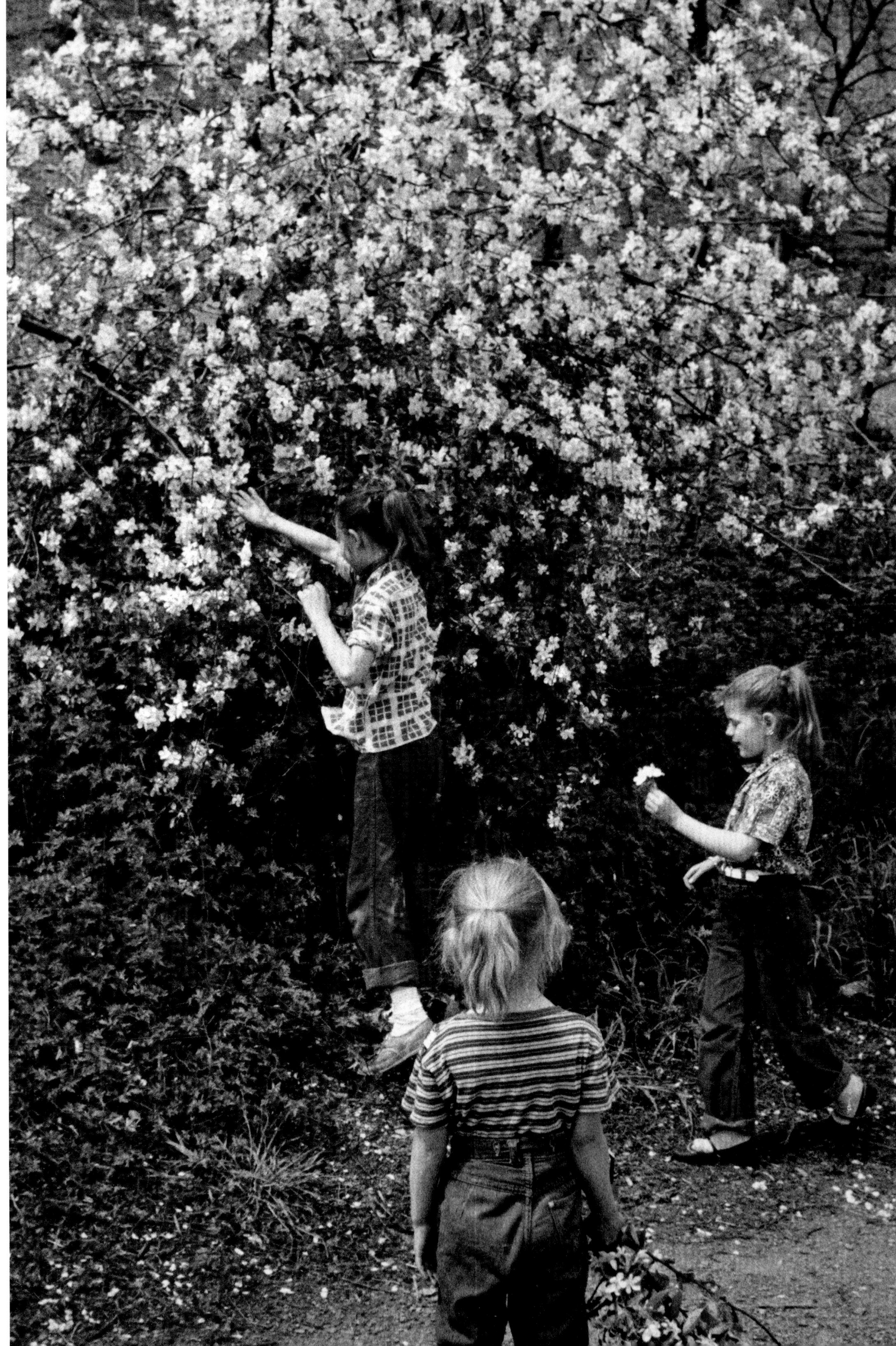

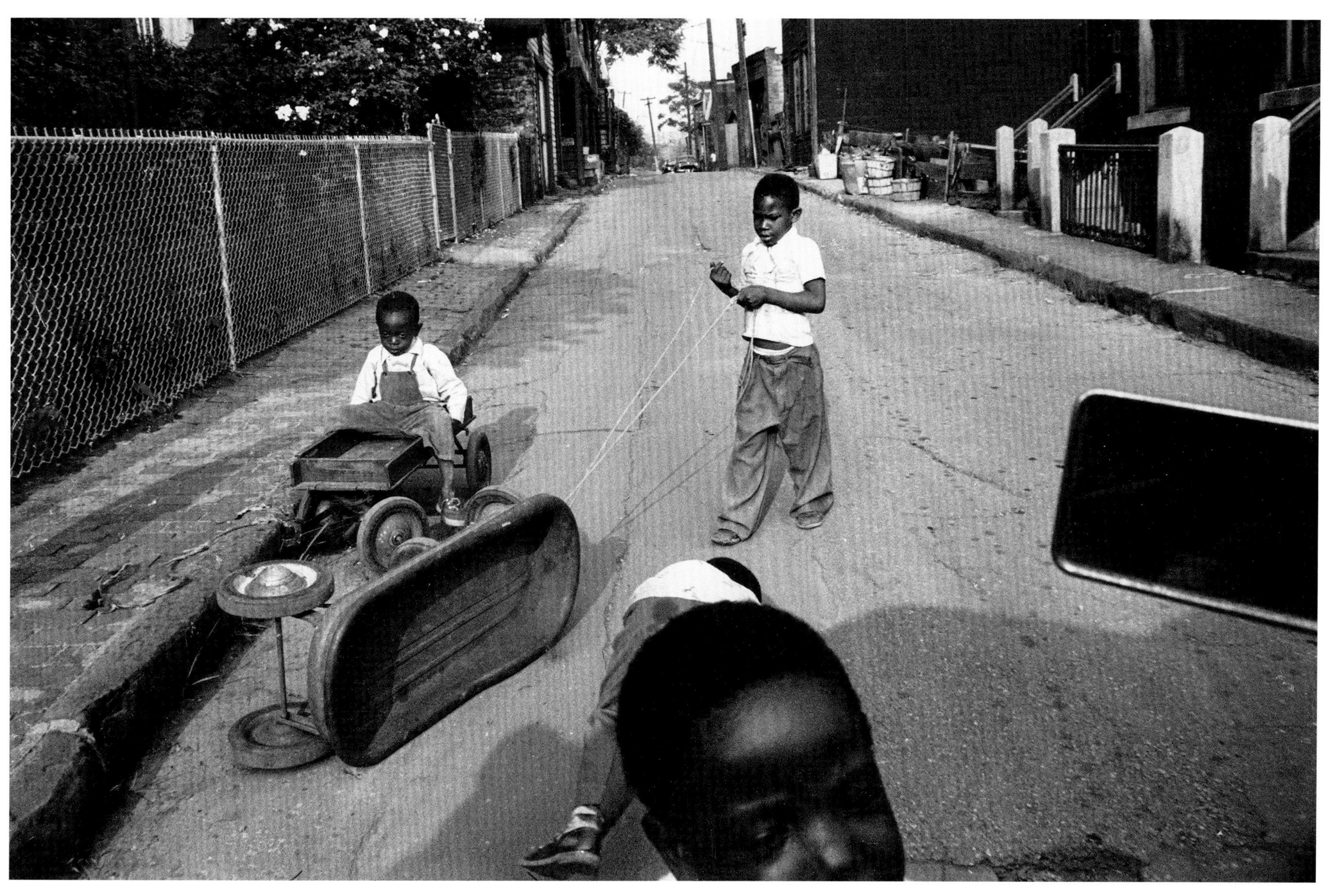

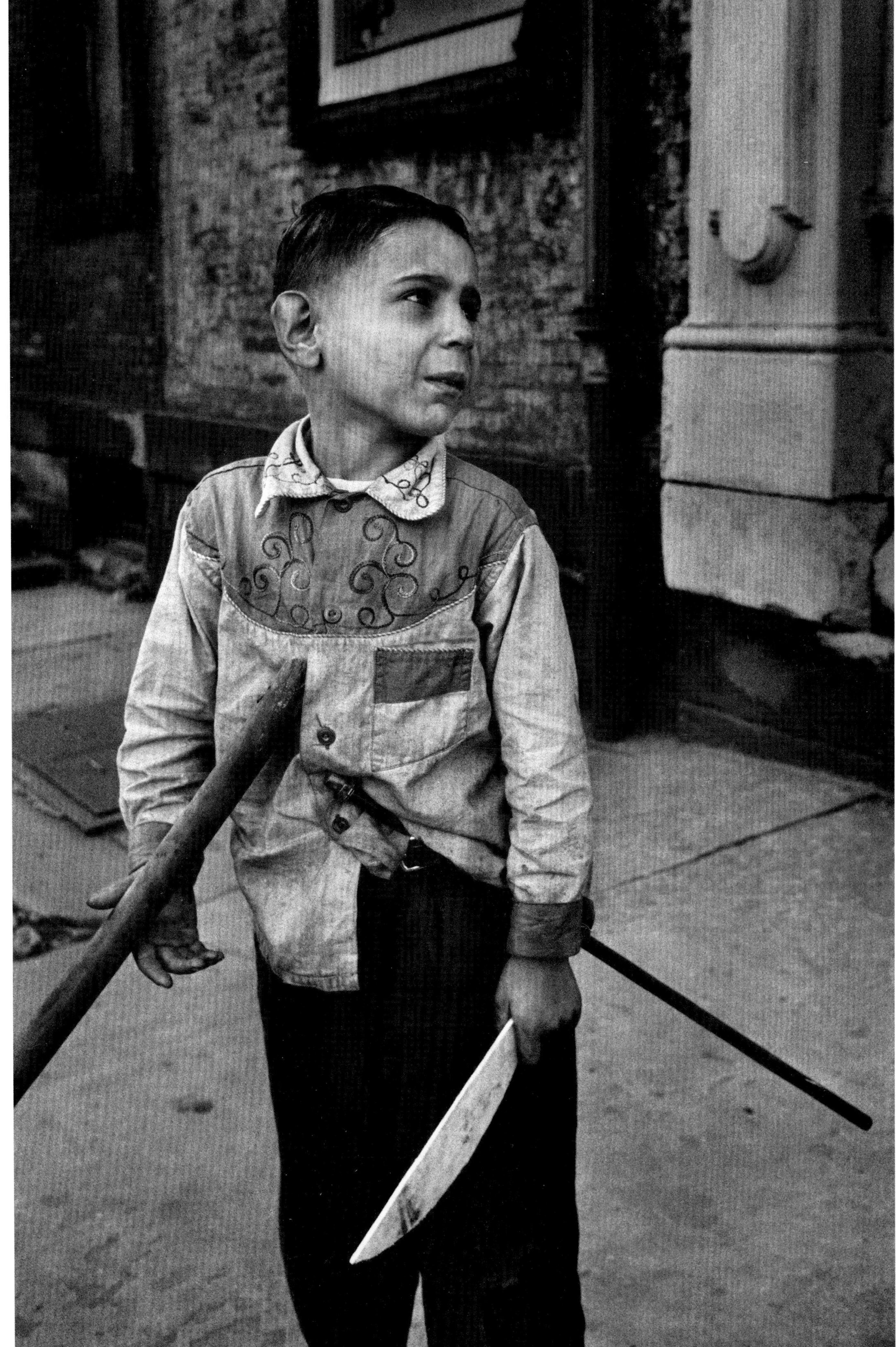

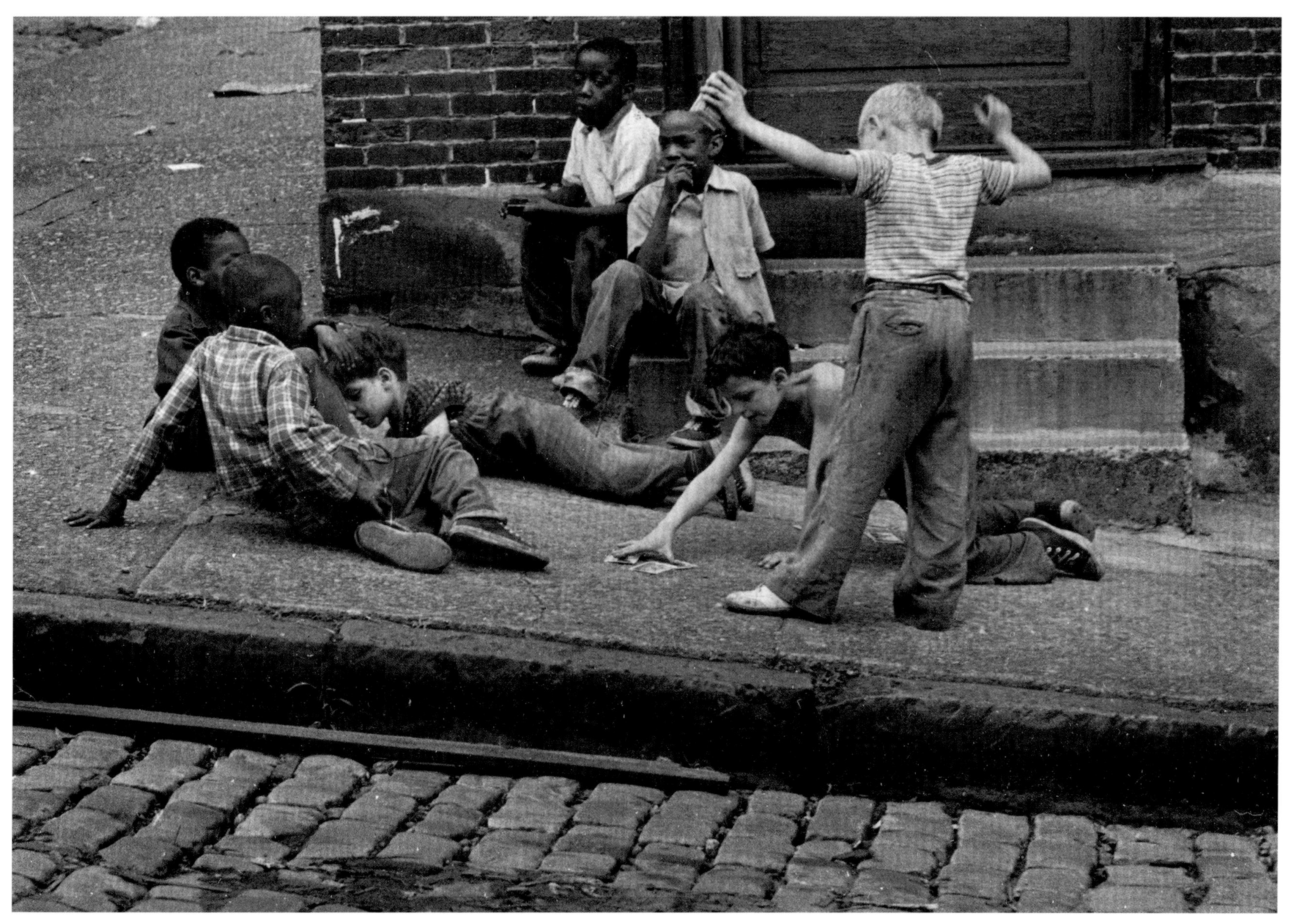

# V

The city as a living entity with it being an environment for—and in turn, an environment being created by—the people who give it heart and pulse. I will observe, with intimate photographic scrutiny, these individuals as I encounter them during participation in the daily life of the city. (Yet, I will respect their ethical right of non-invasion of privacy). Unlike other essays of mine, such as The Nurse-Midwife, I will not, this time, (photographically) know any individual as a complete person. For the individual, in my present essay, is a part of the teaming into the teeming whole that is the city, singular, and—Pittsburgh, the City of, is my project and is the individual to be known.

From Smith's 1956 application for a fellowship from the John Simon Guggenheim Foundation
—"Plans for Use of Fellowship"

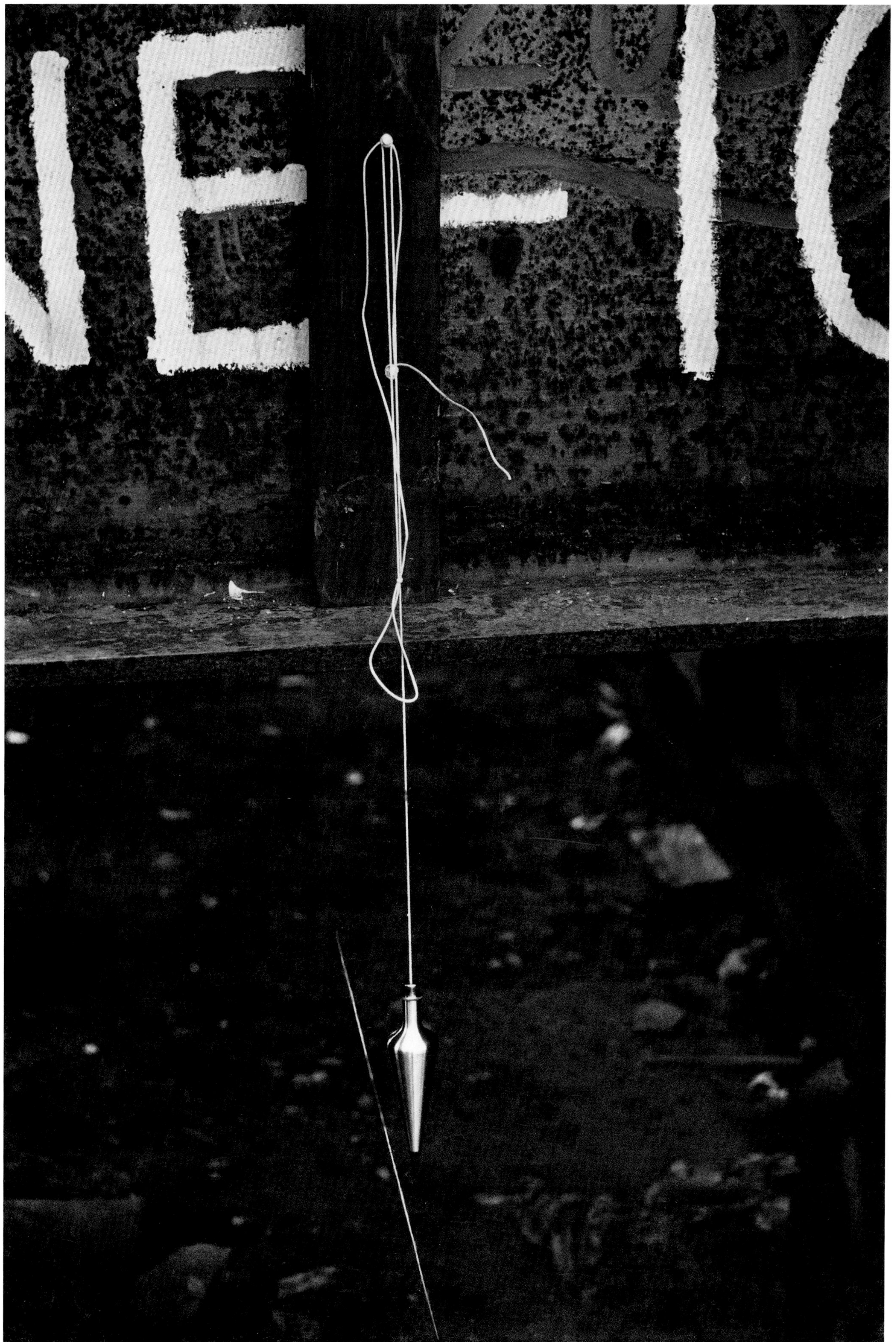

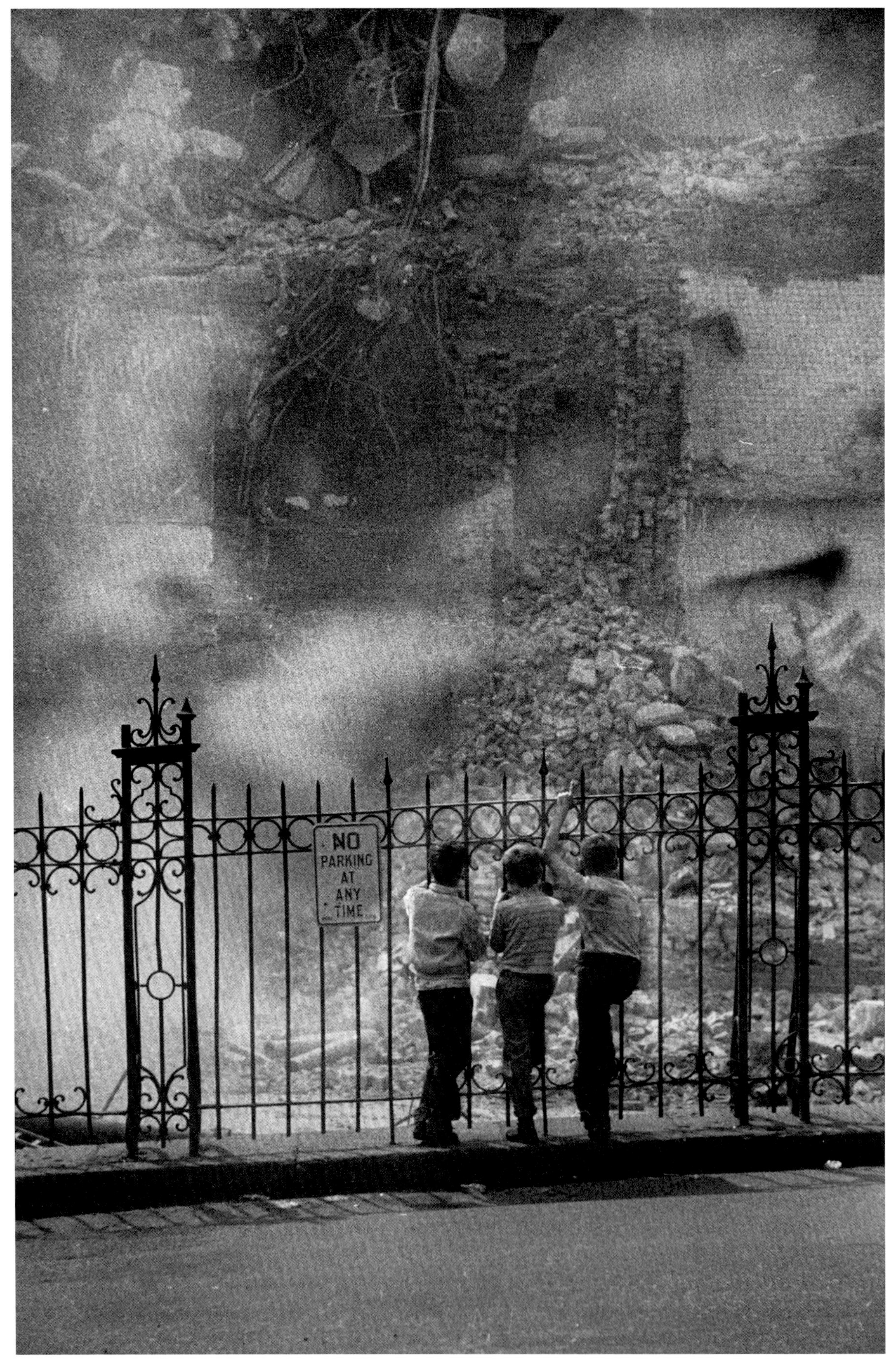
NO
PARKING
AT
ANY
TIME

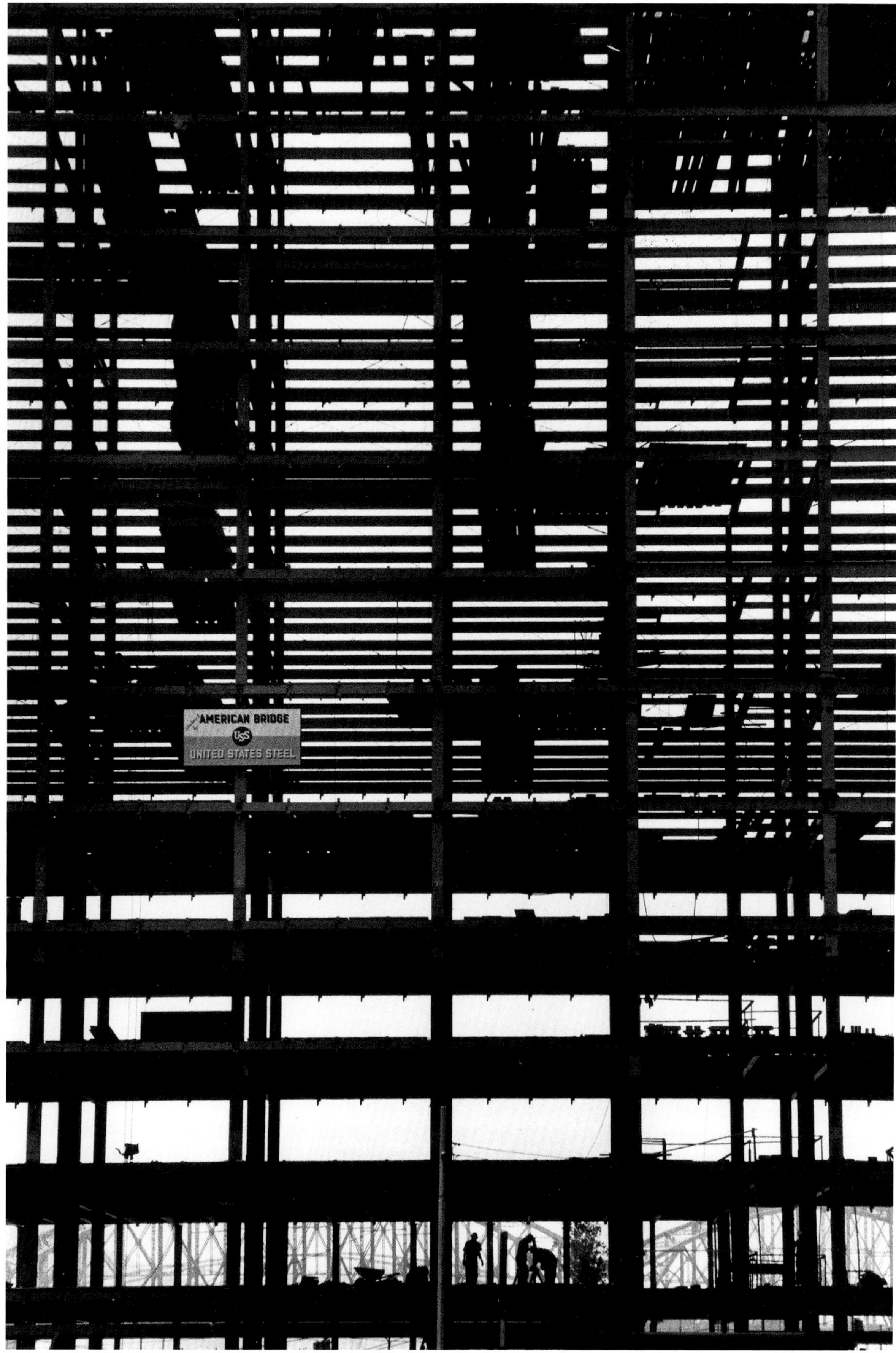
AMERICAN BRIDGE
USS
UNITED STATES STEEL

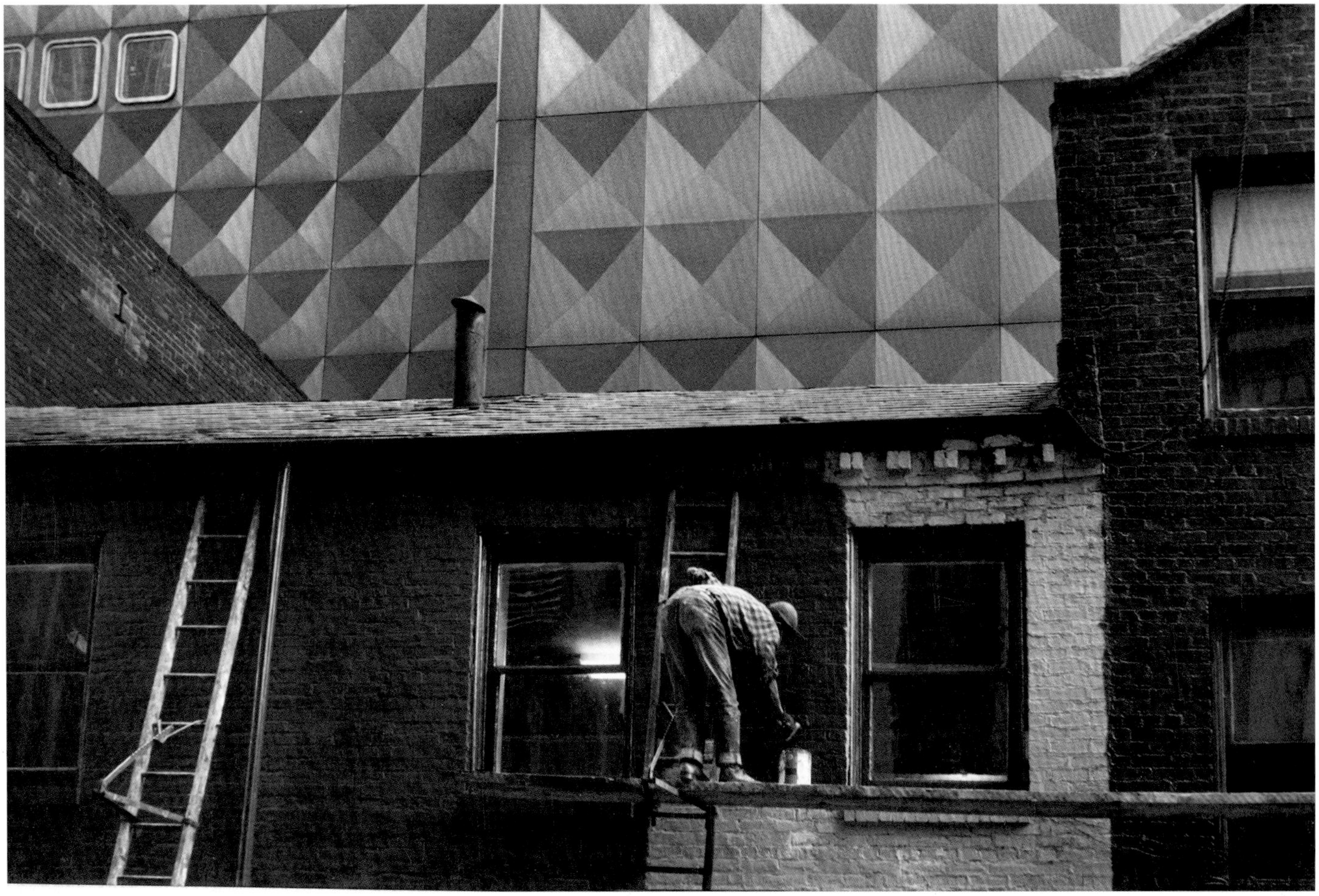

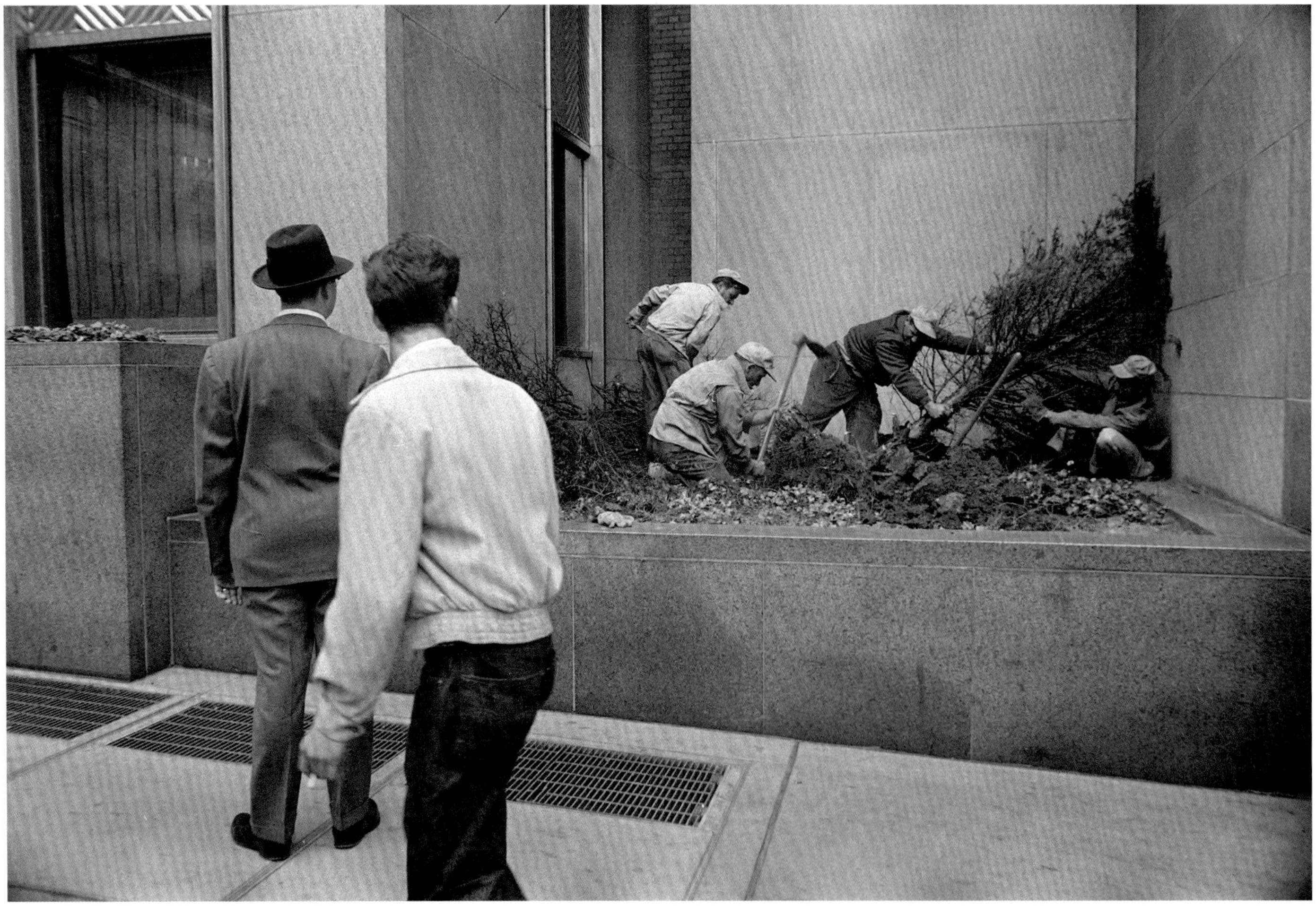

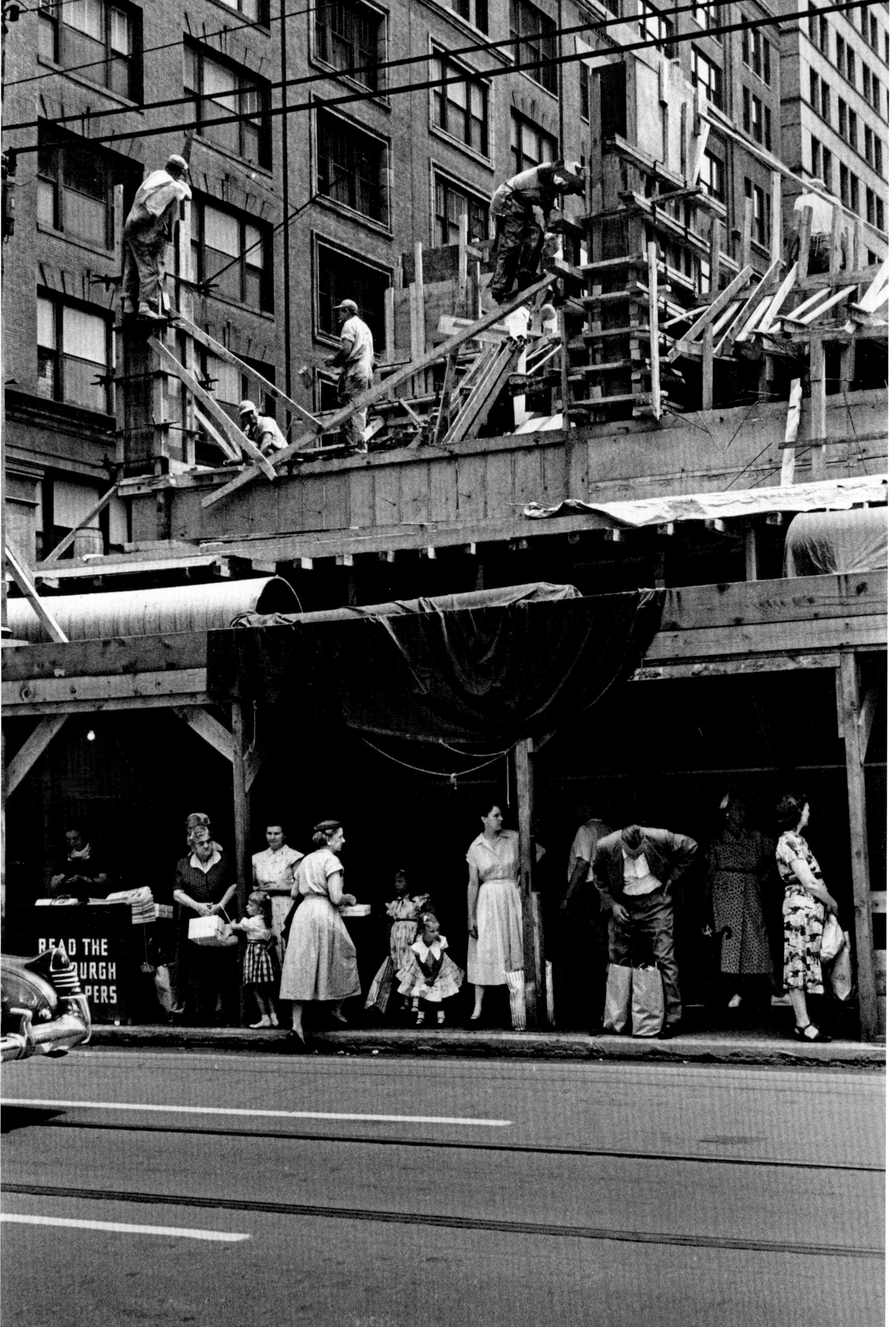

READ THE
URGH
PERS

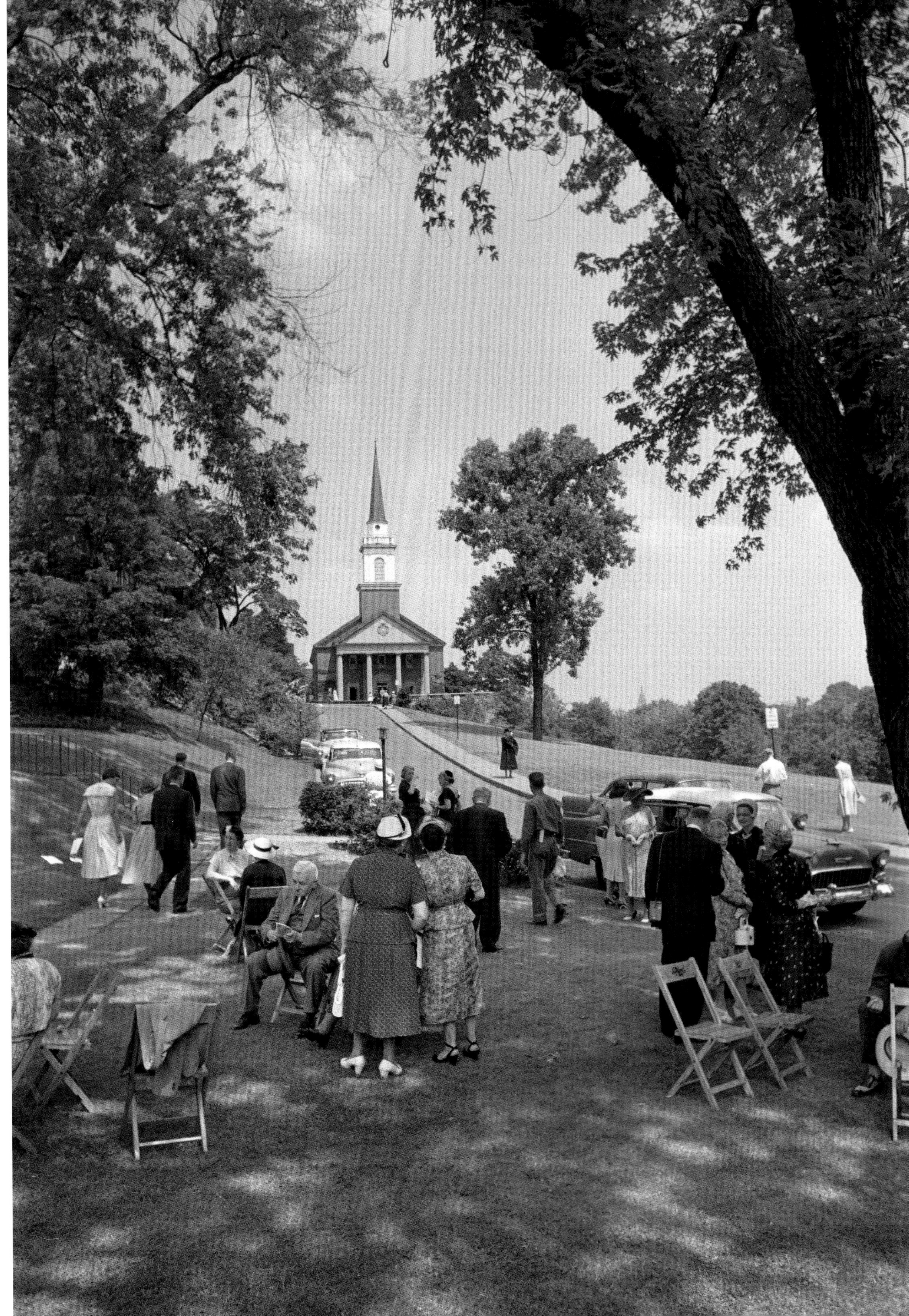

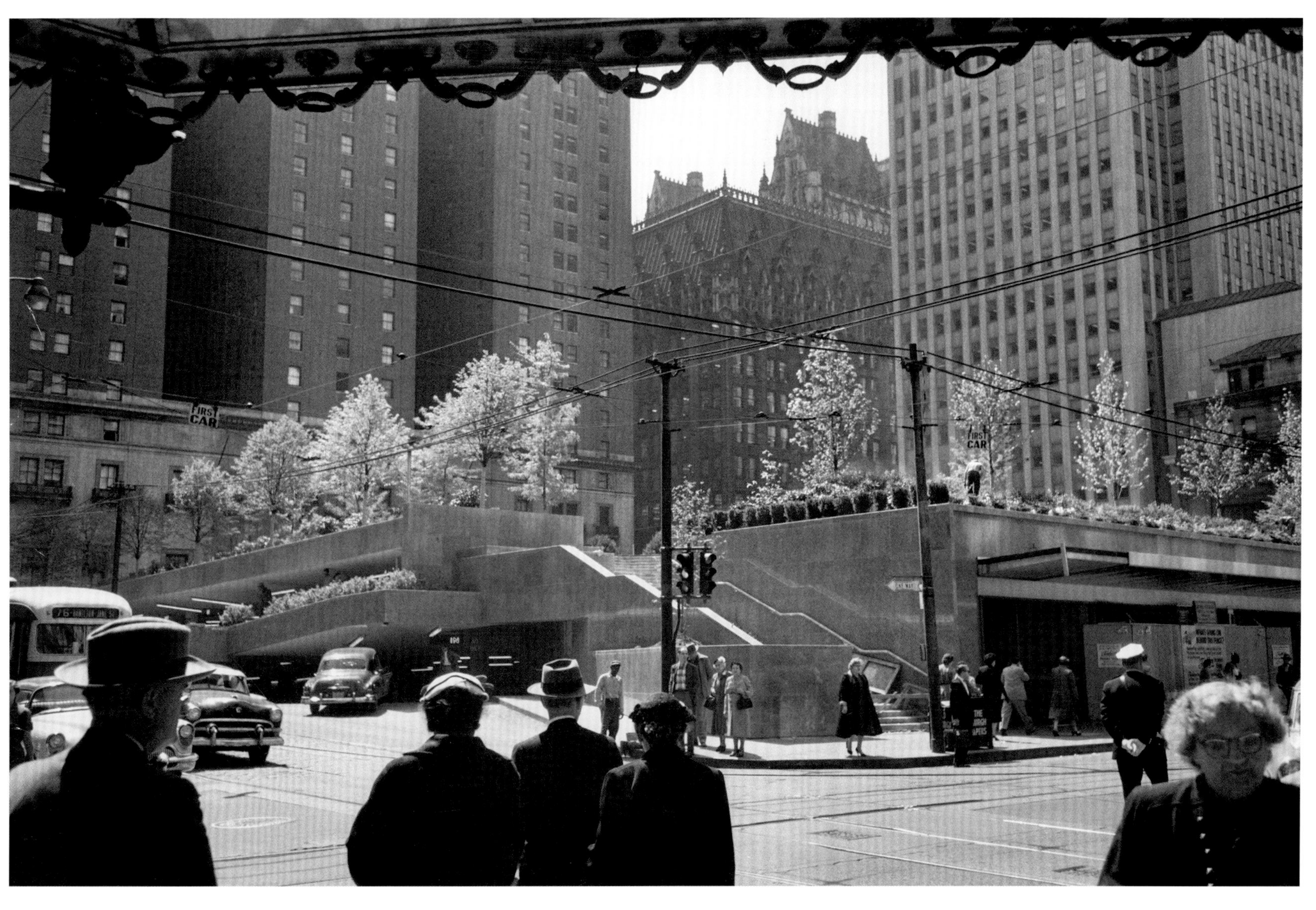
FIRST CAR
FIRST CAR
76

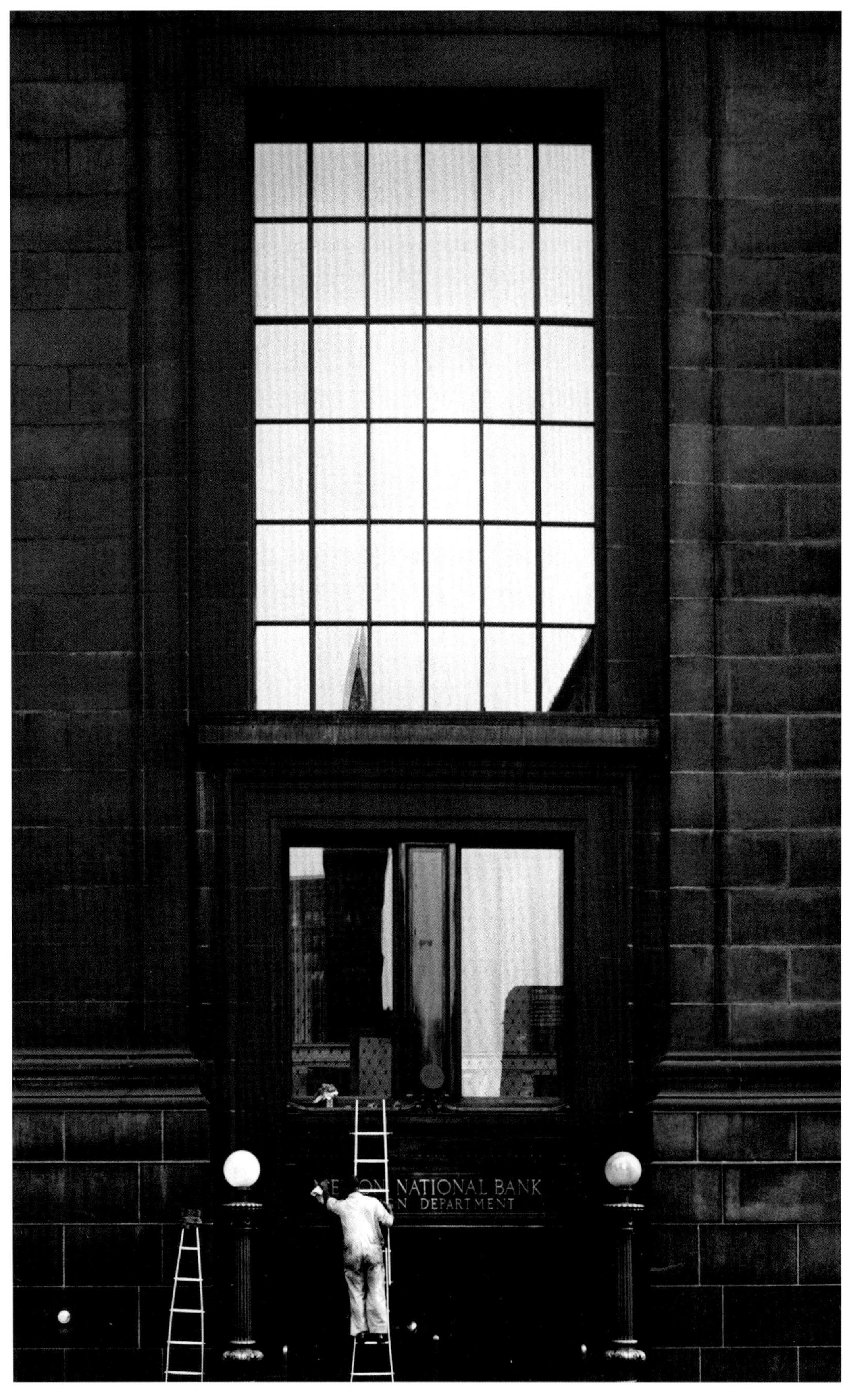


ELON NATIONAL BANK
N DEPARTMENT

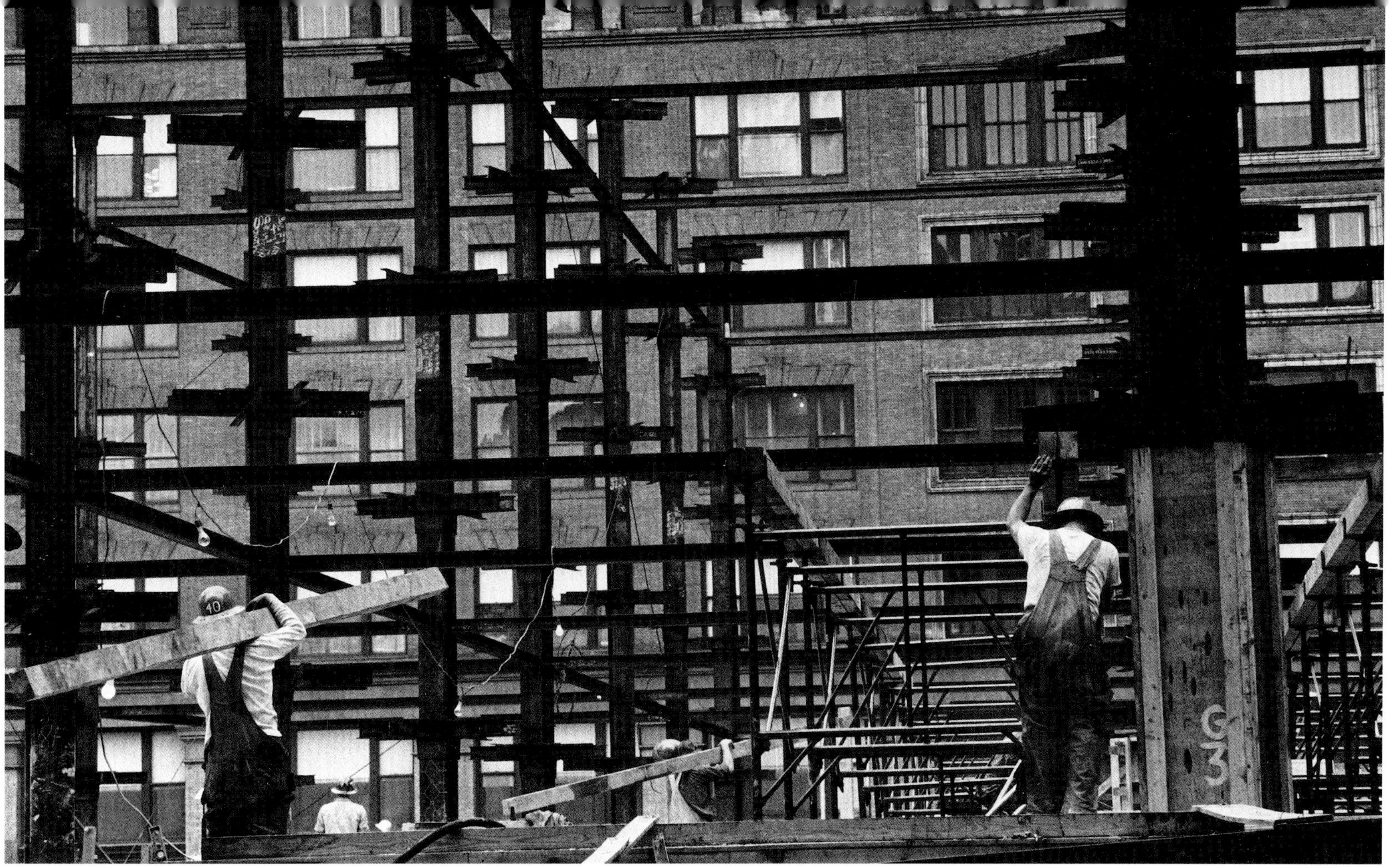

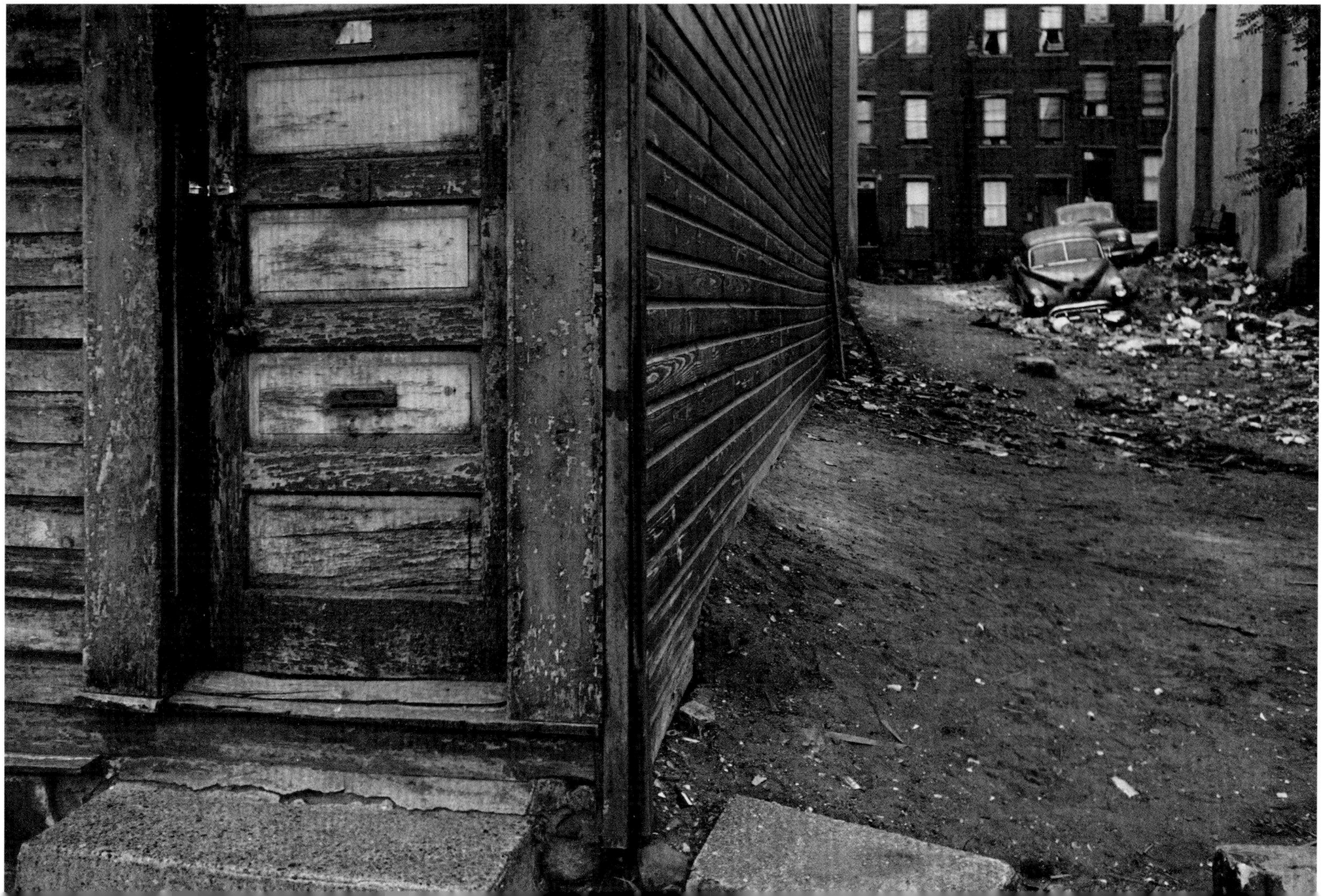

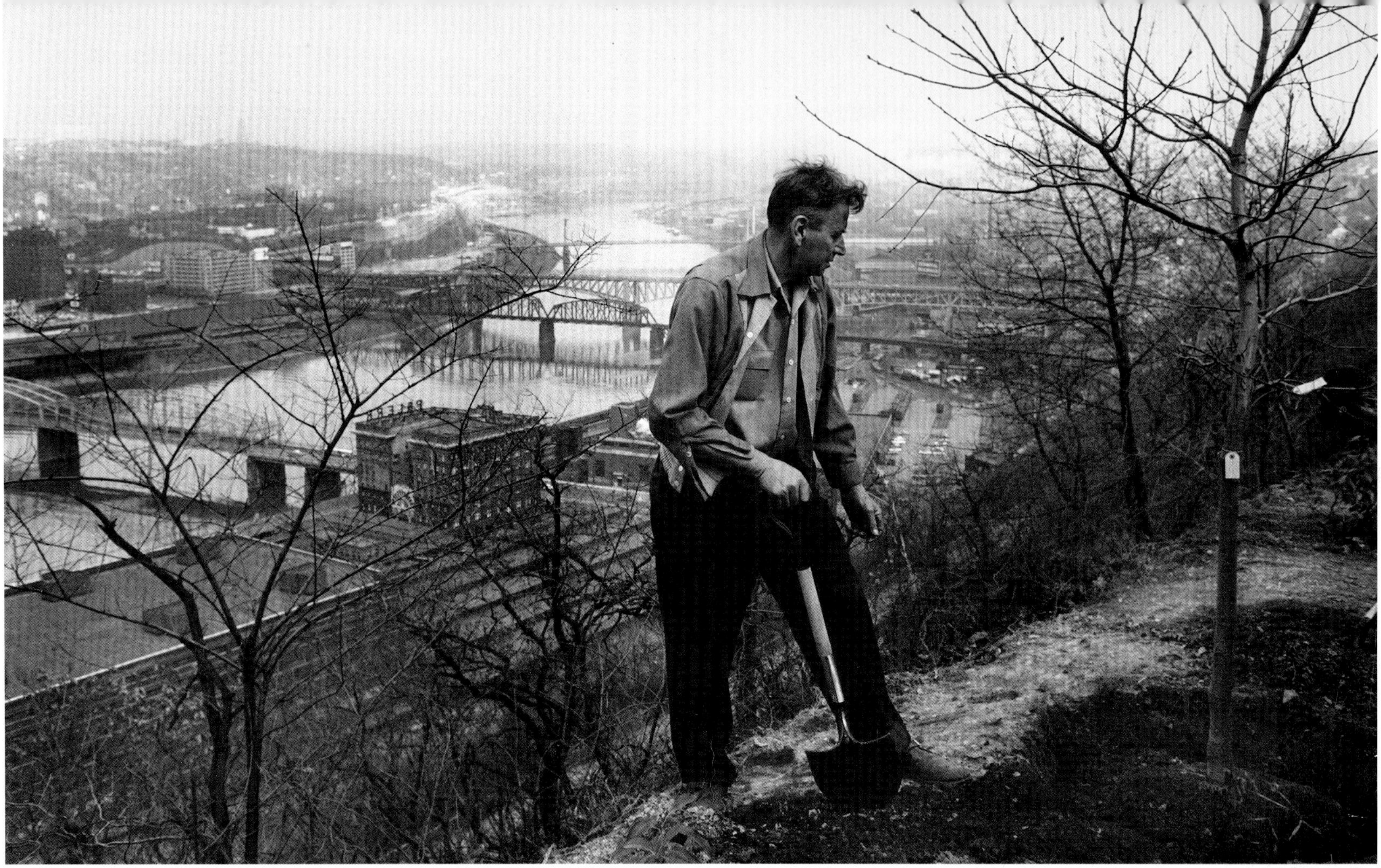

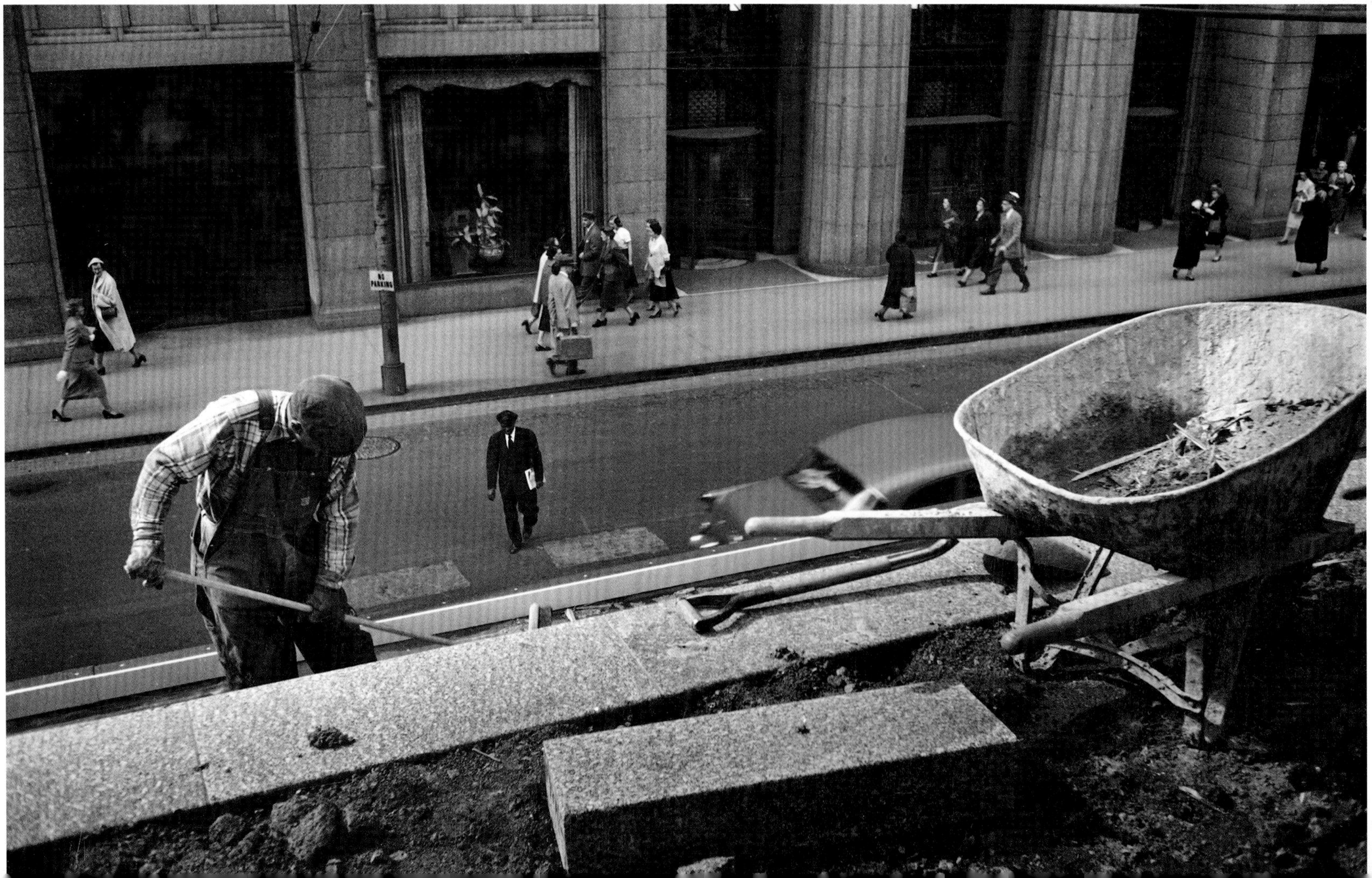

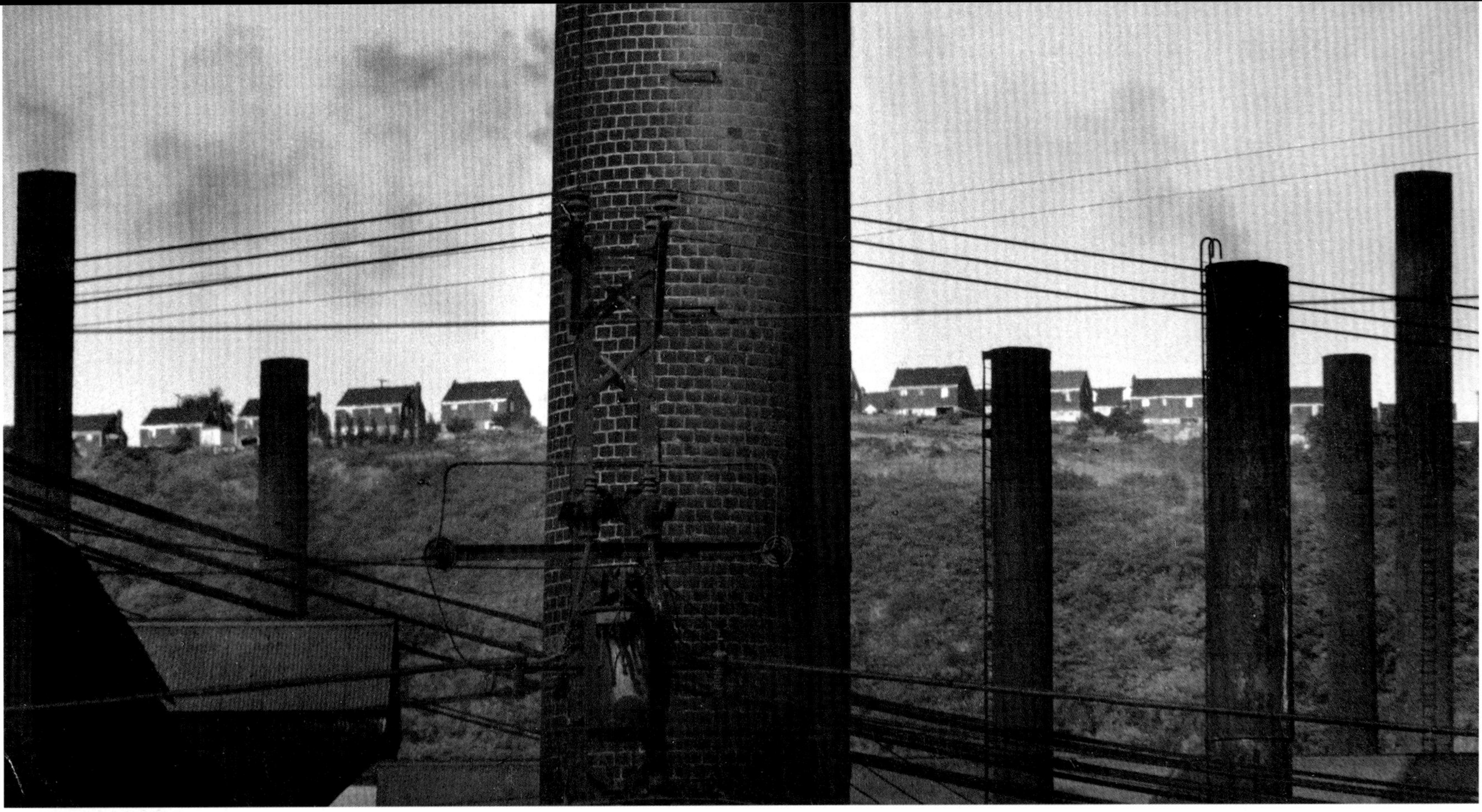

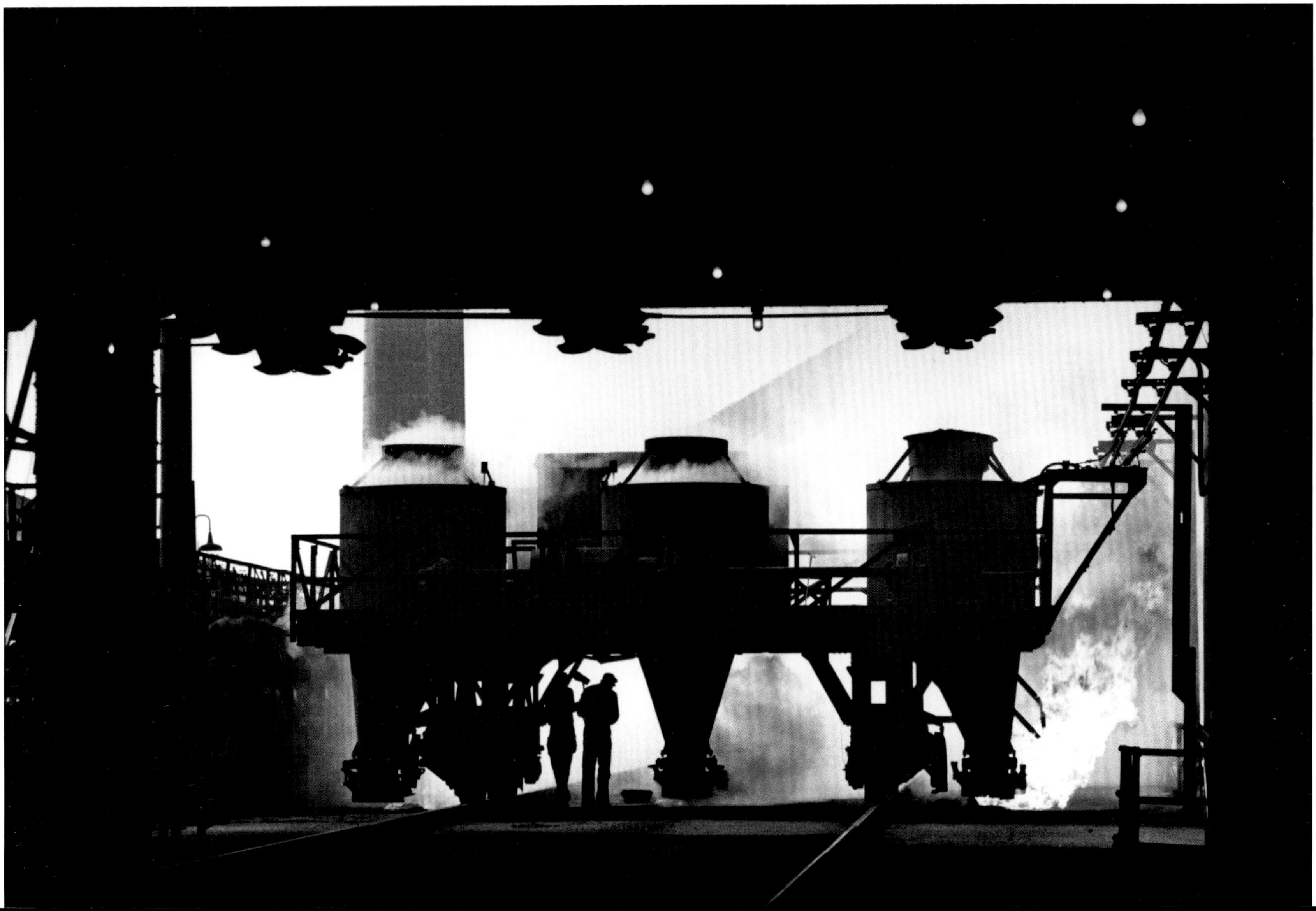

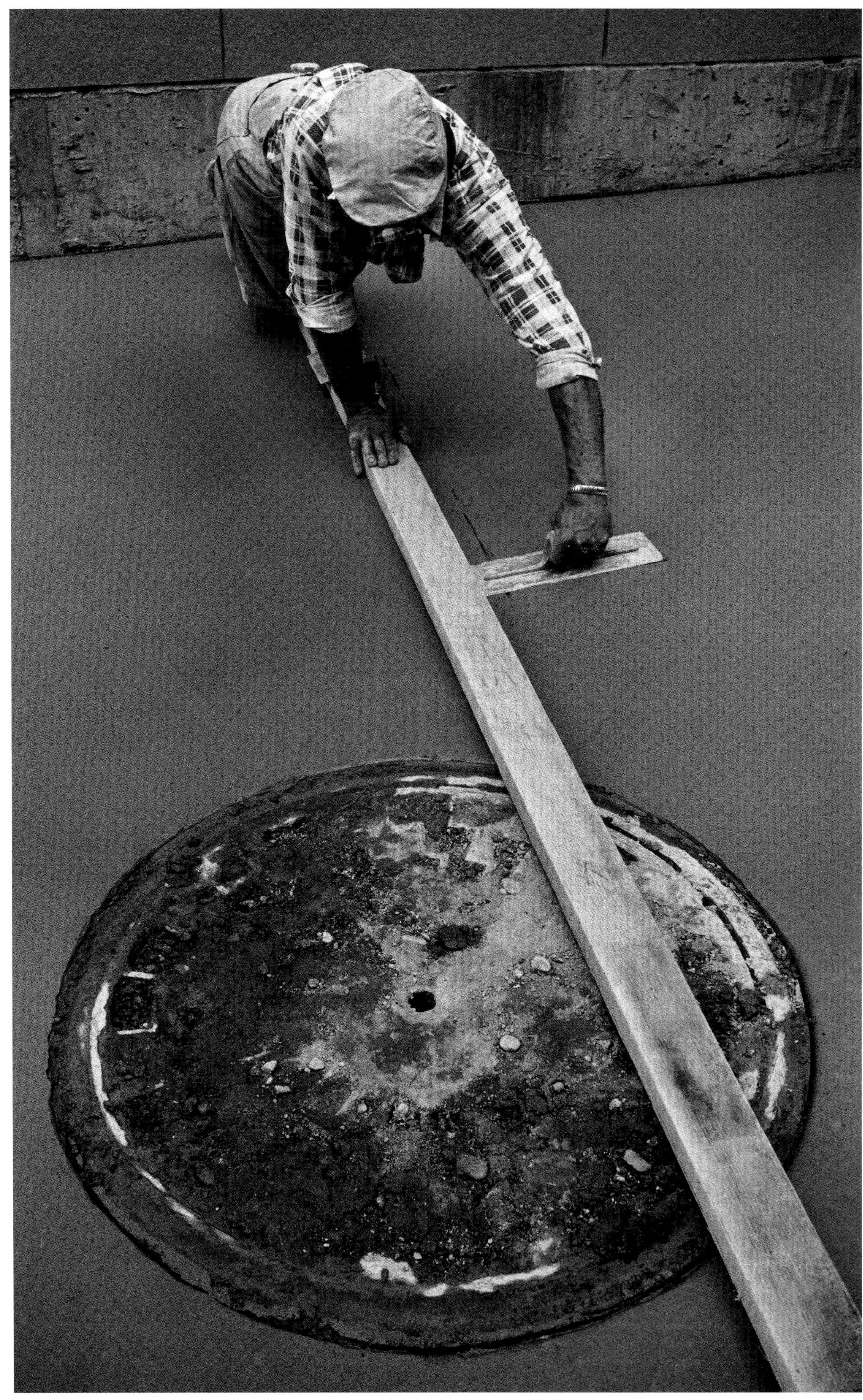

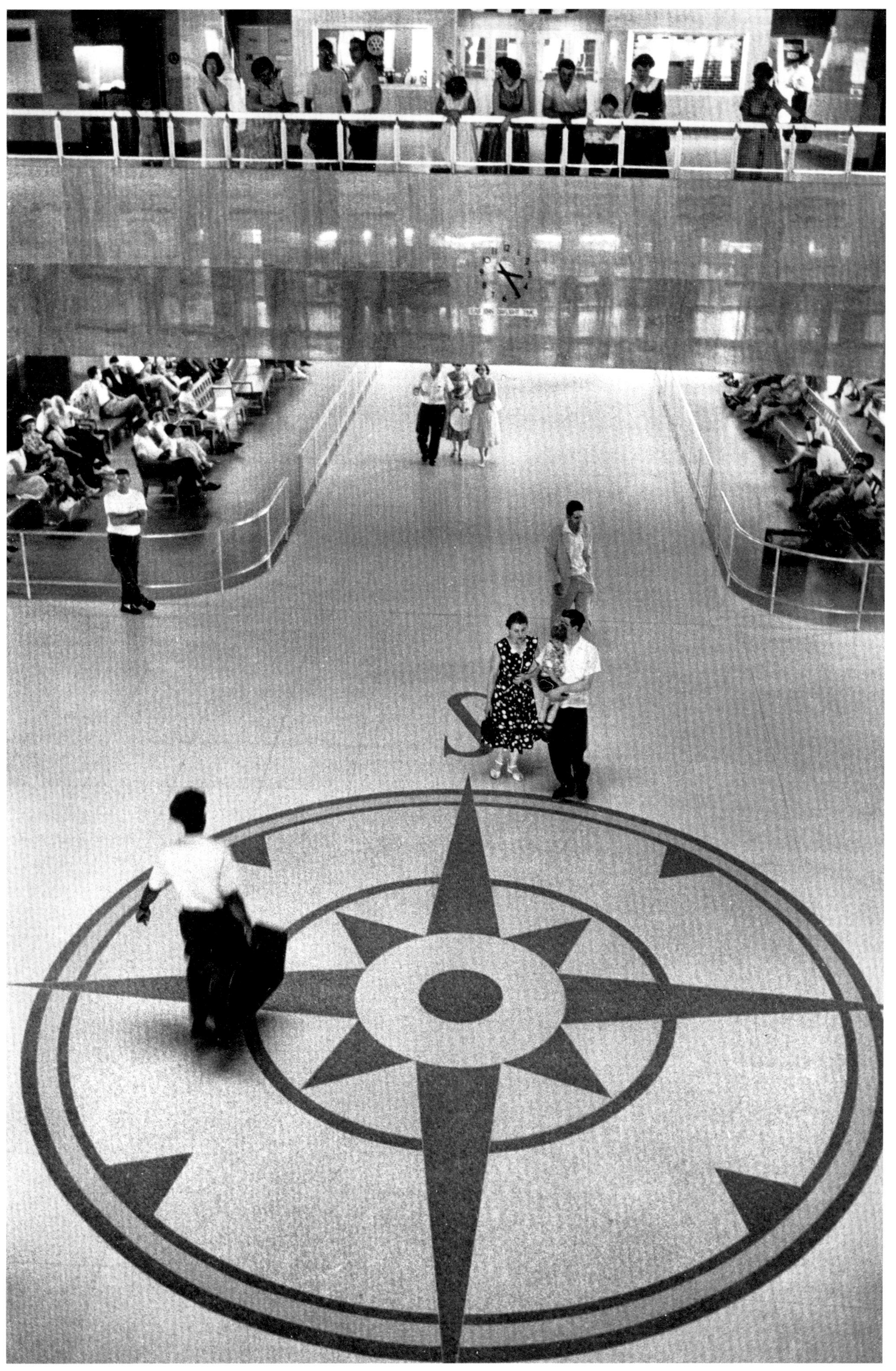

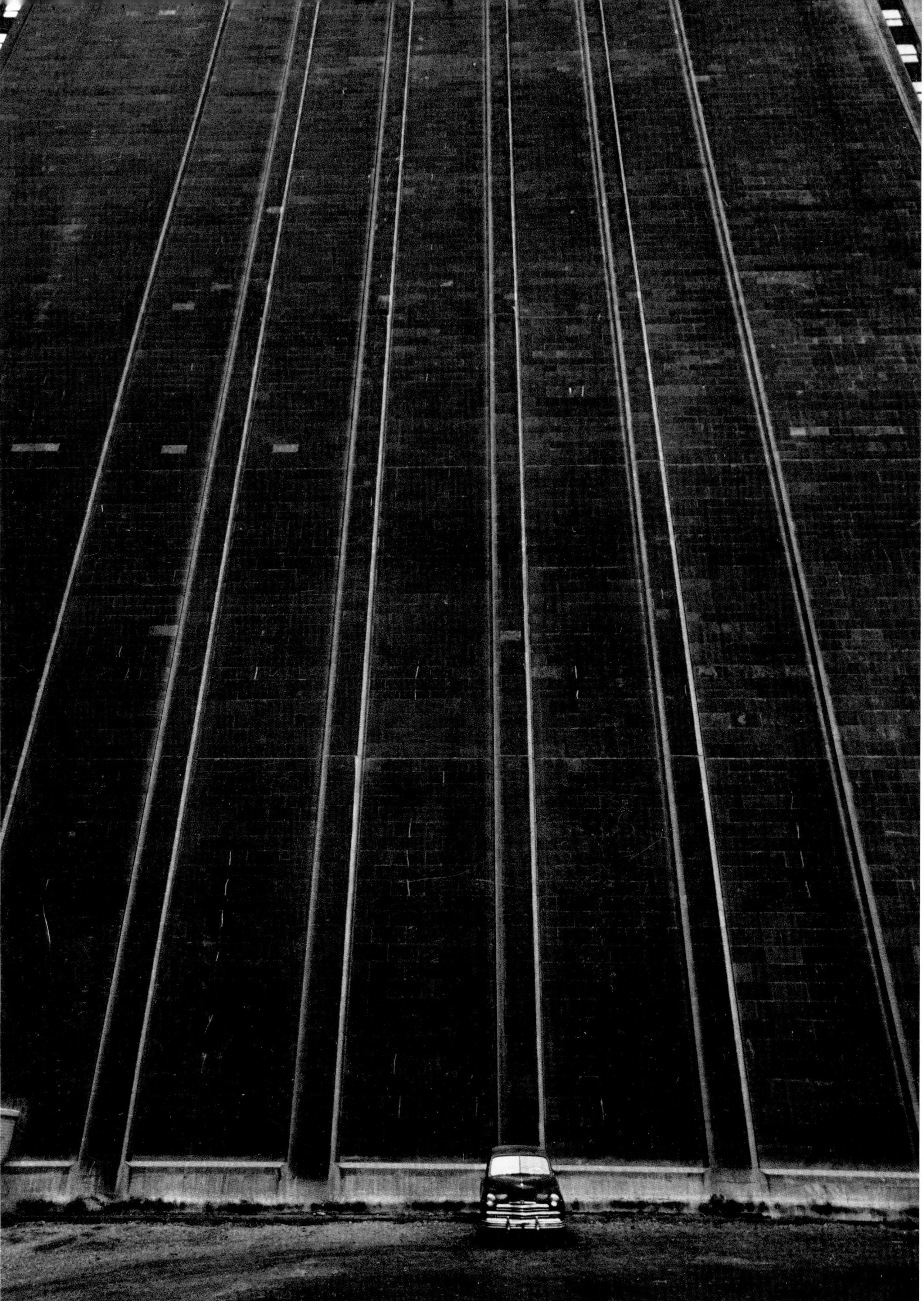

# VI

I also accept my responsibility as to indebtedness in a society of finances wherein too many (not all) take profit and loss as God and the Devil and the worst sinner of all is he who does not get his payment check to the bank on time. And the great big bank can threaten the weak little individual but the little individual can only beg and weep if a great big company owes him money and takes six months or a year to pay it. Oh well—outburst for many reasons.

Excerpt from Smith's letter to his uncle Jesse Caplinger, 5/17/58

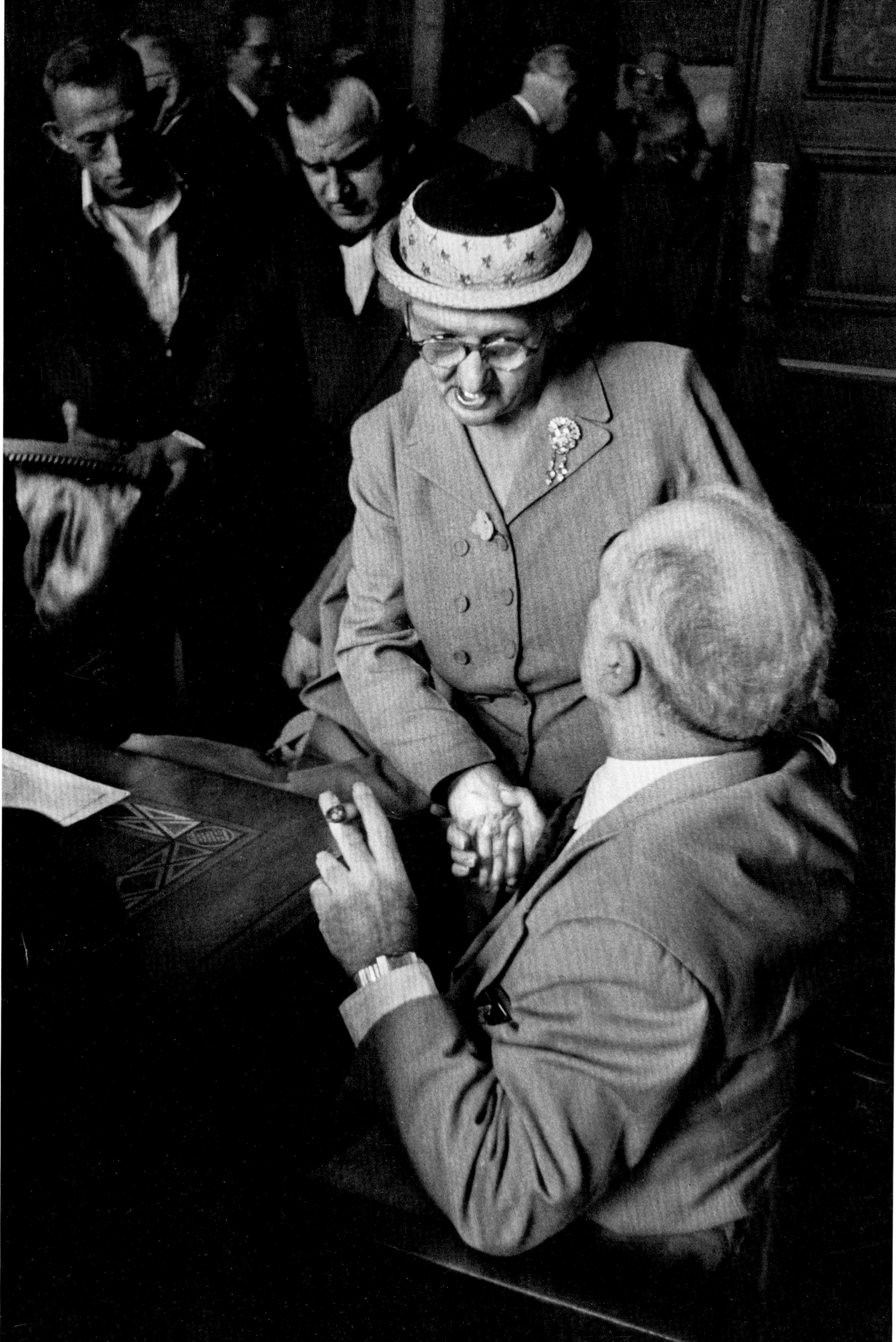

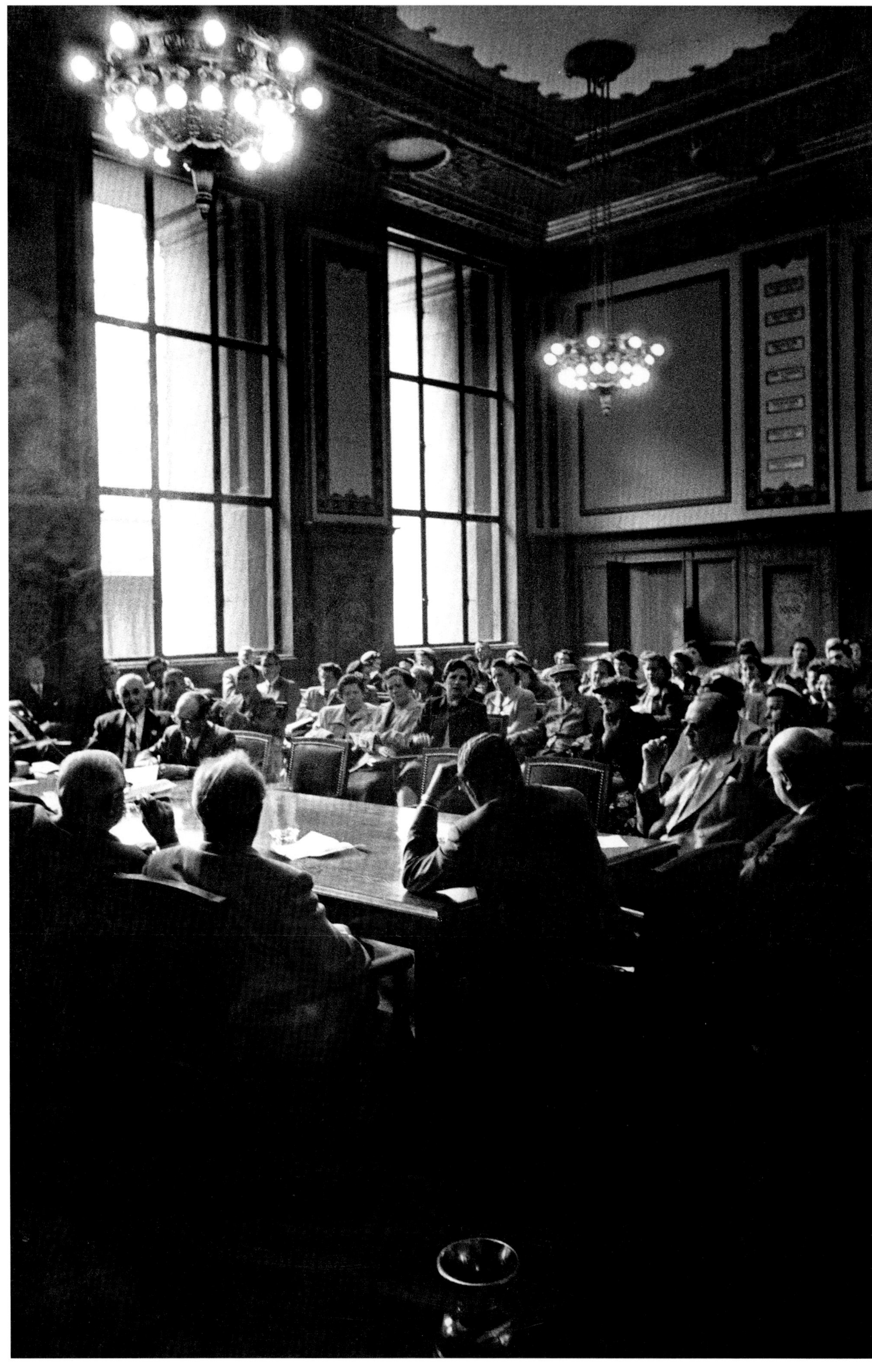

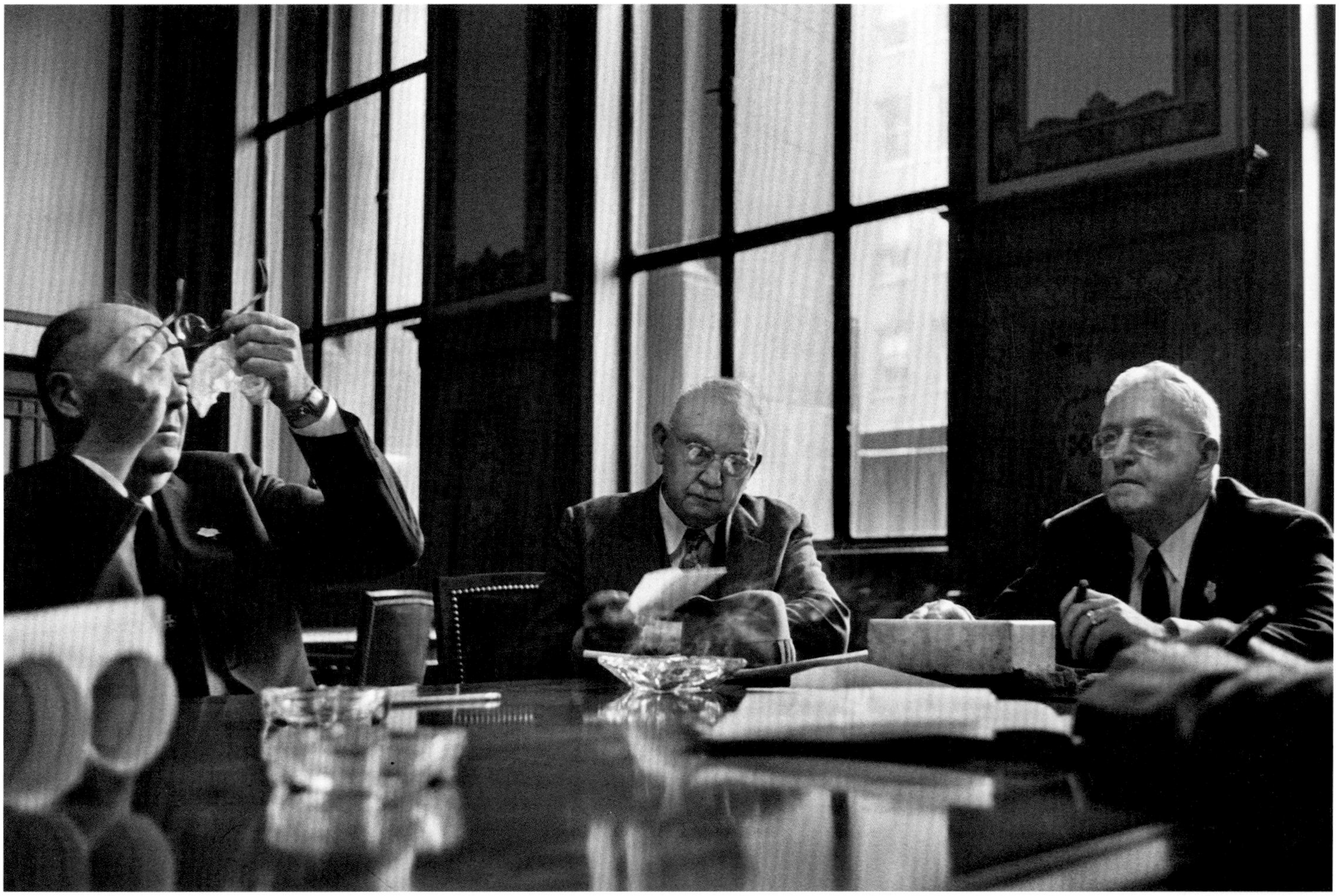

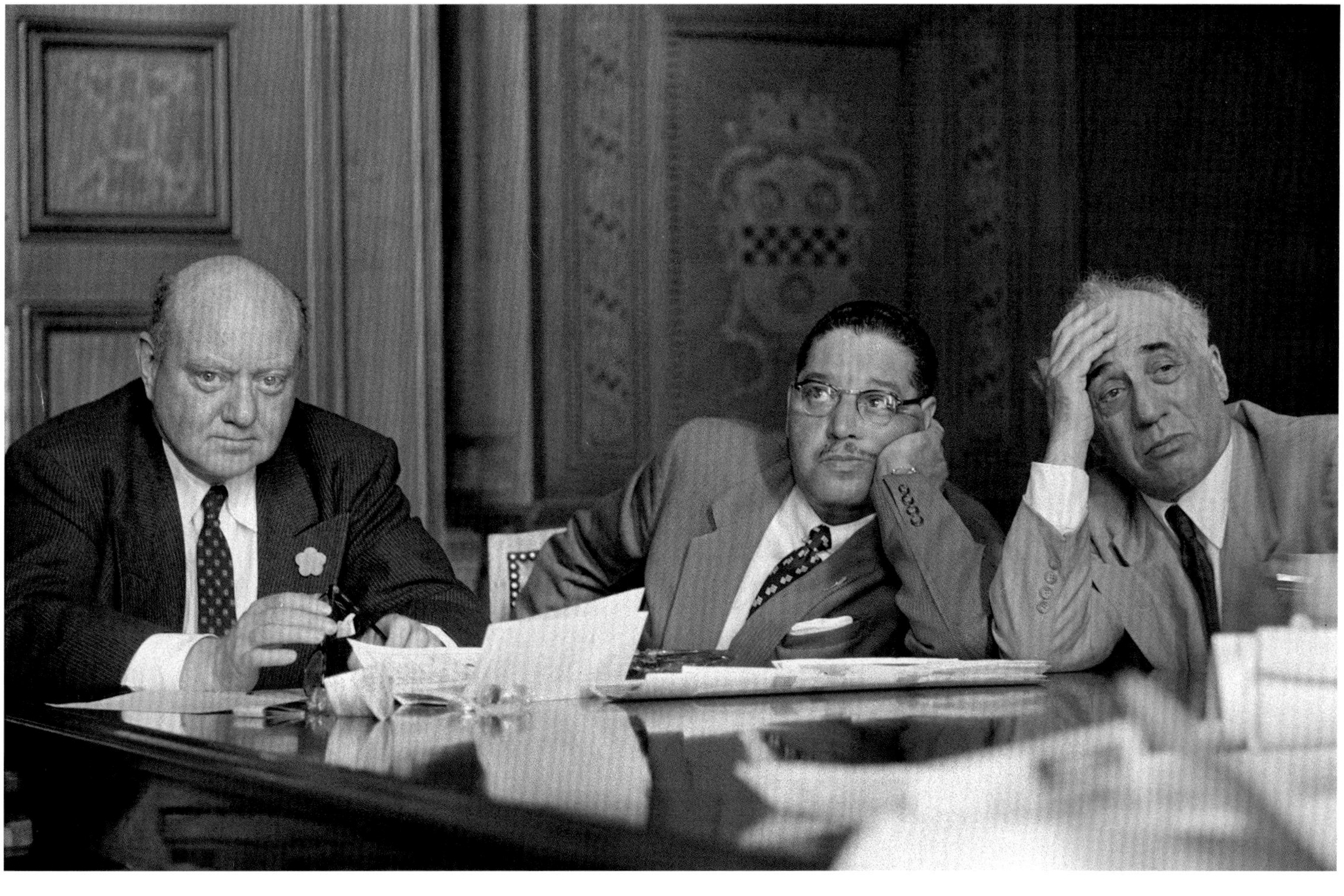

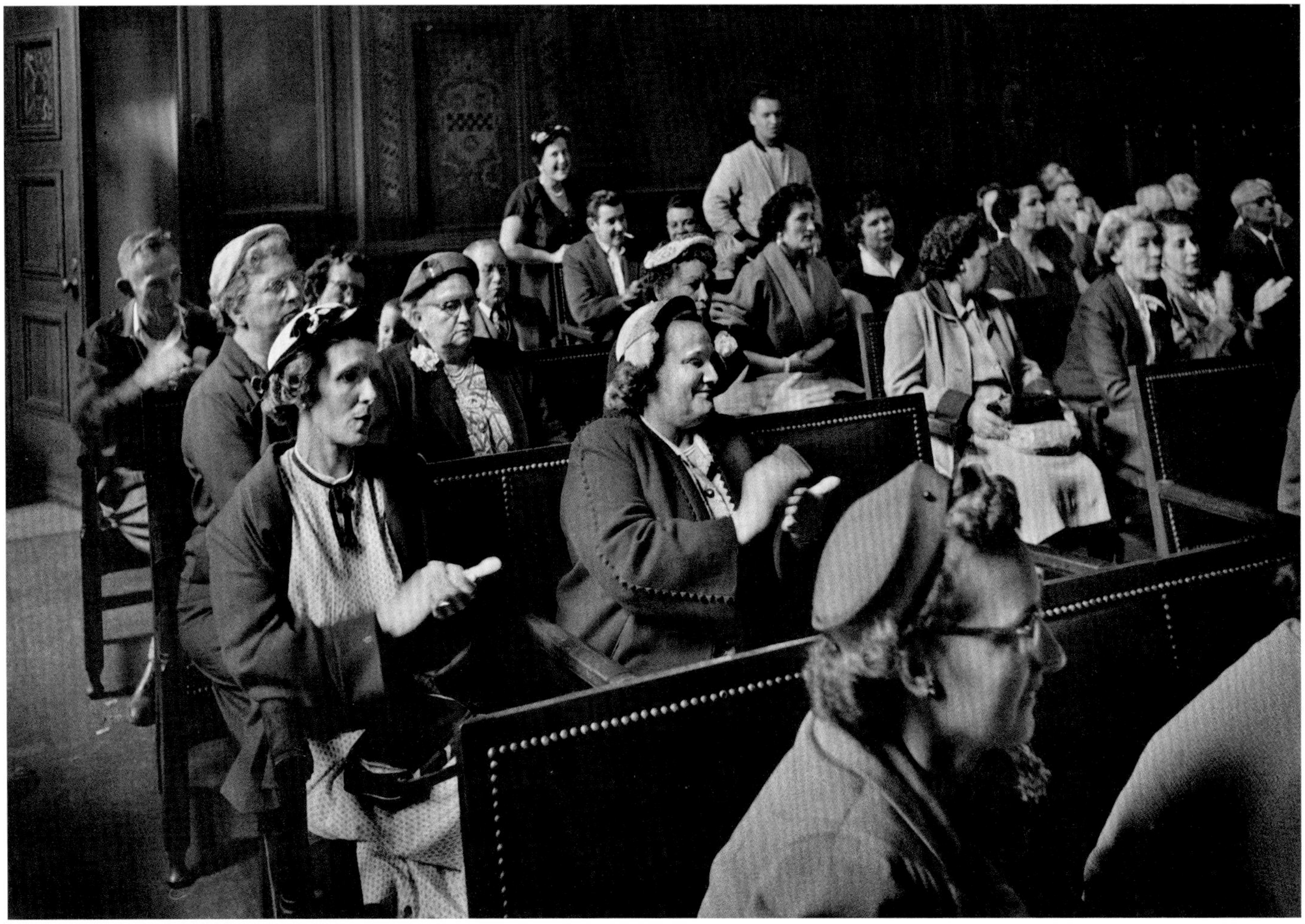

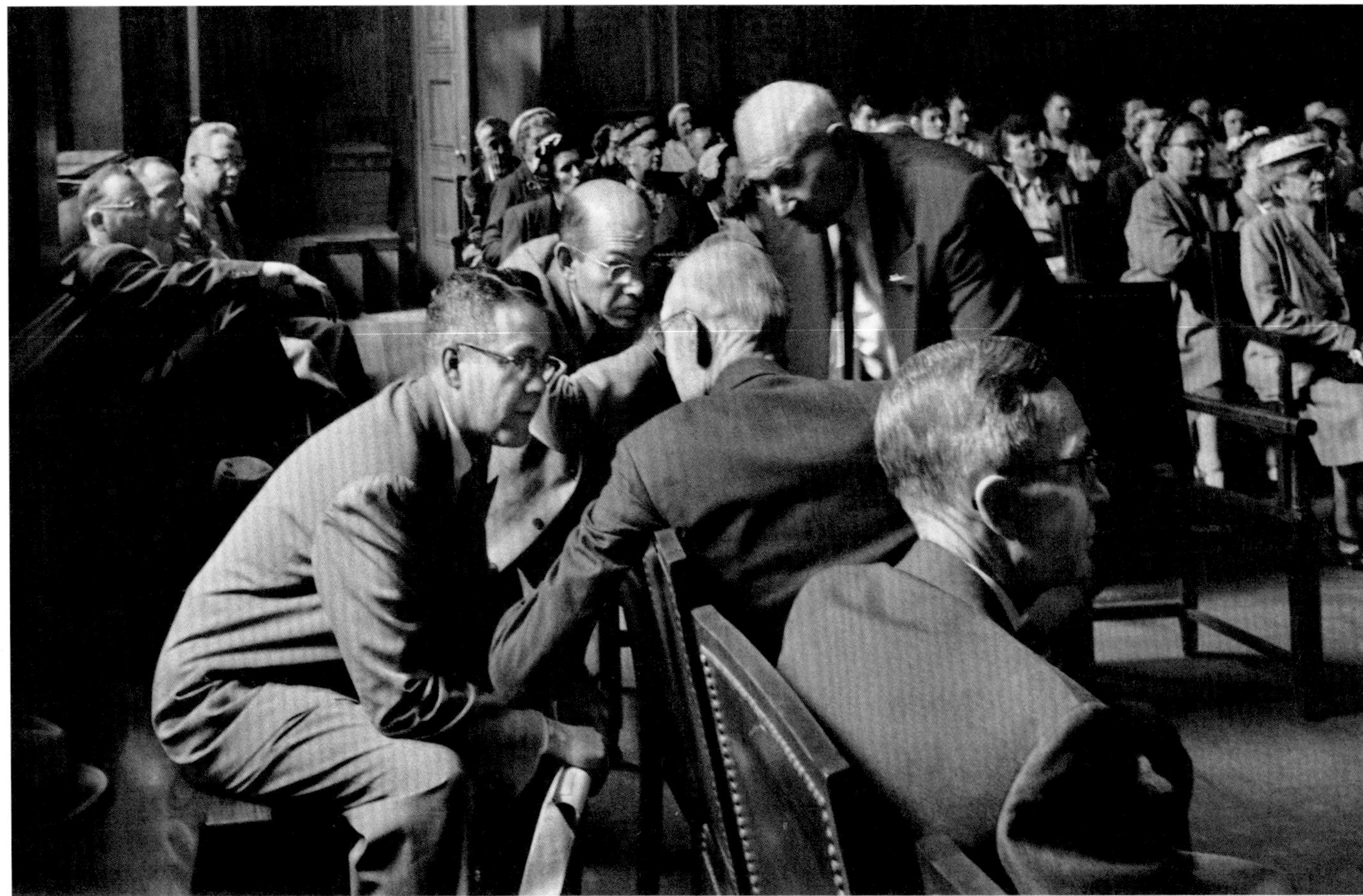

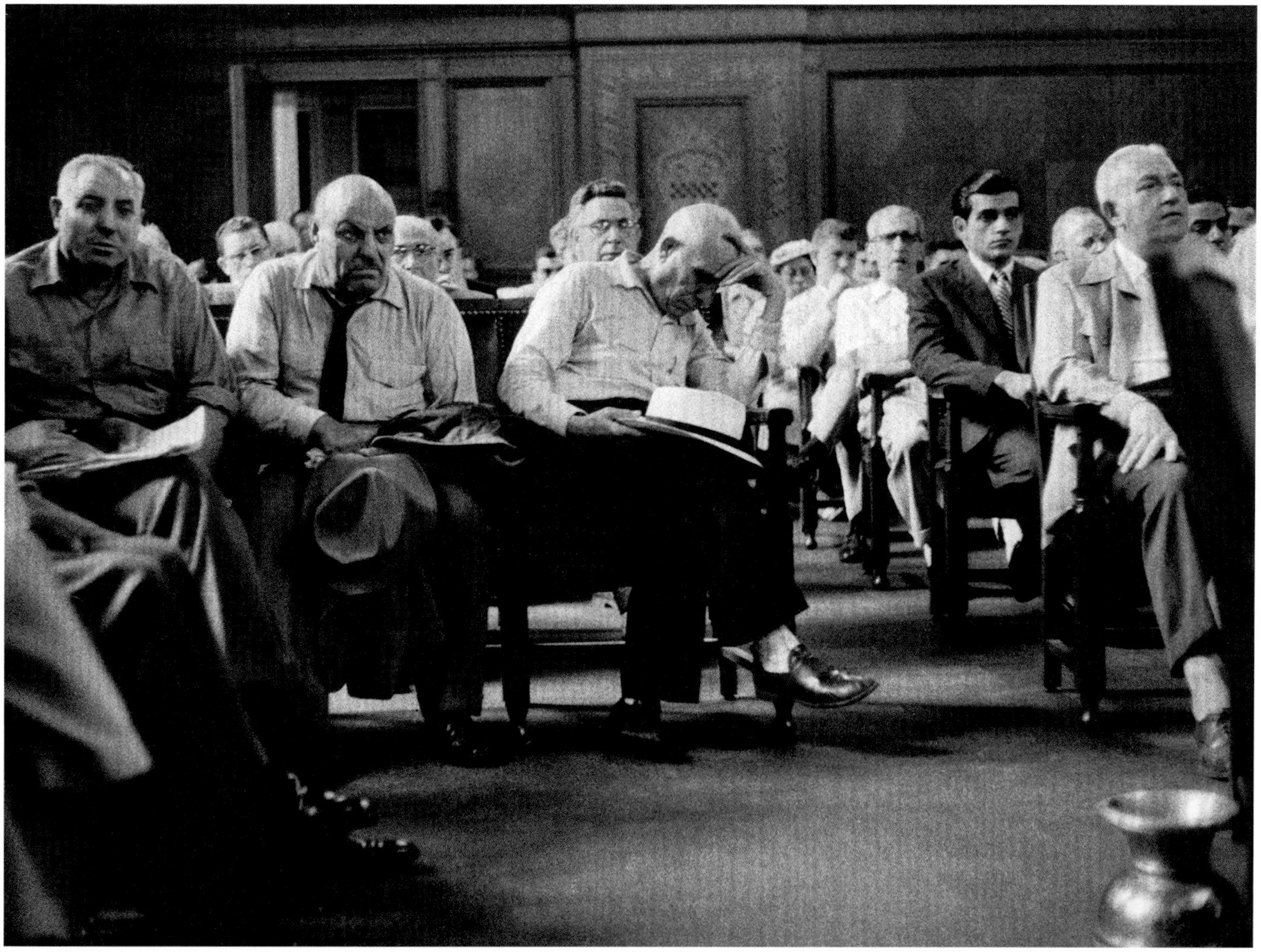

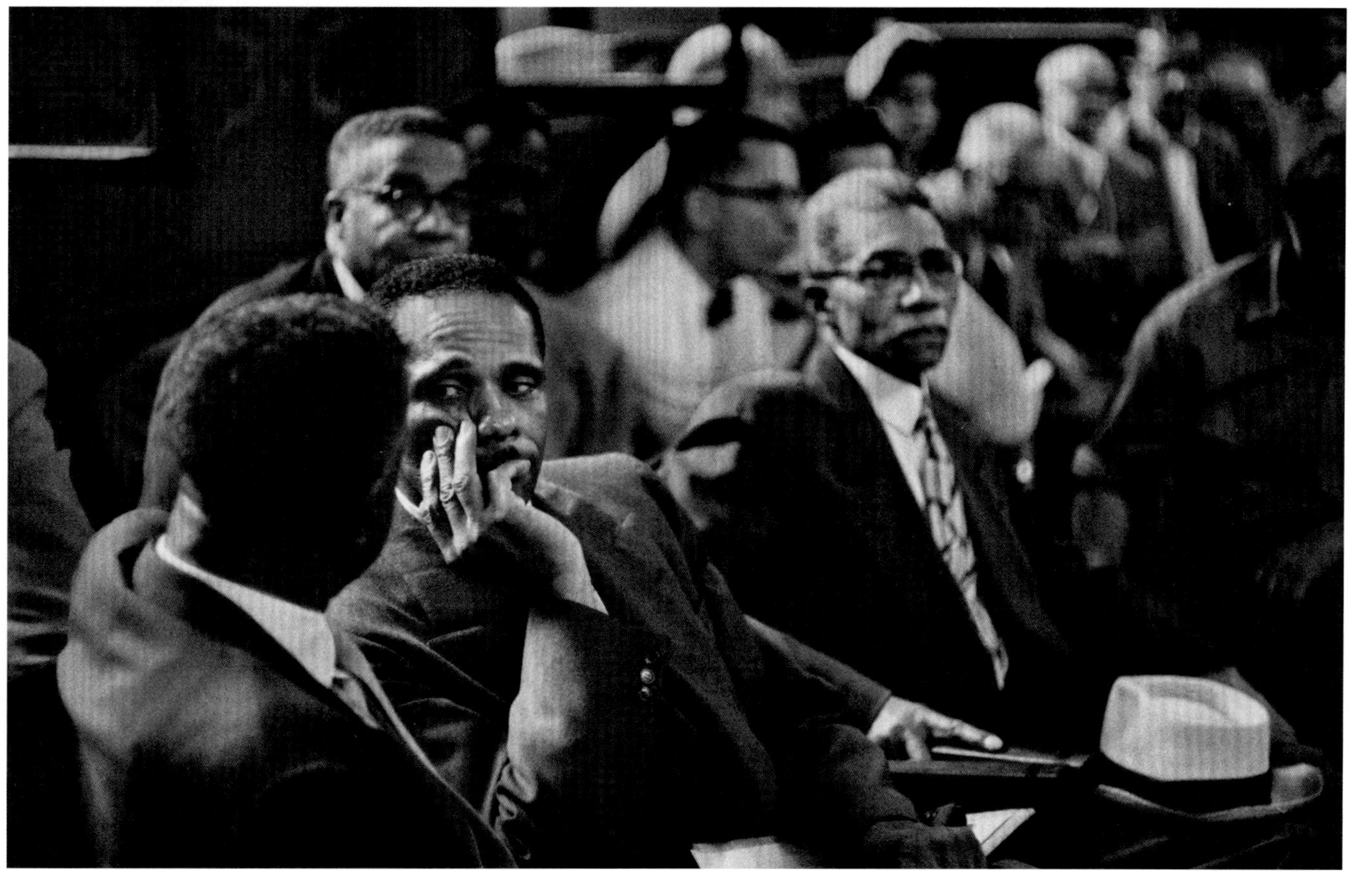

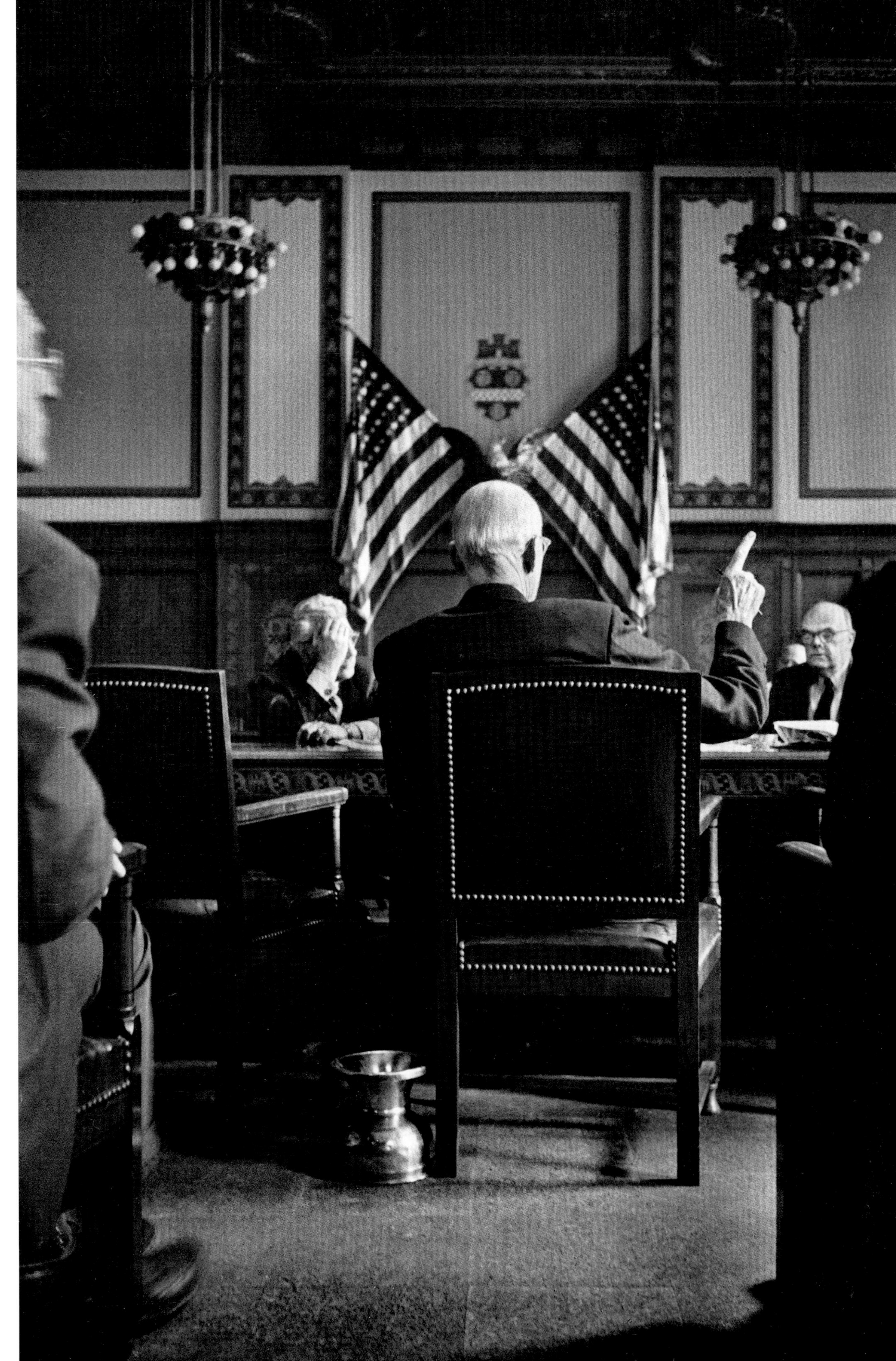

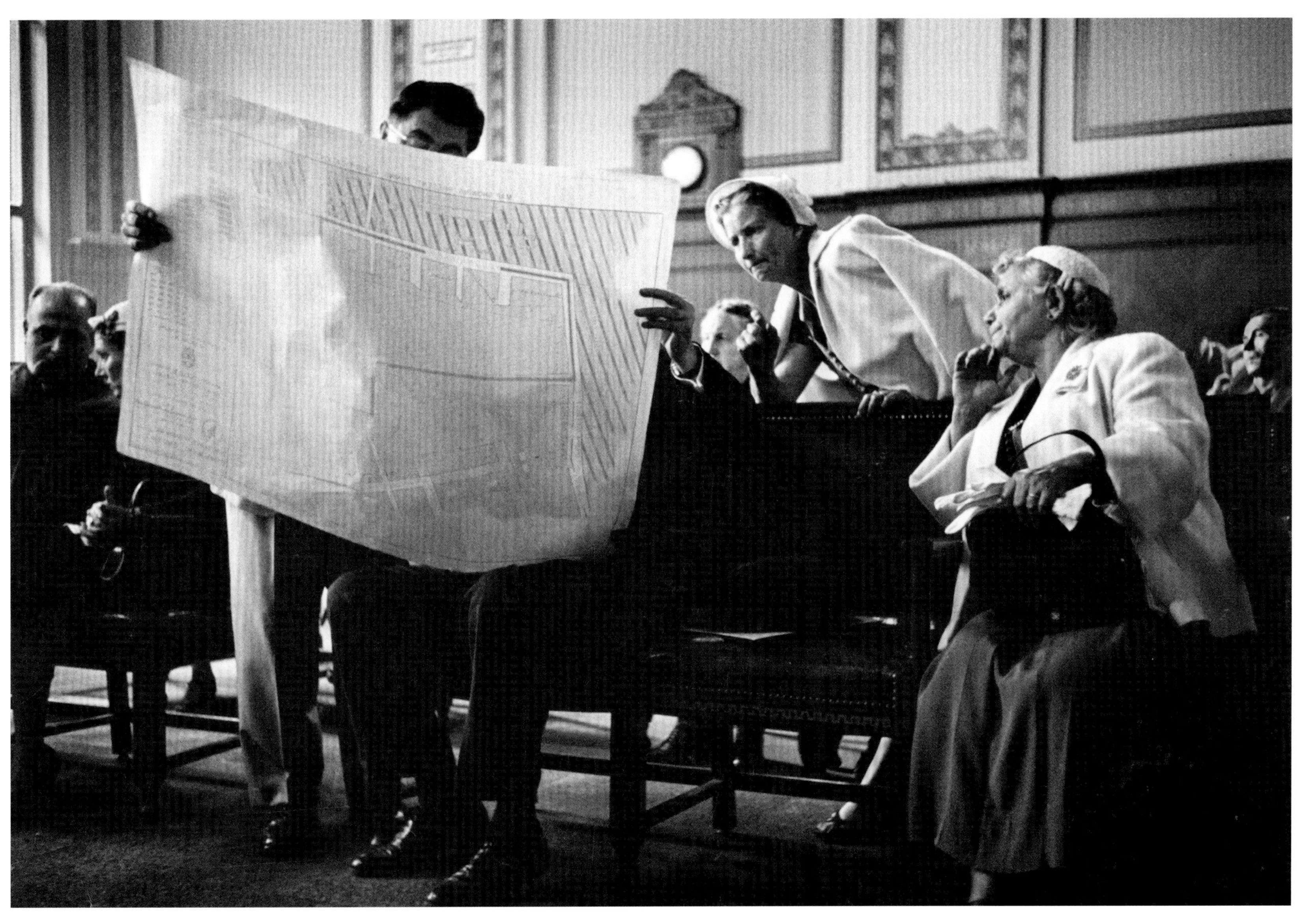

[101]

# VII

I have photographed research at Gulf's laboratories. A dance at the U. of Pittsburgh. Two shovels sticking
in the ground by a freshly planted tree, with the business skyline and the river as background . . . A street-
car in a rainstorm. A block party. The reflection of a Bessemer furnace in the safety goggles of a worker.
A little Negro boy and girl smiling at me, clutching a doll without a head. A Negro group around a street
sign of a street named PRIDE. Another street sign, (part of a series: one of the several sub themes within
the essay proper) of a street named DREAM, which has as other elements, a rural mail box and a car—
(it could be a horrible picture, yet it is one of the most delightful in humor and in symbol, but avoiding
cliché other than in comment upon cliché)—Patterns of construction in the building of a new parking
garage. These, in a listing may indicate that I did not impose any narrow limitations of subject matter, yet
I doubt if even a full listing that extends to all 11,000 photographs I have so far made could give a clear
concept of the execution of the project. And even the number of photographs made might lead to
mis-conception of my pictorial approach.

From Smith's 1956 application for a fellowship from the John Simon Guggenheim Foundation
—"Plans for Use of Fellowship"

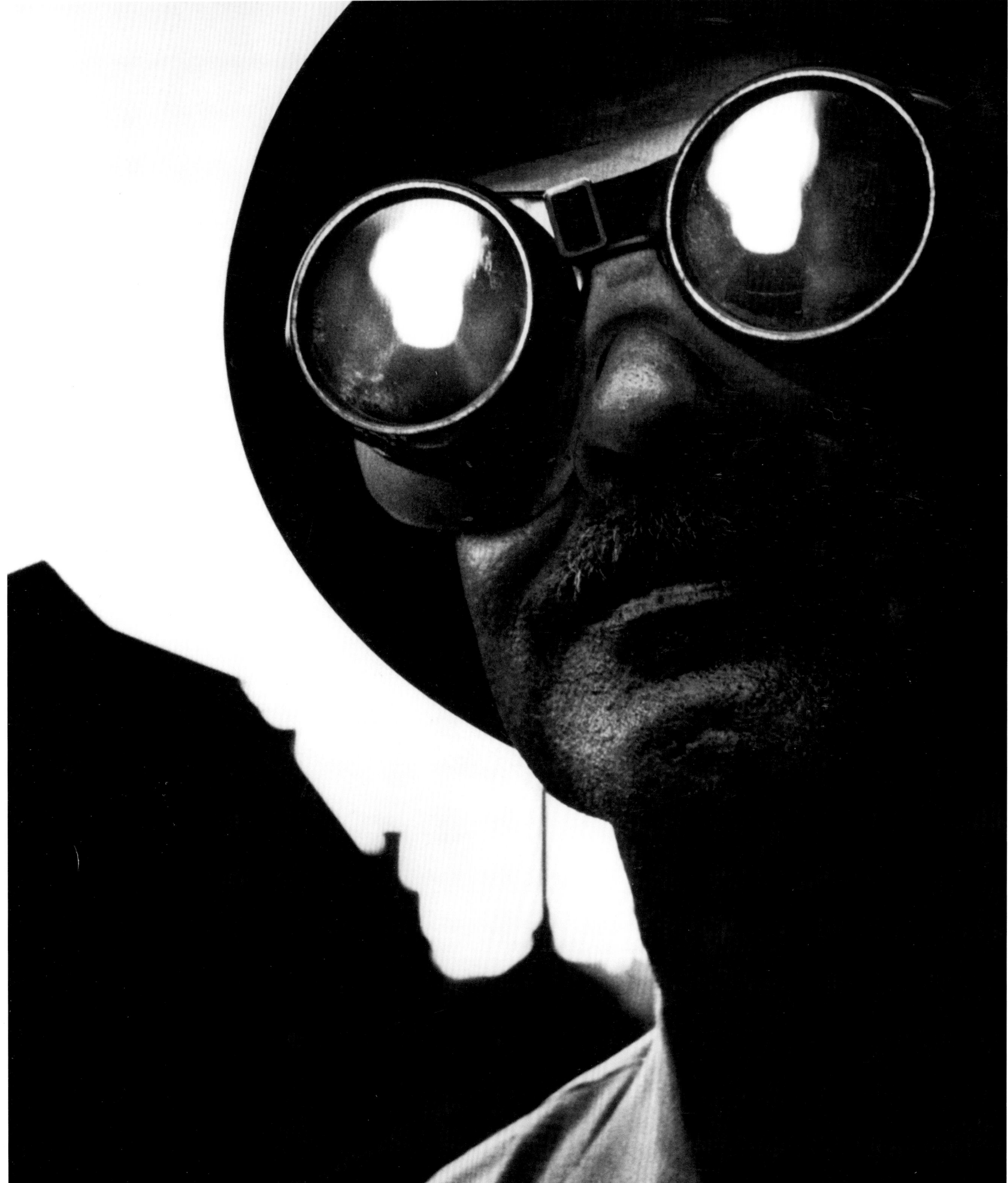

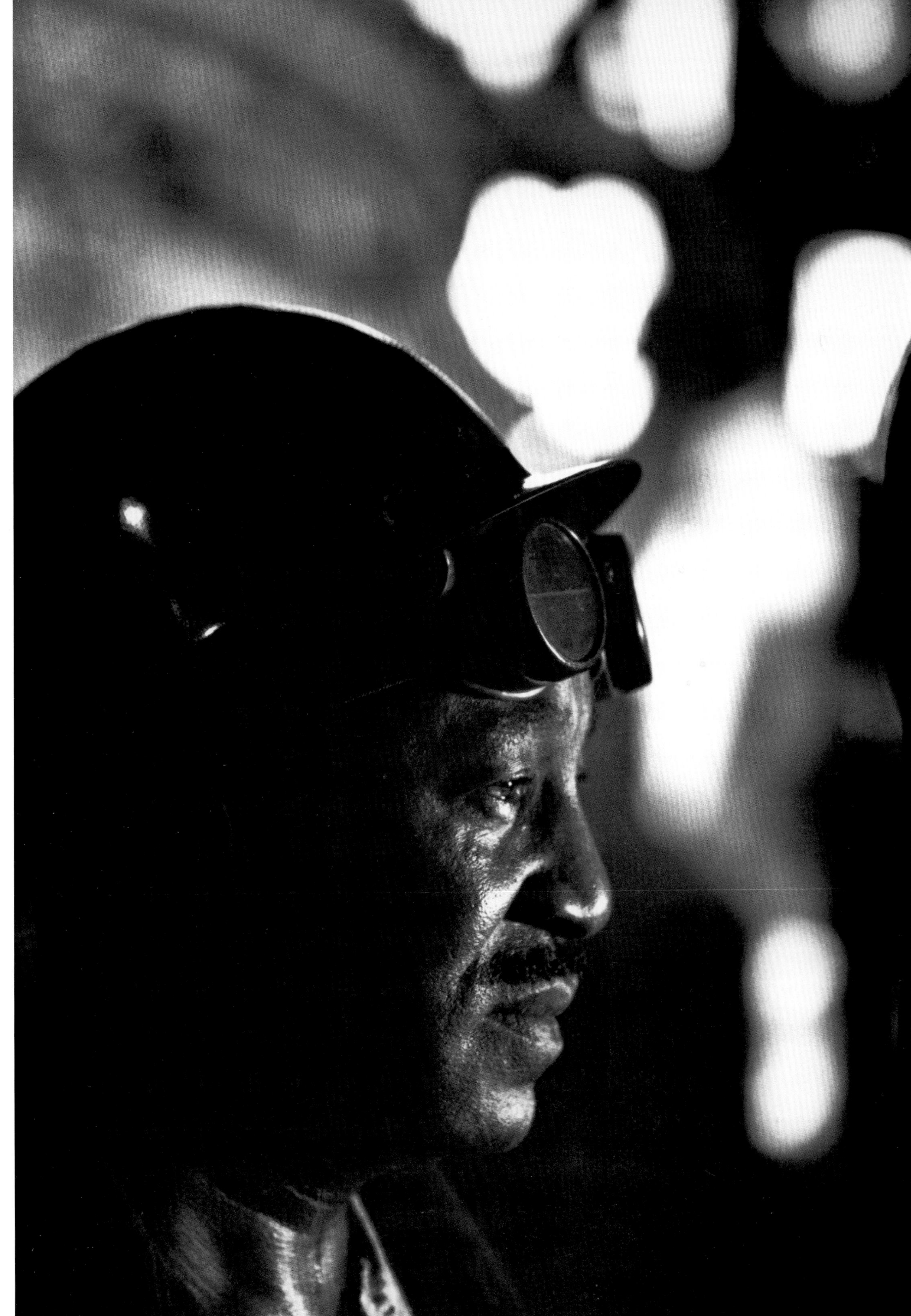

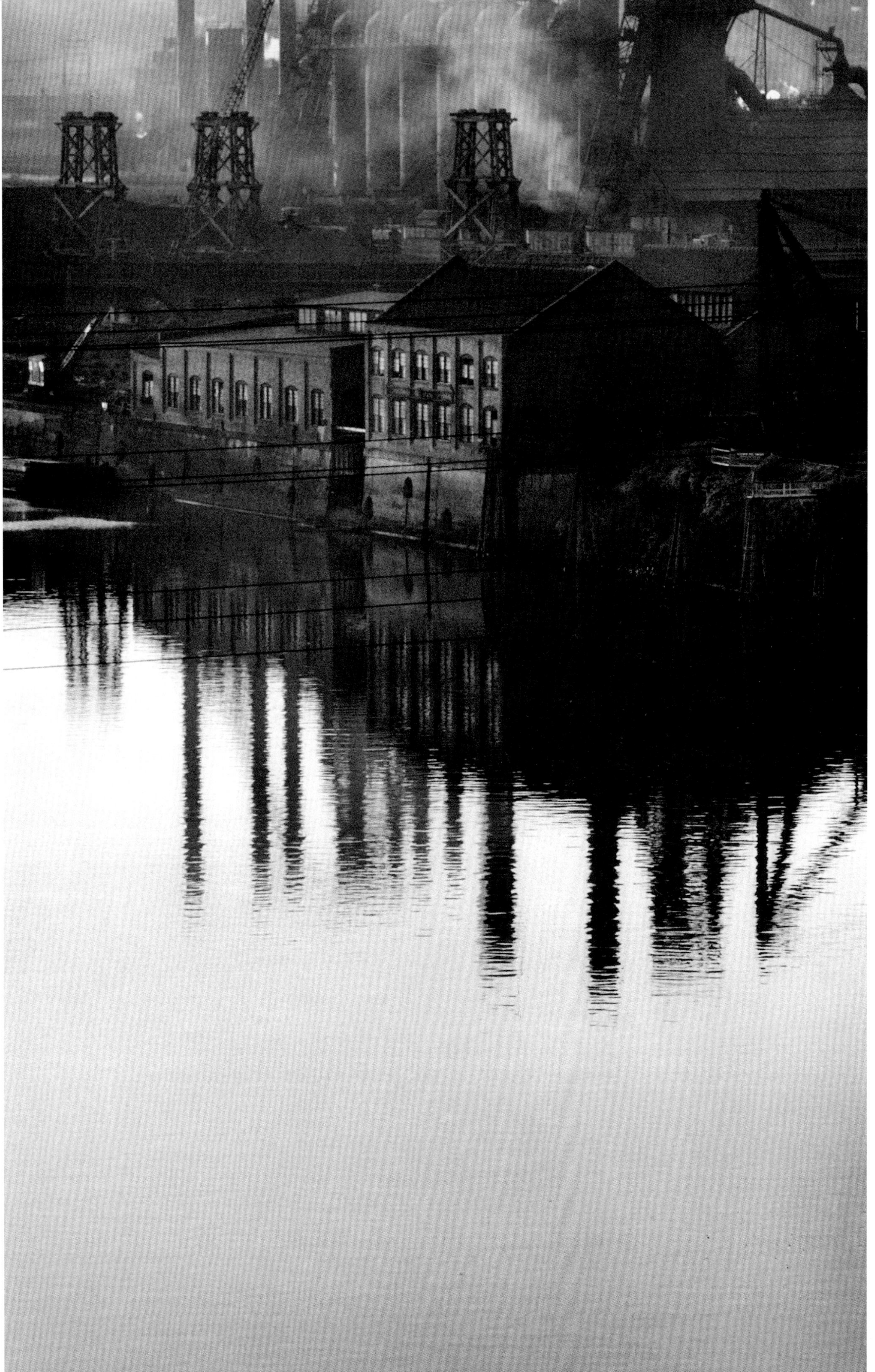

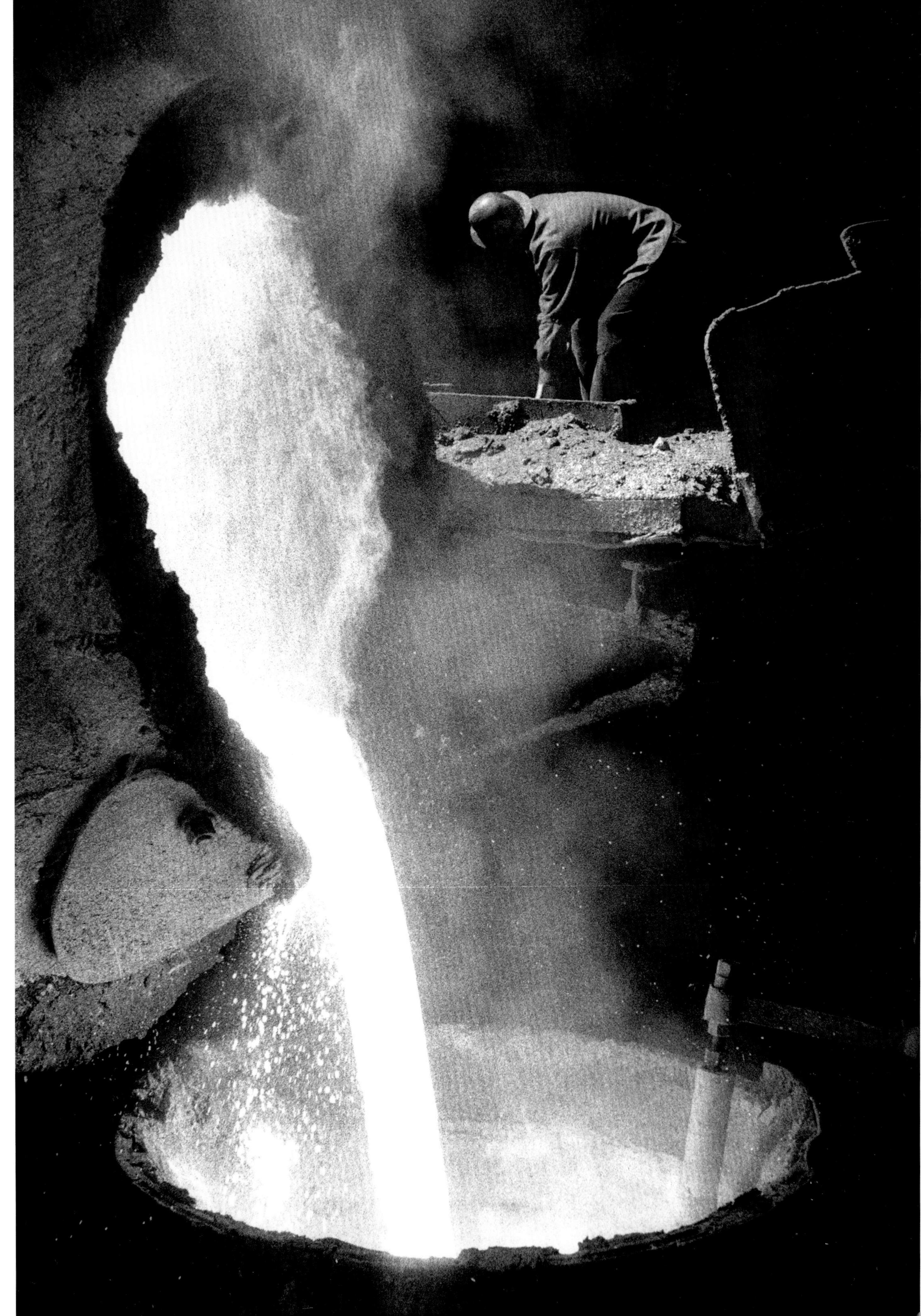

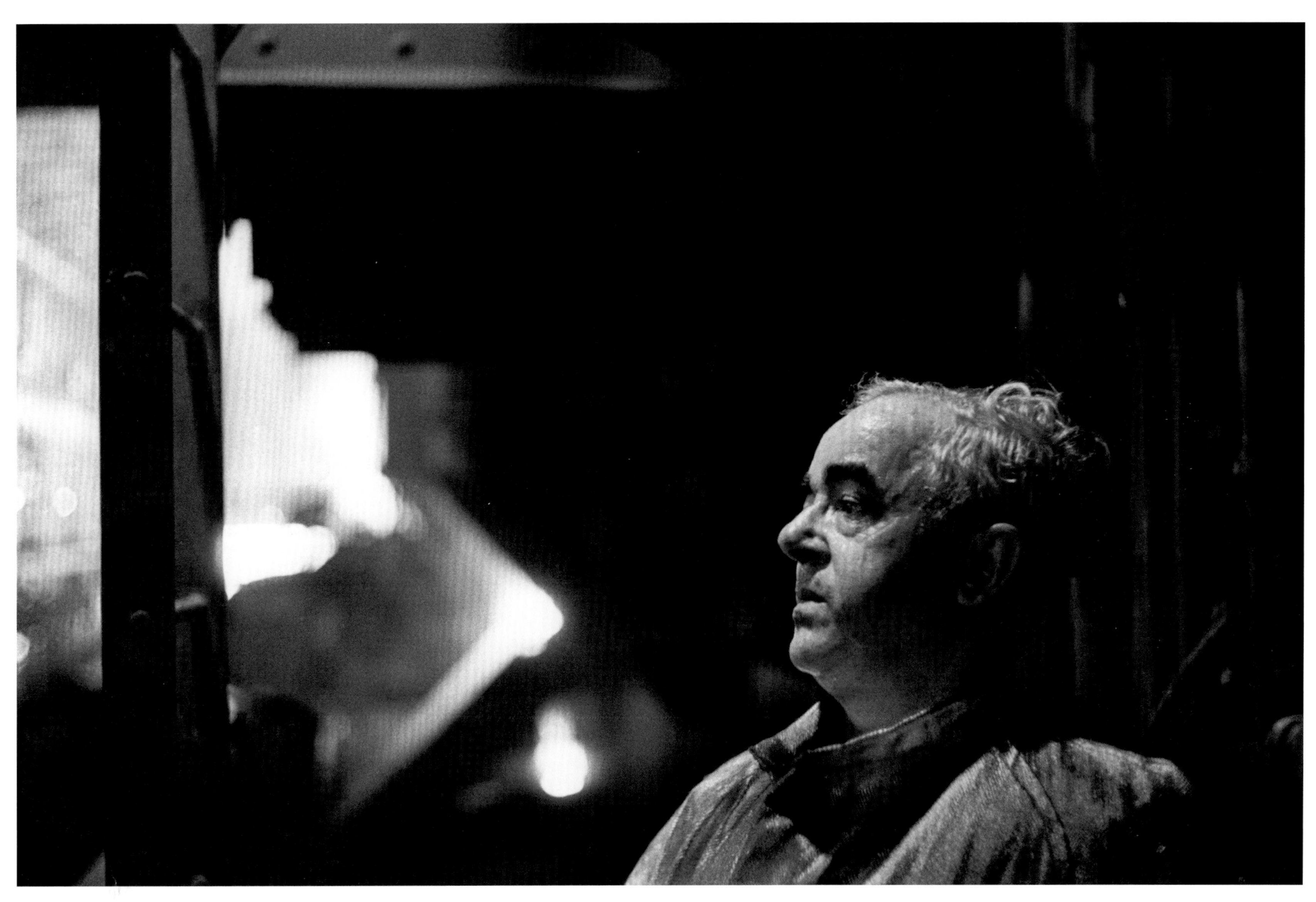

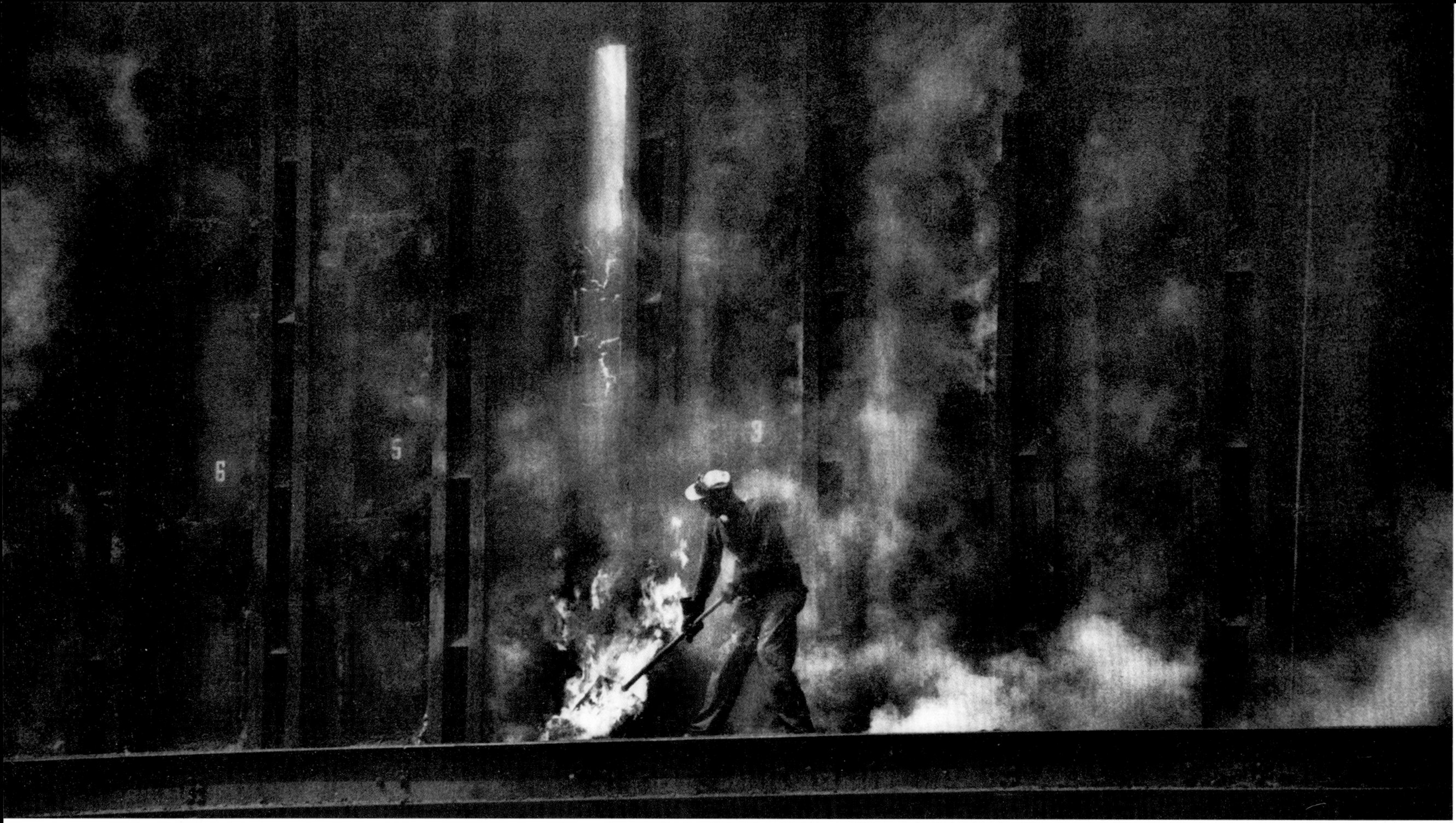

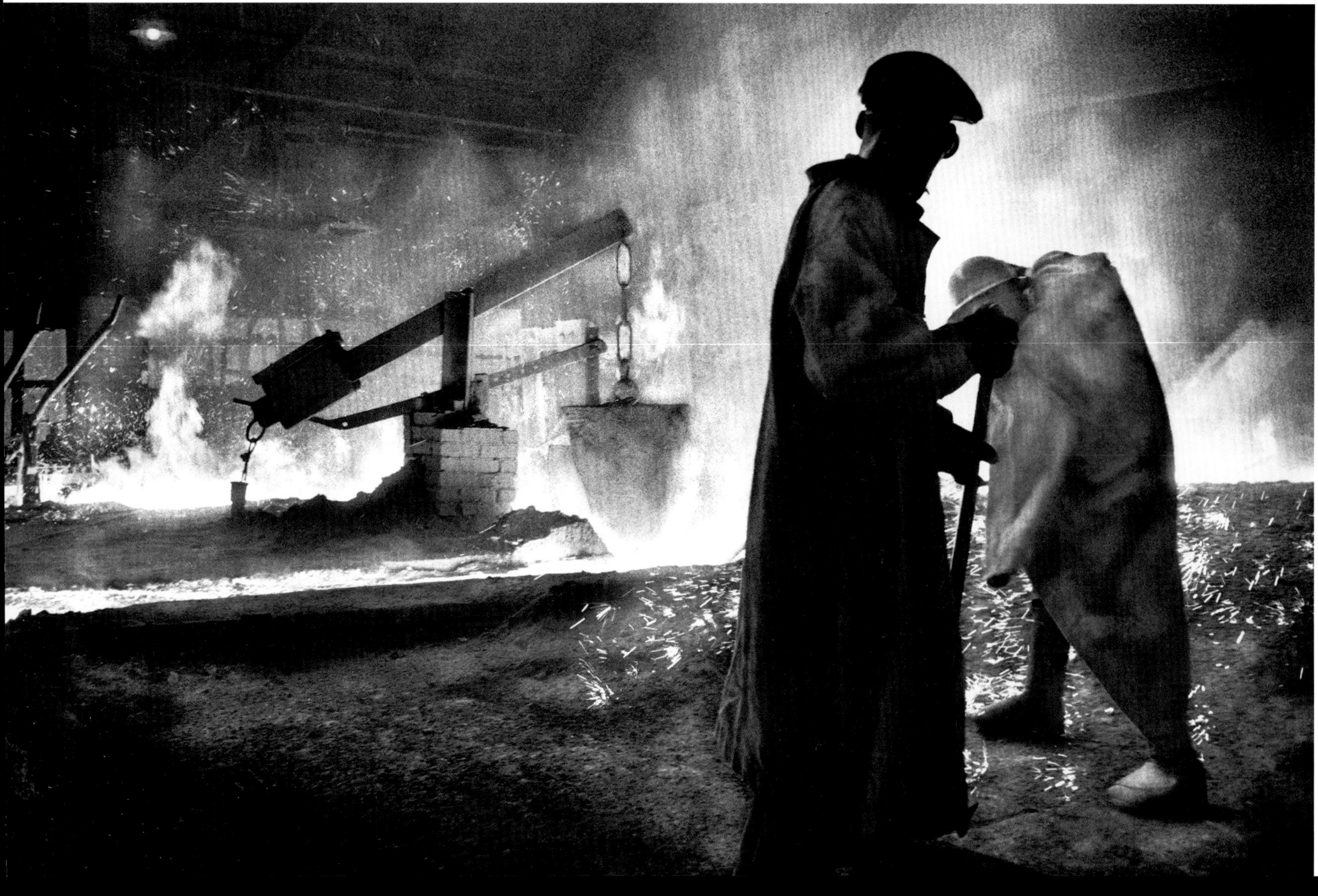

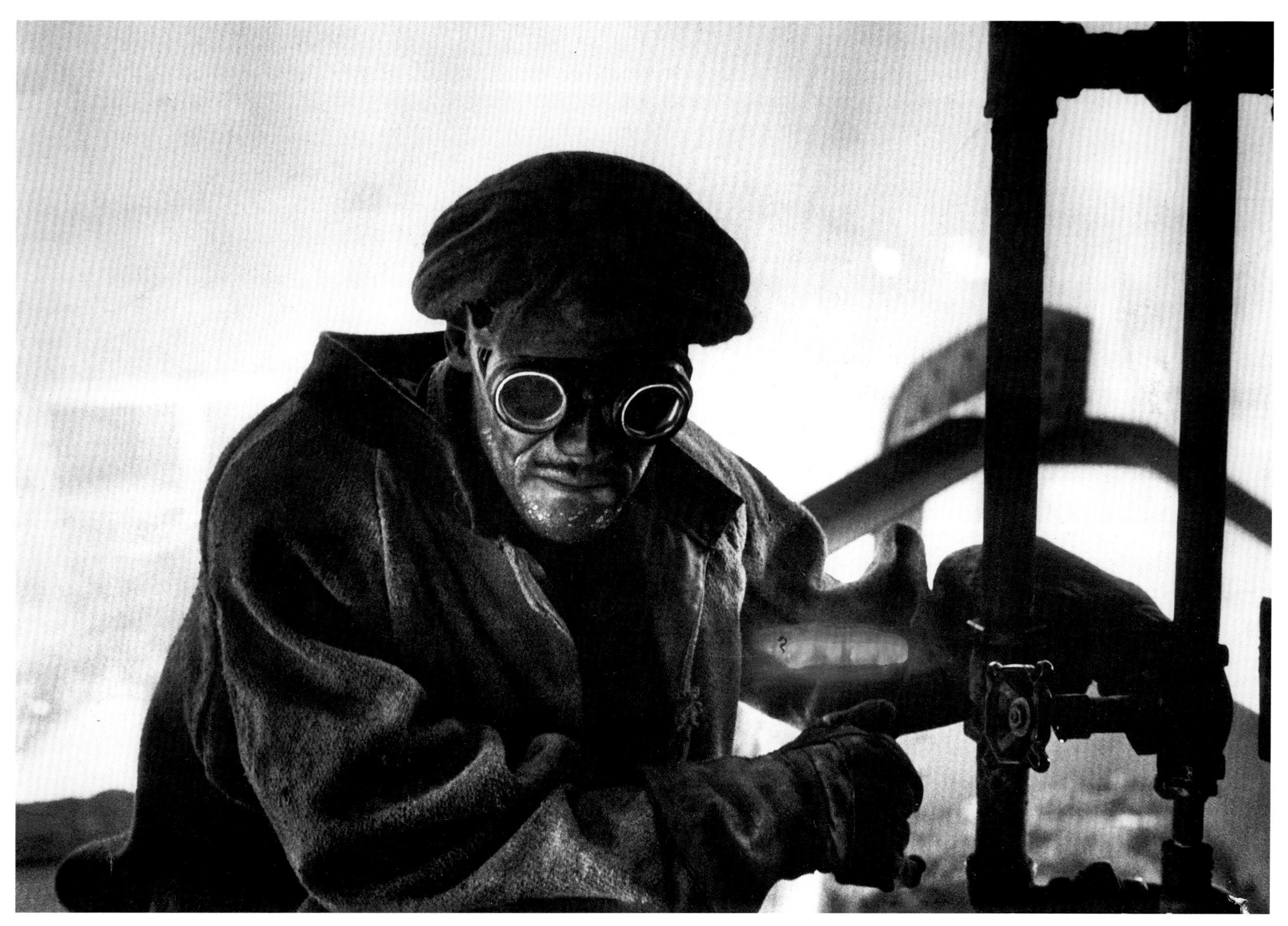

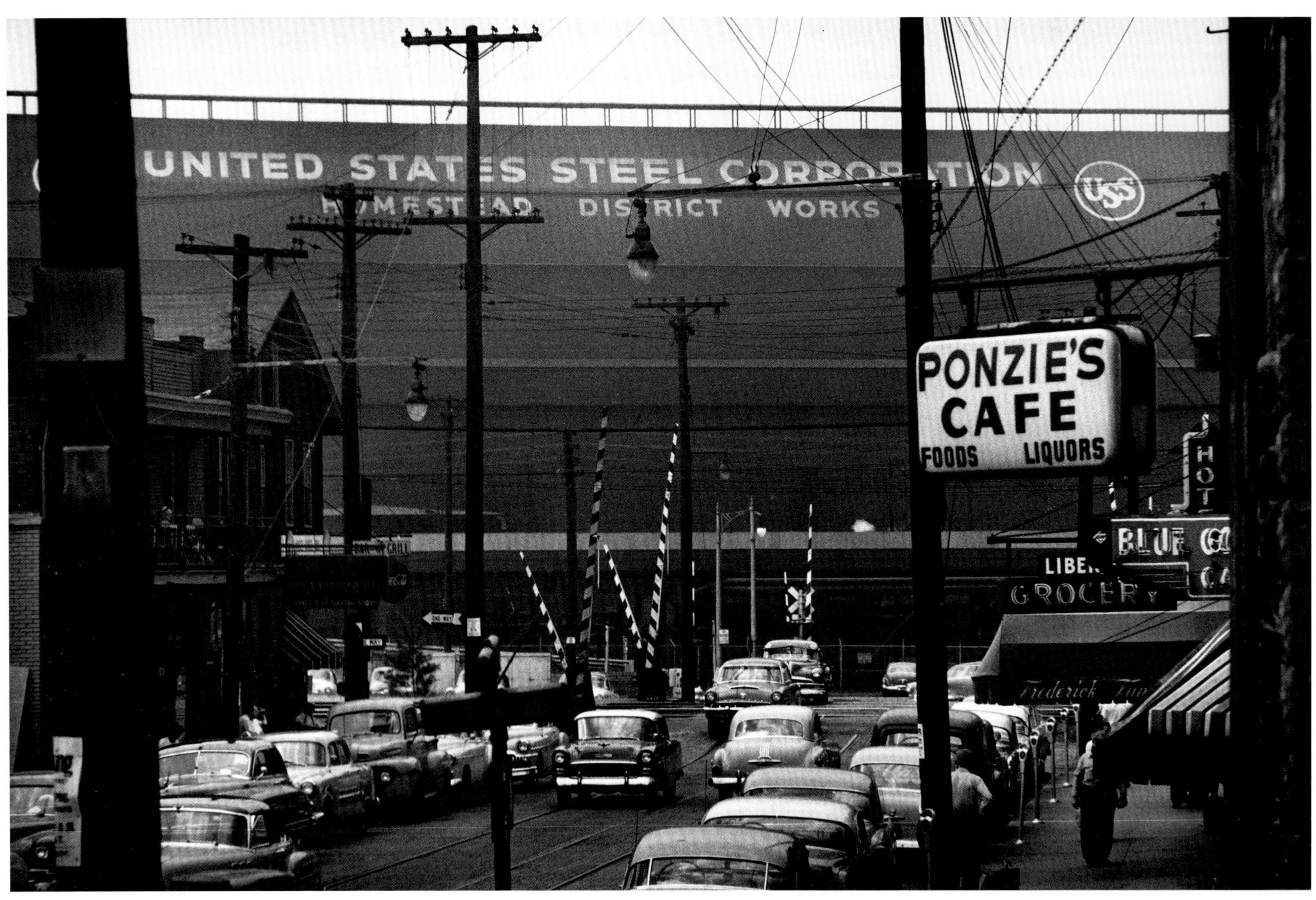

UNITED STATES STEEL CORPORATION
HOMESTEAD DISTRICT WORKS
USS
PONZIE'S
CAFE
FOODS LIQUORS
HOT
BLUE
CA
LIBER
GROCERY
Frederick
ONE WAY

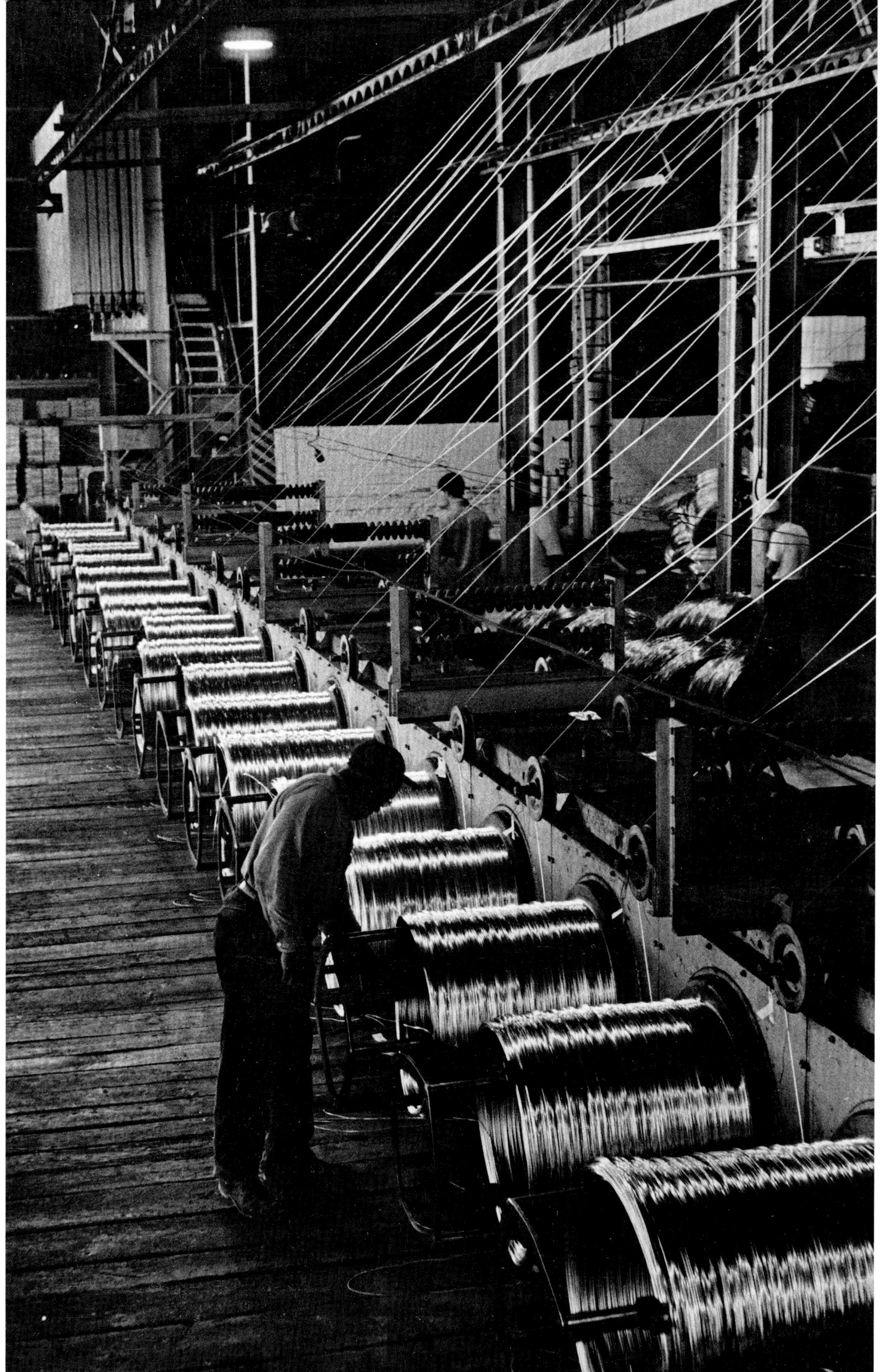

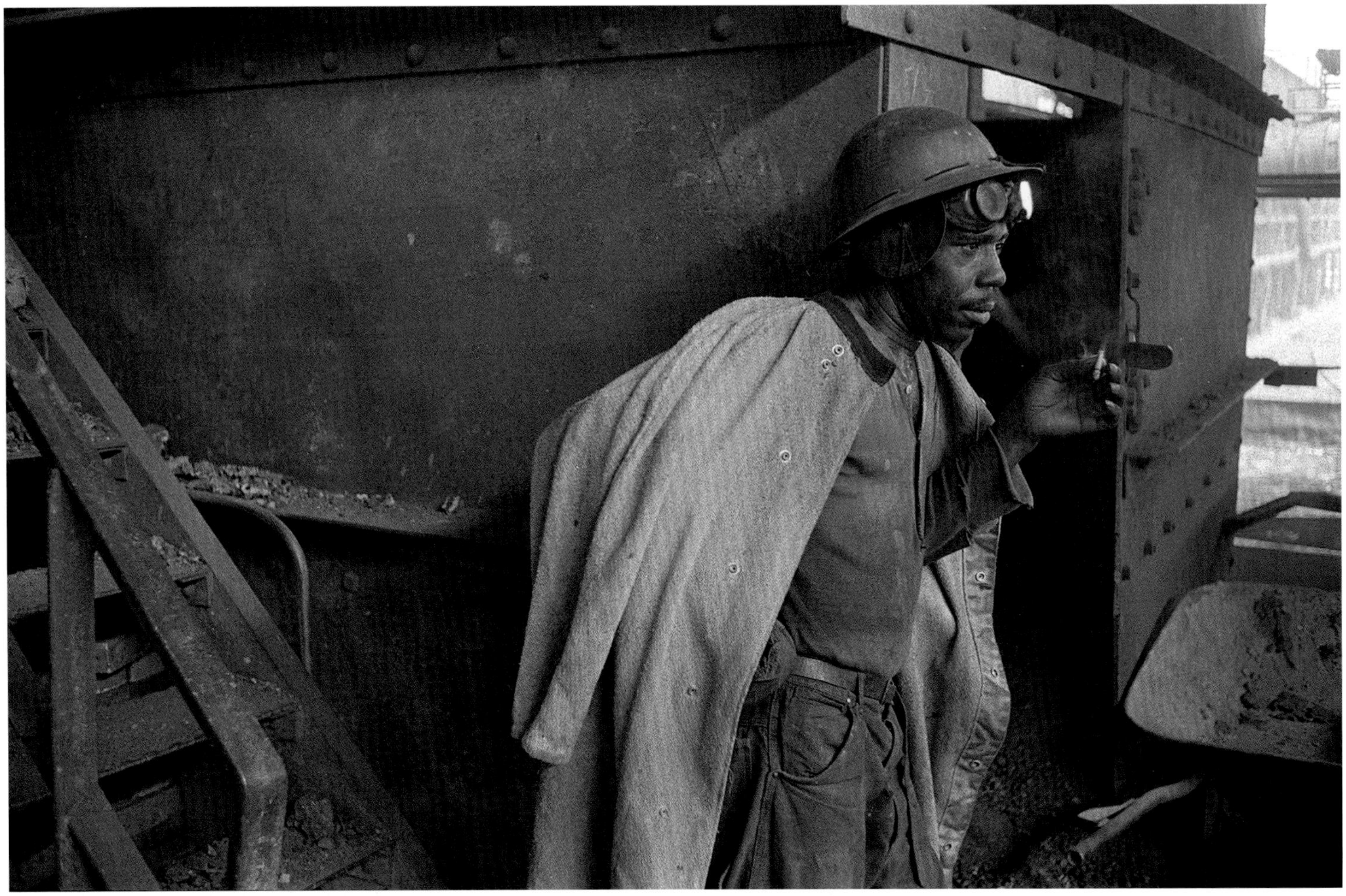

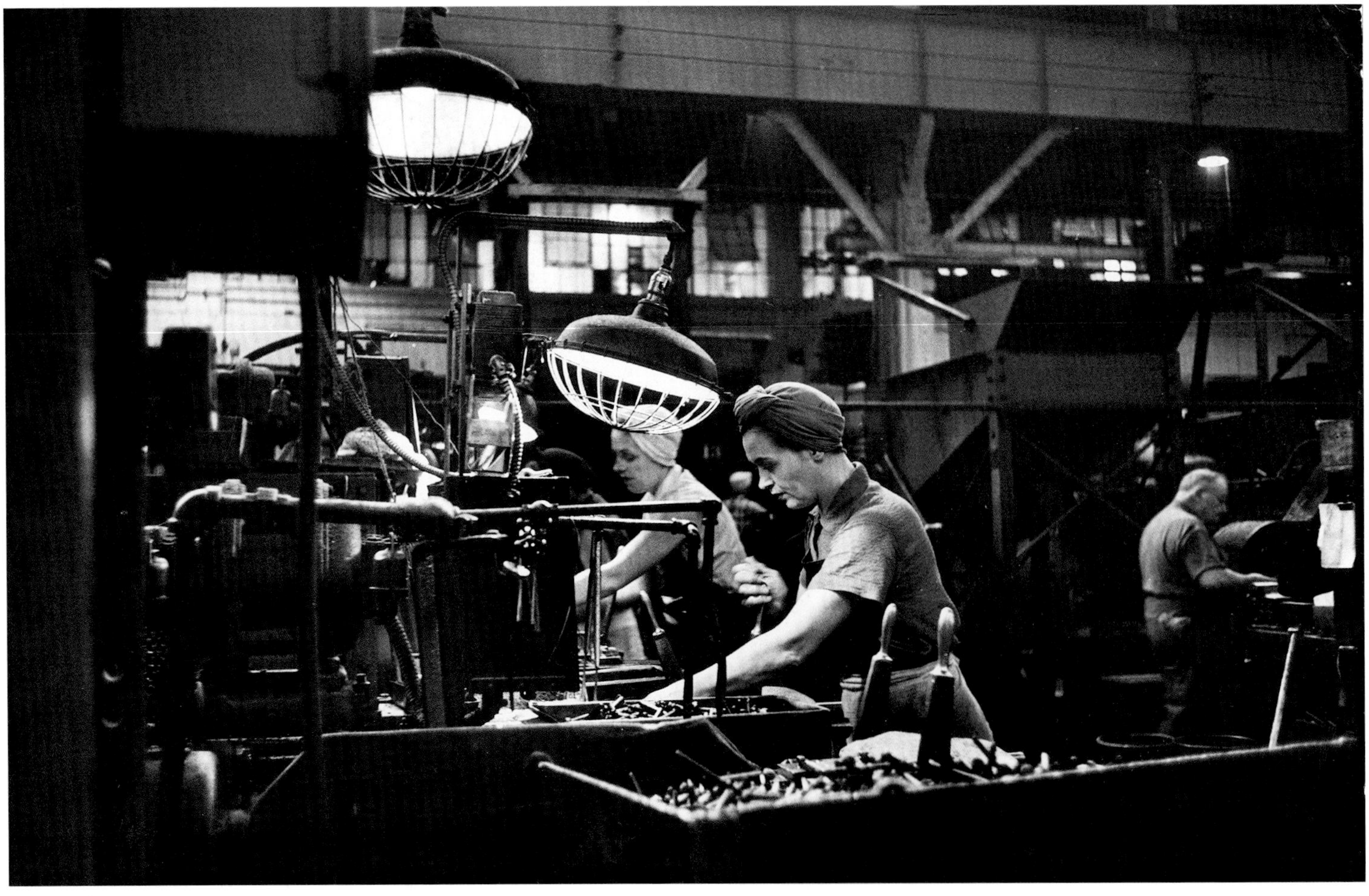

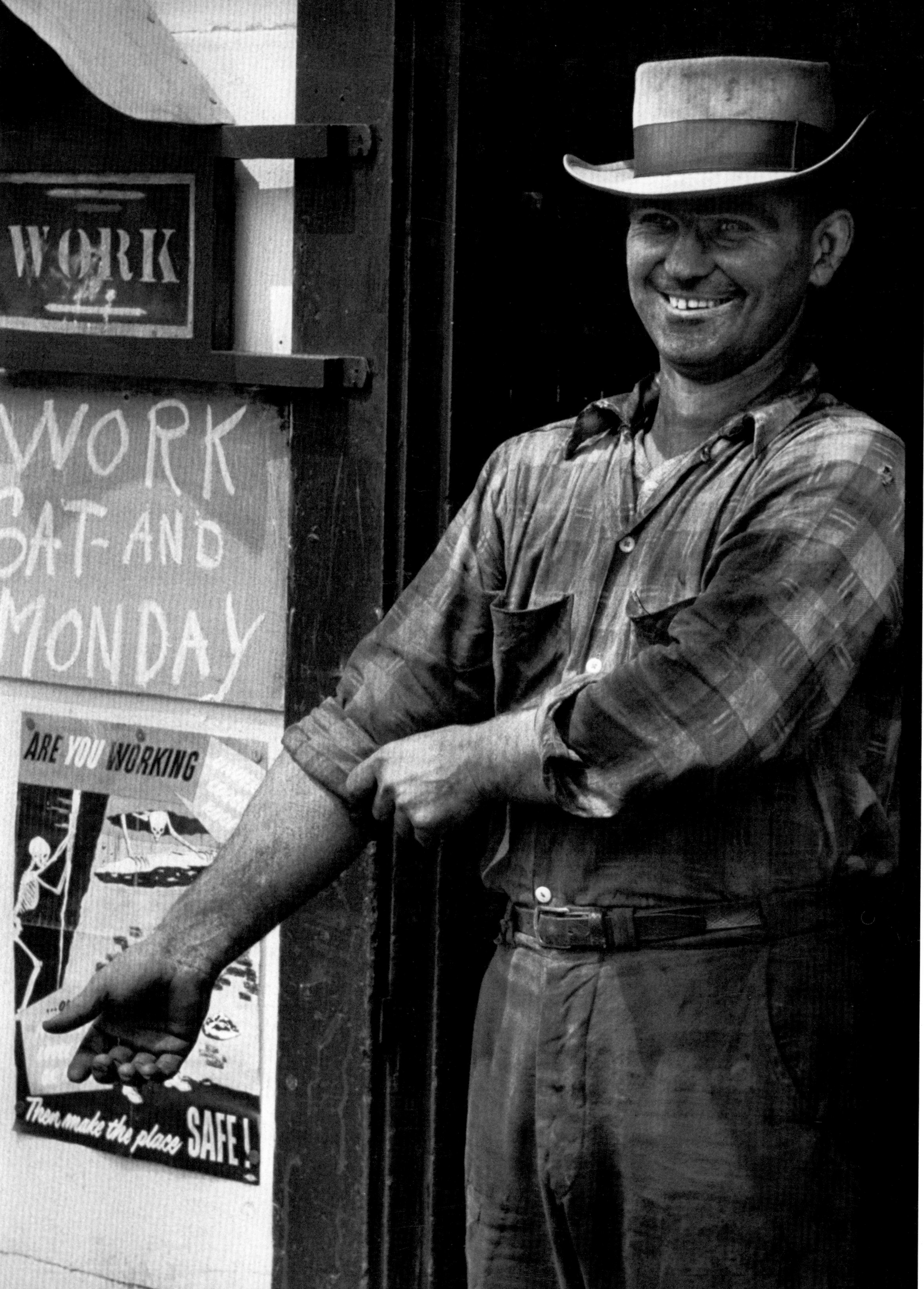

WORK
WORK
SAT-AND
MONDAY
ARE YOU WORKING
Then make the place SAFE!

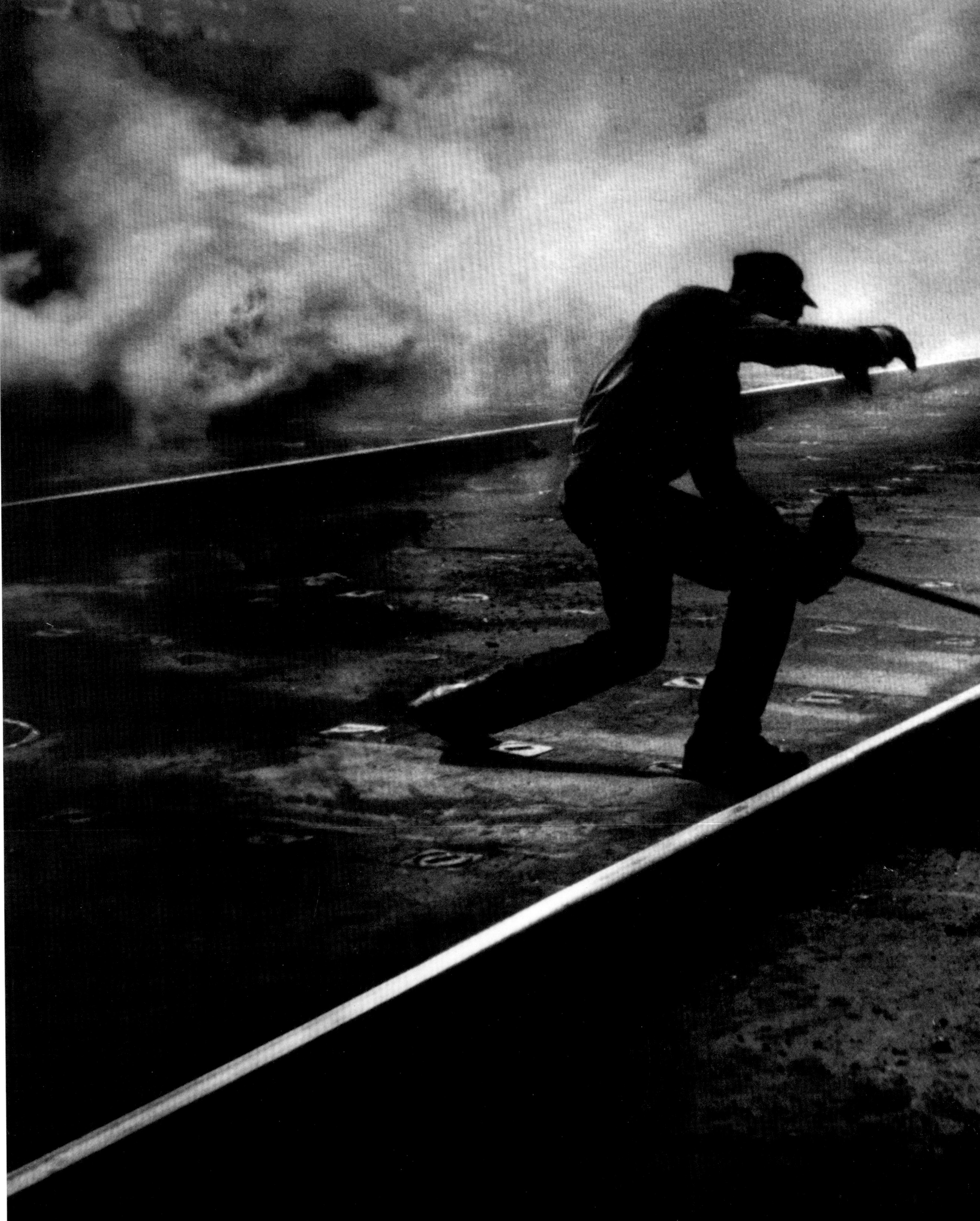

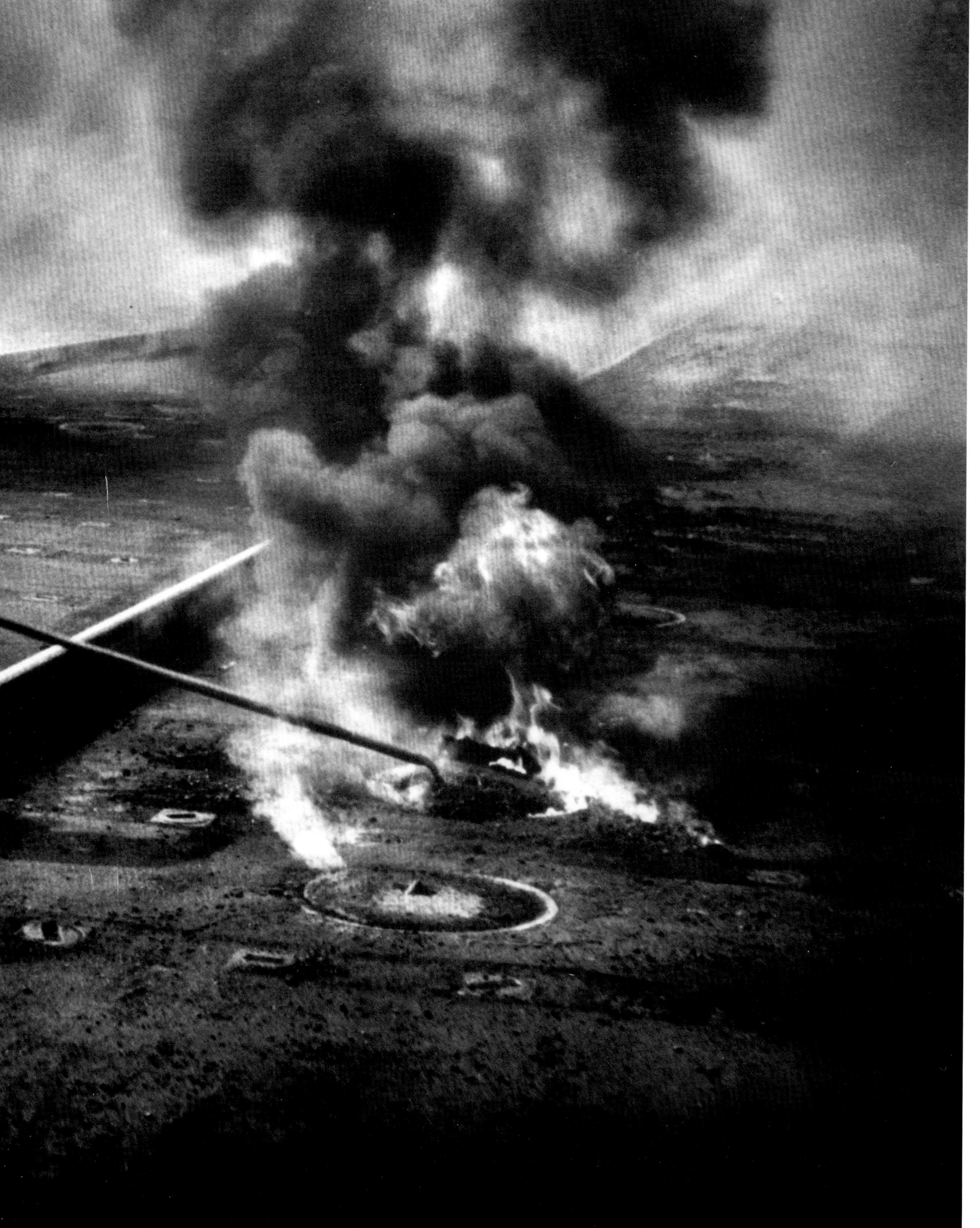

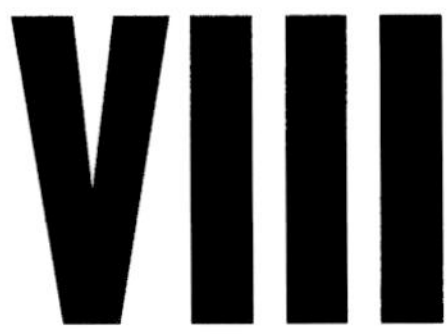

# VIII

The Pittsburgh project—the dream (the very real dream that was also a plan, and a hard plan to bring completion to) has come to twilight many times in the past months, but never quite has it come to banishment. The negatives accomplished, and I would estimate that I have prints made from around two thousand negatives—but so much, so much is yet to complete and since I started the project broke and in very poor health, the year of intensive financing of a project that was not much less than a life-time size endeavor. The outside problems have been quite terrible . . . but, slowly, I think I am still holding many things of project, and of me, together.

Excerpt from Smith's letter to Minor White, George Eastman House, March 21, 1956

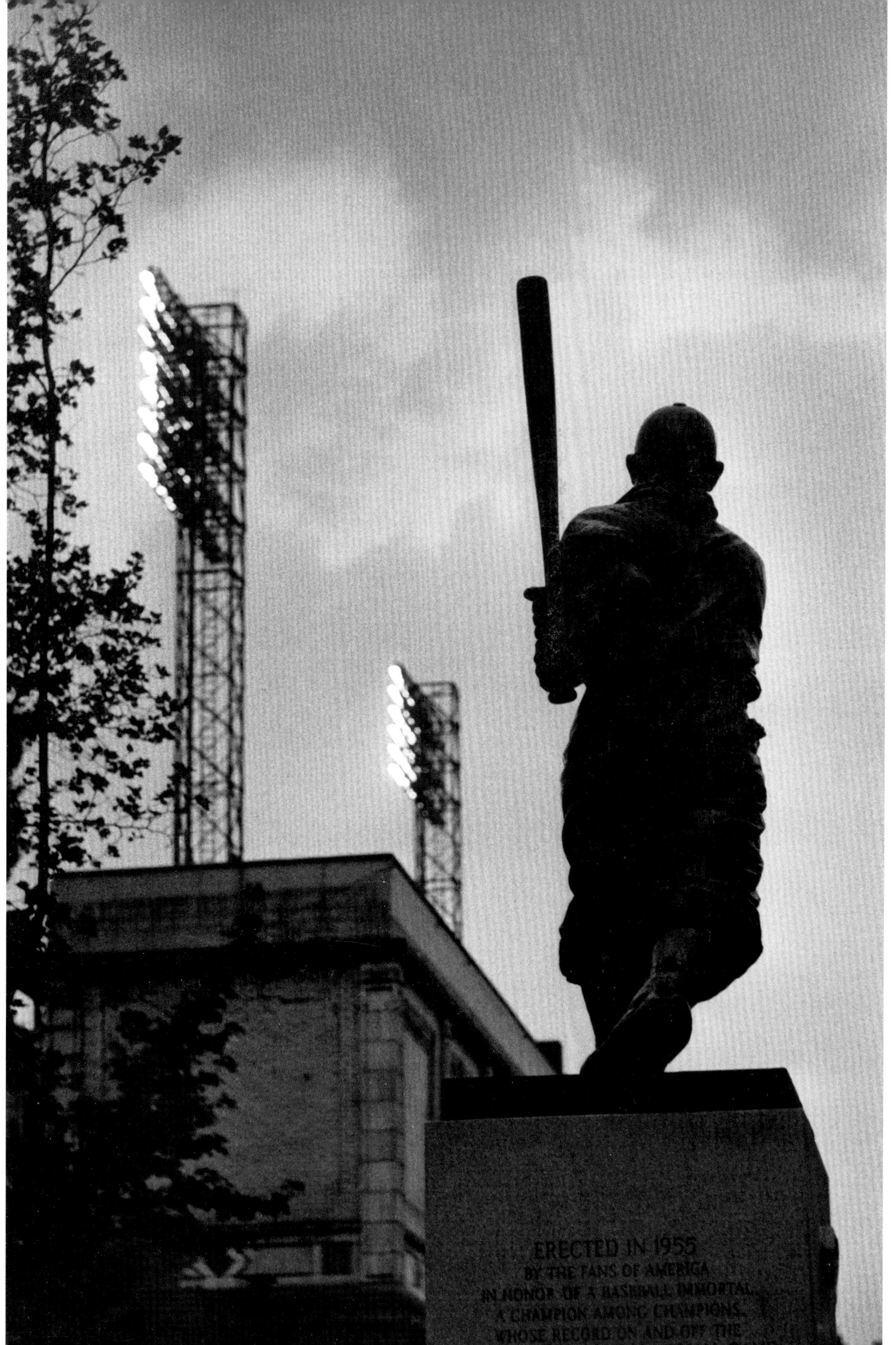

ERECTED IN 1955
BY THE FANS OF AMERICA
IN HONOR OF A BASEBALL IMMORTAL
A CHAMPION AMONG CHAMPIONS
WHOSE RECORD ON AND OFF THE

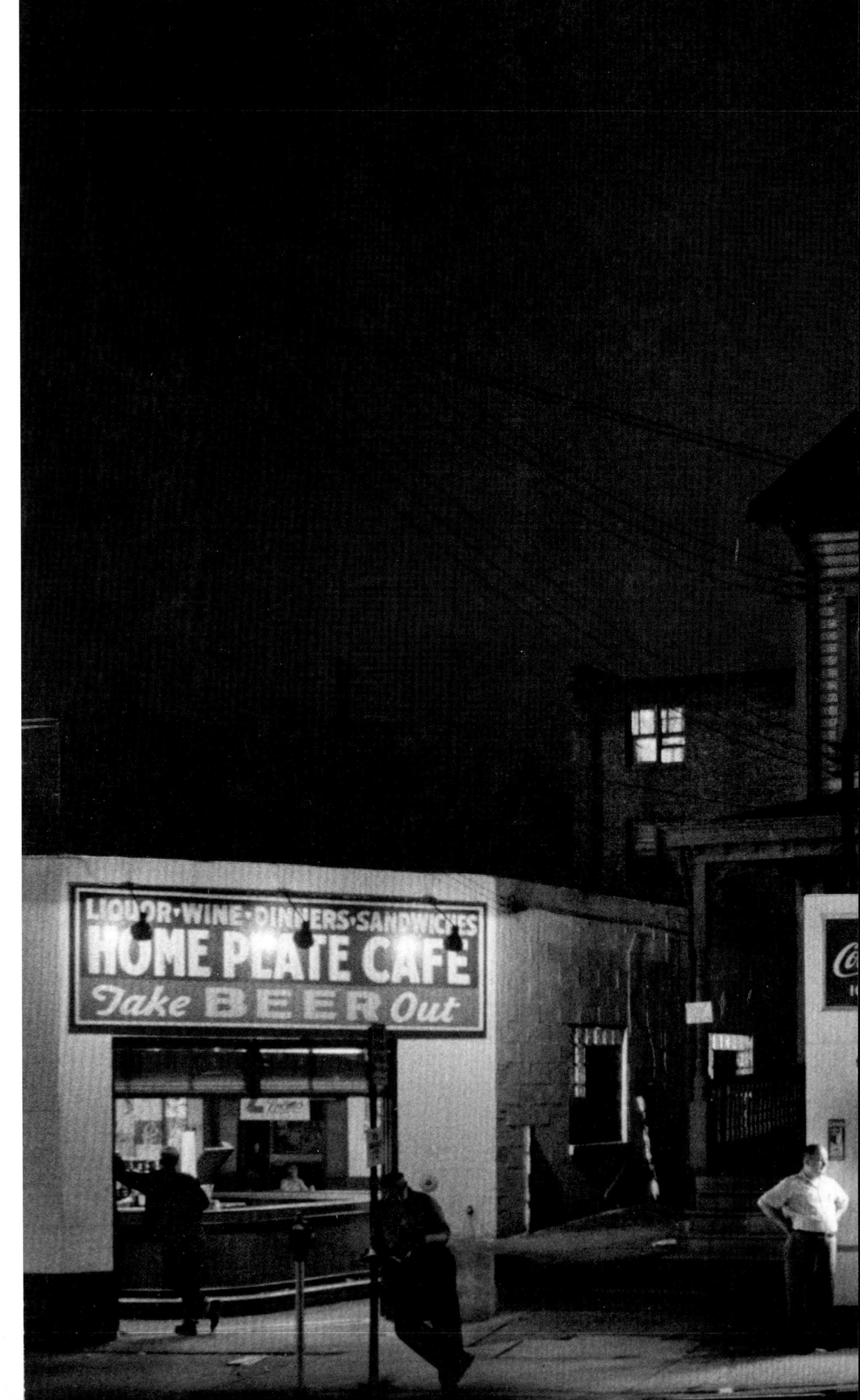
LIQUOR · WINE · DINNERS · SANDWICHES
HOME PLATE CAFE
Take BEER Out

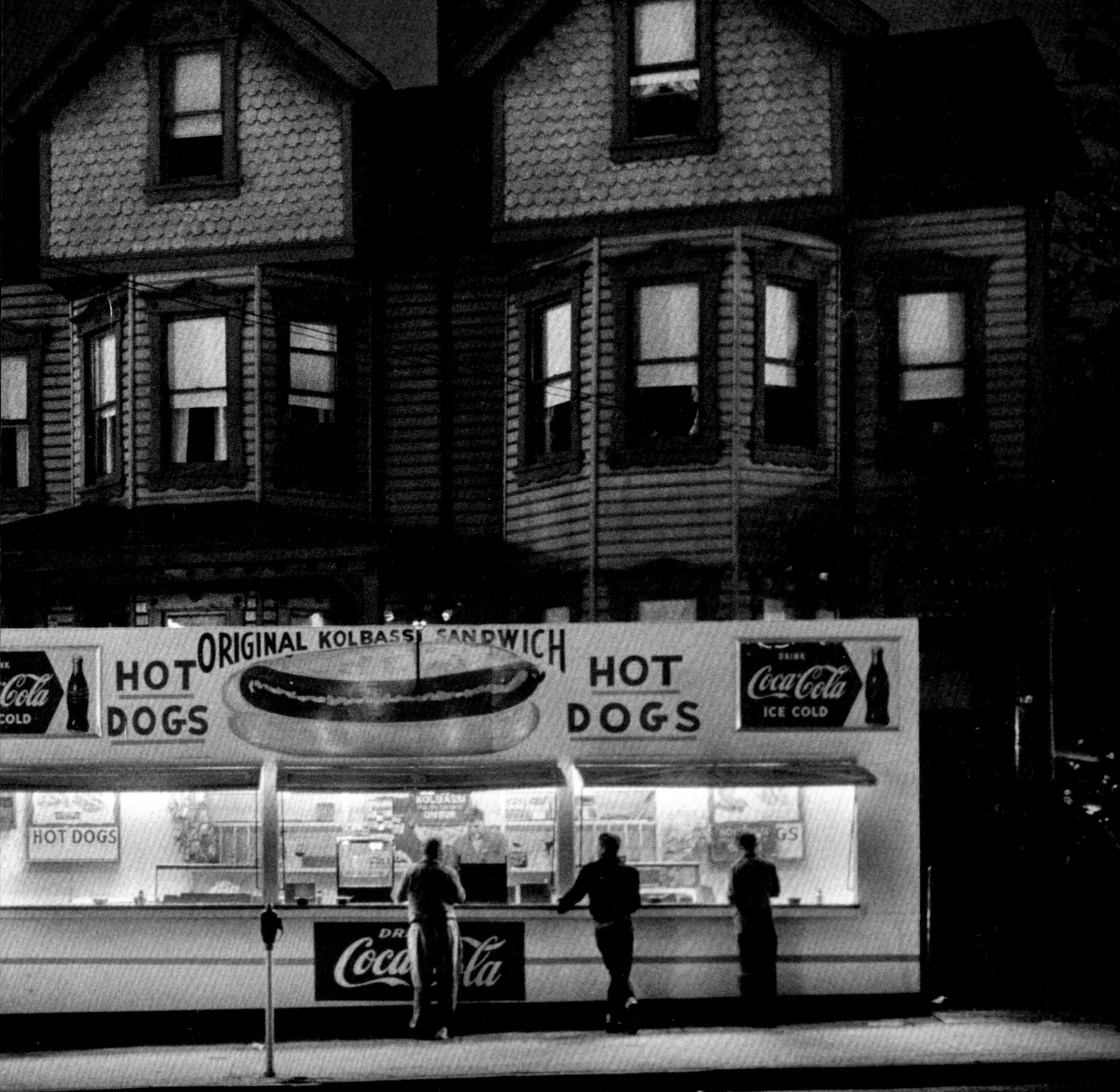

ORIGINAL KOLBASSI SANDWICH
HOT DOGS
HOT DOGS
DRINK Coca-Cola
DRINK Coca-Cola ICE COLD
HOT DOGS
DRINK Coca-Cola

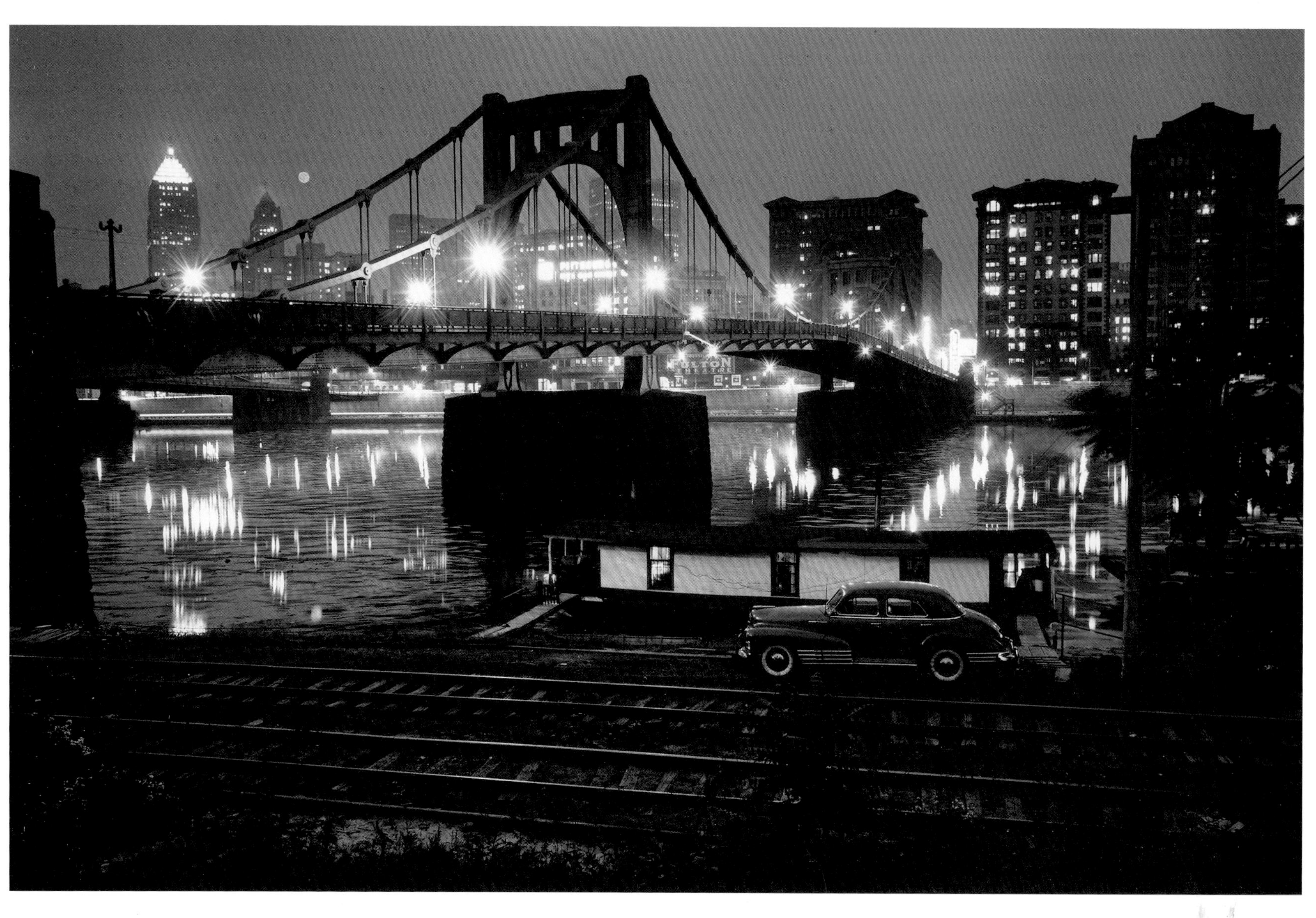

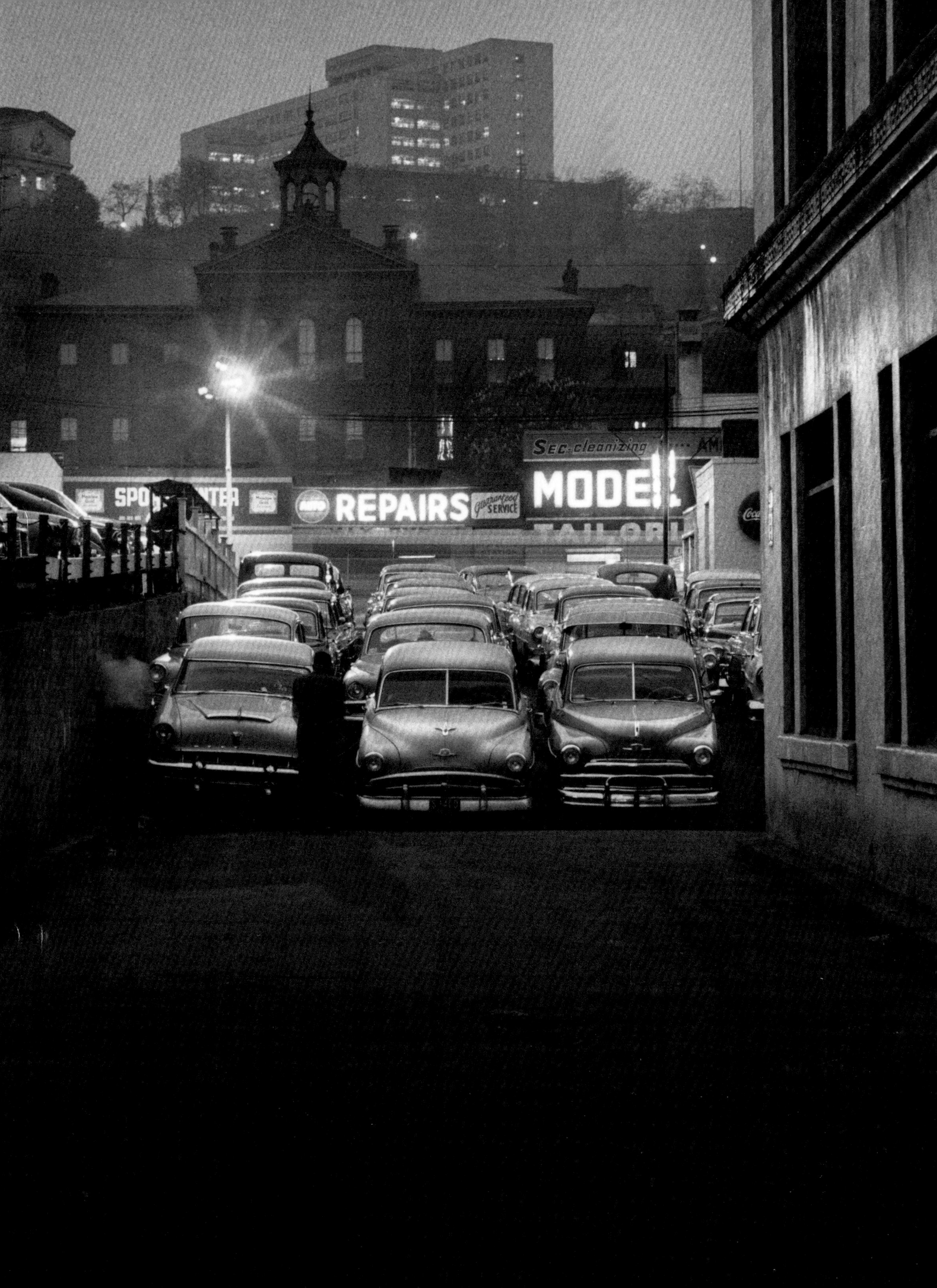
SPORT CENTER
REPAIRS
Guaranteed SERVICE
Sec-cleanizing .... AM
MODEL
TAILOR
Coca-Cola

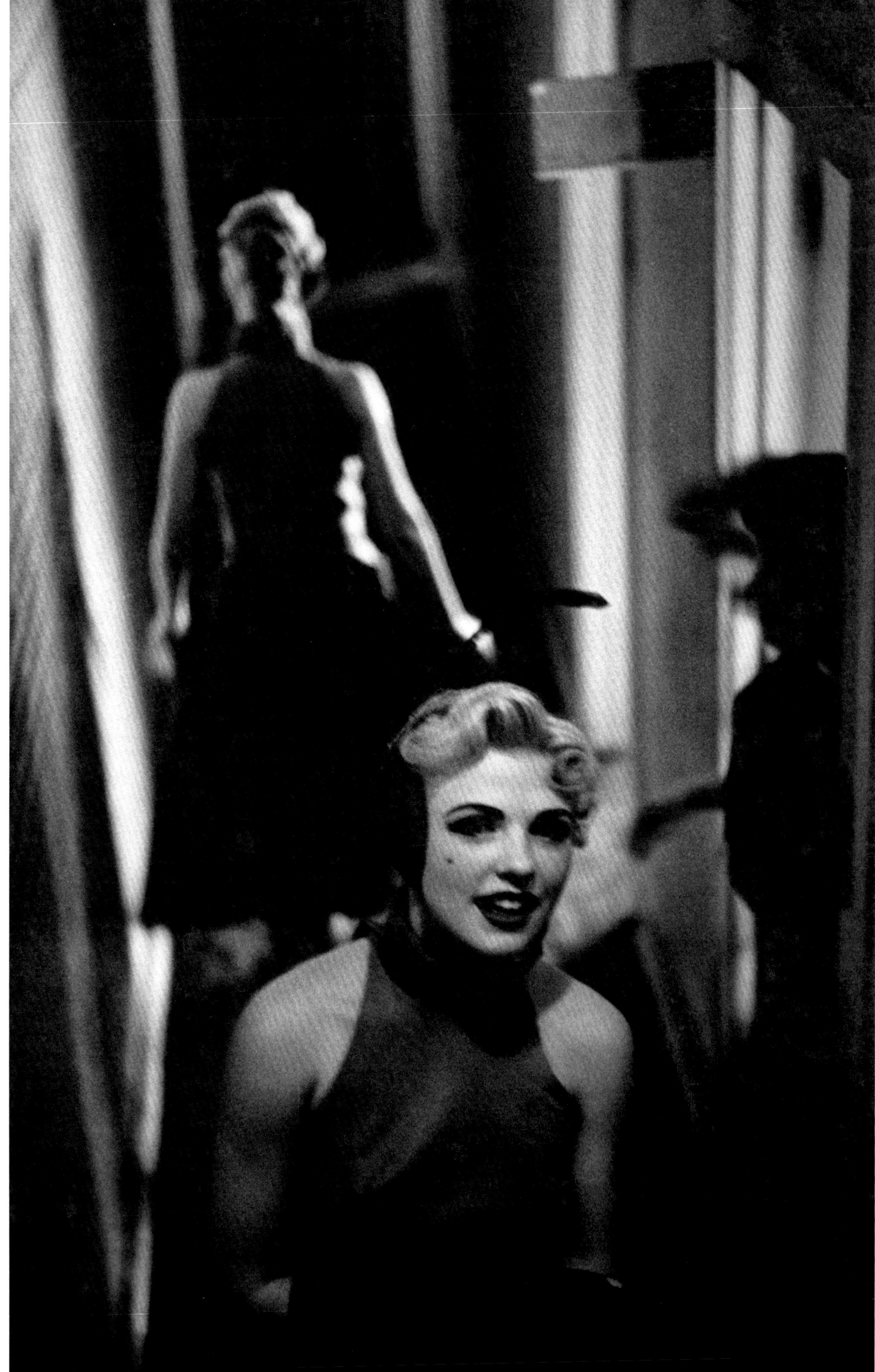

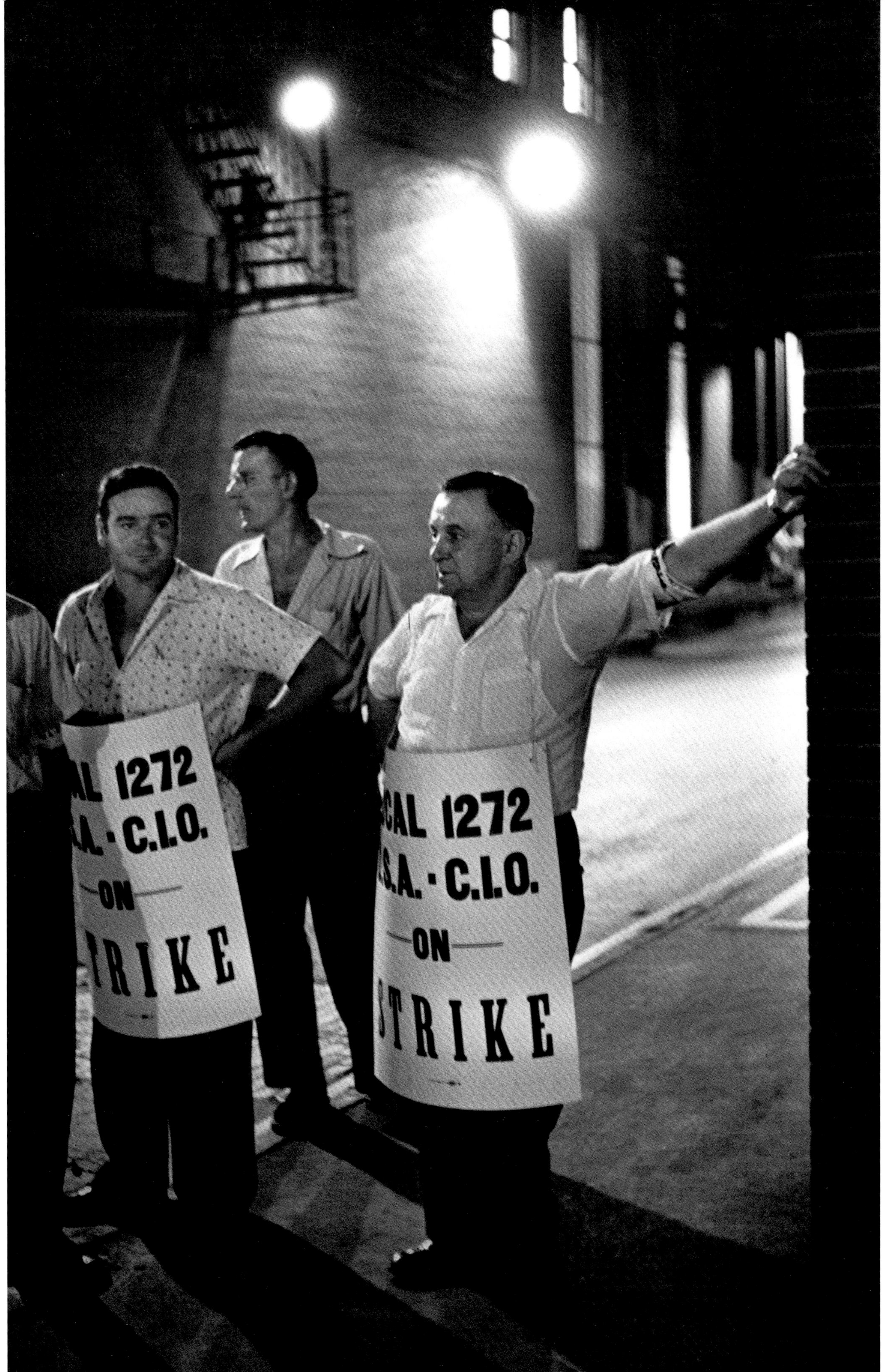
CAL 1272
A. - C.I.O.
ON
TRIKE
CAL 1272
.S.A. - C.I.O.
ON
TRIKE

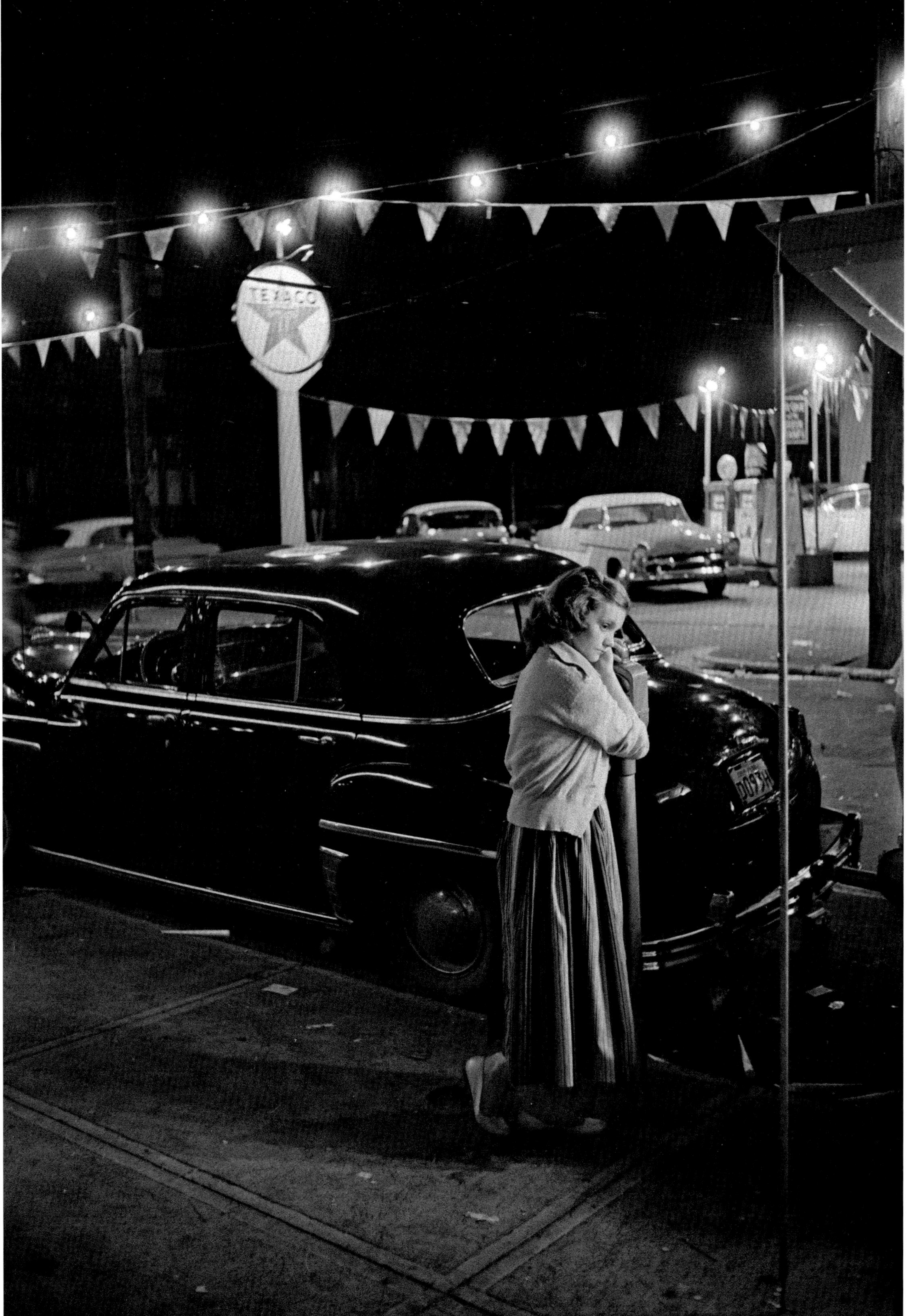

TEXACO

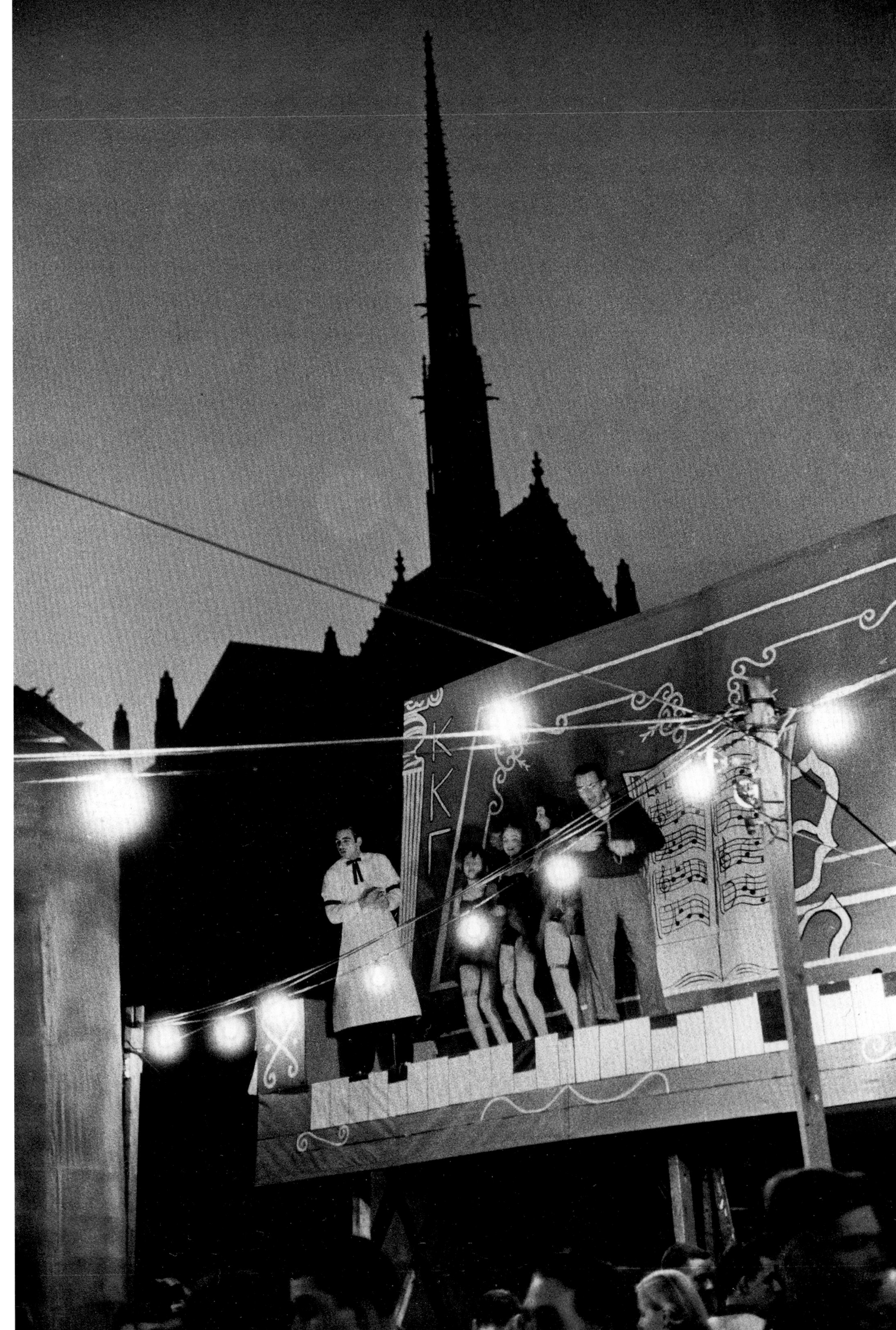

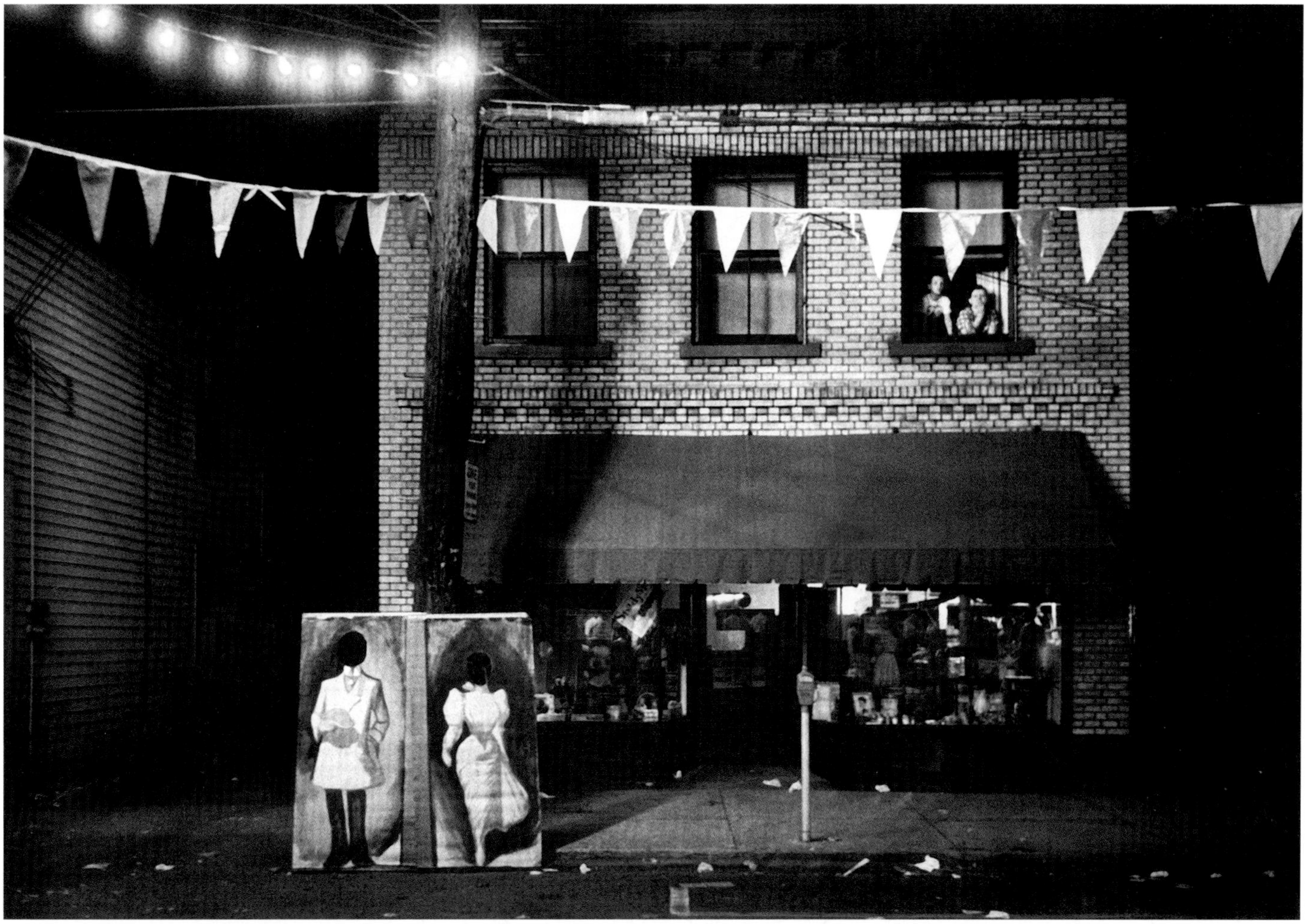

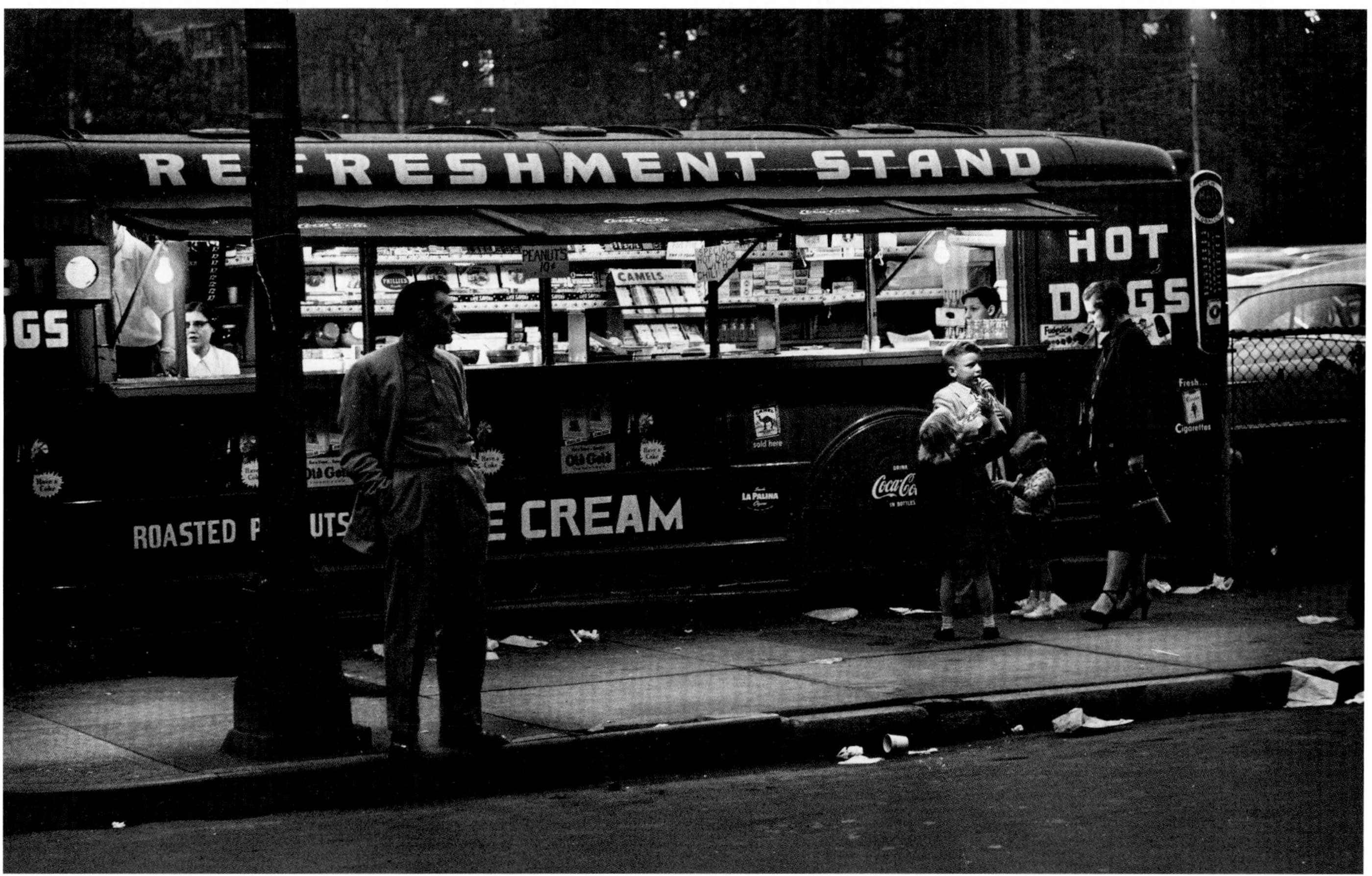REFRESHMENT STAND
HOT DOGS
DGS
ROASTED PEANUTS
CREAM
CAMELS
PHILLIES
PEANUTS
10¢
Old Gold
Coca-Cola
IN BOTTLES
LA PALMA
sold here
Fresh...
Cigarettes

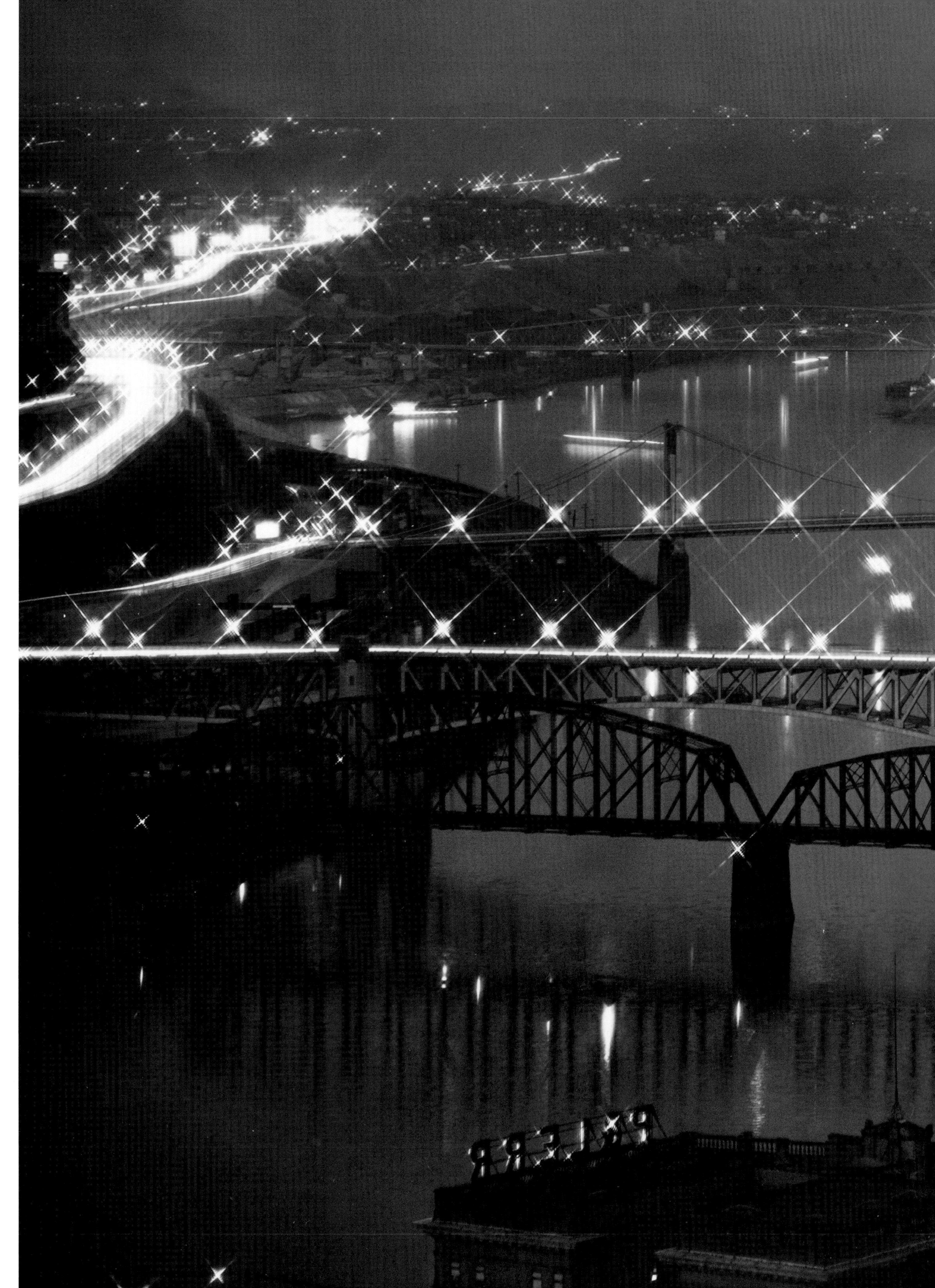

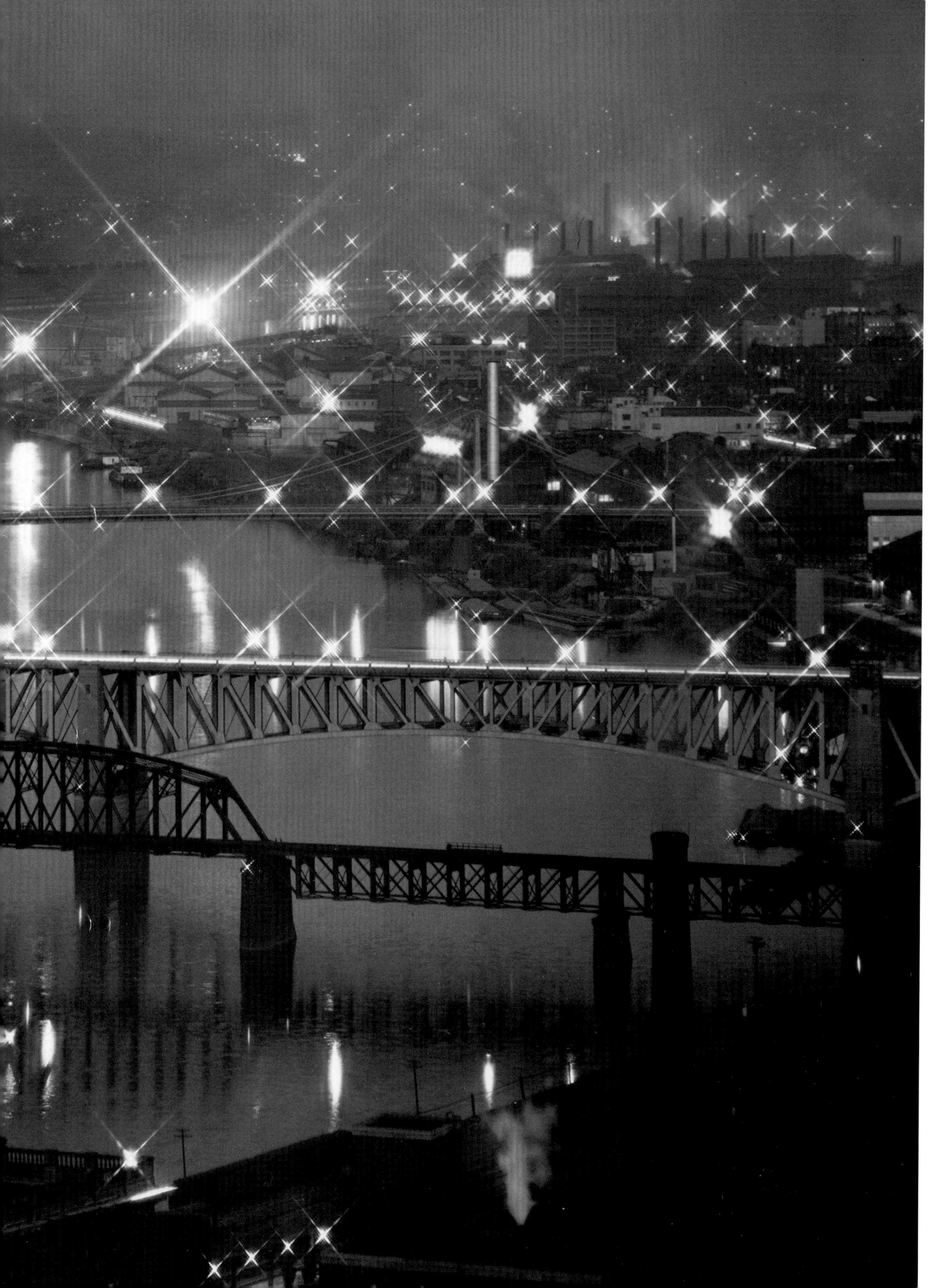

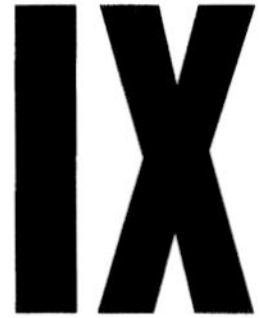

W. EUGENE SMITH: I have now printed somewhere between 200 and 300 negatives of the 2,000 negatives I consider worthwhile and valid to the project.

PHILIPPE HALSMAN: What in the world would anybody do with 200 prints?

WES: The prints so far still represent mere portions of the chapters, incidents, sub-essays within the whole of the project—the 200 printed are a synthesis of that whole, indicating the breadth of it.

PH: How can this be financed? Is there any way, in American today, to pay a man back for his work?

WES: Time and pay? I don't know. It is not a new problem. How long did it take Joyce to do *Ulysses*? *Finnegan's Wake*? And what were his returns? I could never be rested within myself without doing this.

PH: But what of the photographer who does not have financial means?

WES: I don't. Sometimes it seems I financed it from the lining of my stomach. As for others—if asked, I will advise them not to do it—and I will hope they do.

PH: What if nobody sees it?

WES: The goal is the work itself, and with any real finality, the artist is never sure if he is or isn't finished.

Excerpt from Smith's interview with Philippe Halsman regarding the Pittsburgh project, 1957

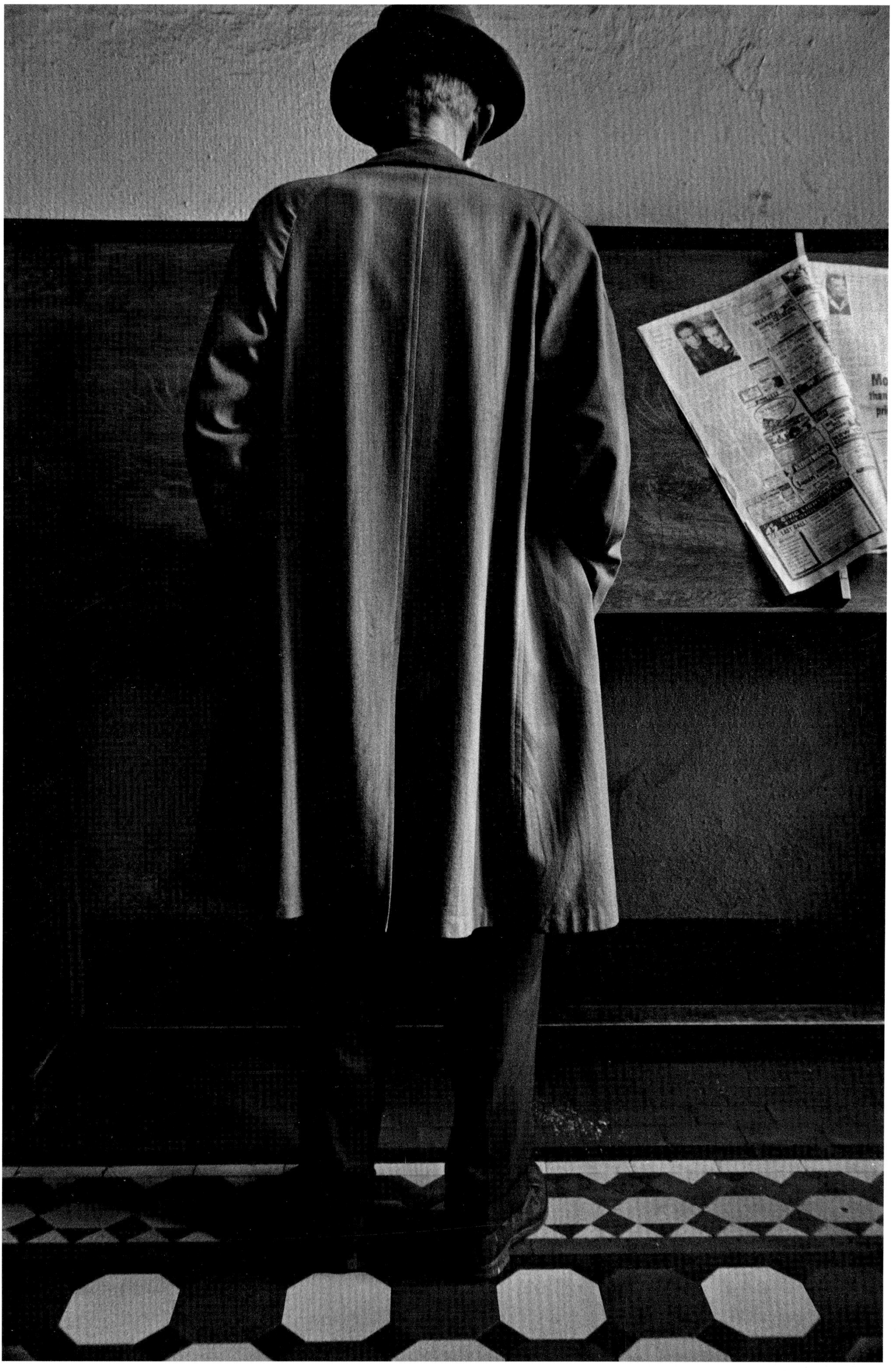

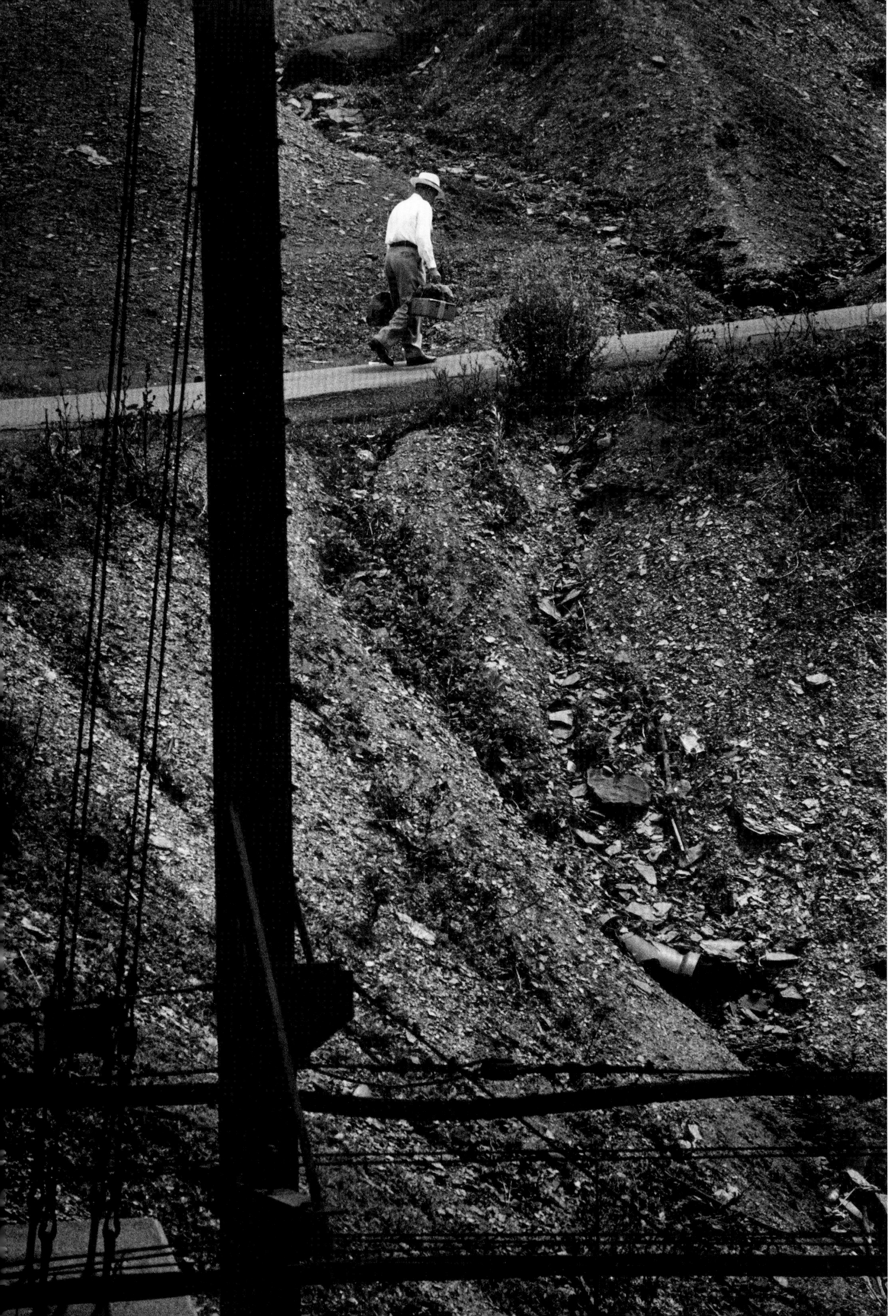

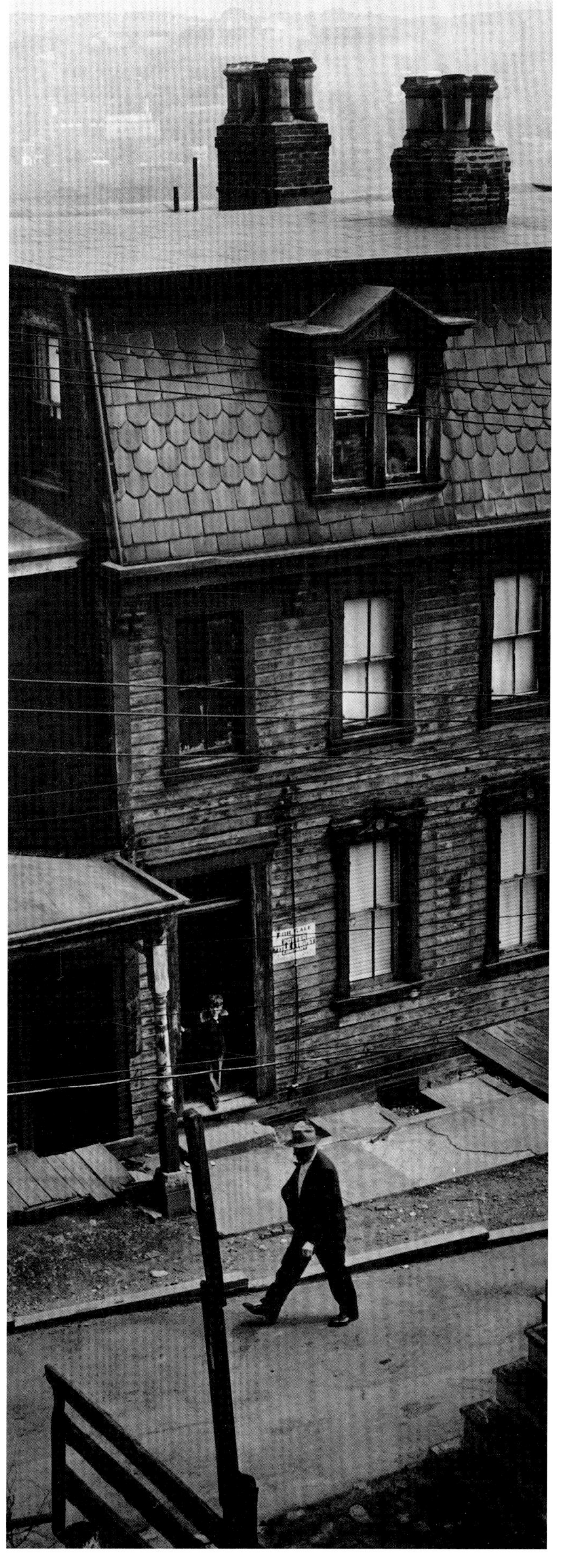

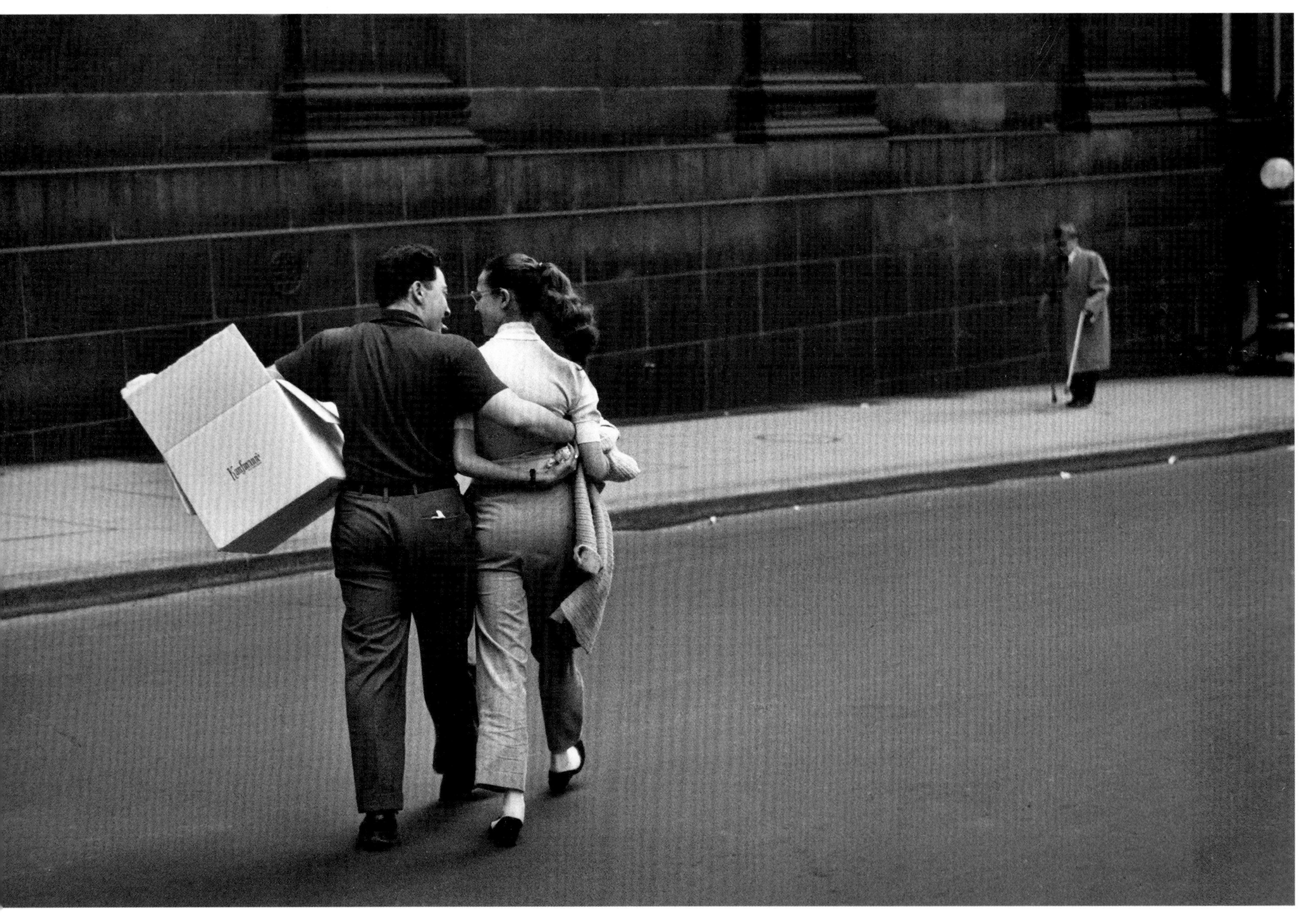

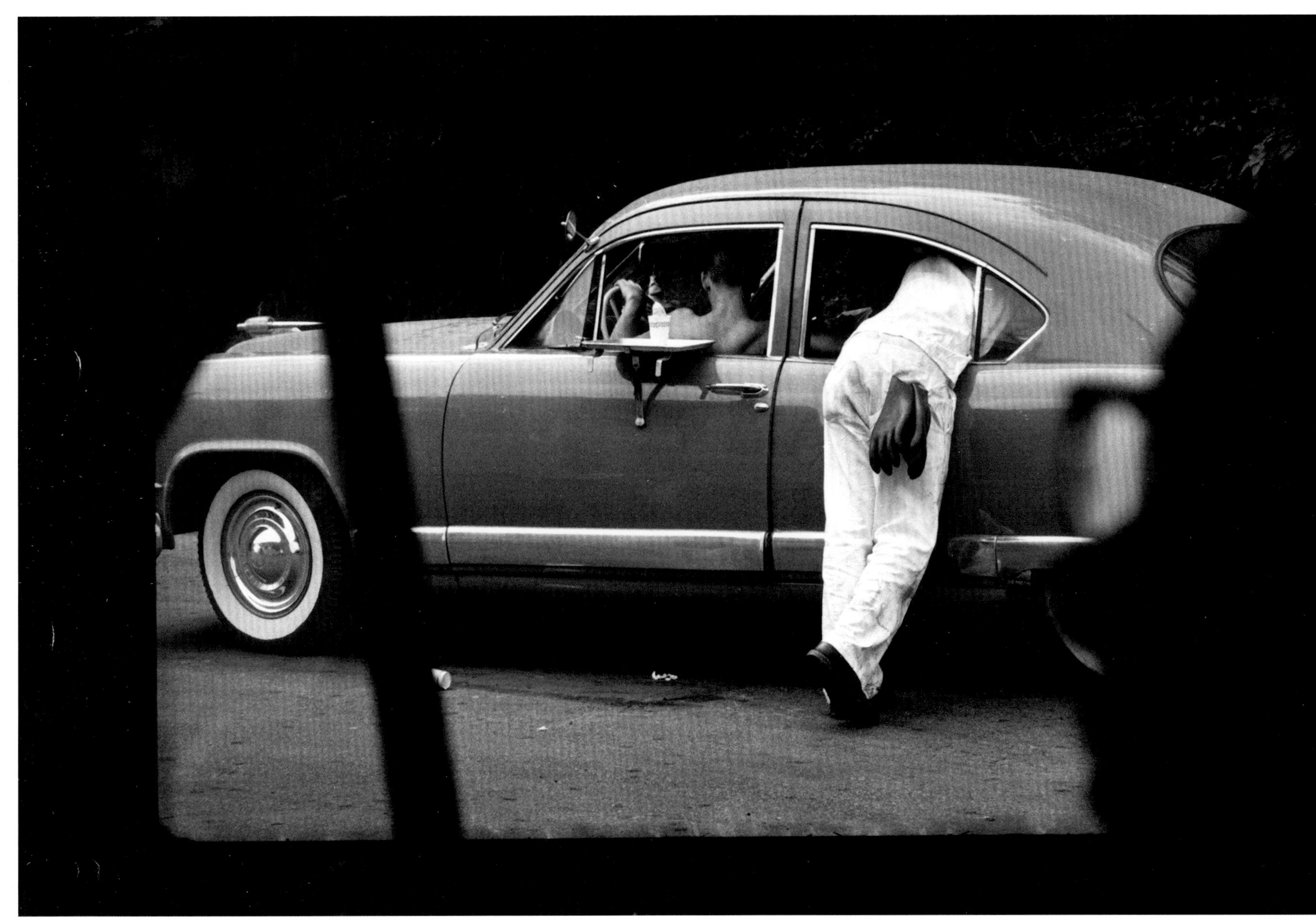

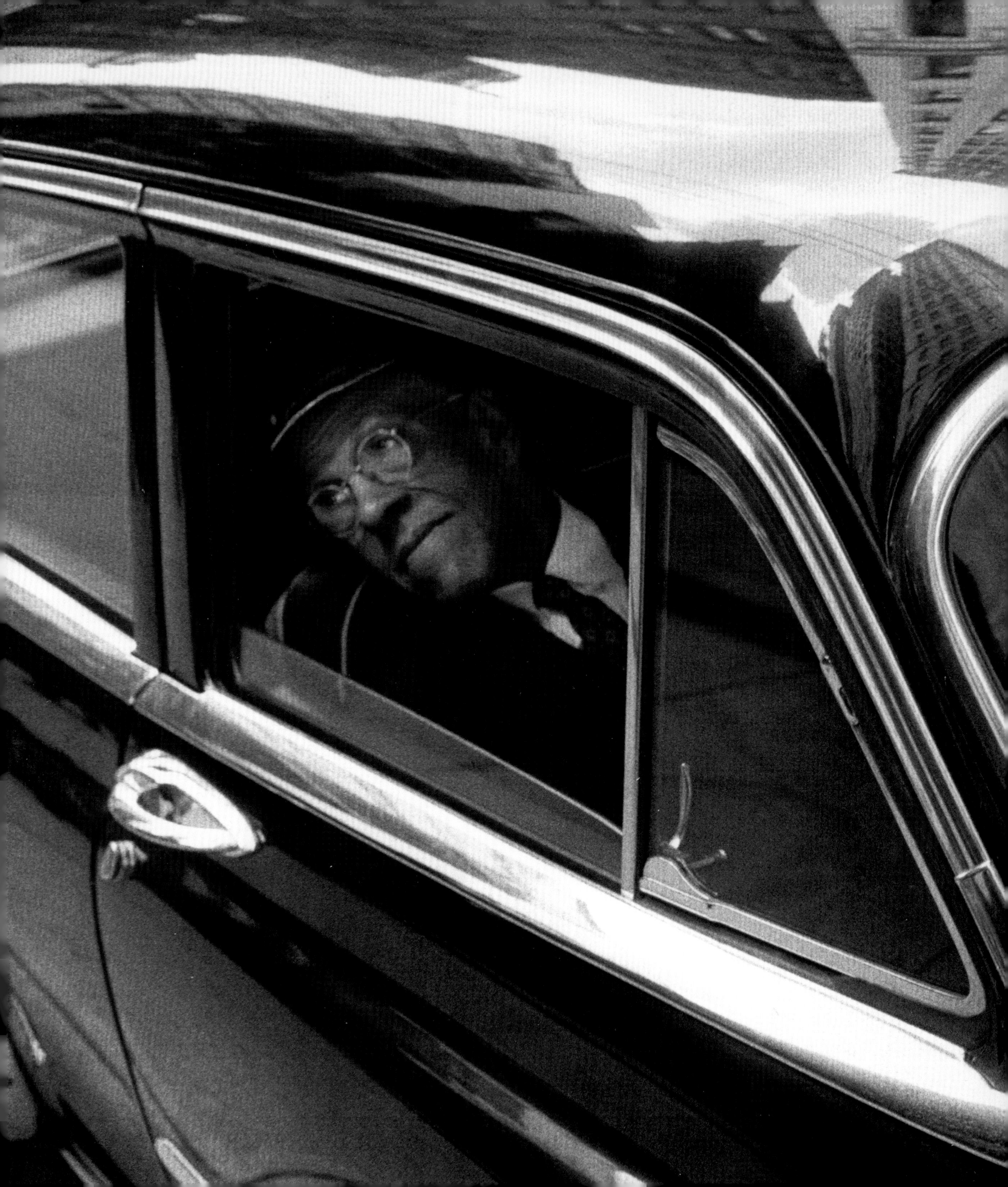

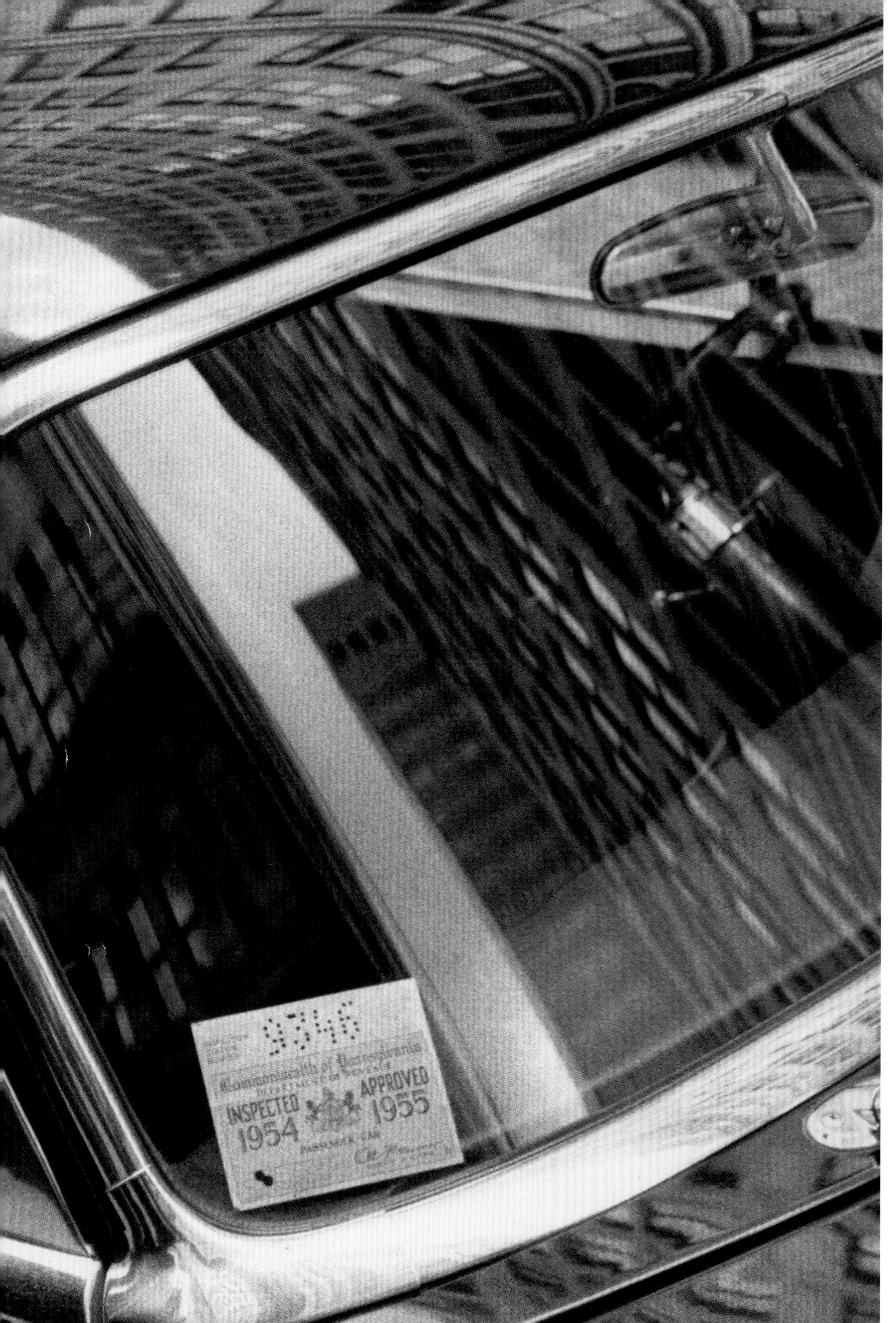

9346
Commonwealth of Pennsylvania
DEPARTMENT OF REVENUE
INSPECTED
1954
APPROVED
1955
PASSENGER CAR

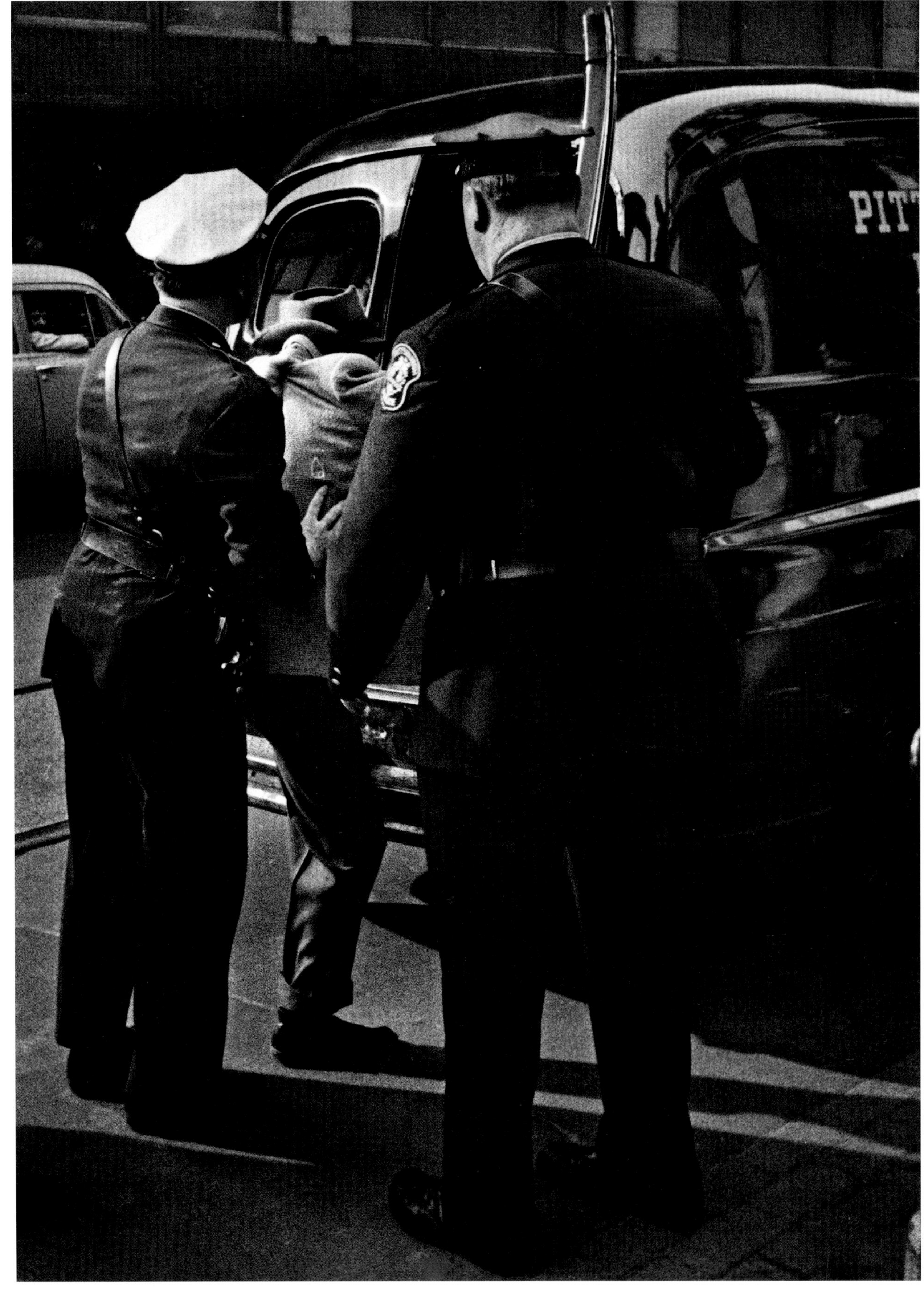

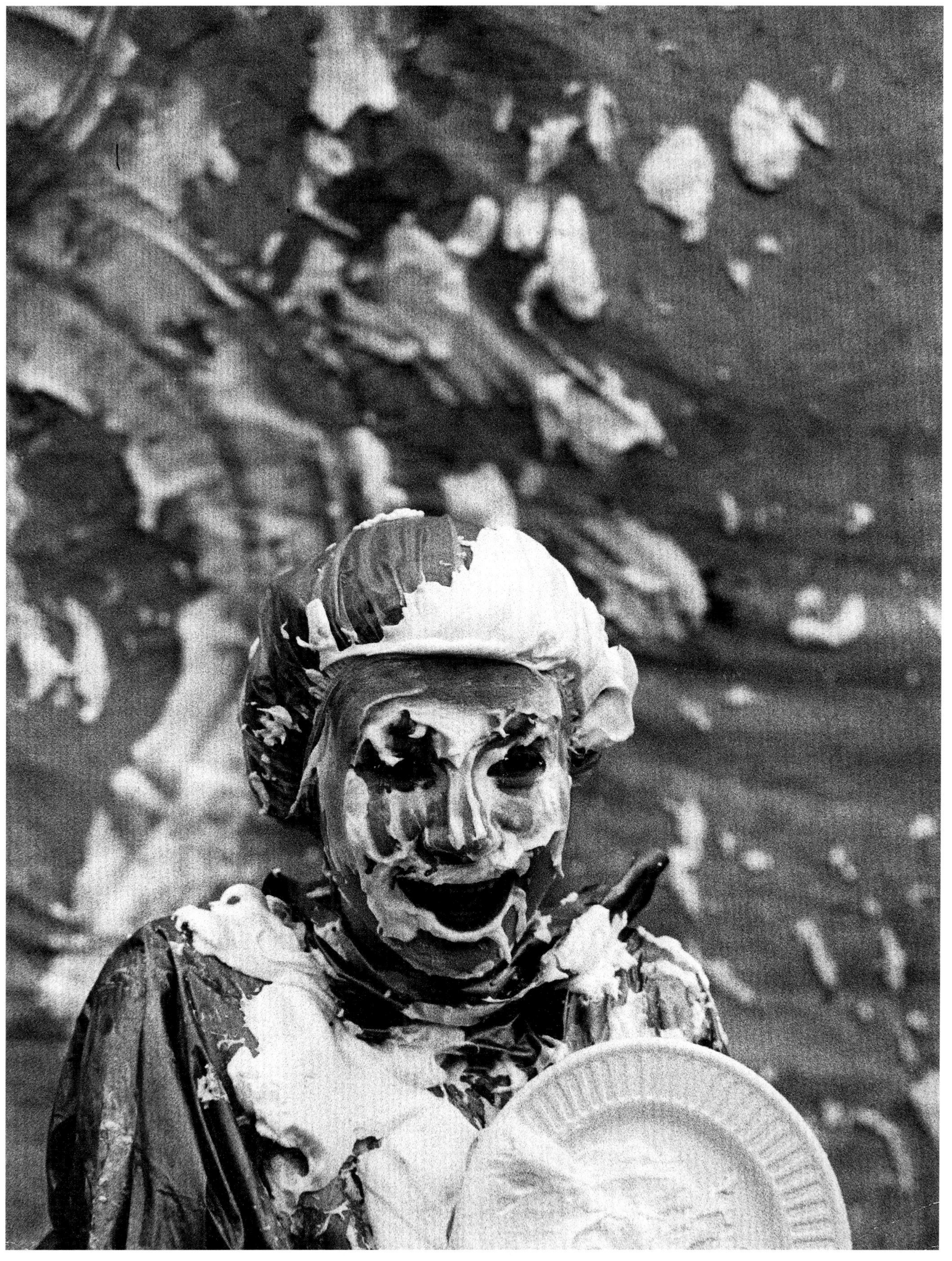

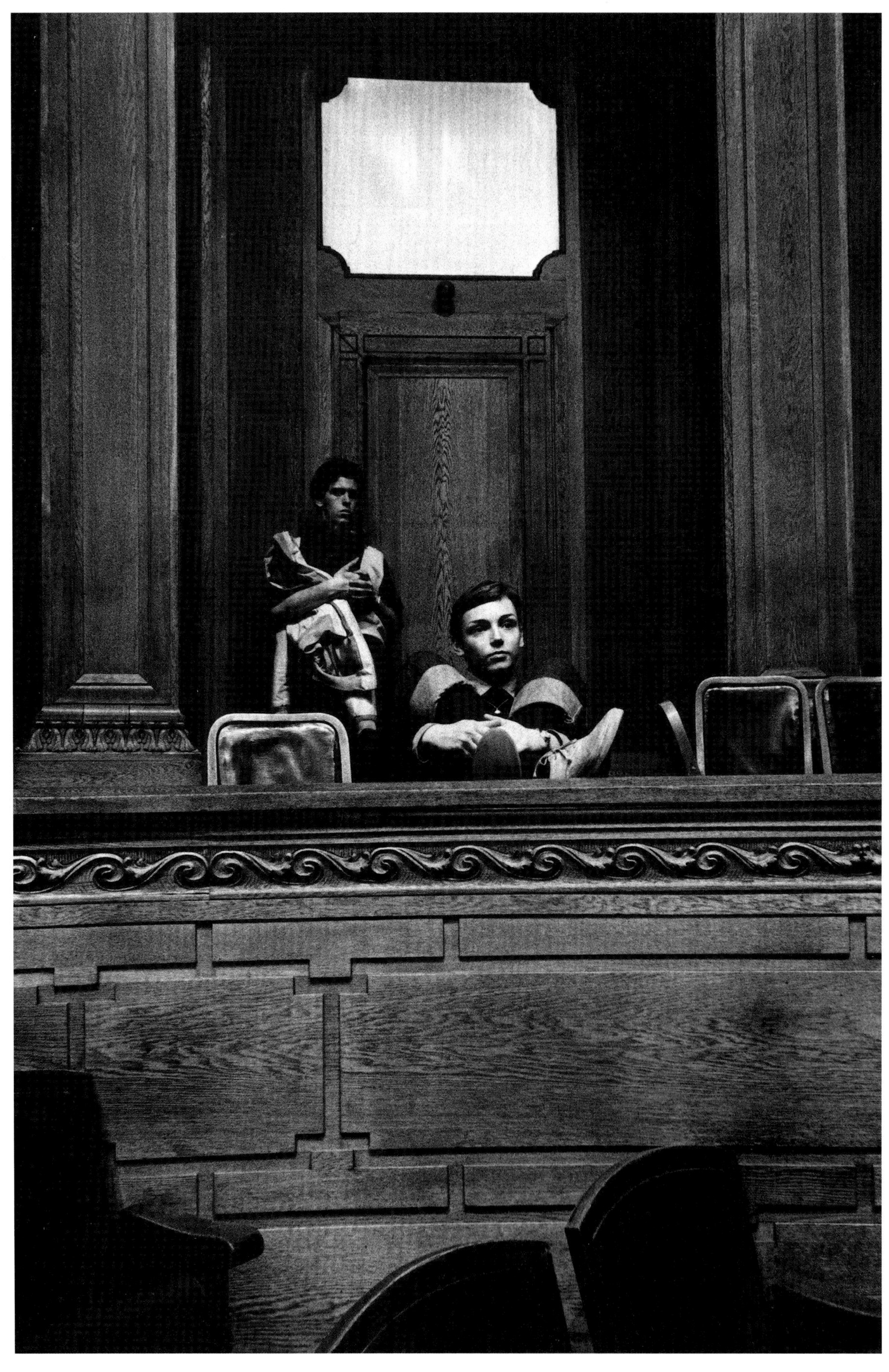

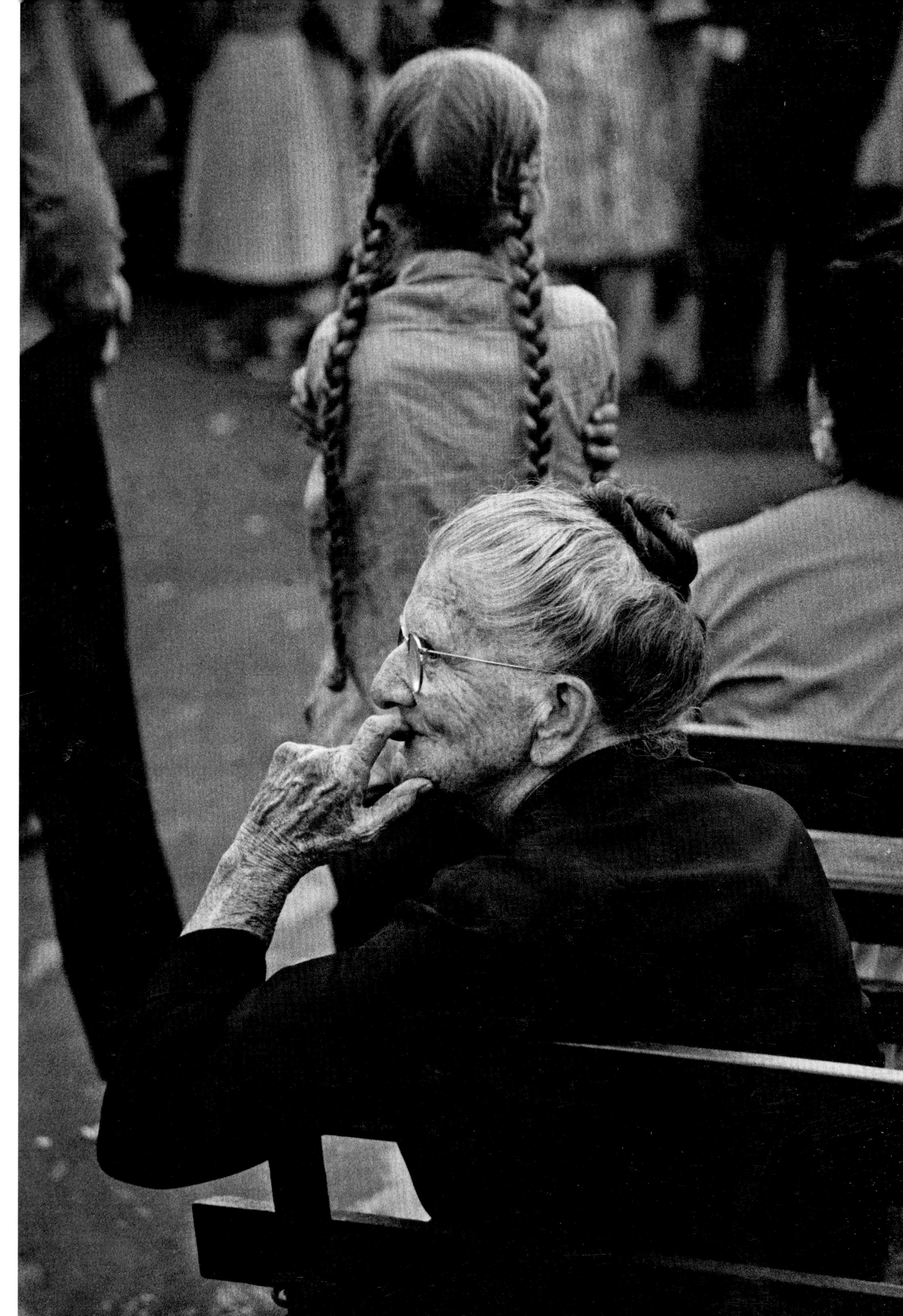

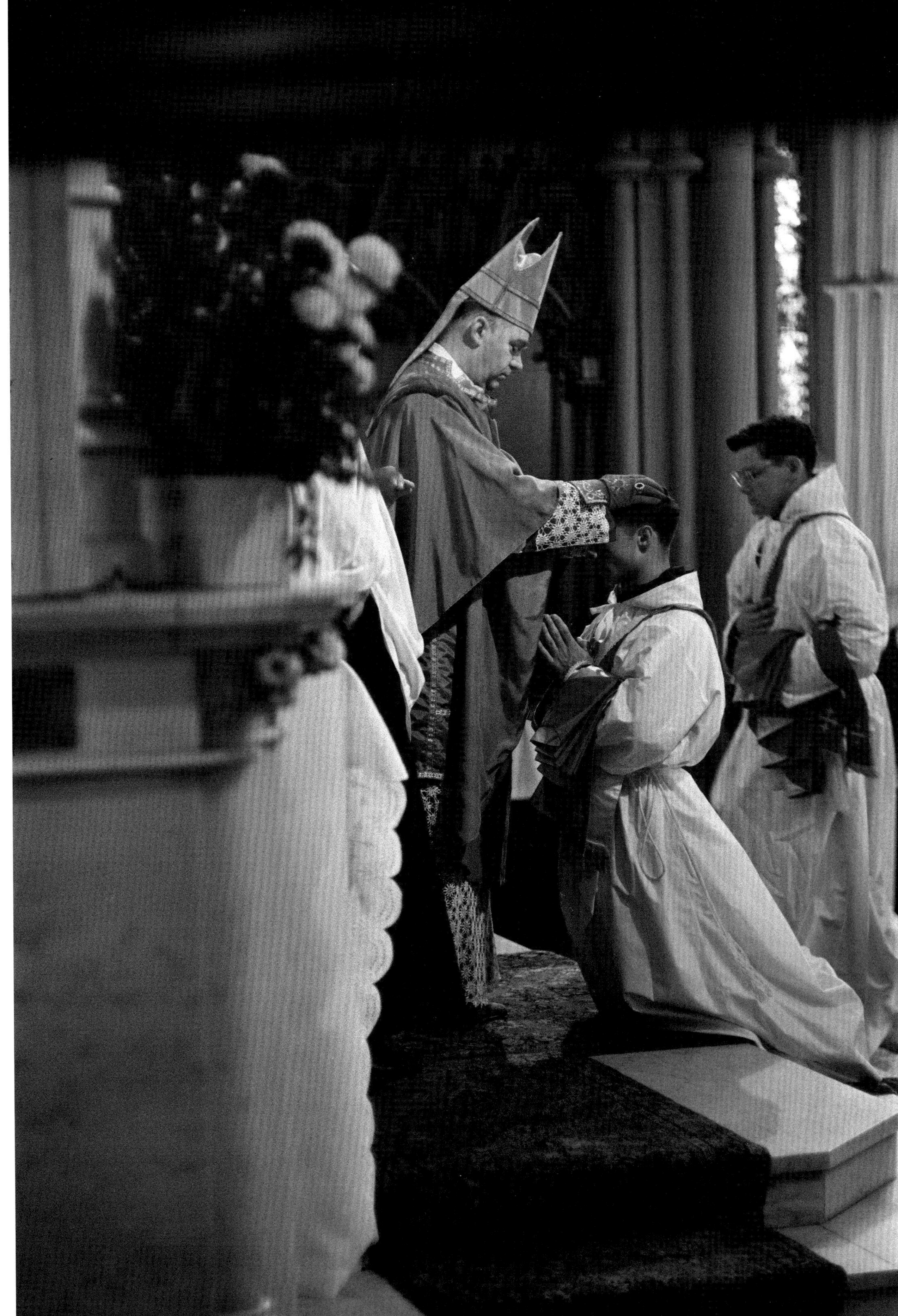

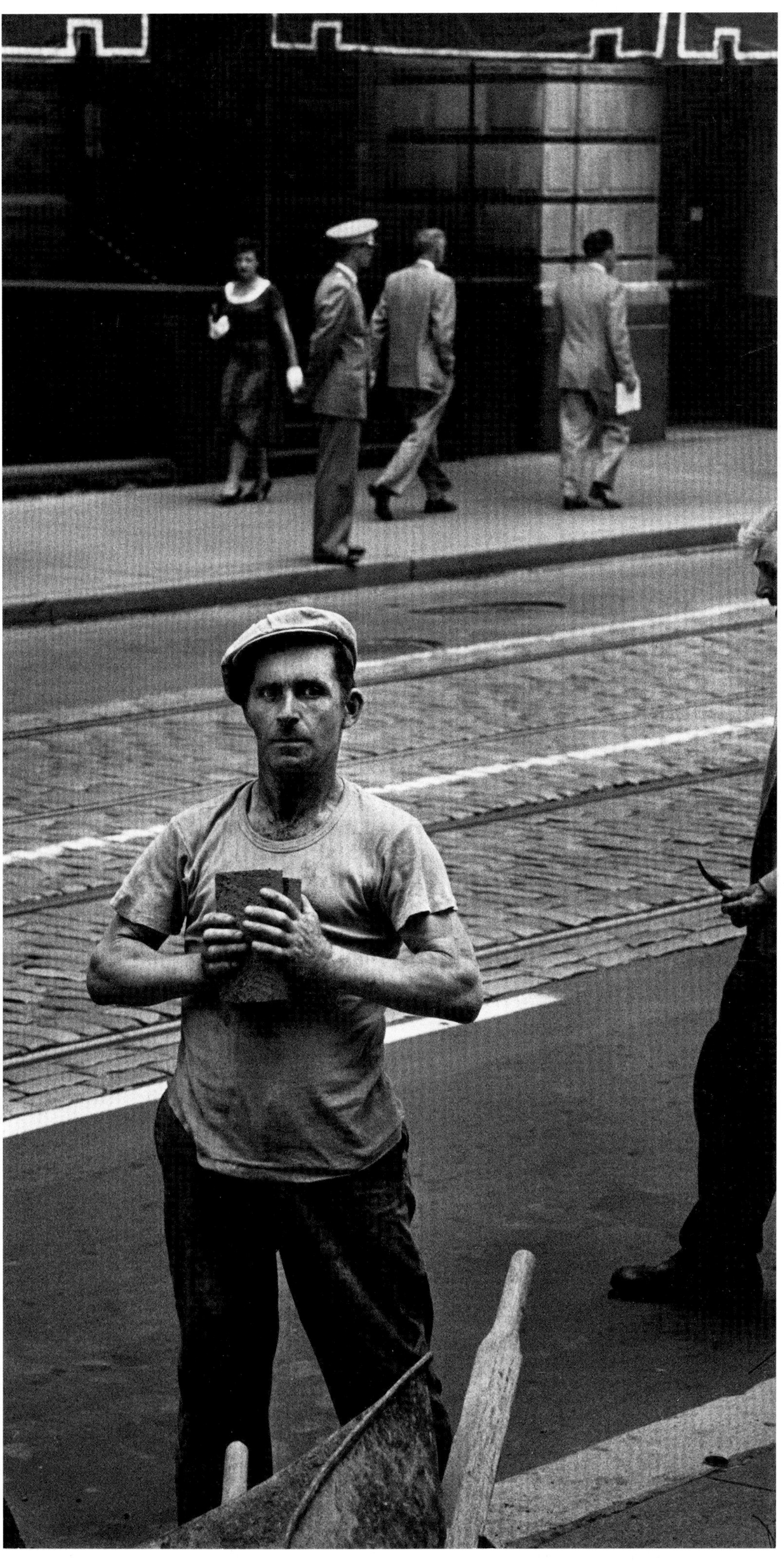

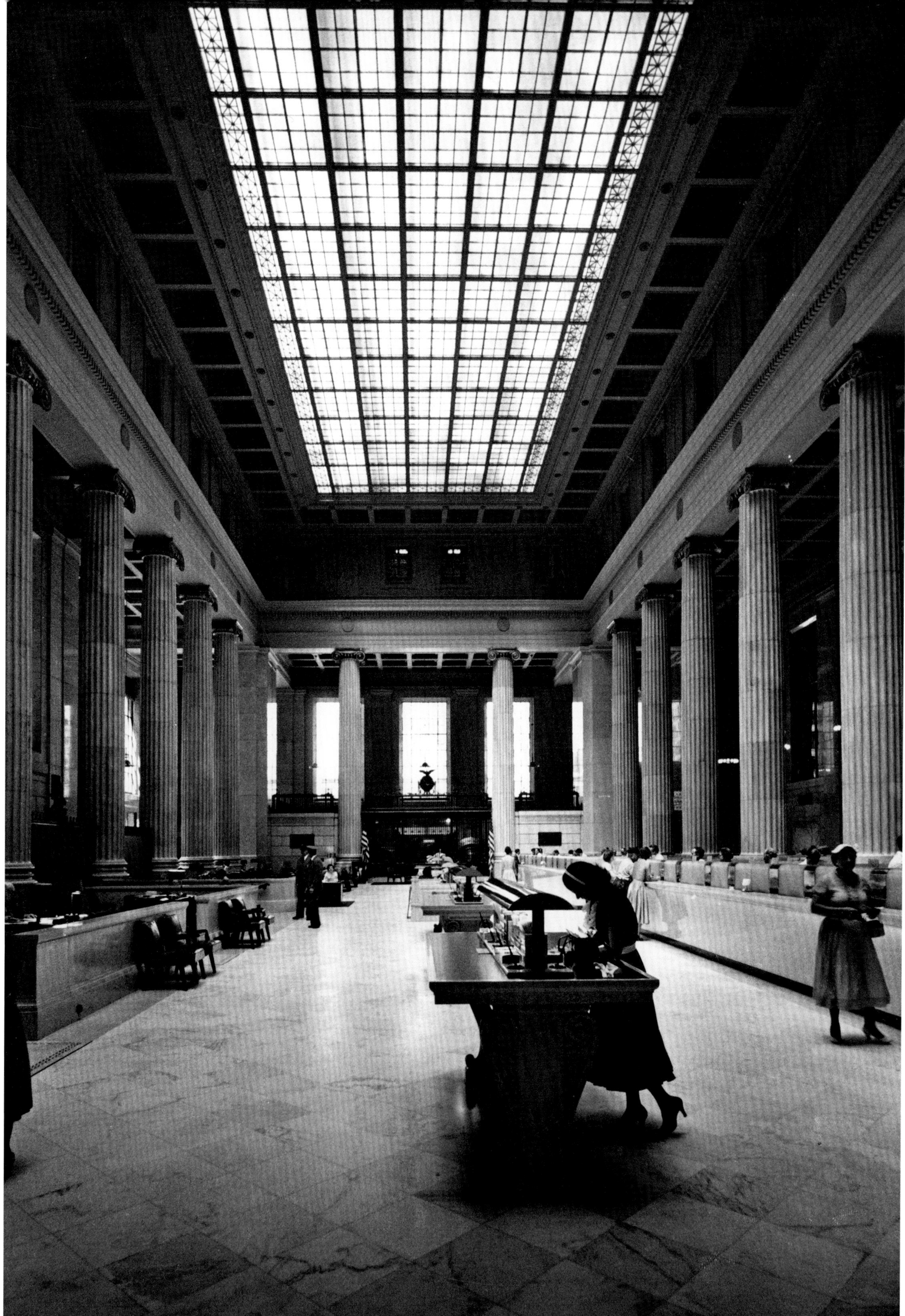

# X

Would these photographs, read without words, would they cause a recall and intensification of your experience of life in Pittsburgh? Or, would you see an alien experience—as if it were almost of a different planet, as you have remarked of your reactions at other times in seeing great magazines presenting "facts" of your city? Tell me—I desire to know, I must know—have I enforced so much individuality into this most individual statement, or poem, that I have lost most others in what finally must stand as an effort in communicating to them a distillation of my experience of that city? However, no matter how greatly I desire you to sense strongly the character essence of Pittsburgh, I would emphatically have you (or the unacquainted reader) find it a human experience transcending any narrow label of Pittsburgh by landmark alone—which to me would also fail as essence of Pittsburgh.

Excerpt from Smith's letter to his friends and photographic assistants in Pittsburgh, Fran Erzen and Leon Miller, April 8, 1957



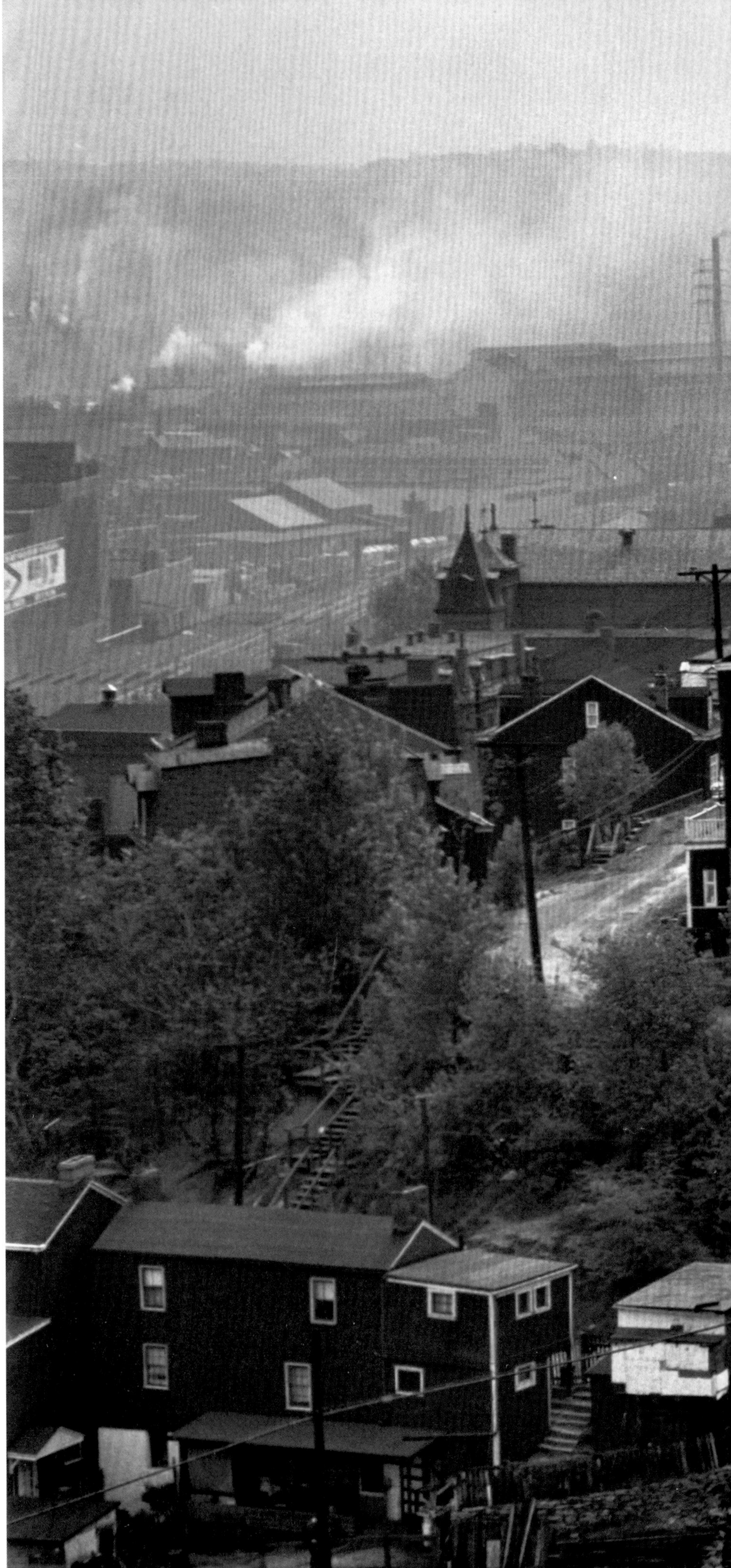

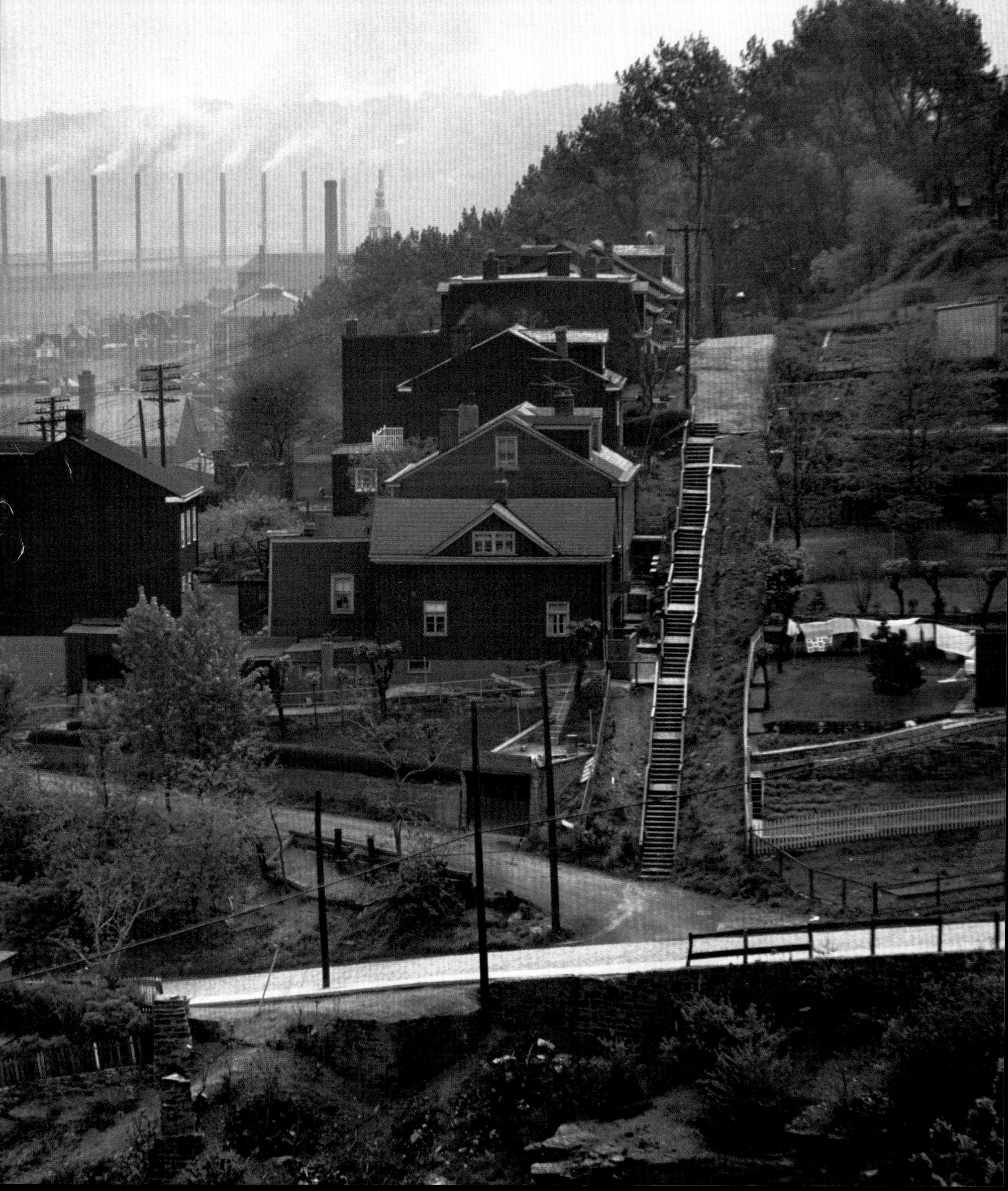

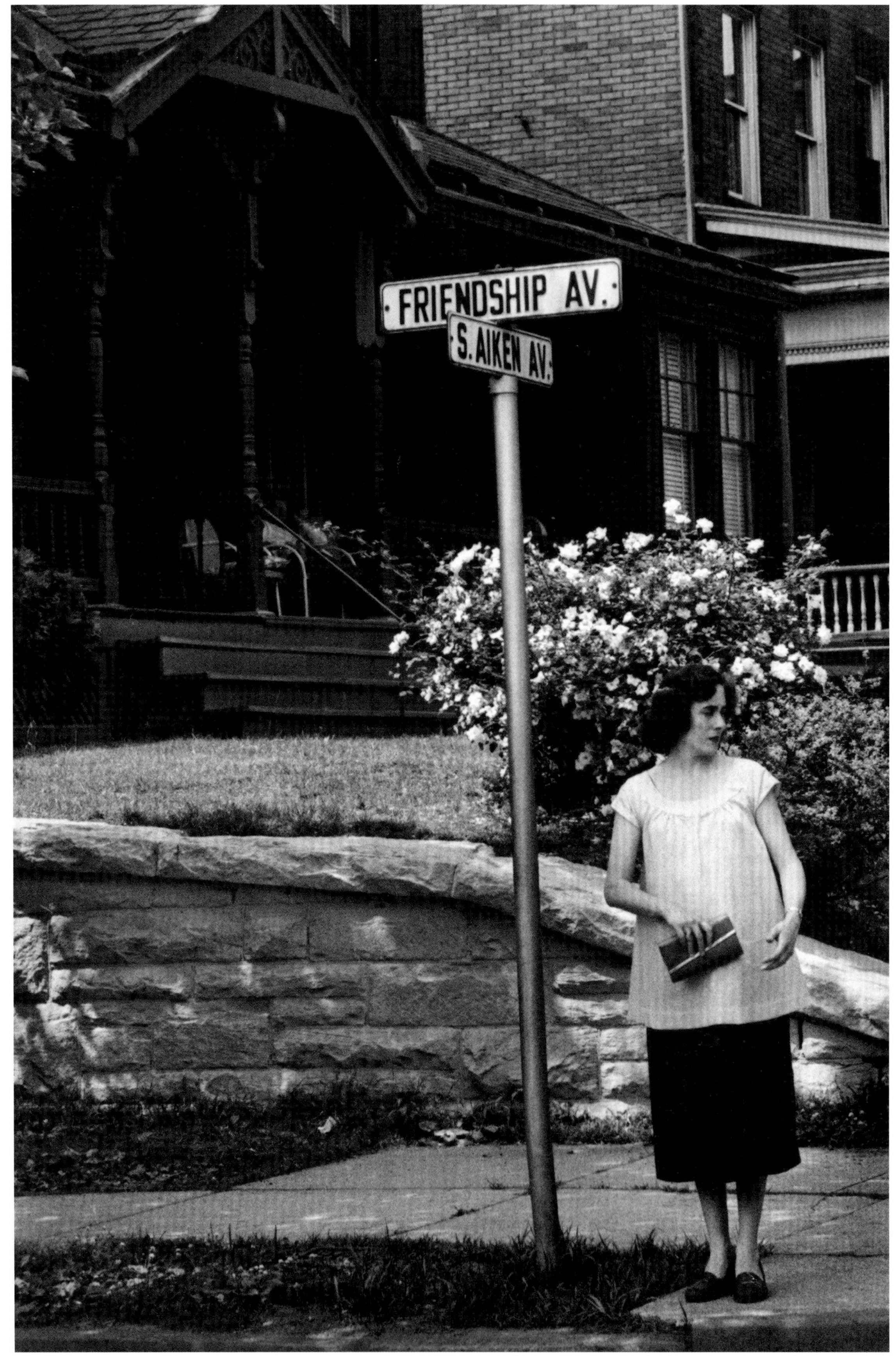

FRIENDSHIP AV.
S. AIKEN AV.

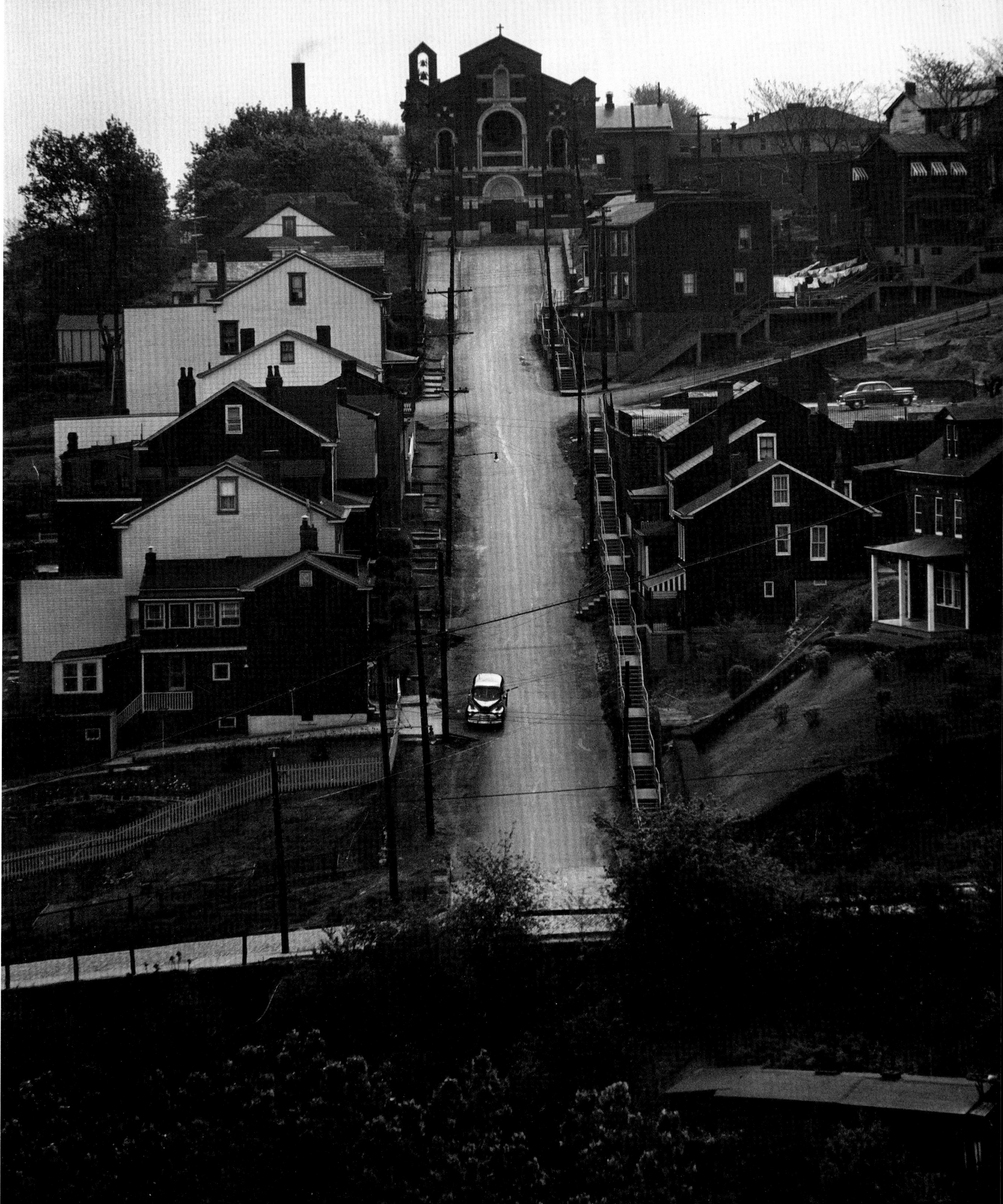

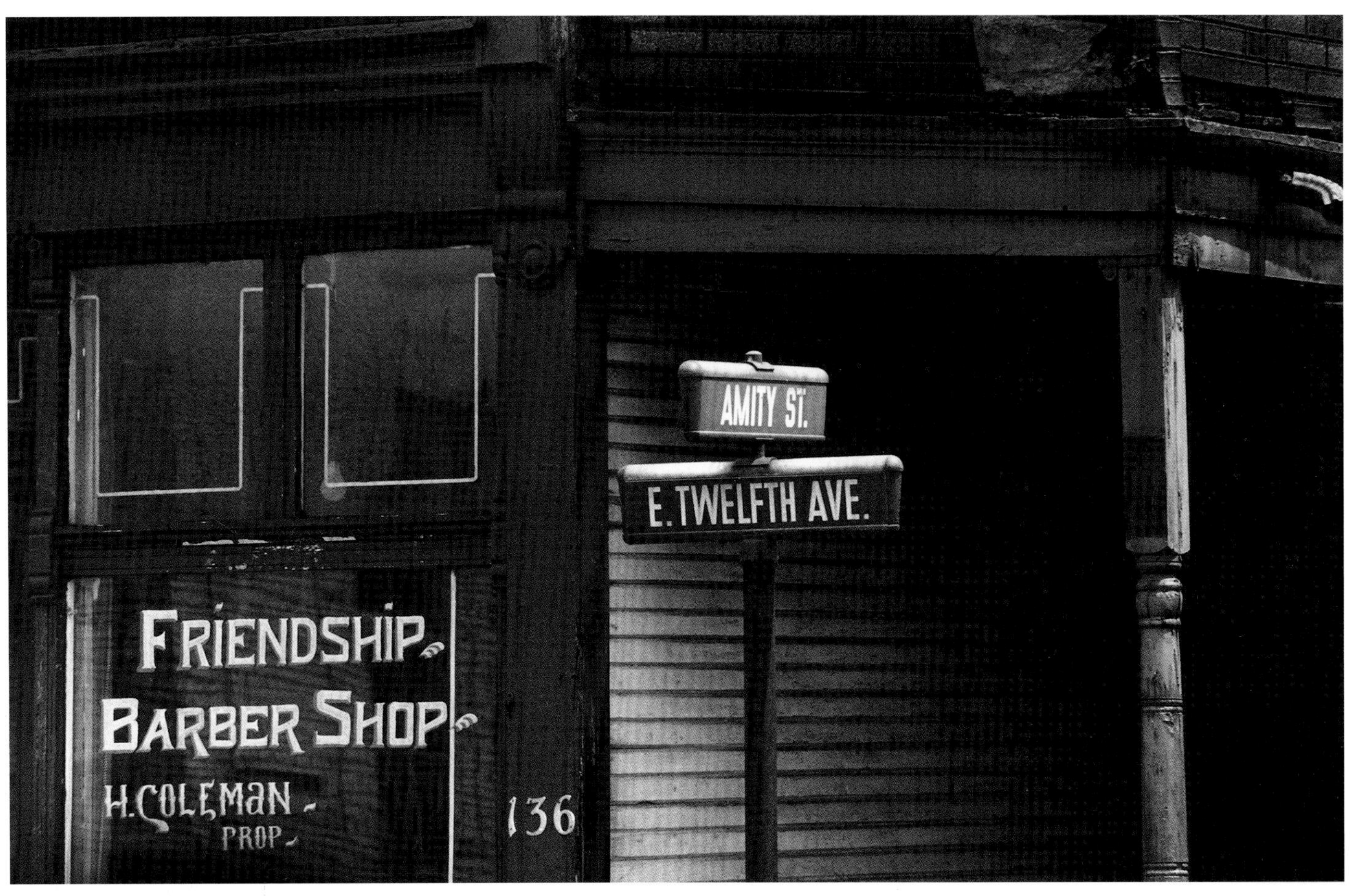


AMITY ST.
E. TWELFTH AVE.
FRIENDSHIP
BARBER SHOP
H. COLEMAN
PROP.
136


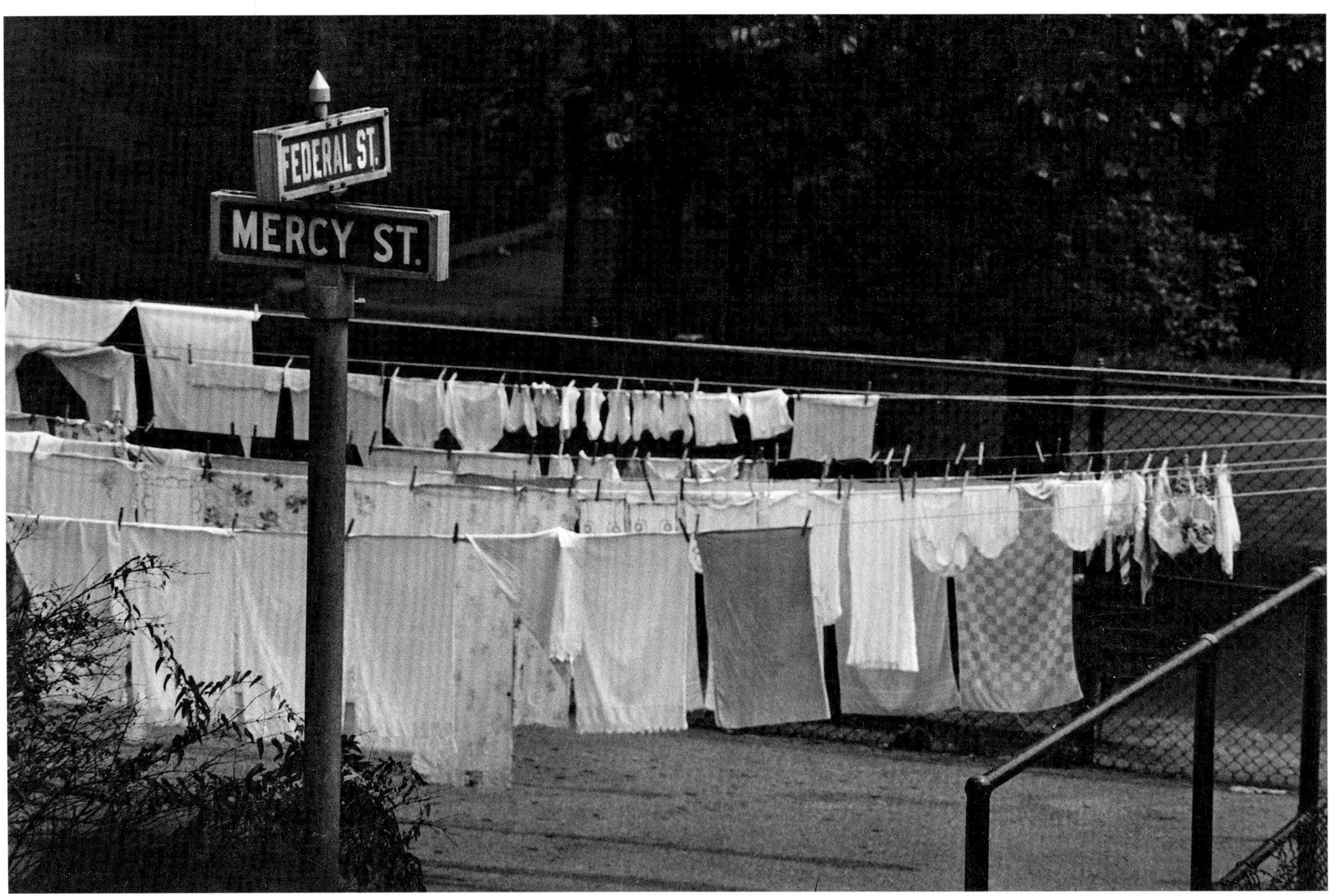


FEDERAL ST.
MERCY ST.

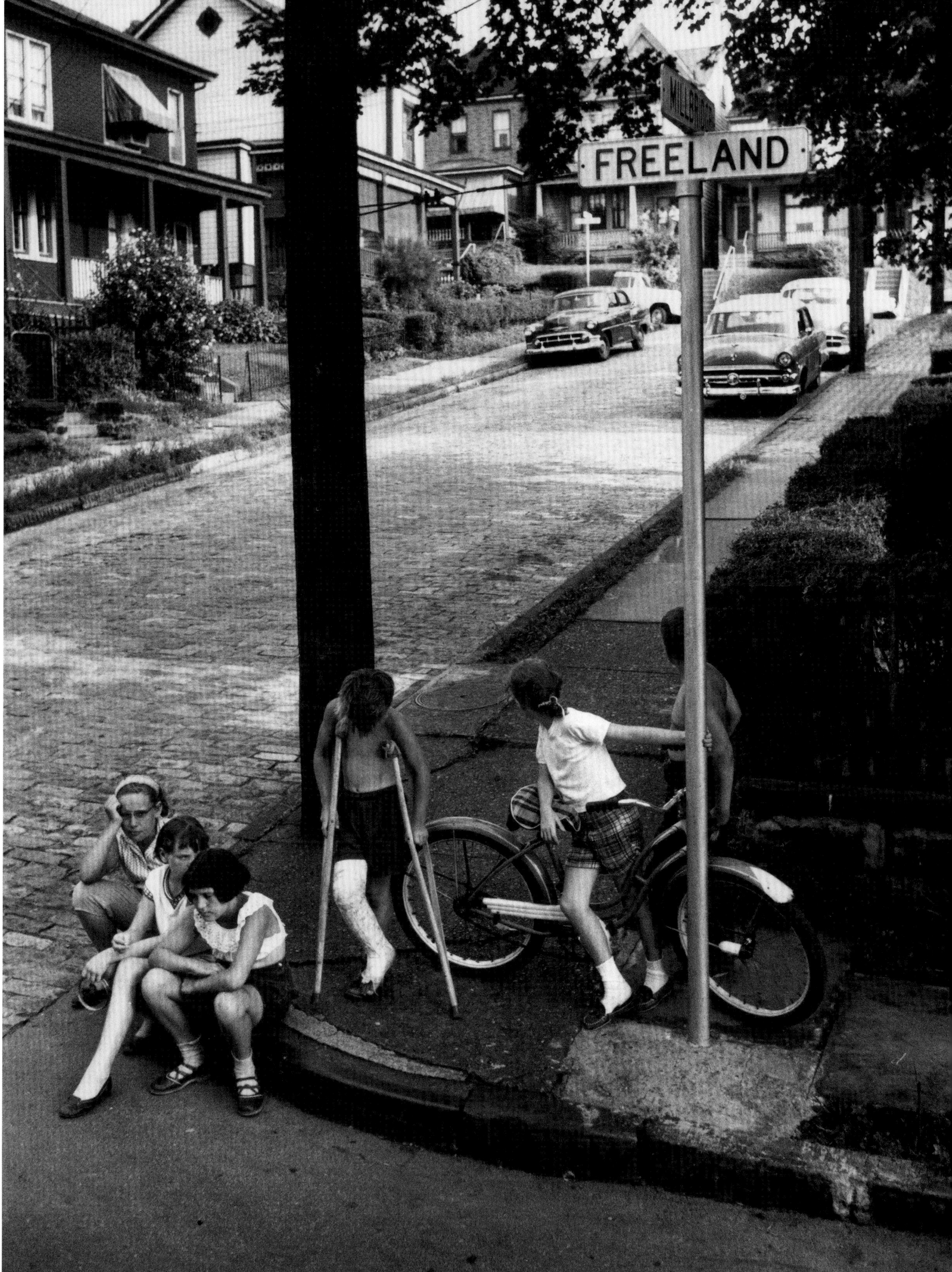
MILLBROOK
FREELAND

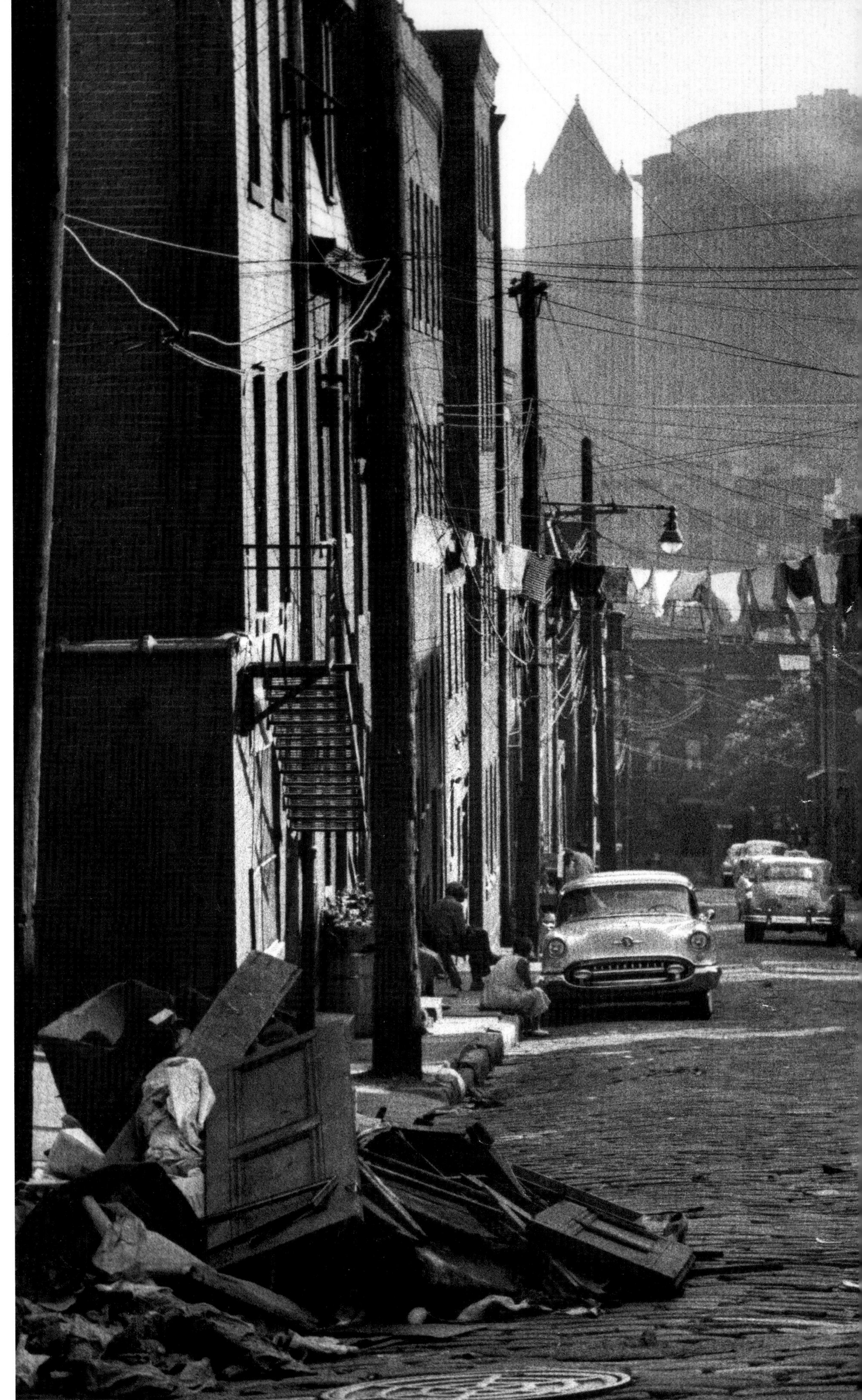

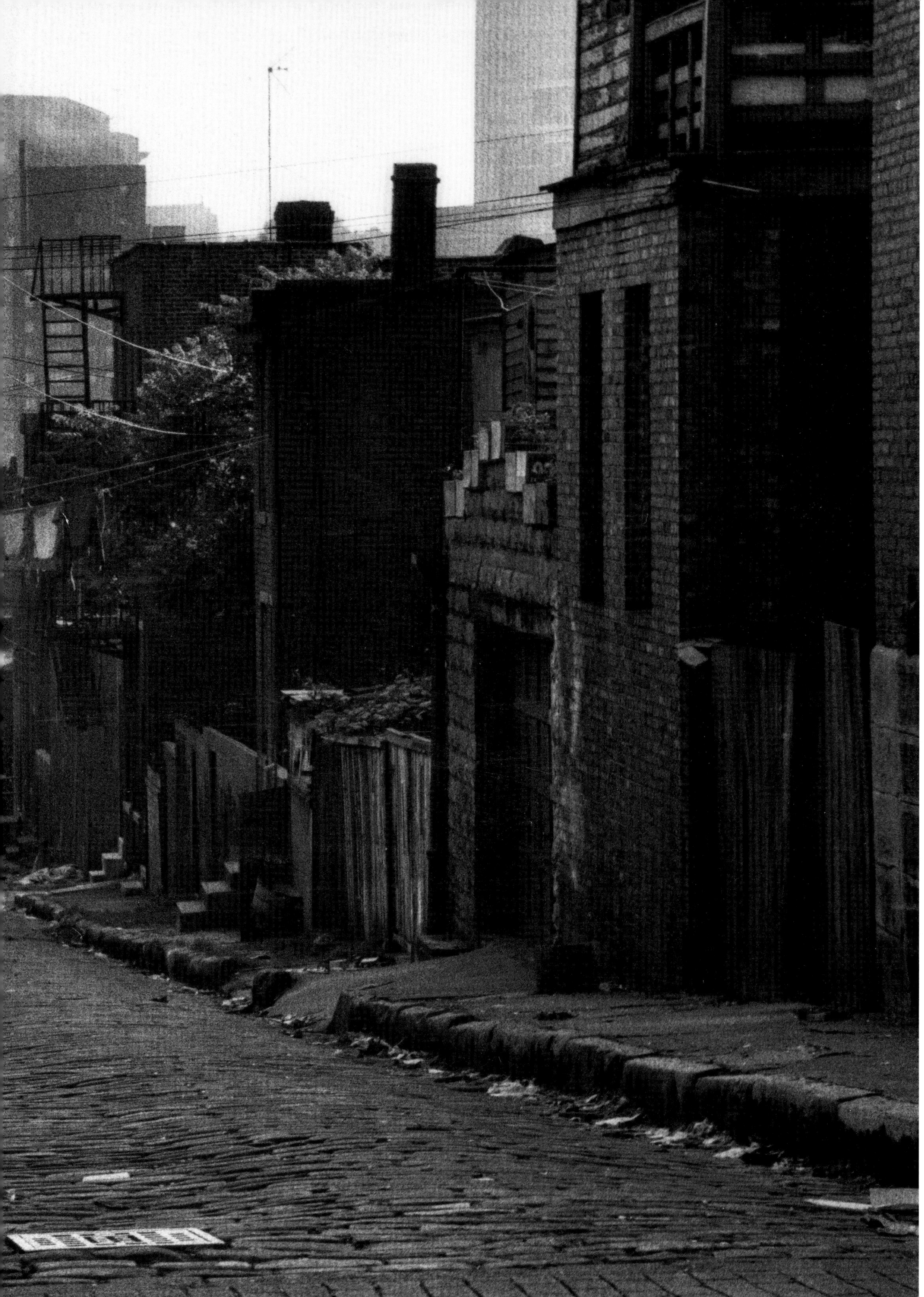

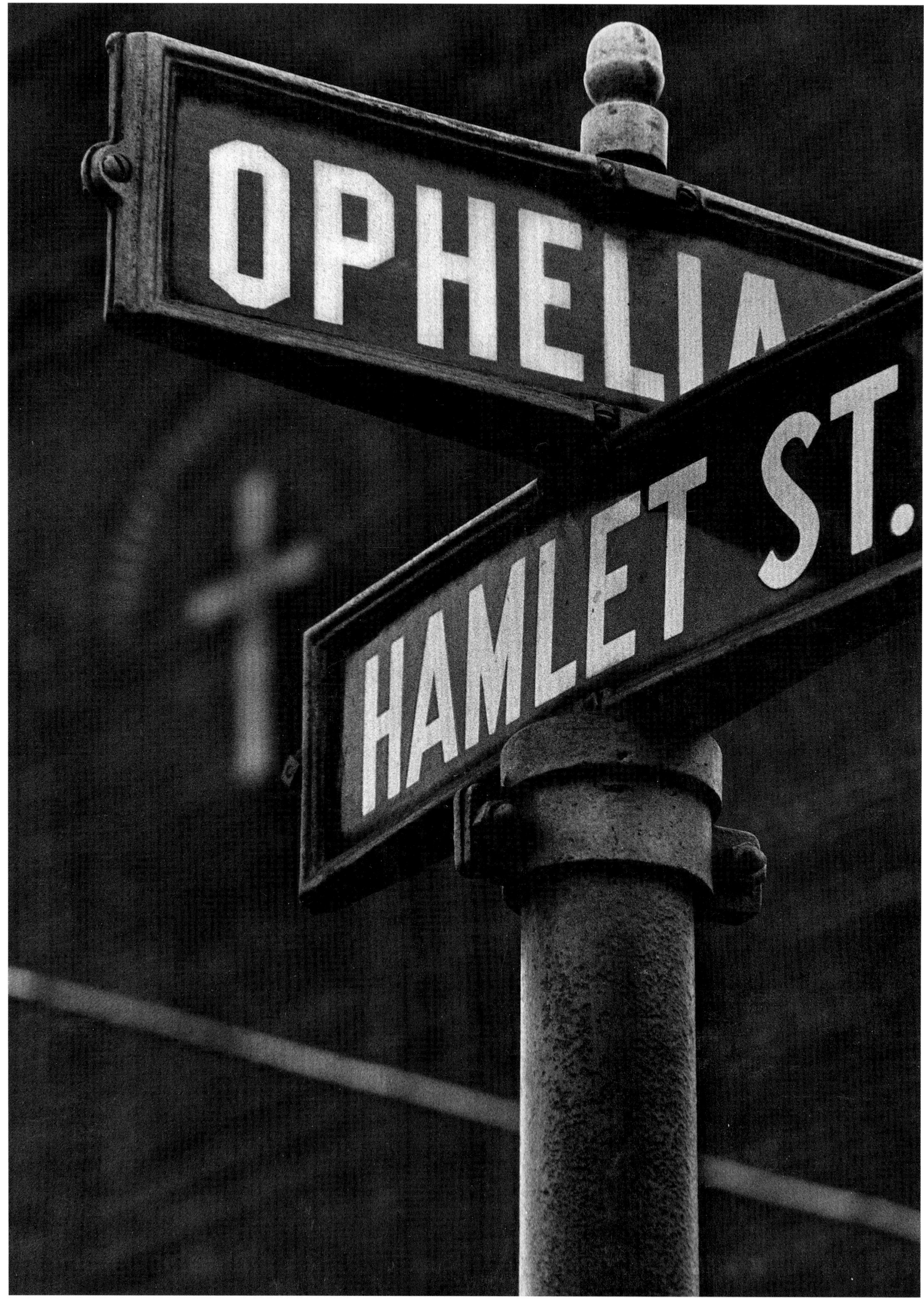

OPHELIA
HAMLET ST.

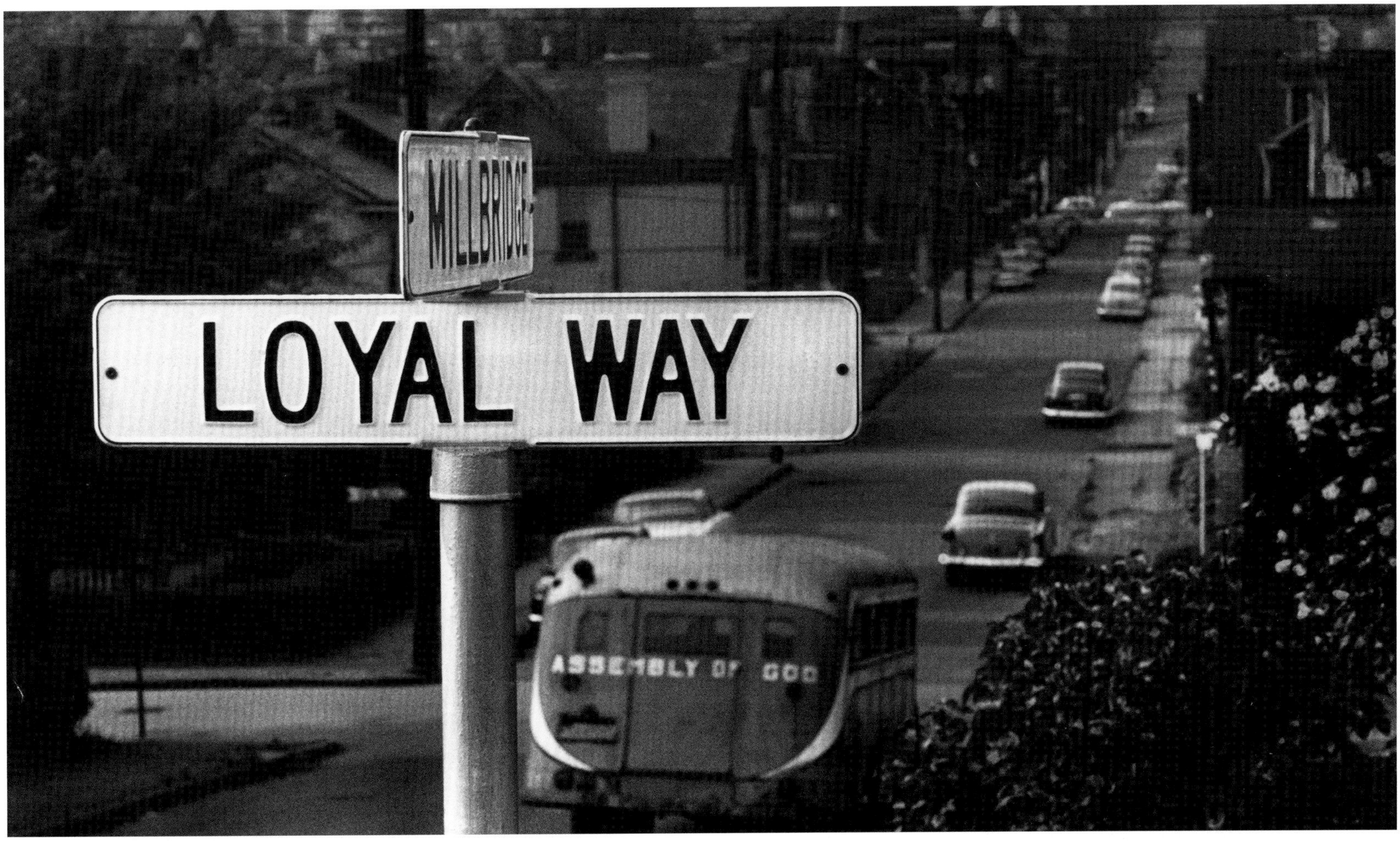

MILLBRIDGE
LOYAL WAY
ASSEMBLY OF GOD

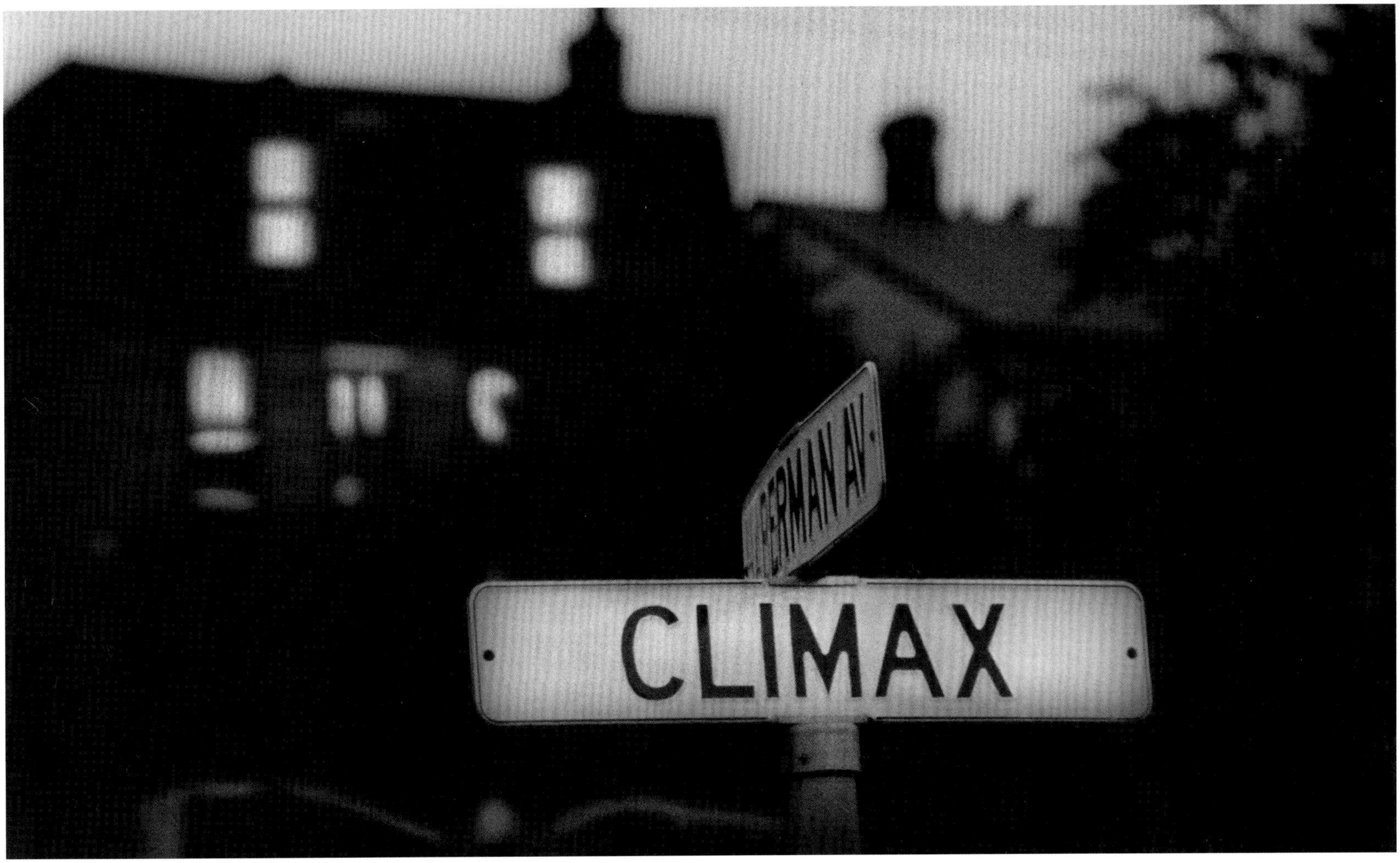

GERMAN AV
CLIMAX

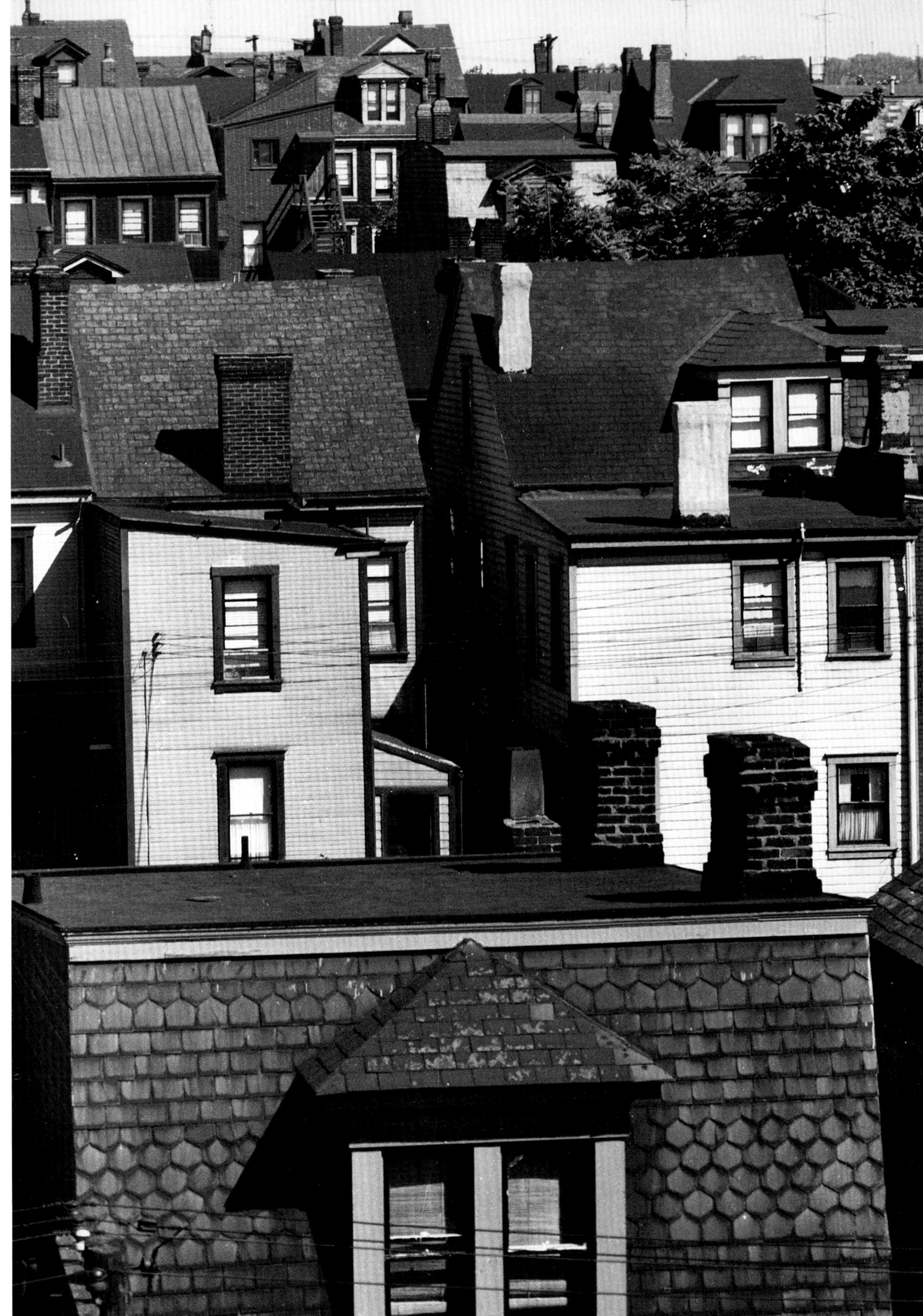

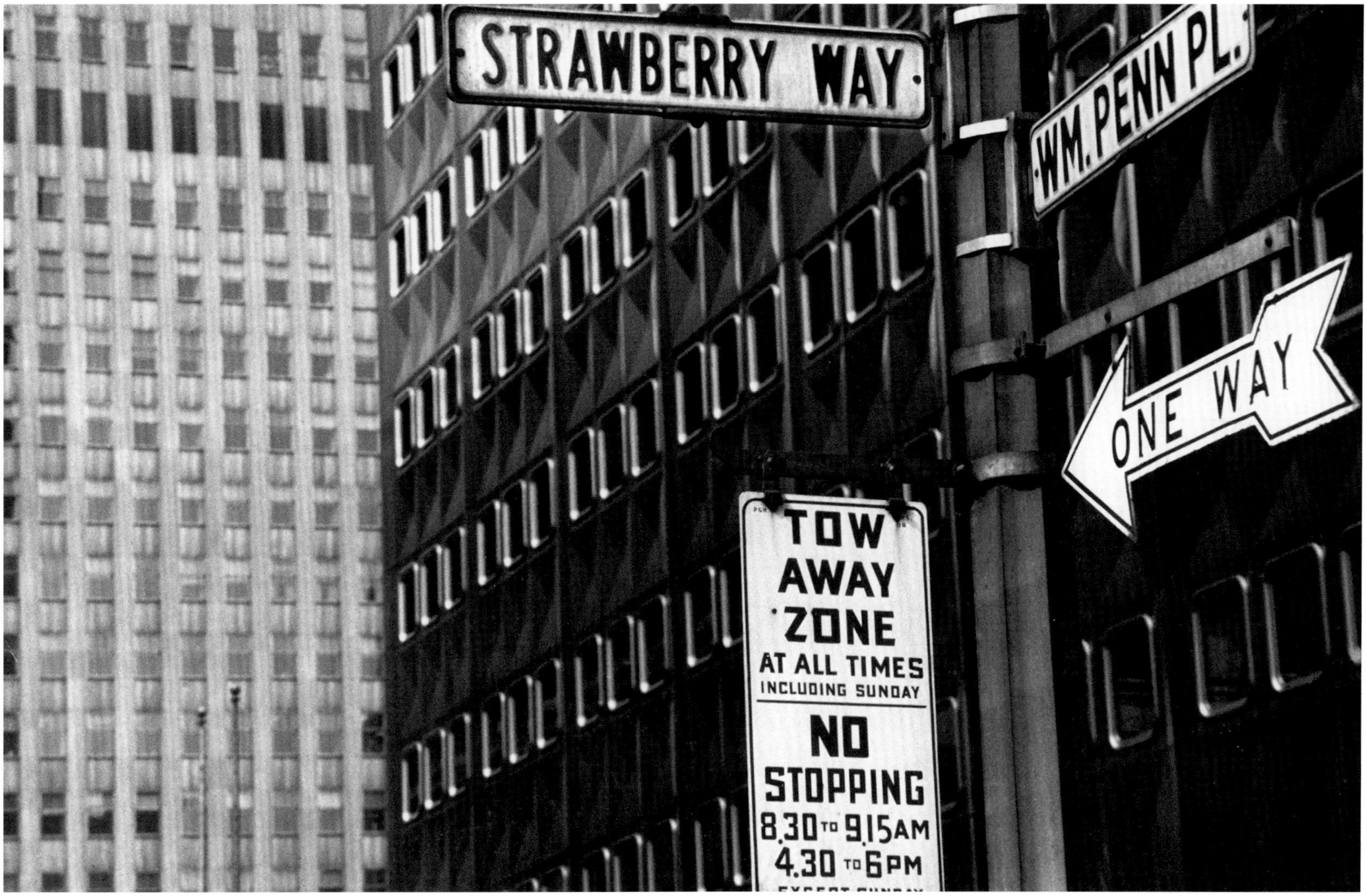

STRAWBERRY WAY
WM. PENN PL.
ONE WAY
TOW
AWAY
ZONE
AT ALL TIMES
INCLUDING SUNDAY
NO
STOPPING
8.30 TO 9.15 AM
4.30 TO 6 PM

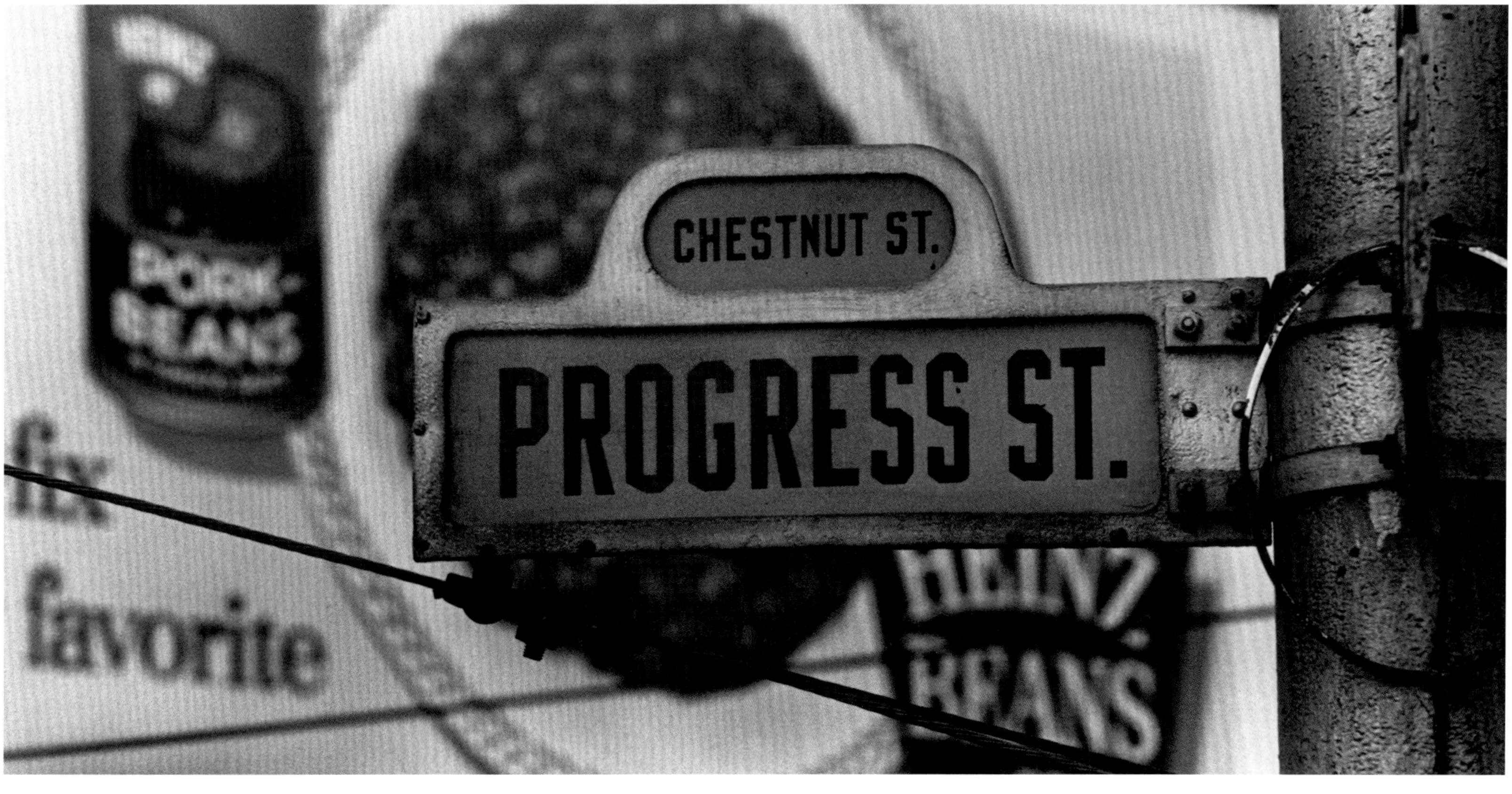

CHESTNUT ST.
PROGRESS ST.
fix
favorite
HEINZ
BEANS

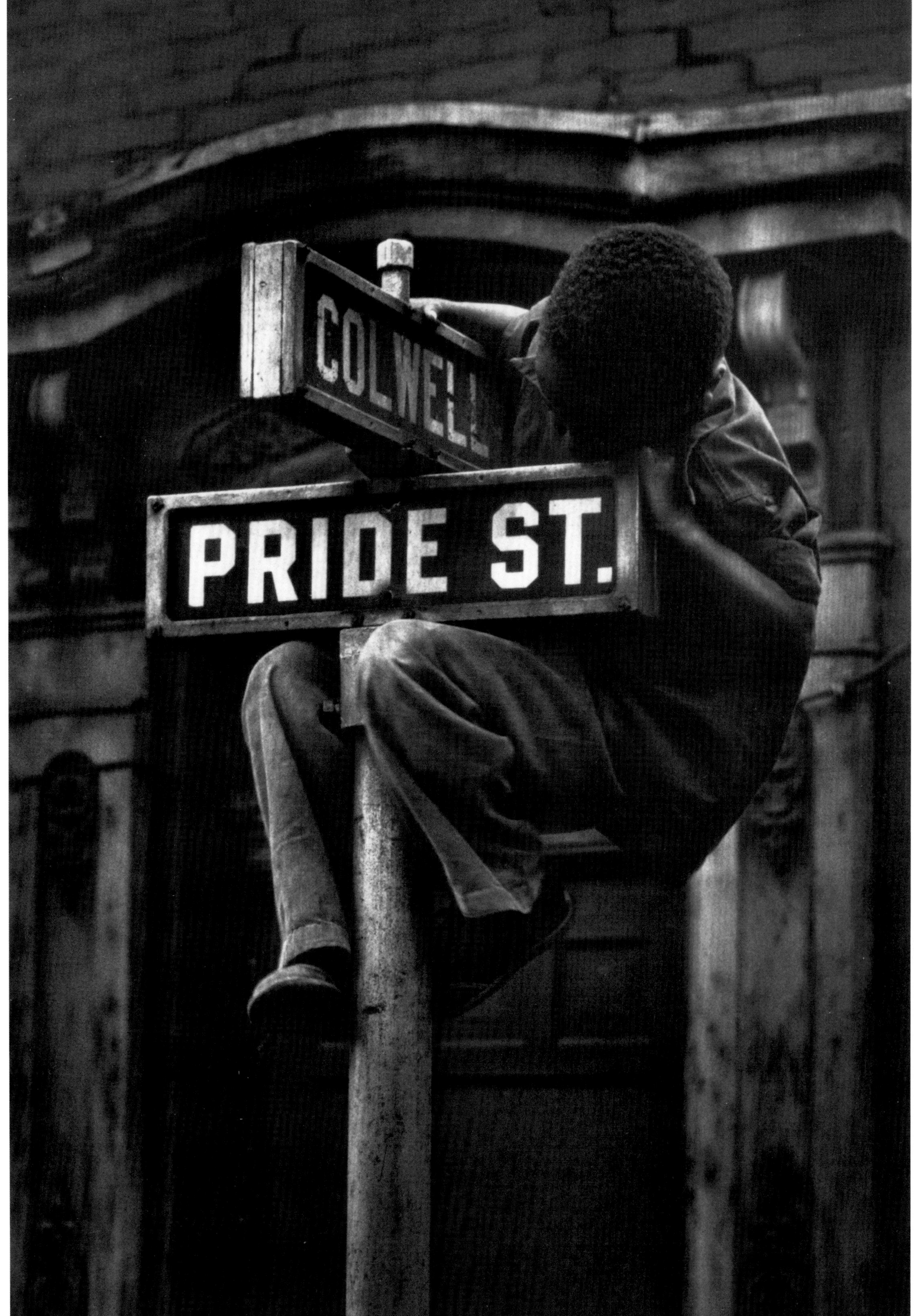
COLWELL
PRIDE ST.

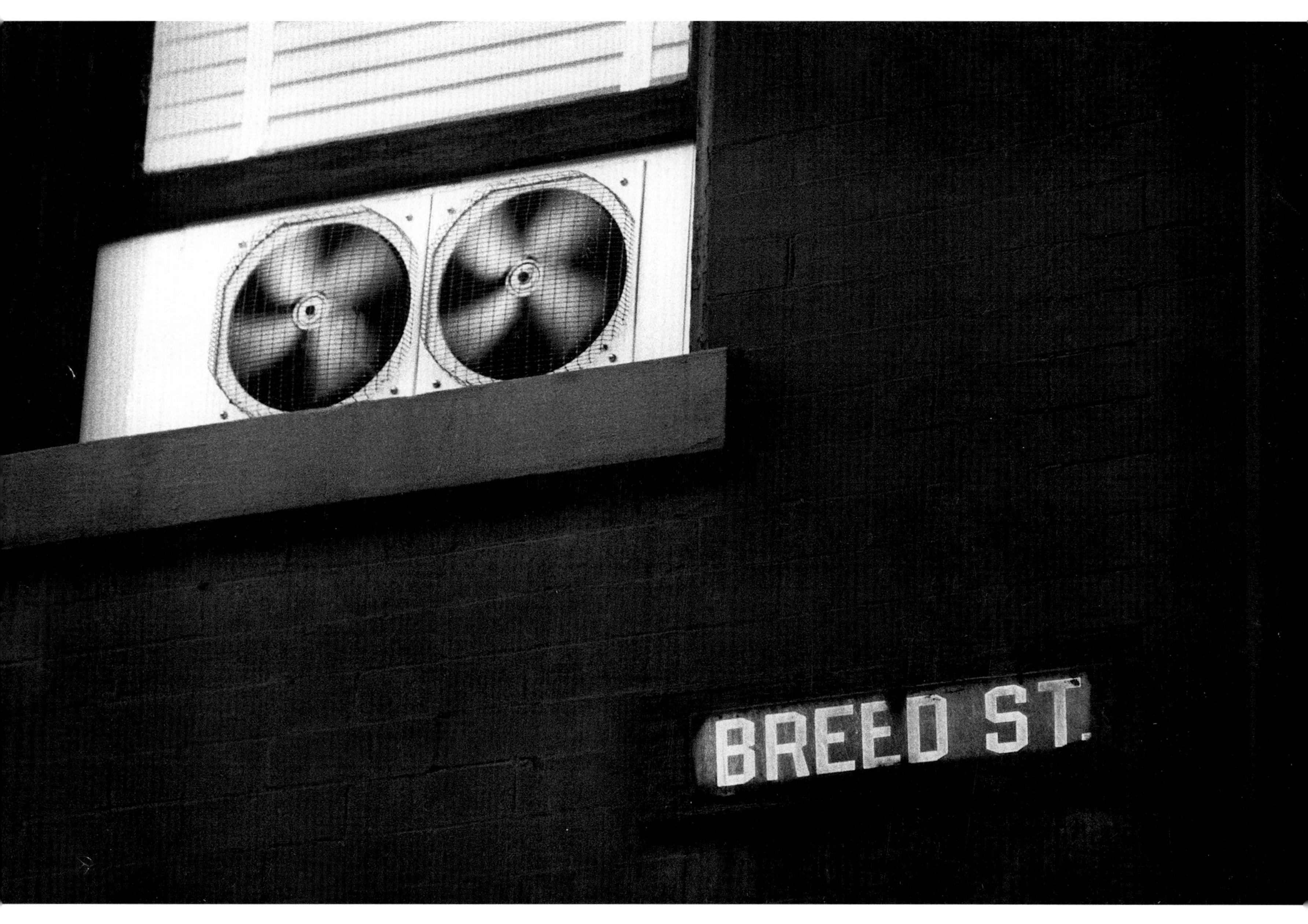
BREED ST.

June 23, 1958

Dear Uncle Jesse,

I have been sitting here just staring. How, once again, to letter a sheet of paper with words that just sit sunk in my seemingly eternal sad song muck.

A few hours ago I finished as best I could in trying to patch up the word part of a long essay. The seemingly eternal, certainly infernal, Pittsburgh project—the sagging, losing effort to make the first of its publication forms so right in measure to the standards I had set for it that its publication would create the historical precedent allowing me to truly start the climb back into human shape and away from the condition of ashes within ashes. I remain—ashes within ashes. And weeks more desperately tired, and my own effort destroyed through my own failure at being able to both ward off the eager buzzards of bedevilment, and to have the stamina and the creative effort living enough to carry through to the completion. And whatever the hells I was sitting on and no matter the how of my distractions by and against the buzzards—all of bedevilment is no excuse. Having fought through four years trying to do, then to protect, then publish this version precisely my way—and having gained the direct right, although against time, I very bluntly could not work my way through the onslaughts with enough workable strength to complete it right.

So———it is a failure, and blunts my chances of recovering, for there will be no precedent working for me, there isn't the physical strength necessary, there isn't . . . a chance???? I don't know—I have infinite patience to try again, continue to try, that is—and how far can the lame and unfreshened horse continue to gallop, no matter the fiber of his courage?

. . . Whatever else, this past week ended the Pittsburgh era of attention—whatever else . . . yes . . . whatever else, and whatever is the residue from its trials and from its failure.

So, let us ride with the sign of the crossed fingers. I'll do my best to see you Monday. I'll even shave, and bring a smile.

Gene


Letter from Smith to Jesse Caplinger

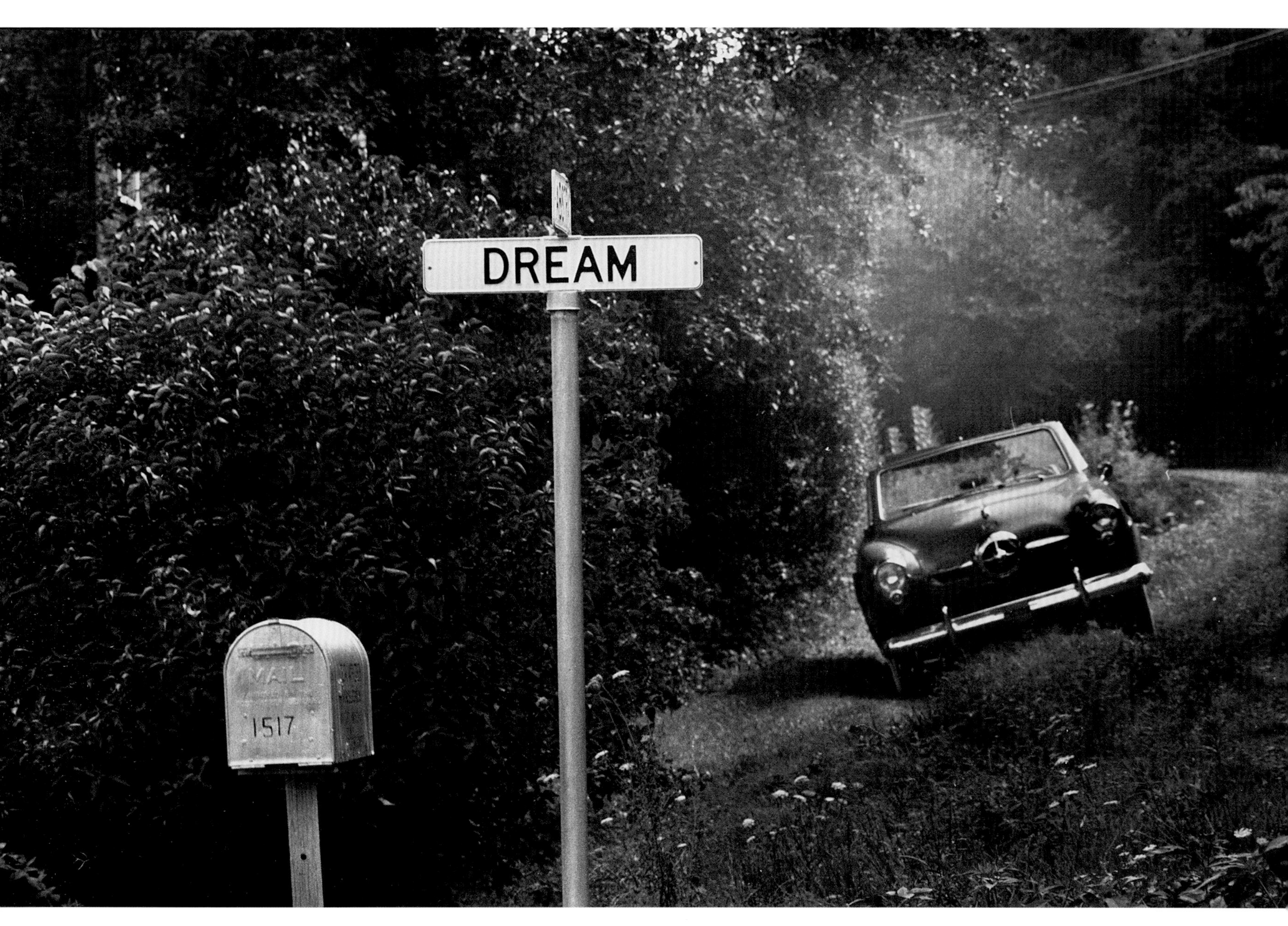

DREAM
MAIL
1517

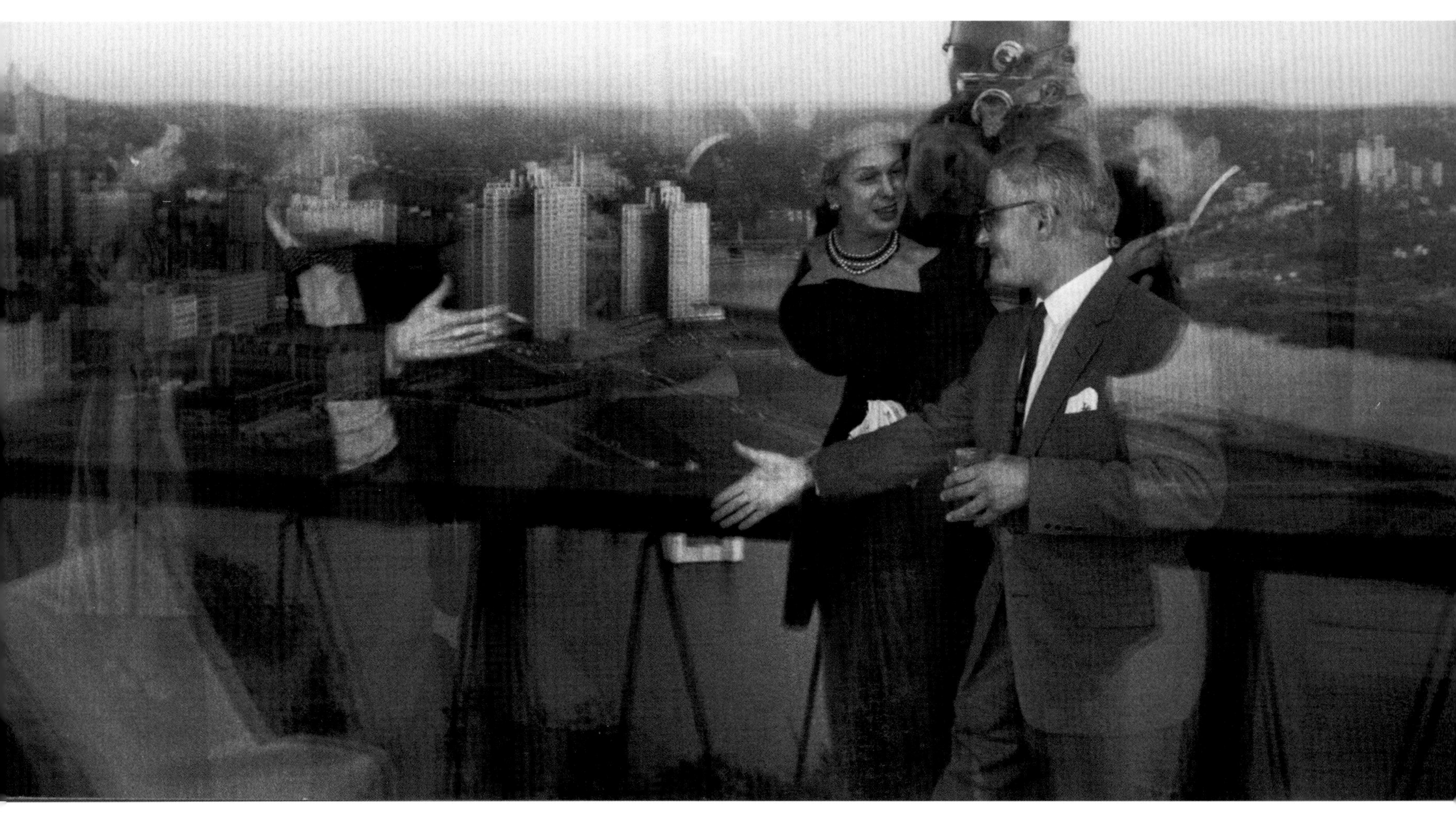

# "MAN-BREAKING CITY": W. EUGENE SMITH'S PITTSBURGH

BY ALAN TRACHTENBERG

W. EUGENE SMITH went to Pittsburgh in 1955 asking for trouble. He came to the city on a simple or at least finite job: to make a group of pictures for a volume on the history of the city edited by Stefan Lorant. From early in the twentieth century Pittsburgh had fascinated photographers, its steel mills, smokestacks, bridges, hillsides covered with wooden frame houses. Smith's assignment would give him a place among a small group of outsiders who came and went, like Lewis Hine, Alvin Langdon Coburn, Margaret Bourke-White, E. O. Hoppe, Edward Weston, and a remarkable insider who deserves to be better known, the local street photographer of the 1930s, Luke Swank; they all contributed to the popular image of Pittsburgh as a rough, tough, hard-working city of few amenities and pleasures (Brodsky and Benedict-Jones, 146–54). But Smith had another plan in mind. It had little to do with Pittsburgh as such.

"Let it be clear," he wrote in February 1956 to John Morris of Magnum, the agency that had arranged the contract with Lorant, "that from that first breakfast I had an essay—for itself, and as a tool against *Life*—as my driving ends, regardless of my conscientious respect for my obligations to the needs of Lorant" (Maddow, 58). Driven as it were by his own private imp of the perverse, he conspired with himself to take all of Pittsburgh as subject for a hitherto-untried photo-essay of epic proportion; he would photograph the city as if it were a single collective person, "the city as a living entity" (1956 Guggenheim application). With such ambitions, how could he sit still for the Lorant assignment? Smith fated himself to undergo Pittsburgh as an ordeal and to watch helplessly as it ended, in his words, as "debacle" (Johnson, 9).

As a photographer and magazine editor in Germany in the 1920s, Lorant had pioneered in shaping the photo-essay as a vehicle for "human interest" reportage of everyday life. Lorant was in a sense "father" of the kind of photojournalism Smith practiced, adding an ironic twist to the conflicts that ensued in Pittsburgh (e.g., over first-publication rights) (Hughes, 354–361). What Lorant wanted from Smith in Pittsburgh was "to show life at present." His list of subjects (a loose "script") included "Steel industry," "Nationalities and their clubs," "Libraries," "Life on the river," "Life in parks," and "Department stores" (Smith's pictures indeed fall in general under the twenty-five such headings). Lorant himself designed rather pedestrian layouts for Smith's pictures in the final chapter, "Rebirth," a narrative by Democratic Mayor David Lawrence, of the alliance between big business and government.

"One morning looking out of a window, I wondered what the hell I was doing in Pittsburgh. Mine was no love affair with this city, and I felt no crusade for the Mellons to give me cause and desire" (Maddow, 57). Apart from his driving wish to produce something that would justify his break with *Life,* the tenor of the Lorant project, its commitment to praise and celebration, seemed an increasing irritant to Smith. "After all," he commented in an interview in April 1977, shortly before his death in 1978, "Pittsburgh was proud of itself, for the strides it had made against pollution. That's the reason why I photographed it with all the smoke—because men's miracles are seldom perfect, and they were calling the salvation of Pittsburgh 'a miracle'" (Hill and Cooper, 270). Lorant published about fifty of Smith's pictures in the "Rebirth" chapter, but there's no record of what he thought of them, whether he detected sarcasm about "miracle," or scorn toward the "crusade for the Mellons," or the absence of love. "It was a cold place and I photographed it coldly," Smith remarked in 1977.

For all its rhetoric of "rebirth" the Pittsburgh process of demolition and rebuilding obeyed a cold-hearted commercial vision in the first place. Richard King Mellon, scion of the wealthiest banking family in the city (and country) and a powerful corporate leader, founded the Allegheny Conference on Community Development (ACCD) as early as 1943, foreseeing a coming crisis in the city's future; deterioration of the environment threatened the downtown business district and the economic competitiveness of the region as a whole. The ACCD fostered a coalition between business and government, specifically between Mellon and Democratic Mayor David Lawrence, the principal players who "precipitated," in the words of historian Roy Lubove, "a dramatic expansion of public enterprise and investment to serve corporate needs; it established a reverse welfare state" (Lubove, 106). The aim was to use "public power or investment to promote private economic ends," thus shaping the Pittsburgh Renaissance as a revival less of the city as a whole, all its neighborhoods and all its citizens, than of the wealth of its private sector and the sightliness (for the sake of a logo) of its skyline (Lubove, 111). Low-cost housing was among its most glaring neglects (Lubove, 130). Viewed from within the city, managerial indifference took its toll, as we see in wide-angle juxtapositions Smith made yoking derelict regions of the city with the sleek corporate towers of the Golden Triangle, the center viewed from the perspective of squalid residential areas. Visible contradictions of "rebirth" and "miracle" infuse his pictures with what can only be called hysteria. "Hysteria," writes Lincoln Kirstein, "the enemy of nihilism, a clean suggestion that things have gotten out of hand, smolders in Smith's most memorable prints" (Kirstein, np). Things have gotten out of hand: a nice epigraph for W. Eugene Smith's Pittsburgh.

One goal of the ACCD was to inform and educate the public and the wider world about the Pittsburgh "rebirth." What better instrument than photography? In 1950 the committee invited Roy Stryker to conduct a photographic survey of the changing city. Once director of the famous 1930s Farm Security Administration (FSA) documentary photographic project and presently head of a similar corporate project at the Standard Oil Company, Stryker enlisted a crew including Esther Bubley, Arnold Eagle, Sol Libsohn, Russell Lee, Eliot Erwitt, Clyde Hare, and Richard Saunders, which came and went and in about three years created the Pittsburgh Photographic Library (PPL) of some 30,000 images. An image library fit perfectly the ACCD concept of "rebirth" as civic improvement; pictures were culled for local exhibitions, brochures, books such as Lorant's, and stories about the "miracle" in *Life* and *Fortune* (Schulz and Plattner, 3–26). A selection of PPL pictures, published recently as *Witness to the Fifties* (1999), shows the Stryker documentary ethos and aesthetic with perfect clarity; indeed, clarity of vision emerges as its most striking feature. Typically made with large-format cameras under conditions of light chosen by the photographer to show the scene with utmost visibility and sharpness of focus, the pictures convey a sense of quiet, of distance and detachment and undisturbed emotion. Without angst or signs of violated holiness in the landscape, most of these Pittsburgh pictures please the eye with a quiet beauty of facticity, splendid "documents" of what a camera lens can see and record at this place and time. Does it go too far to say that their cool documentary style plays a bit too comfortably like a song to the beneficence of big business, of the "reverse welfare state" by which Pittsburgh achieved a new image and its poorest inhabitants the same old raw deal? The Stryker collection stands in relief, in any case, to Smith's rage of images, paid for (he said somewhere) by the lining of his stomach. Smith's small-format Pittsburgh pictures made a year or two after the Stryker project seem by contrast like molten emotion poured from an open cauldron. His experience of Pittsburgh, while in one sense "cold," in another burns with conflict: a struggle of light and dark, light struggling to free itself from the serpent of darkness. "I like pictures that surmount the darkness," he said in the 1977 interview (Hill and Cooper, 263).

An obsession threatening to spiral out of control, Pittsburgh didn't end for Smith; it just stopped, broke down, an act as arbitrary as its beginning. "To portray a city is beyond ending," he confessed in the opening paragraph of his 1959 publication, "Labyrinthian Walk"; "to begin such an effort is itself a grave conceit." At best the result will be "a rumor of a city, as meaningful and as permanent" (Smith, 99). Rumor, clamor, din: a gargantuan fragment survives, 17,000 negatives and hundreds of work prints, one of the most haunting monuments to an unrealized intention in the history of photography. An overgrown field of negatives and images and pieces of texts, some fiercely lucid, some densely occluded, they simply constitute W. Eugene Smith's Pittsburgh: a testimony to the presence of man and camera, to the drivenness of his desire to make his being there known in light surmounting darkness in pictures. Smith had come to Pittsburgh with his demons in high gear; one feels them in the fraught darkness and noir ambiance of the pictures. Usually dismissed (especially by Smith himself) as a botch, a stop-gap measure, "Labyrinthian Walk" nevertheless reveals something important of Smith's unique gifts as a historian of his times, driven, as Lincoln Kirstein has written, "to capture what he'd actually lived" (Kirstein, np). Unsuccessful as it is, the scale of the pictures especially inadequate to carry the difficult dialectical message of the prose, "Labyrinthian Walk" reveals an intention, the form of a vision in process.

Throughout the Pittsburgh project, the shooting, printing, testing of alternate layouts, Smith held to the goal of an "essay—for itself," as if bearing a fragile chalice before him. He might have arranged the pictures in sequence in a book, as his friend Robert Frank was doing in the same years (*The Americans* appeared in 1958). But this alternative probably never occurred to Smith. Remarks he made about Frank and photojournalism in the 1977 interview help explain the hold of the photo-essay upon his imagination, as well as his difference from Stryker's crew of large-format documentists. While "photojournalism is documentary photography with a purpose," he says, the word "documentary" can do mischief by giving people the wrong idea that the outside or surface of things is enough for a picture: "it can give some people the idea that you can make absolutely dull pictures of the ingredients of something instead of the heart of something" (Hill and Cooper, 258). Along with superficial photography, photography of surfaces, there's also highly personal photography, like Frank's. "A journalist has to thoroughly understand the subject and you have to interpret that subject, keeping true to what it is." Frank "photographs only for himself," which, he adds, "is fine" (Hill and Cooper, 271).

The distinction has the force of singling out what makes "essay" indispensable for Smith. It's a mode of understanding, of knowledge, of coherent interpretation; it links artist-journalist to world and to audience. "An essay has to be thought out, with each picture in relation to the others, the same way you would write an essay. Perhaps the writing of a play comes closer" (Hill and Cooper, 266).

The importance of "essay" was its vision of coherence, its promise of meaning. "Essay," too, holds nihilism at bay, the encroaching pools of darkness which threatens to swallow light in many of the Pittsburgh pictures. "Essay" gives proof of the artist's victory over the disequilibrium of Pittsburgh's money-driven "rebirth" of the 1950s, industrial capitalism putting on a new clean hard-edged face, leaving the core of misery and desecration untouched.

In a letter in 1954 Smith spelled out a credo of the "essay" as a form of intelligence.

> The gravest responsibility of the photo historian or journalist is the search through the maze of conflictions to the island of intimate understanding, of the mind, of the soul, amid circumstances that both create, and are created by—and then to render with intelligence, with artistic eloquence, a correct and breathing account of what is found; and popular fancy, myth can be damned. Meaning: get to the guts of matter and show the bastards as they are (Maddow, 54).

Smith was not a reformer in the mold of Lewis Hine, his greatest precursor in Pittsburgh, who in collaboration with progressive social scientists and economists showed industrial and domestic conditions that cried out for change (Stange, 47–88; Trachtenberg, 164–230). But reform, the re-forming of consciousness by recognition of the truths of human existence at this time and place, had been even before Pittsburgh the inner need satisfied (sometimes frustrated) by his photo-stories for *Life* (Willumson, passim). Pittsburgh was his chance to raise the ante, to show what the essay form might accomplish in way of grandness of subject and greatness of theme. Grand and grandiose, yes, and individualistic: but the furthest from mere ambition or egotism.

Smith cracked under the pressure of Pittsburgh in part because he made ultimate demands on the possibilities of the essay form as a vehicle of high individualist art. What had attracted him to the job offered by Lorant was not the precise assignment, "to show life at present," but a much weightier conception: "The relationship of industrial to man, theme and counter-theme through the history of such a city, can be a wonderful challenge" (Maddow, 55). What he wanted was, in short, the opportunity to produce a major interpretive work, a treatise-sized essay on man, machine, and society. Lurking in the background was surely his experience (including the shattering of his own body) of mechanized violence in World War II. With its blast furnaces menacing sky, air, and workers, its polluted air and begrimed landscape, Pittsburgh would have seemed the perfect place to investigate "theme and counter-theme" of American industrial power, its dark Satanic metal-making mills which forged the great war machines of 1917 and the 1940s, in the process desecrating nature and the human spirit. The Pittsburgh assignment seemed Smith's chance for a major cumulative statement about the history of his times, of what he had actually lived. He described his work there as "participation rather than observation. The antithesis of mere reaction." He saw himself engaged in a "de-veiling of the mysteries." "I have not been content," he wrote, "to remain merely a 'seeing' photographer." In Smith's private writings during his Pittsburgh agon flows the passion of a visionary; hysteria drives his need to be a "symbolization of the universal" (Hughes, 363).

Although faithful to Lorant's script in regard to subject-matter, he was less interested in documentation in the usual sense than in something more personal, in a poetry more of his own soul than of the place as such, certainly not celebration of "rebirth" or anything as deceptively straightforward as "information." Smith sought the city as a "living entity," as if a fictive character in its own right. "I will not, this time, (photographically) know any individual as a complete person," he wrote at the outset of the project. "For the individual, in my present essay, is a part of the teaming into the teeming whole that is the city, singular—and Pittsburgh, the City of, is my project and is the individual to be known." In many ways he himself is the figure who represents the city: himself in the act of portraying and "essaying" the city, captured often in self-portraits on reflecting surfaces in that very act. He also speaks of "the people who give the structural image of static stone and bracing steel the facts of heart and pulse" (Maddow, 56).

Like Lewis Hine, who preceded him in the mills and streets of Pittsburgh by almost fifty years, Smith kept an eye on labor, the "pulse" which brings the city's stone and steel to life. Unlike Hine, however, he purposefully diminishes the role of people as individuals. With few exceptions, he portrays his workers not in their individuality but as laboring bodies; in his magnificent, demonic pictures of steel-making, workers are abstract figures swathed in darkness, silhouetted against flame and smoke, faces averted. Smith's decision to seek knowledge of the city itself rather than of its individuals comes from his guiding insight, that to know a city means to take its people as integers or emblems, performers in the larger drama of his own experience. "A City Experienced; Pittsburgh, Pa.," he titled a collection of his proof sheets submitted for copyright in 1956. "Unlike other essays of mine such as The Nurse-Midwife," he wrote, "I will not know any individual as a complete person." The city itself "is the individual to be known."

Jim Hughes remarks about "Labyrinthian Walk" that "[w]hile the Pittsburgh essay was a powerful and accurate visual portrait of an industrial city in the throes of change, its greater significance lies in its being a symbolic rendering of the artist himself" (Hughes, 392). The number of self-portraits, portrayals of himself at work prowling the city with his camera, taking the light and dark as given, using a compass to note the fall of light at particular times and places so he could return there and recover his feeling at that place, suggests that like Baudelaire in Paris, Smith sought semblances of himself. The portrait of himself shooting a social gathering of well-heeled citizens through a plate-glass window which also reflects the skyline of the city behind him offers itself as symbol of his entire enterprise in Pittsburgh.

Drawn to tableaus and silhouettes rather than individuals, to spaces deep and shallow, fragmented into isolated parts, Smith conveys an experience of brokenness, aloneness, and mutilation, a place drained of nurturing emotion, where "love" and "dream" are mocking street signs. Faces are bored, indifferent, empty, as if accomodated in their own unimportance (as Ben Maddow remarks) within the order of Pittsburgh; some show signs of a rage about to vent a mad fury. Even the play of children seems often grim and strangely mechanical, crippled, joyless, empty of the spiritual adventure of childhood. His people perform their tasks, go about their routines, as if under the spell of the place where grudging labor dominates over the free expression of pleasure. Social distance, racial difference, a pattern of inclusion and exclusion, endanger the coherence and wholeness of the city as he experiences it. The new buildings give off signals of unchallenged corporate power; old stone baronial mansions loom like darkened wicked presences; the rickety homes of the poor cling precariously to hillsides, accessed by long steep wooden staircases. Their dark shadows and deep spaces bring contradiction into focus, and in the ambiguity of the small recorded dramas on streets and porches, Smith's pictures might be stills from an unedited film noir of the era. A weird nighttime beauty rises from the region of the mills, the unquenched fires of their furnaces, the shining railroad tracks snaking their way into mysterious recesses, shadows of workers tending the flames, a glimpse of an exhausted sweating face, a barge churning a roiling wake on the dark poisoned waters of the once lovely Monongahela river. The Golden Triangle and its sparkling lights seem far away, remote, another world. Ben Maddow is just in describing Smith's vision as of "a city that for all its mechanical energy lies soporific in its banal culture" (Maddow, 61). There is no exaltation in Smith's Pittsburgh.

"Labyrinthian Walk," a journey marked by narrow pathways and dead walls: the figure of "labyrinth" summarizes both his experiences of Pittsburgh and his gropings toward a formal expression of that experience. He spoke of "inter-weaving many photographic themes," each of which "could be individual photographic stories," but woven together, would project an epic totality, "gigantic and complex" (Johnson, 6). In other random notes he reached for literary analogies: in a letter to Minor White in 1956 he wrote, "Pittsburgh, in a special way—perhaps a Thomas Wolfe way . . . is the most complex photographic literature, and the richest in scope and depth of theme and characterization I have ever . . . well, wrought" (Johnson, 6). Drama was another analogy: "A comparison to the playwright probably comes closest to illustrating the way of my thinking in building a work," and claimed literary more than photographic precedents for his Pittsburgh ambition: "Photographic essays must reach beyond their realization as now achieved—it is imperative" (Johnson, 7). Music, too, was a constant and necessary source of inspiration about composition. The analogies—woven tapestry, novel, drama, musical statement of theme and counter-theme—all elicit a struggle toward a new form. Combining image and text in new ways, he would achieve a new "whole as a third medium" (Johnson, 9). Bringing to mind Sergei Eisenstein's theory of "montage," "third medium" suggests cinema as yet another analogy and inspiration.

Pittsburgh occasioned Smith's most extreme enactment of a pervasive modernist-romantic myth in the post–World War II period: the misunderstood male artist, driven to exceed all limits of previous art, prepared to destroy himself as testimony of his worth. Smith risked his soul in Pittsburgh, risked personal and professional wreckage that he seems to have courted as a form of perverse self-justification. Eventually the entire tortured experience seemed to him a fateful parable: the angelic artist doomed to suffer abuse and defeat. He invoked Icarus, son of Daedelus: "Mine would not be the first wings to melt near the sun" (Hughes, 358). In the excruciating four years of shooting, printing, struggling to resolve thousands of Pittsburgh images into one perfect and unchangeable design of image and text, Smith often likened himself to the boy who flew too close to the sun, a mythic role which would turn bitterly prophetic as one publisher after another refused him the autonomy he demanded. "Other than that, Icarus," he mordantly quipped, "how was the flight?" (Hughes, 392). In the end Smith saw Pittsburgh as "debacle," and his obsession a "wry and tragi-comic satire of my whole intent" (Johnson, 9). But he won something as well, something glimpsed even in the flawed "Labyrinthian Walk." Pittsburgh, he more soberly reflected, was "an extraordinarey experience," and "the resultant set of pictures is (in its own way), the finest set of photographs I have ever produced" (Maddow, 194).

Smith's idiosyncrasies, his inner voices, his self-destructive impulses, belong as much to the age as to his personal history. The apparent ease of living and social tranquility of the 1950s disguised underlying tensions about to erupt in the revulsions of the next decade, and in his Pittsburgh pictures Smith caught glimpses of a world at odds with orthodox versions of American reality. Pittsburgh materialized for him as a composite symbol of volcanic forces beneath the placid façade of the times, "a turbulent debate," he put it in the opening text of "Labyrinthian Walk," "teeming evolution within the equilibrium of paradox" (Smith, 99). Too colossal a symbol, he came to realize, too much for one frail man driven to witness with his own eyes the outer edges of his horizon of nightmare. What he finally put into print in 1959 was a mere handful of the two to three hundred images boiled down from the two thousand he had selected for the much grander unrealized "essay," an admission of personal limits, and of exhaustion beyond describing, but still, the hint of a more complex, richer symphonic coherence that remains immanent in the collection from which this volume is drawn.

The 1959 publication embodies a predicament of the times, the challenge to eye and mind of a new enigmatic social landscape coming into view in the 1950s. The sense of hidden menace Smith infuses into the essay clarifies what Kirstein means when he speaks of Smith as uniquely "attuned to his time." Smith lived the inner tensions of the history of his times with an intensity rare (though not unknown) among his peers, including poets, jazz musicians, filmmakers, and "action" painters. His gift was that he was able with the camera to give adequate expression of his experiences, true accounts of what he actually lived. Kirstein ranked him with Brady, Atget, and Cartier-Bresson as historians, major interpreters of their day.

"Labyrinthian Walk" discloses an intention, a walk in search of a historical Pittsburgh commensurate with the artist's experience of paradox, the coexistence, as in the opening triad of images, of education for war (the ROTC troops parading in a park), love (a mere street sign, a shadowed cliché), and a figure of paradox itself, the tightly-framed close-up of the head of a steelworker, his helmet a black halo, his goggles reflecting the explosive burst of fire from a furnace. An image of blindness, or of preternatural vision? Hell or redemption? In an interview late in his life Smith said of this ambiguous opening image: "I wanted to show that the worker was fairly well submerged beneath the weight of industry; the anonymity of the worker's goggles and factory behind him told the story. Still, I did not want the worker to be entirely lost as a human being" (Kobre, np). The three opening images, Smith explained, establish themes which play together as counterpoint in the rest of the essay.

The opening image suggests yet another reading, not contradictory but supplemental: an identity of worker and artist, Daedalian figures linked fatefully to fire (light); their eyes burn like frightful furnaces. Daedalus's most famous artifice was, of course, the labyrinth, a maze of winding passages and blind alleys at the heart of which brooded the monstrous Minotaur, half-man, half-bull, who demanded the tribute of human sacrifices. No one who crossed the threshold of the maze had hope of escaping the beast's looming jaws. Eventually, clutching Ariadne's thread to secure his way out, Theseus slew the beast and freed the city of the scourge. Earlier, according to myth, Daedelus himself had contrived an escape, but at a cost. Of feathers and wax he fashioned wings for himself and his son Icarus, who ventured too near the sun. "Other than that, Icarus, how was the flight?" Smith suffered Pittsburgh as an Icarian debacle. The ordeal also delivered a Daedelian triumph. Dipped in the acid of rueful perception of an unregenerate world, the best pictures give witness to what he called finally, unconsciously evoking Minotaur, "the man-breaking city" (Maddow, 61).


WORKS CITED

Hill, Paul, and Thomas Cooper, eds. *Dialogue with Photography.* New York: Farrar, Straus, Giroux, 1979.

Hughes, Jim. *W. Eugene Smith. Shadow and Substance: The Life and Work of an American Photographer.* New York: McGraw-Hill, 1989.

Johnson, William S. *W. Eugene Smith: Middle Years.* Tucson: Center for Creative Photography, University of Arizona, 1984.

Kirstein, Lincoln. "Afterword." *W. Eugene Smith: His Photographs and Notes.* New York: Aperture, 1969.

Kobre, Ken. "A Last Interview with W. Eugene Smith." *Photoplex,* Fall 1997 (www.gigaplex.com/ photo/kobre/smithqu.htm).

Lorant, Stefan. *Pittsburgh: The Story of an American City.* Pittsburgh: Esselmont Books, 1999.

Lubove, Roy. *Twentieth-Century Pittsburgh. Vol. 1: Government, Business, and Environmental Change.* Pittsburgh: University of Pittsburgh Press, 1996.

Maddow, Ben. *Let Truth Be the Prejudice. W. Eugene Smith: His Life and Photographs.* New York: Aperture, 1985.

Schulz, Constance B., and Steven W. Plattner, eds. *Witness to the Fifties: The Pittsburgh Photographic Library, 1950–1953.* Pittsburgh: University of Pittsburgh Press, 1999.

Smith, W. Eugene. *W. Eugene Smith: His Photographs and Notes.* New York: Aperture, 1969.

Smith, W. Eugene. "Labyrinthian Walk." *Photography Annual 1959.* New York: Ziff-Davis, 1959.

Stange, Maren. *Symbols of Ideal Life: Social Documentary Photography in America, 1890–1950.* New York: Cambridge University Press, 1989.

Trachtenberg, Alan. *Reading American Photographs: Images as History, Mathew Brady to Walker Evans.* New York: Hill and Wang, 1989.

Willumson, Glenn G. *W. Eugene Smith and the Photographic Essay.* New York: Cambridge University Press, 1992.

# W. EUGENE SMITH'S PITTSBURGH LAYOUT FOR PHOTOGRAPHY ANNUAL 1959

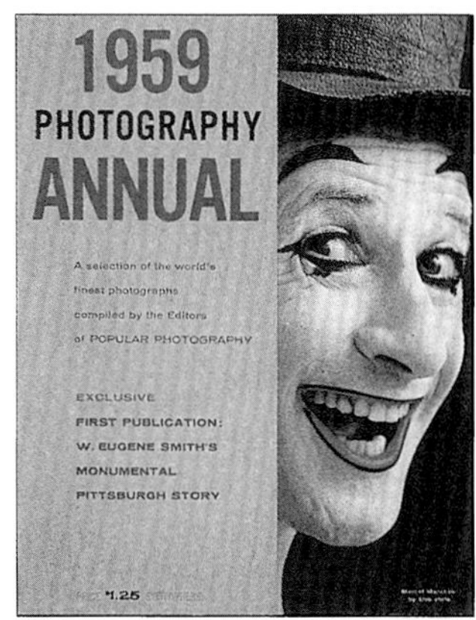



THE FOLLOWING is a reproduction of the eighty-eight Pittsburgh images Smith published in *Popular Photography's Photography Annual 1959*. Editor Bruce Downs gave Smith total control over the creation of the layout. Despite this freedom, Smith never completed it to his satisfaction and in his letters and speeches afterward was extremely critical of the published piece overall, especially the text.

In lectures for the rest of his career, Smith often returned to this version of his Pittsburgh work as an example of his "many layered" or "Faulkner-like" approach to editing. Of the opening picture of the steelworker with flames reflected in his goggles, Smith said, "I needed a picture of man submerged underneath industry, but not lost." Though this was one of the last pictures he made in Pittsburgh, sometime in 1957, he had made the photograph knowing it would be his opening image.

The two pictures opposite were meant to offset the themes of the first picture: "The checker game we play with ourselves—ROTC headless-heads lost in the cherry blossoms—we go on heedlessly—training for peace in pursuit of love—this is a contradiction." The remainder of the essay was intended "to elaborate on themes stated in the first spread." In a 1970 interview, he said, "From the opening three pictures you could go in any directions, sets up vibrations between each other that allow you to think as deeply as you wanted from there."

The only other spread Smith commented on was the second; he described it as an "amplification of humanity in this—hands touching—the theme of love from a new approach—man and his livelihood—Smoky city—moon in the city at night—dream of clearing smoke—a contradiction—stairways—more disclosure of the feeling of the city."

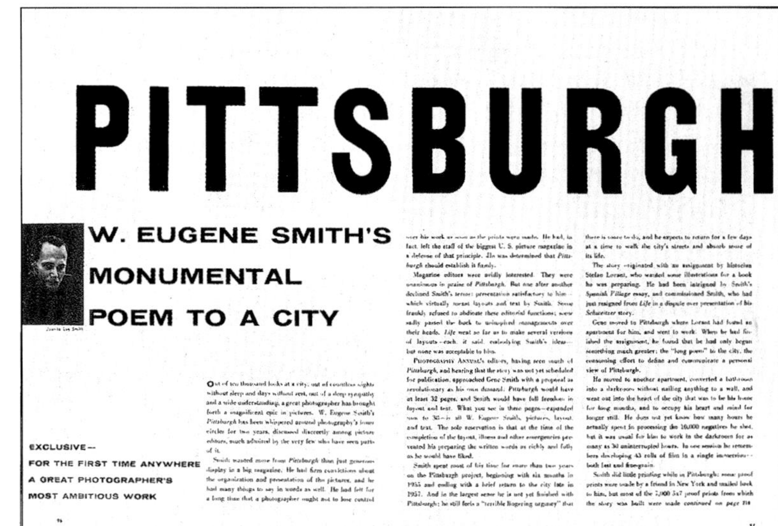



All quotations are from taped or transcribed materials in the W. Eugene Smith Archive at the Center for Creative Photography, Thè University of Arizona: Smith's speeches at a photojournalism conference in Miami, Florida, April 22–25, 1959, and the Rochester Institute of Architecture, Rochester, New York, January 15, 1965, and his interview with Bob Coombs, circa 1970.

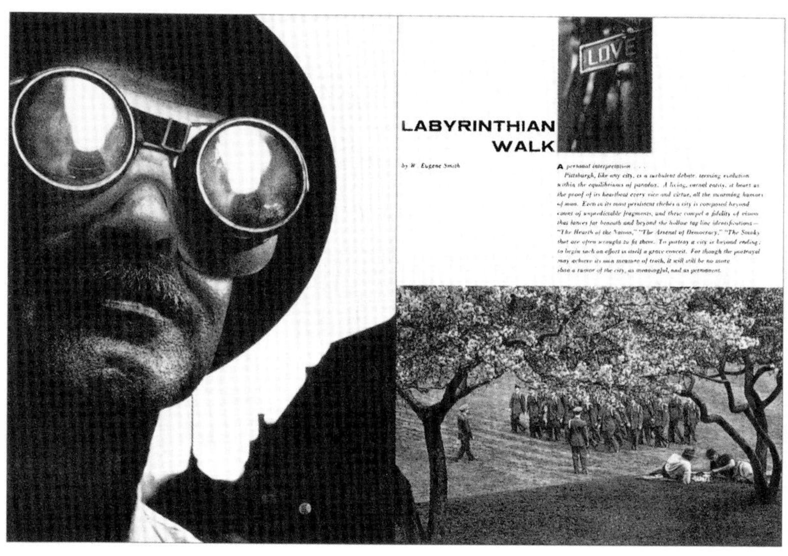
LABYRINTHIAN WALK
by W. Eugene Smith

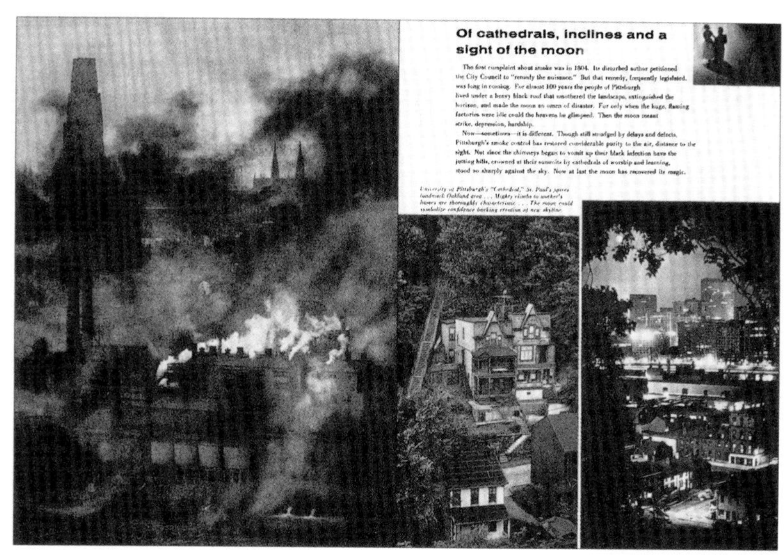
Of cathedrals, inclines and a sight of the moon

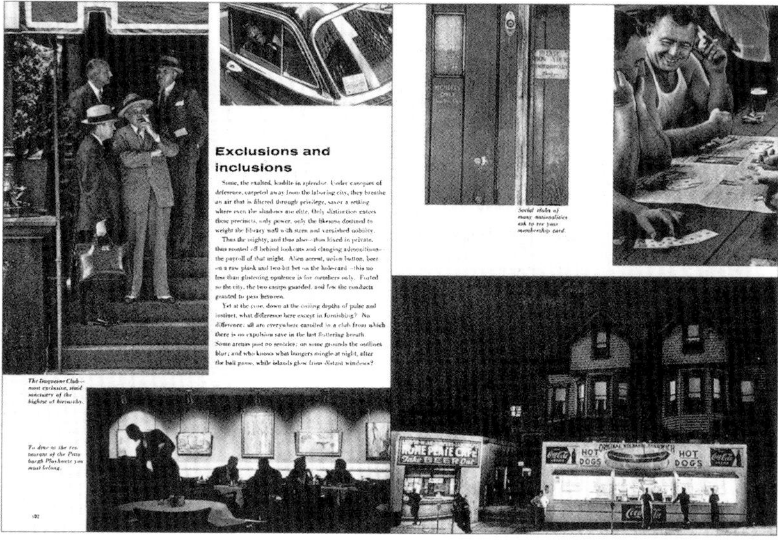
Exclusions and inclusions

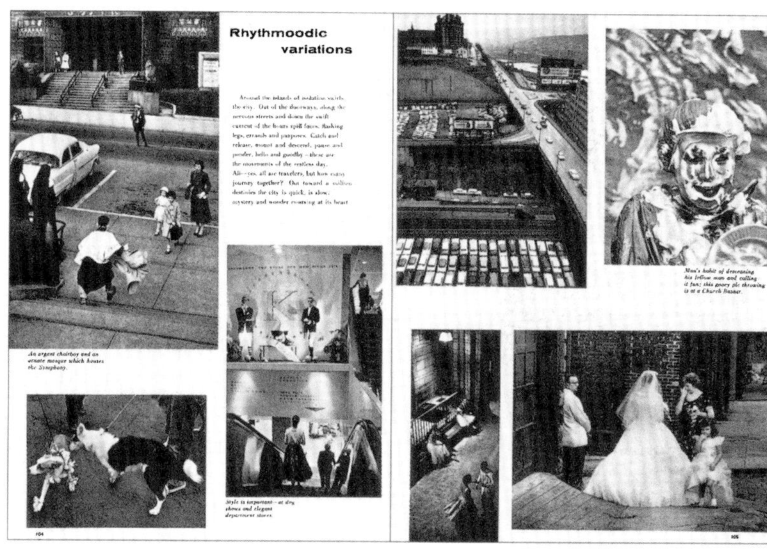
Rhythmoodic variations

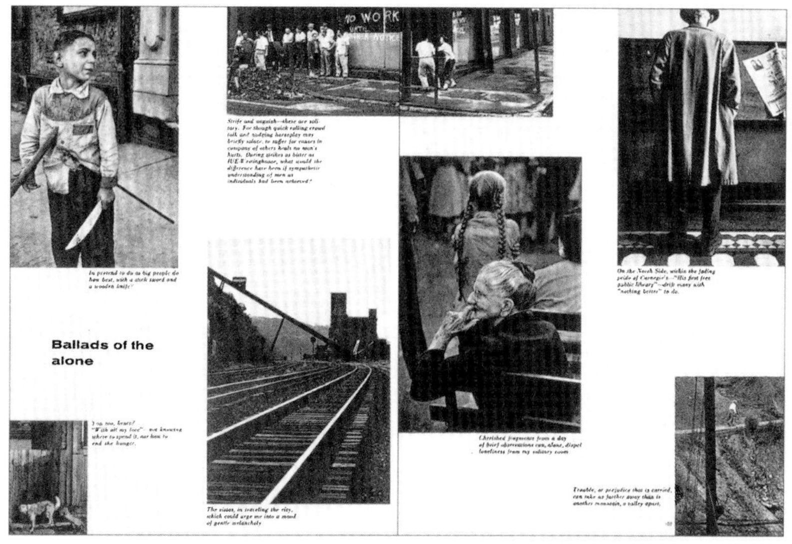
Ballads of the alone

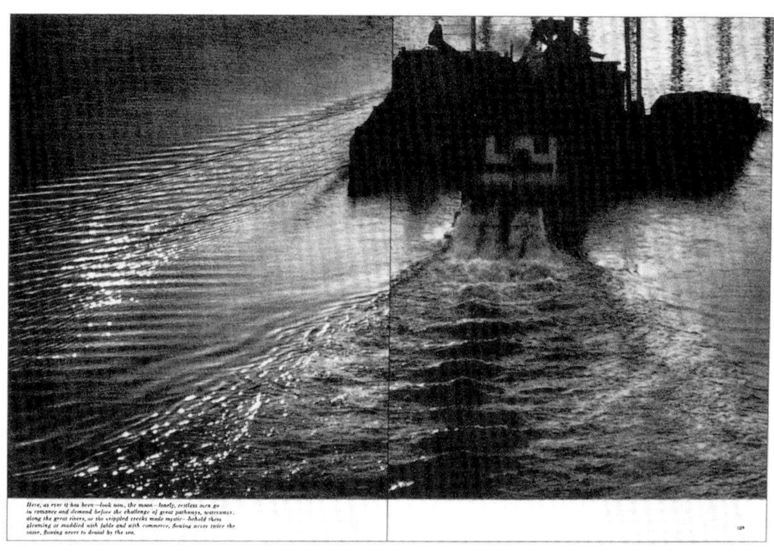

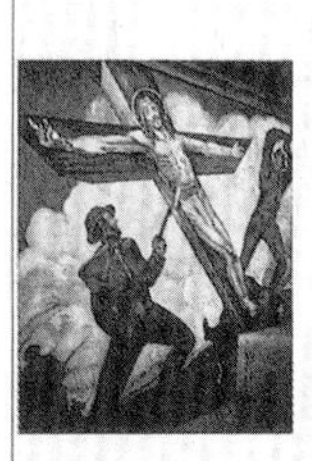
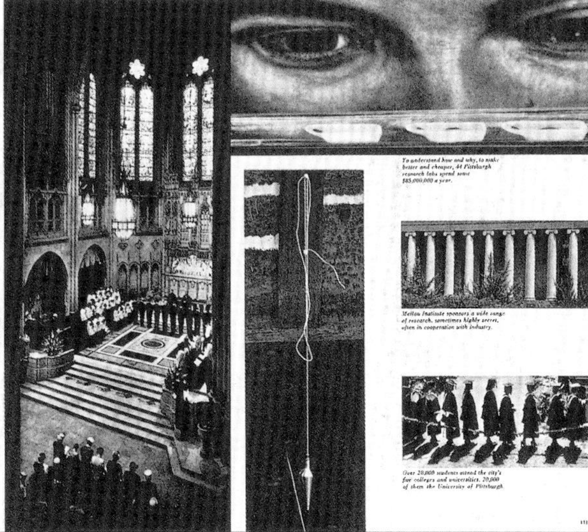
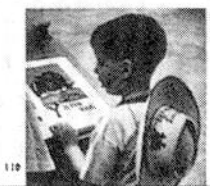
Search—soul,
science, and the
mind for tomorrow

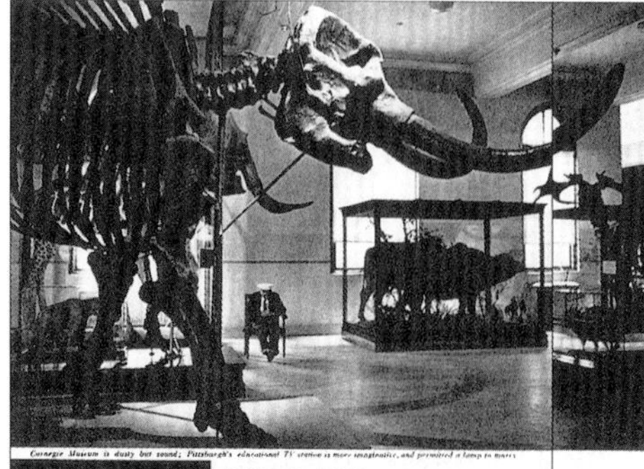
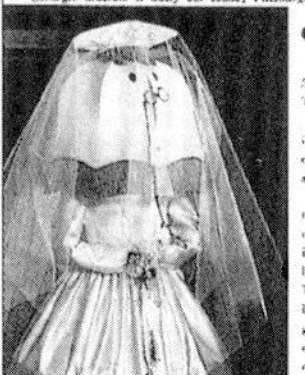
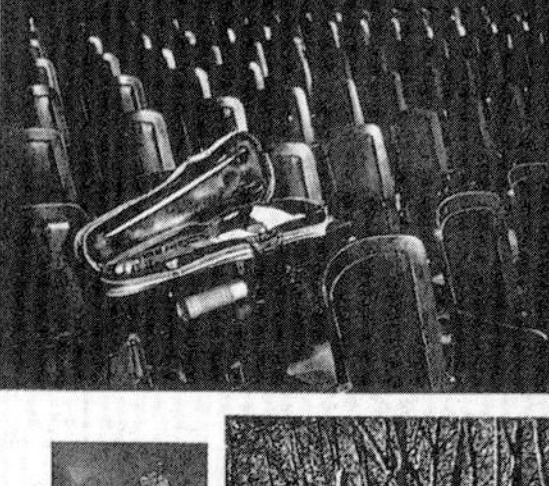
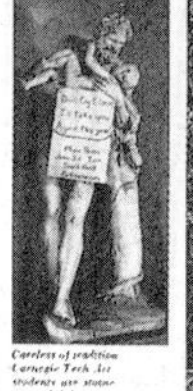
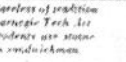
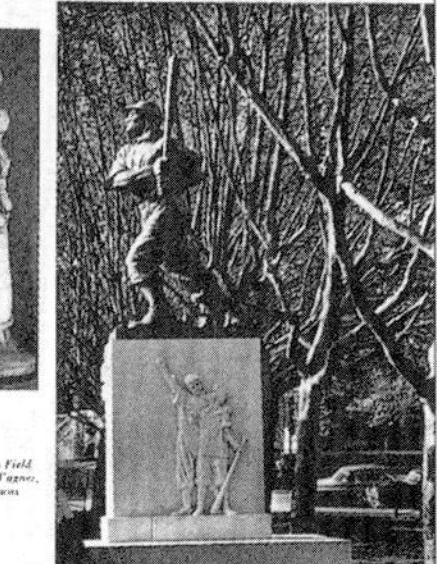
Cultural still lifes

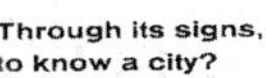
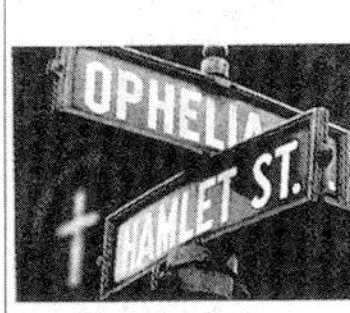
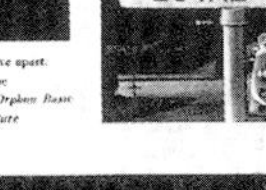
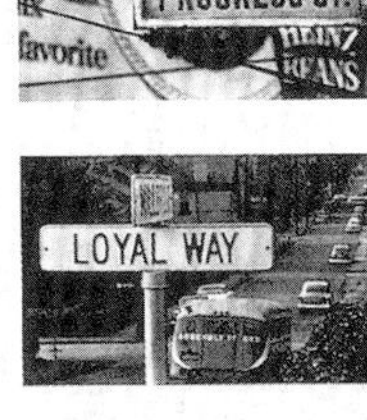
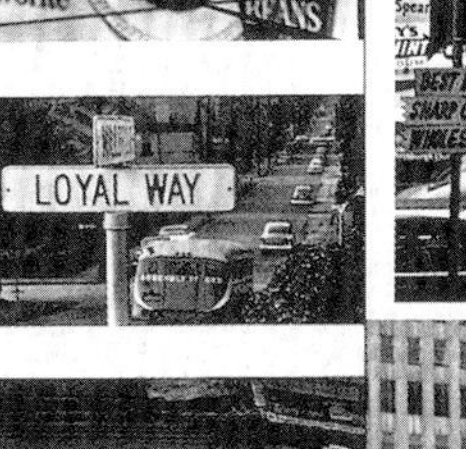
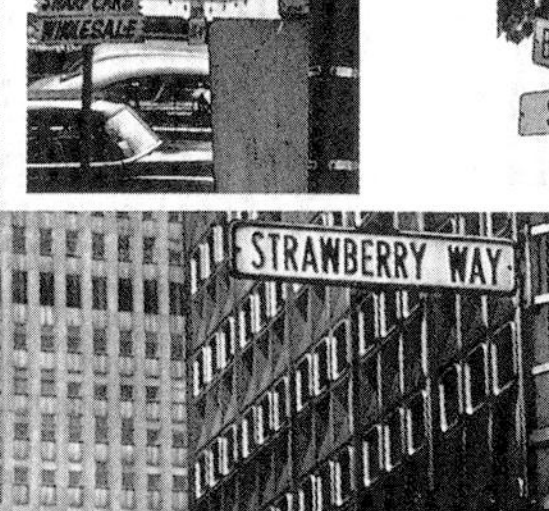
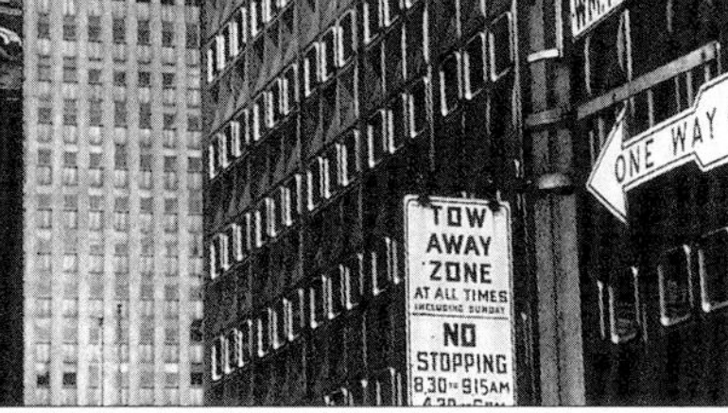
Through its signs,
to know a city?
OPHELIA
HAMLET ST.
CHESTNUT ST.
PROGRESS ST.
HEINZ BEANS
GOLD WAY
LOYAL WAY
SCIENCE
BELTZHOOVER
STRAWBERRY WAY
WM. PENN PL.
ONE WAY
TOW AWAY ZONE AT ALL TIMES
NO STOPPING 8.30—9.15 Am
E. TWELFTH AVE.
FRIENDSHIP BARBER SHOP
136

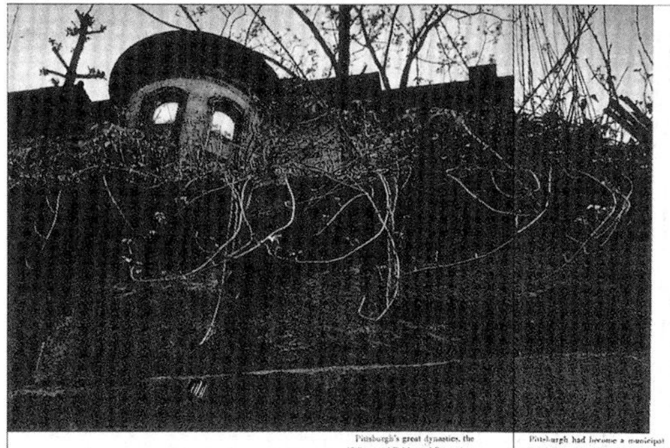
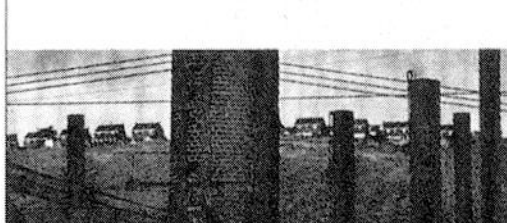
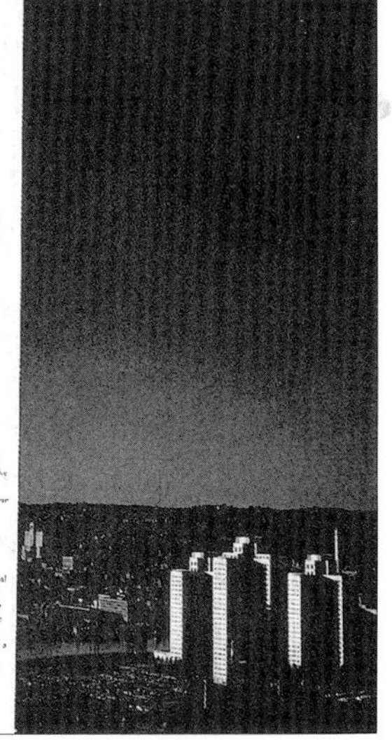
From baron era—and from
present blight arising

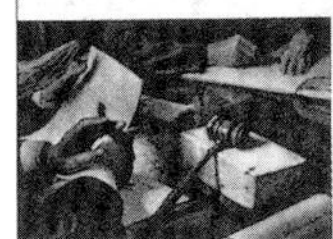
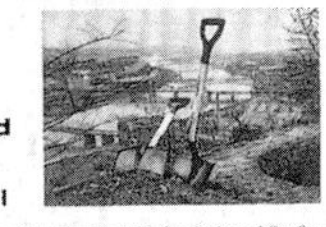
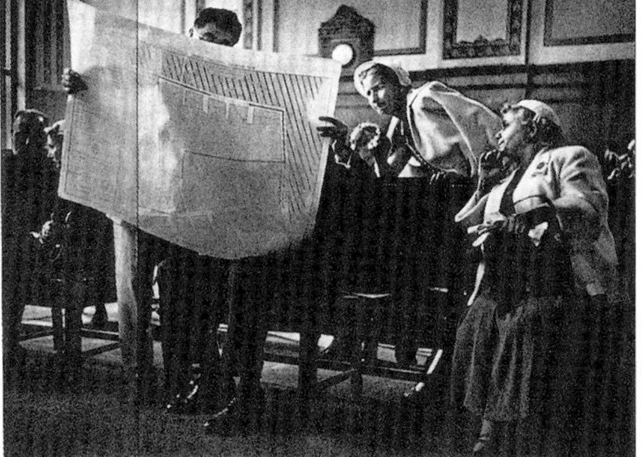
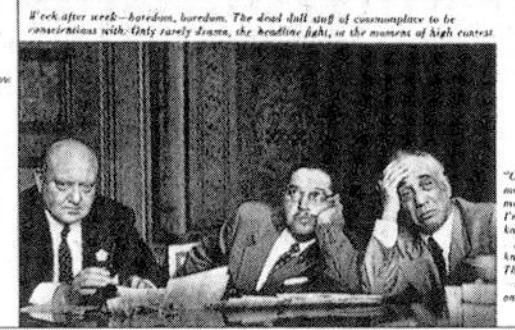
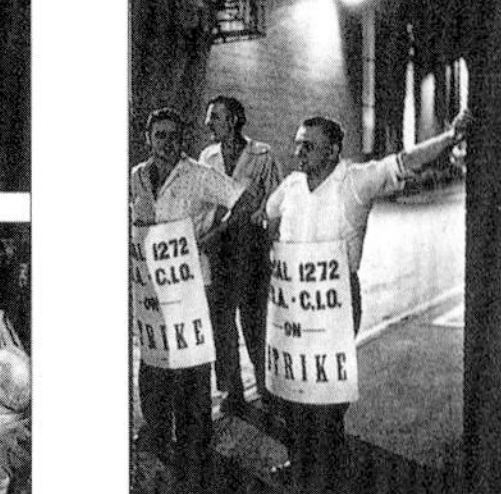
By legal process...to place hand
to shovel,
to stay hand
from shovel

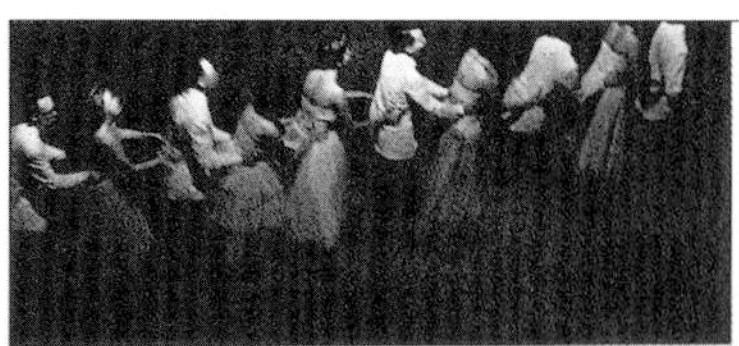
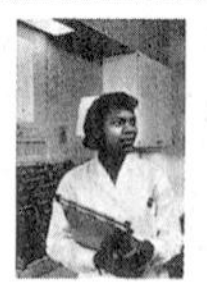
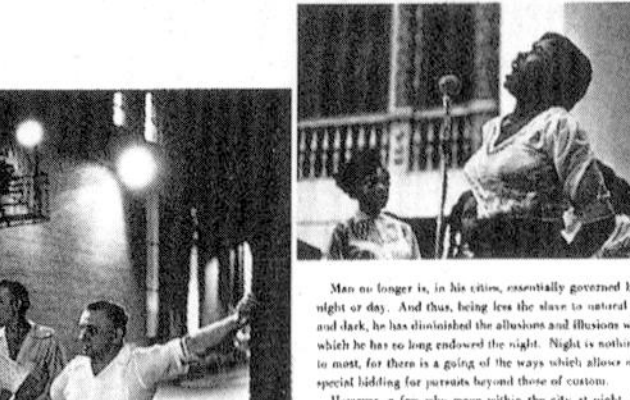
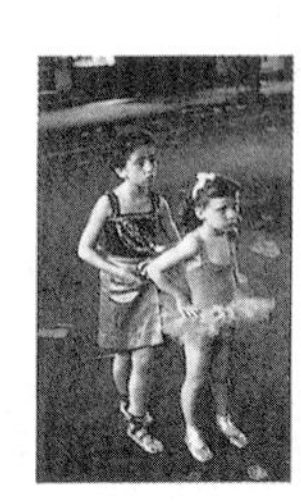
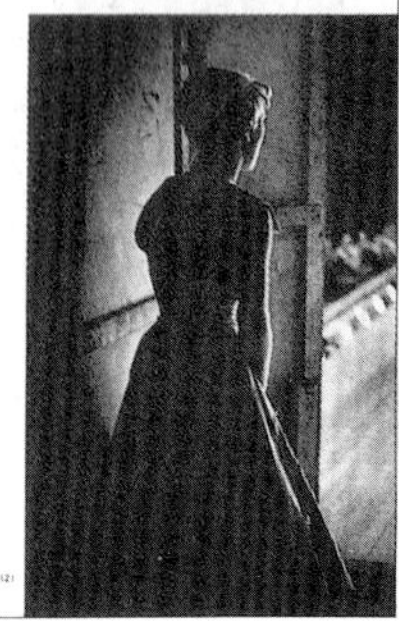
LOCAL 1272
STEEL WKS. C.I.O.
ON STRIKE
Night-
time
is nothing
now

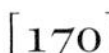

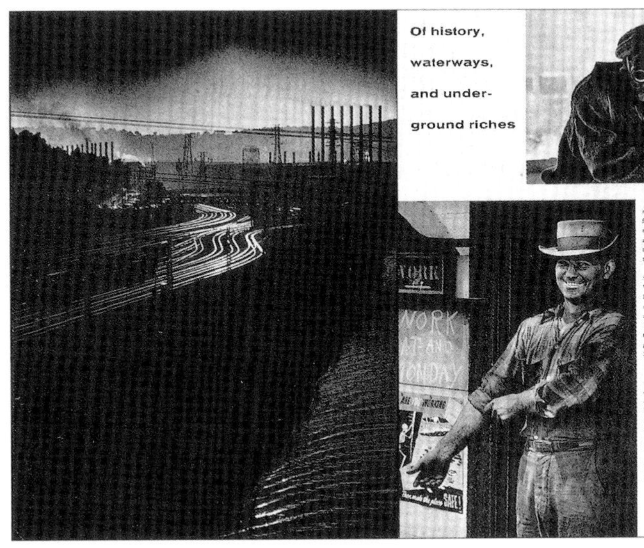
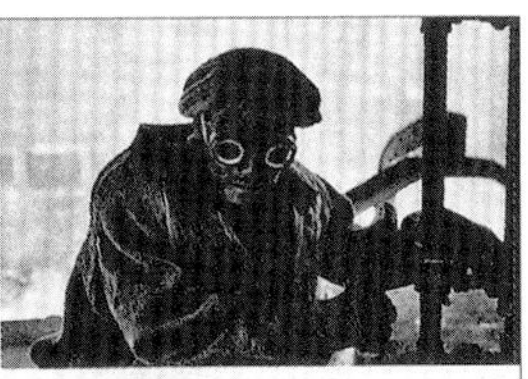
Of history,
waterways,
and under-
ground riches

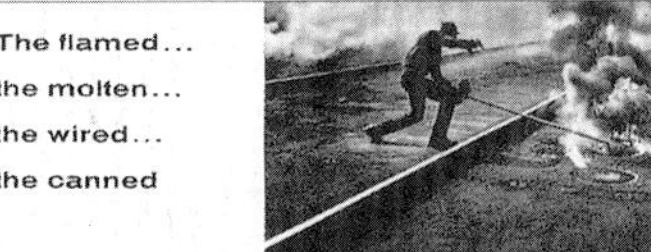
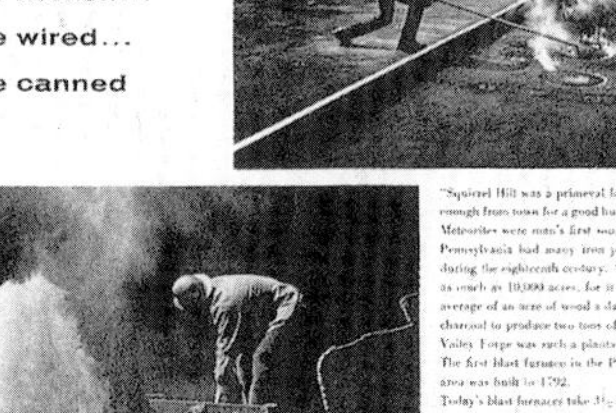
The flamed...
the molten...
the wired...
the canned

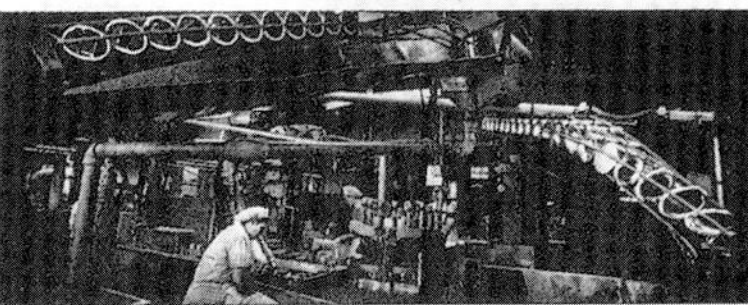

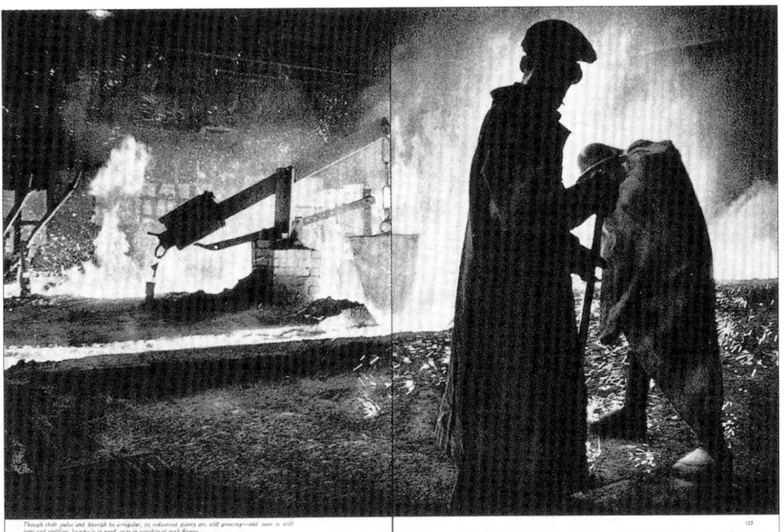

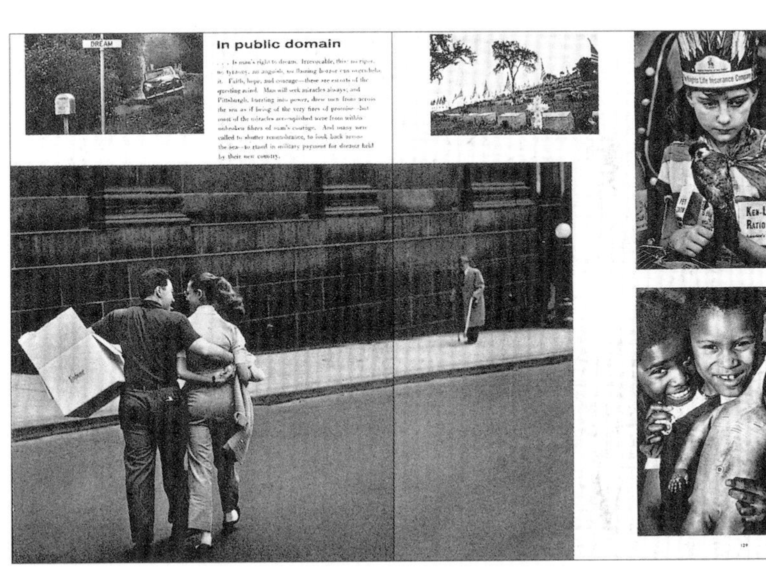
In public domain

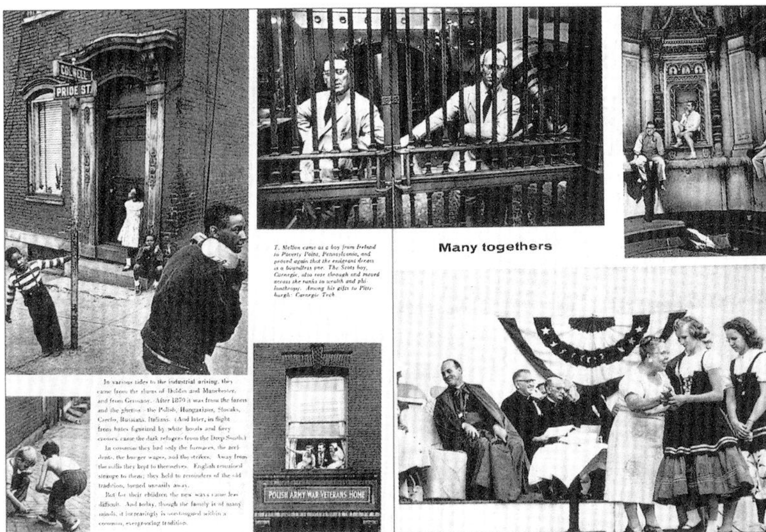
Many togethers

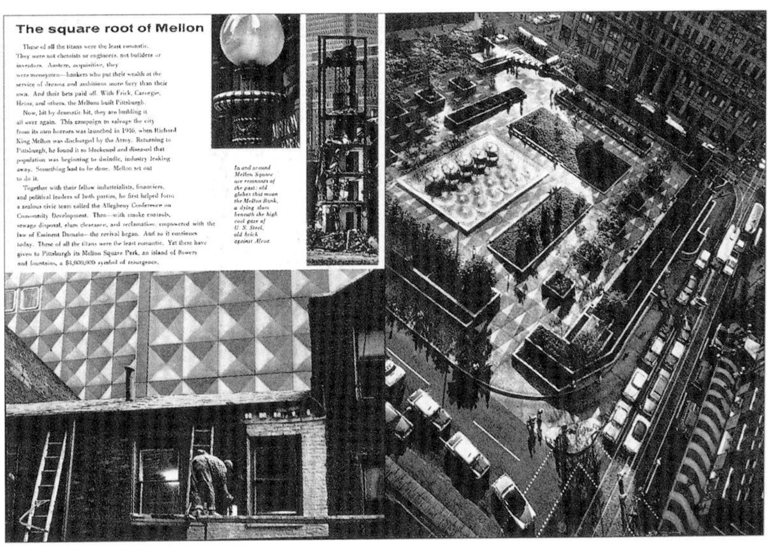
The square root of Mellon

# NOTES TO PHOTOGRAPHS

THERE ARE 1,200 finished master prints from W. Eugene Smith's Pittsburgh project in the collections at the Center for Creative Photography at the University of Arizona and the Carnegie Museum of Art in Pittsburgh. Among those prints, more than 600 different images are represented. Smith stated that there were 200 finished prints that represented "a synthesis of the whole" body of work, but he never indicated which 200 he meant.

Between 1957 and 1971, Smith made five selections of his Pittsburgh images for presentations that can still be documented. First, in 1957 photographer Harold Feinstein, Smith's friend and sometime assistant, sketched a 48-page layout under Smith's instruction that contained 125 images. Second, in late 1958, *Popular Photography* magazine's *Photography Annual 1959* published 88 images in a layout that Smith largely designed, with similarities to Feinstein's sketch. Third, between 1959 and 1961 Smith worked with his assistant Carole Thomas to create a massive retrospective essay of his career to that point. A 350-page dummy of that never-published book survives in his archive. Among approximately 500 photographs there are 59 Pittsburgh pictures. Fourth, in 1969, Smith put together a monograph of 118 pictures that was published by Aperture. Eleven of those pictures were from Pittsburgh. Finally, in 1971, Smith assembled another enormous retrospective of his career, this time in an exhibition of roughly 650 images at the Jewish Museum in New York City. Official records of the exhibition were not kept, but surviving photographs of the museum's walls show that at least 63 Pittsburgh images were displayed in that exhibition. These five occasions form the basis for the selection of pictures that I made in editing this book. I made additional selections from the master-print collections after examining Smith's 6,000 5×7 Pittsburgh work prints, contact sheets, photographs of his layout boards, and voluminous written archive, looking for clues as to his priorities for individual images. Smith often printed an image one way, then flipped the negative and printed it again, using whichever print best fit a given layout. He considered both to be master prints. I also learned a great deal about Smith's methods from interviews with several of Smith's key assistants: Leon Miller and Norman Rabinowitz, both of whom were on the ground with Smith in Pittsburgh; Jim Karales, who was Smith's darkroom assistant for the project; and Harold Feinstein and Carole Thomas, mentioned above.

Early in my research on Smith's work in Pittsburgh, I noted a comment Smith delivered at the Miami Photojournalism Conference in April 1959, after he had failed to achieve his goals for a published essay: "The main problem, I think, is that there is no end to such a subject as Pittsburgh and no way to finish it. . . . Any photographer's short version is bound to be a portfolio only." In deciding how to organize these pictures I took into account Smith's use of the word "portfolio." He was known to sometimes discard magnificent images from his essays in favor of lesser alternatives because the latter served more effectively, he thought, in a given sequence. I made no attempt to achieve or emulate that sort of essay since Smith admitted that he himself couldn't. The book's layout was conceived as a series of portfolios of the strongest individual images, with each section of pictures being influenced and informed by Smith's own topical groupings, though sometimes blended. The sections do not graphically follow the juxtapositions or sequences in Smith's layout. We have included an appendix of Smith's original layout from the *Photography Annual 1959*, which I believe provides the clearest possible glimpse in one document of Smith's grand designs for the "essay" he intended as his groundbreaking magnum opus. He did, however, achieve a remarkable set of prints that, together, may meet his goals for the essay.

# ACKNOWLEDGMENTS

IN 1997 Alex Harris and Robert Coles, editors of *Double-Take,* gave this project a pivotal boost by encouraging and supporting my early work, which appeared in the magazine's Spring 1998 issue as "W. Eugene Smith's Unfinished Symphony." They have my warmest thanks.

My colleagues at the Center for Documentary Studies have been generous with their friendship and support throughout this project. My two editors at CDS, Iris Tillman Hill and Alexa Dilworth, were crucial in helping shape and execute *Dream Street,* and I thank them enormously. Many thanks also to Tom Rankin and Greg Britz for their leadership; Alex Harris and Margaret Sartor for their always helpful advice; Courtney Reid-Eaton and Dan Partridge for their work on the exhibition; and various assists by Lynn McKnight, Bonnie Campbell, Dawn Dreyer, Bill Butler, Alice Huang, John Moses, and Charlie Thompson.

My gratitude goes to Jim Mairs at W. W. Norton & Company for his editorial guidance and ongoing encouragement, and for making this paperback edition possible. Thanks also to Molly Renda for her excellent design of this book.

This project would not have succeeded without the participation of the Carnegie Museum of Art in Pittsburgh. I thank Richard Armstrong for directing the museum's extraordinary efforts. A special mention and thanks are owed curator Linda Batis, who worked with me for four years on the exhibition and was always inspiring in her dedication, diligence, and expertise. Thanks also to curator Louise Lippincott, who was integral in getting the project off the ground, and to the museum's staff, who were all a true pleasure to work with: Arlene Sanderson, Lucy Stewart, Amber Morgan, Marilyn Russell, Richard Tourtellott, Tey Stiteler, Monika Tomko, Meg Bernard, Maureen Rolla, Michael Fahlund, Gerald Farber, Champ Knecht, Dale McNutt, Bill Judson, and Lauren Friedman.

The staff at the Center for Creative Photography at the University of Arizona played many key roles in the completion of this project. My deep gratitude goes to Amy Rule, Leslie Calmes, Dianne Nilsen, Denise Kramer, Marcia Tiede, Betsi Meissner, Trudy Wilner Stack, Pat Evans, Terry Pitts, Nancy Lutz, Cass Fey, Roxane Ramos, Claudine Scoville, and Shaw Kinsley.

At the International Center of Photography, Buzz Hartshorn and Brian Wallis assisted me with their leadership and support, as did Cynthia Fredette who also worked on the *Dream Street* exhibition. I greatly appreciate their efforts.

Smith's former assistants and friends Jim Karales and Harold Feinstein were invaluable to my understanding of Smith and his work; my warmest thanks to them. And also to Leon Miller, Norman Rabinowitz, and Carole Thomas; jazz drummer Ronnie Free, who shared a New York City loft with Smith during the late 1950s; and the painter David X. Young, who lived a floor above Smith in the loft for several years. Smith's biographer, Jim Hughes, was helpful from an early stage, as was William S. Johnson, the original archivist of Smith's work at CCP.

Alan Trachtenberg made a critical contribution to *Dream Street* with a wonderful essay as well as his friendship and consultation during the last year of this book's development. I can't thank him enough. I also thank Glenn Willumson, Walter Kidney, and Tom Hanchett for their contributions.

Smith's son and estate executor, Kevin Eugene Smith, went beyond the call of duty in making this project possible. My sincere thanks also to Patrick Smith, Shana Rasmus, Marissa Scott, Juanita Smith, Margery Smith, and Aileen Smith.

I am very grateful to Robert Frank for his contributions and affirmations of this project. In addition, many thanks go to Robert Adams, Richard Rothman, Rob Amberg, and Jesse Andrews. I am also deeply appreciative of filmmaker Kenneth Love and his wife and executive producer, Barbara McNulty, for making the film *Brilliant Fever: W. Eugene Smith and Pittsburgh*.

I am dearly thankful for the ongoing support and friendship of the Reva and David Logan Foundation of Chicago. And I must thank our friends in Tucson, Carol Buuck and Linda, Dane, and James Armijo, for their invaluable hospitality and contributions of lodging during all those trips to Smith's archive at CCP.

Finally, and most importantly, my very deepest thanks and appreciation are for my wife, Laurie Cochenour—if not for her belief in me and this project, and her roots in the Monongahela Valley, I never would have done this work.

SAM STEPHENSON
*Pittsboro, NC*
2003


This new edition of *Dream Street* was made possible by a generous grant from the Jonathan Logan Family Foundation. My warm thanks to Jon and his staff. Also, much gratitude to the University of Chicago Press, where it has been a pleasure working with Alan Thomas, David Olsen, Jill Shimabukuro, Adrienne Meyers, and their colleagues. I extend my sincere thanks to Ross Gay for contributing a new foreword to this edition. Love and gratitude also to my wife, Courtney Fitzpatrick, and our son, Parker Stephenson.

SAM STEPHENSON
*College Station, TX*
2022

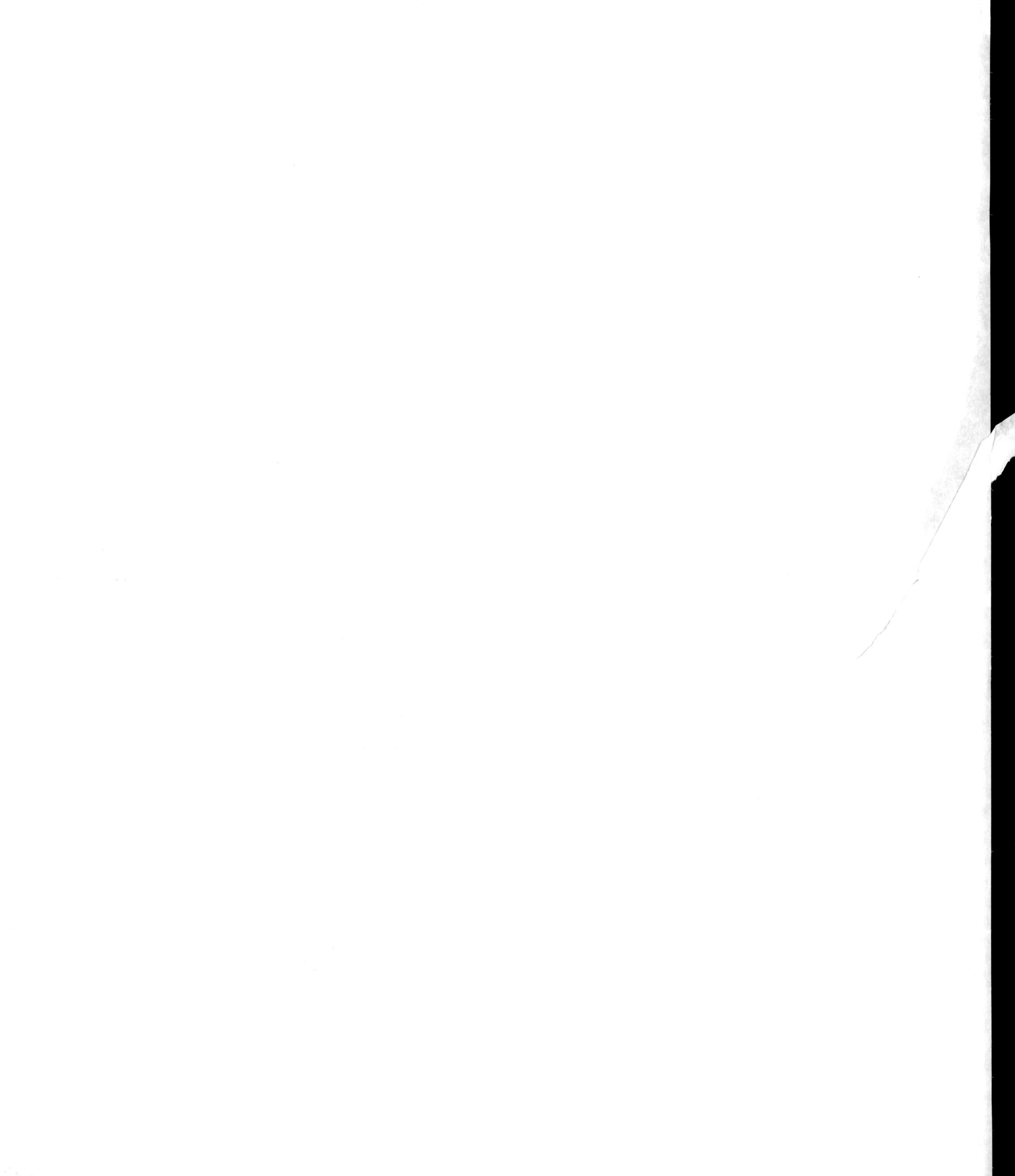